TEXT AND INTERPRETATION

GENESIS

A Practical Commentary

Claus Westermann

Translated by David E. Green

GRAND RAPIDS, MICHIGAN
WILLIAM B. EERDMANS PUBLISHING COMPANY

Copyright © 1987 by Wm. B. Eerdmans Publishing Co.
255 Jefferson Ave. S.E., Grand Rapids, Mich. 49503

Translated from the Dutch edition *Genesis: Een Praktische bijbelverklaring,*
volumes I and II, part of the Tekst en Toelichting series. Uitgeversmaatschappij
J. H. Kok—Kampen, 1986.

Library of Congress Cataloging-in-Publication Data:

Westermann, Claus.
  Genesis : a practical commentary.

  "Translated from the Dutch edition Genesis:
een praktische bijbelverklaring, volumes I and
II"—T.p. verso.
  1. Bible. O.T. Genesis—Commentaries.
I. Green, David (David E.) II. Title.
III. Series.
BS1235.3.W4313 1987   222′.11077   87-24603

ISBN 0-8028-0106-4

CONTENTS

CONTENTS

PREFACE

This translation and explanation of the book of Genesis for the series *Text and Interpretation* is based on my commentary on Genesis which was published in Germany (*Biblischer Kommentar* I, Neukirchener Verlag, 1974-1982). There one can find the philological reasoning behind the translation, the religion-historical background, and a consideration of the literature published on this book of the Bible (with the appropriate references). There one also finds summaries of the different parts of Genesis, and an account of the related problem complexes.

I am grateful to the editor and publisher of this series for the opportunity to make the results of my work available to the public in a condensed and more popular form. It is my personal conviction that the scientific study and exegesis of a book of the Bible will serve to build a bridge between ancient texts from the past and the living word from Scripture in the present.

C. Westermann

INTRODUCTION

"In the beginning God created the heavens and the earth." In the period extending from the Middle Ages to a time in which horizons are constantly shifting, the opening words of the first book of the Bible have gained a new meaning. Today there is mention of the possibility that mankind will destroy the earth, and people explore regions well beyond the reach of the planet earth. The problems and perils of present and future generations are increasing in scope to such an extent that the solution of these problems and the aversion of these threats seem still possible only on a worldwide scale. Increasing numbers of organizations and institutions are today called into being whose activities extend far beyond national boundaries and whose reach is worldwide. After a period of many thousand years shaped by distinct peoples and groups of peoples and their politics, it seems that an era is now approaching in which mankind as a whole will be the determinative category.

There is, therefore, good reason for us to reflect on the roots, the *genesis*, of mankind.

The function of Genesis as a book of the Bible is to take those who read it and those who hear its message to the things of the beginning. The Bible, because it speaks of God, is concerned with the reality of what has happened from the beginning and is now. It gives a report of everything from the beginning to the end and covers all that is. Its lines run from the beginning of the world and mankind through the center (which is Christ) to the end. After all, its reference is to him who said of himself: I am the first and the last.

In Christian churches this universal horizon of the Bible has often been somewhat neglected, a neglect that is manifest, for example, in the fact that the Creation is not celebrated in the calendar of the Church. God's mandate to the people, his creatures, and to the rest of creation was misjudged and distorted. Of the Prehistory, only the first three chapters of Genesis played a significant role, and chs. 4-11 remained obscure. In this way, chs. 3 and 4—one dealing with transgression against God and the other with transgression against fellow human being—were torn apart, a fact that had unprecedented consequences. The connection between the Creation and the Flood

ix

was never grasped, let alone taken to heart. People deemed the patriarchal stories as suitable for children—but did not hear their real significance.

Genesis tells the story of the beginning of the world and mankind in the dim reaches of primeval history, and of the beginning of community in the patriarchal narratives. The book is also the prelude to the story of a people whose history begins in the Exodus, but not only that. It tells us that Israel is a part of humanity and shares in the attributes of being human with all other created human beings. On top of that, it says that because of God's blessing the earth belongs to all peoples (ch. 10) and that not only the people of Israel but also many other nations descend from the patriarchs Abraham, Isaac, and Jacob. For God's blessing is universal, and the family as the basic unit of every human society is universal.

A feature of the present time is that questions, ideas, and problems which go beyond the boundaries of one's own people—and even one's own church—have come more conspicuously to the fore than in preceding periods. As a result, Genesis acquires an importance it has not had heretofore.

The special importance of Genesis for the history of Israel and, beyond that, for the history of Christian churches lies primarily in the fact that the God who saved and preserved Israel, to whom the people cried in their distress, and who was honored in their songs, was the God of the beginning, the Creator, who holds the world in his hands, gives life to people, and calls them to live. Their trust was in this God because the beginning and the end was in his hands, his power.

When in the Primal History and the patriarchal narratives a clear line is drawn (in the genealogies) from one generation to another— from Creation to Abraham, Isaac, and Jacob, a line that proceeds in Jacob's sons to the different tribes from which the people of Israel were constituted—it becomes in the story of Genesis a path on which God accompanies his people from generation to generation. Indeed, this is a fundamental given in Genesis. Here history gains an aspect of which we have almost completely lost sight: the life of people in this world cannot continue unless it is borne onward by the blessing of God who sustains this life. This silent spring and vital current lies at the root of every history—also the specific history of God with his people, the history referred to in Genesis by the promises made to the patriarchs. When at the end of Genesis, in the Joseph story, peace is restored in a family because one of the brothers is prepared to guarantee the safety of another brother (43:9), we have an allusion to that of which the New Testament speaks, at the same time illustrating the path that leads from Genesis to the New Testament.

THE BOOK OF GENESIS

The Bible comprehends the acts and the words of God from beginning to end. The book of Genesis speaks of the beginning, the Revelation of John of the end. In both the first and last books of the Bible, God is concerned with all of humankind, with the whole world, with all creation. The God who is Alpha and Omega, beginning and end, is the same God whose work comprehends everything—all that was, and is, and is to be.

It is the purpose of the book of Genesis to tell of the origin of all things. It is the "Book of Beginnings." As such it falls into two parts: in chapters 1–11, the "Primal History," it speaks of the beginnings of the world and of humankind; in 12–50, the "Patriarchal History," it speaks of the beginnings of the human community, and so of human history.

The Primal History extends from the creation of the world (ch. 1) and humankind (chs. 2–3), through the threatened destruction of the world in the Deluge, and its preservation (chs. 6–9), to the expansion of the human race over the earth, in the Table of Nations (ch. 10) that introduces human history. It is God's blessing (chs. 1, 5, 10) that makes it possible for humanity to spread out and to become the family of nations; it is human transgression of God's limits (chs. 3, 4, 6, 9, 11) that endangers the human race throughout its history.

The Patriarchal History (chs. 12–50) grows out of the Primal History (chs. 11--12). It begins with the patriarch Abraham (chs. 12–25), continues in the story of the brothers (Jacob and Esau, chs. 25–36), and then, in the story of the twelve sons (Joseph, chs. 37–50), moves from family history to the history of the peoples who were one day to spring from the twelve sons. The Patriarchal History is concerned to present the Primal History of the human community: all forms of human community are based on the family. The elementary forms of human community focus on events involving parent and child (chs. 12–25), brother and brother (chs. 25–36), father, brother and other brothers (chs. 37–50).

As in the events of the Primal History, so in the Patriarchal History it is God from whom everything proceeds, and in whom everything has its goal. Just as God creates the world and humanity (chs. 1–3), so—with Abraham and Abraham's family, together with the Primal History of the human community—he begins the story of his people, in whom "all the families of the earth" should be blessed (12:1-3). The way of the people of God, which began with the call of the patriarch Abraham, has its goal in the sending of the Son, whose way, whose life and passion took place for "all the families of the earth."

In the book of Genesis is the beginning of God's way with the world and humankind, the way on which he leads them, through the midpoint in Christ, to the end towards which and for which he created them.

THE ORIGIN OF THE BOOK OF GENESIS

Genesis has come down to us along a path of more than three thousand years and in a foreign language. There is, therefore, a scholarly interpretation of the book which helps to translate it for us, to make it comprehensible. Mere translation from Hebrew into a modern language is not sufficient; to explain what is strange to us, we also draw on linguistics and historical studies, with their related fields such as archaeology, Near Eastern studies, and the history of religions. We can make use of these various aids with gratitude. When we tackle the problem of interpreting the book of Genesis at the end of the second millennium A.D., we must question and learn from the long succession of previous exegetes of this book in order to be responsible interpreters for our own generation. In our exegesis, we must never forget that all interpretation of Scripture is part of a process; there can never be one definitive interpretation.

Throughout the history of the interpretation of Genesis, it has therefore been impossible to answer definitively the question of how this first book of the Bible came into being. This question, too, is always in process. No other book of the Bible is so deeply rooted in the early history of the human race. At the beginning of its development stand individual stories that were told and passed down orally for a long time—in many cases for centuries—before being written down. We cannot trace the path of these oral traditions; here scholarly investigation meets its limits. We can only draw certain inferences from the written form in hand, nothing more.

But even this written form did not come into being in one piece, all at once, the way a book is printed. Instead it developed gradually, over a period of centuries in a series of individual steps—only a few of which, again, we can reconstruct. In its present form, however, there is one thing that Genesis does reveal: the components that we can see in it were once independent, once existed separately. This is certain in the case of the Primal History (chs. 1–11) and the Patriarchal History (chs. 12–50). But we can progress a few steps further by distinguishing between the two stages of oral and written origin. In the Patriarchal History, for example, the Joseph story (chs. 37–50) can be clearly distinguished from the preceding section (chs. 12–36): it is one long, homogeneous story that moves in a straight line from the quarrel between the sons of Jacob in chapter 37 to the final reconciliation in chapter 50. In this way it shows its written origins, and for this reason it has often been called a novella. On the other hand, in chapters 12–26 we can clearly distinguish the individual stories (ten to fifteen verses on the average) from which the larger whole was fashioned, drawing on the connecting material, the genealogies and itineraries, which were also at one time transmitted independently. We can also distinguish the Abraham story (chs. 12–25) from the Jacob-Esau story (chs. 25–36); each was once independent. Separately from the Patriarchal History, the Primal History (chs. 1–11) was also formed out of individual stories that were once transmitted independently, as several parallels between the stories demonstrate convincingly.

A later stage of development is signaled by the union of the Primal History and the Patriarchal History. This union clearly indicates written transmission. It reveals the intention of an author who, by joining the Primal and Patriarchal Histories, sought to create a historical work in which both would present the earliest history of Israel. It is also easy to see, however, that other hands have been at work in this historical composition, which comprises Genesis, Numbers, and parts of Deuteronomy. In a period of pentateuchal scholarship that is just now ending, investigation has focused entirely on the written sources from which the Pentateuch was fashioned. Recently the classical "Documentary Hypothesis" has again been questioned, or at least reformulated, because the importance of oral tradition vis-à-vis written sources has been increasingly recognized.

With regard to Genesis, I will simply restate the position that I put forward in my *Genesis 1–11* (Minneapolis: Augsburg, 1984). The Primal History grew out of the union of the earlier (tenth–ninth century) Yahwistic source and the later (sixth–fifth century) Priestly source. The Patriarchal History is likewise a composite work; here, however, the earlier Yahwistic Patriarchal History has incorporated a series of additions (which do not, however, constitute a continuous "Elohistic" source). This earlier Yahwistic patriarchal narrative has been linked with the later Priestly narrative. The Yahwist (J) and Priestly sources (P) can also be distinguished here as in the Primal History. The Joseph story (chs. 37–50) is an independent, homogeneous narrative by an anonymous author of the early Monarchy; it was appended to the Jacob story, which comprises most of chapters 46–50. This complex origin of Genesis can only be sketched briefly here. The purpose and distinctive characteristics of J and P will be dealt with below. I refer the reader to my commentary for my discussion, and also for bibliography, the positions of previous exegetes, and detailed analysis.

THE PRIMAL HISTORY   1–11

INTRODUCTION

To speak of God means to speak of totality. Therefore the first eleven chapters of the Bible deal with the whole—the totality of the world and humanity. This totality is presented as a story with a beginning and an end. Genesis 1–11 speaks of the beginning; but these chapters already suggest that the totality will one day have an end. Neither the world nor the human race is eternal; God alone is eternal.

The Primal History (chs. 1–11) constitutes a single complex in which each individual unit has its place and meaning. Observing the primary rule of all biblical exegesis, that every text must be interpreted in its context, we must examine each unit in these eleven chapters in its place in this complex, and assign it its meaning there. We violate this rule when—as frequently happens in ecclesiastical tradition—we consider only the Creation and Fall to be important, and treat the other texts in Genesis 1–11 as insignificant.

This context comprises two kinds of material: narratives and lists. The lists are the genealogies in chapters 4, 5, 10, and 11. Against the regular, invariable flow of these genealogies, the narratives of particular events stand out in relief. These include the narratives of the Creation (1:1–2:4a, 2:4b-25) and the Deluge (chs. 6–9), as well as those of sin and punishment (3:1-24; 4:1-16; 6:1-4; 6:5–9:28; 11:1-9).

The Creation story has its reflex in the story of the Deluge. It says that in spite of all disasters, God the Creator holds his creation in his hands; at the end it promises the continued existence of his creation (8:20-22).

The reflex of human transgression against God in chapter 3 is the transgression against a brother in chapter 4. In addition, we have the other stories of crime and punishment, each with its particular features.

Alongside the narratives, and in conjunction with them, the genealogies give the sense that in them the blessing of the human race at its creation is unfolded: in the sequence of generations, the blessing operates in the depths of time (ch. 5) and the broad expanse of space (ch. 10). The blessing of the Creator continues to work in the history of the human race.

So the primal events constitute the prelude to history: God works in human history in particular events (deliverance and judgment) as well as in the ongoing blessing realized in the sequence of generations.

THE DEVELOPMENT OF THE PRIMAL HISTORY

The material preserved in the first eleven chapters of the Bible touches on the profound questions of the beginning of the world in the early history of the human race. Despite the clear differences, we have in the biblical Primal History something that the Bible shares with other human religions at an early stage of their common history. For just this reason, this material can have significance for the future of humanity. It is not just a matter of "religio-historical parallels" in the sense that certain texts in Genesis 1–11 exhibit similarities to texts from other areas and religions. Far more important is the fact that the principal themes of Genesis 1–11 are encountered in the early histories of peoples from all over the earth, and that in them is expressed something common to all human history. These many and varied questions and answers about origins are also reflected in the biblical tradition. What we read in these eleven chapters is the product of a long process of growth, in which we must distinguish two stages, oral and written. In both stages many voices have been harmonized, just as in the New Testament gospels. The former theory of historico-critical exegesis, that such a harmonization demands that we distinguish "authentic" from "secondary" texts, can today be considered obsolete. The recognition that the biblical texts attained their present form through a gradual process of growth restores to them the dignity of the word of God, as it arises from God's actions on behalf of his people in their history; in its changes can be realized its variety and richness. It is just this harmonization of many voices that constitutes the reliability of their witness.

This holds true for both the oral and written stages. For the written stage, we can agree with generations of scholars that Genesis 1–11 is a composite of two written works, J (the "Yahwist," tenth–ninth century), and P (the "Priestly source," sixth–fifth century); the details will be discussed in the conclusion. In the case of the oral stage, however, research is still very much in flux. Hermann Gunkel and others first recognized that J and P are not authors in our sense of the word, but are primarily tradents who fashioned the traditional materials into a single work, a cohesive Primal History. They worked not only as tradents, but as authors and theologians as well.

Three tradents contributed to the final written form—J, P, and R (Redactor). But innumerable voices shared in the oral stage, for stories are passed from mouth to mouth. In this process we should not consider only the narrators. Every oral narrative has its place in and for a particular community. Those who hear it contribute directly or indirectly to the ongoing development of the narrative. Recognition of the significance of the oral narrative for the origin of Genesis (as well as of the patriarchal narratives) has paved the way for a new understanding of the development of the Genesis traditions. These narratives had already existed for decades, even centuries, before being written down—not as a tradition known and handed on by only a few people, but rather as an element integral to the life, thought, culture, and religious faith of the people of Israel and their forebears. It was an indispensable element of their history; they lived with these stories. This is the real sense and significance of the term "tradition history" that dominates Genesis research today.

OUTLINE OF THE PRIMAL HISTORY: GENESIS 1–11

1:1–2:4a (P)   Creation of the World and Humanity
         1-2   Introduction
        3-31   Creation of the World and Humanity
               3-5 Light; 6-8 Festivals; 9-10 Earth and Sea; 11-13 Plants;
               14-19 Stars; 10-25 Animals; 16-31 Human Beings and
               Food
      2:1-4a   Conclusion: God Rests on the Seventh Day
2:4b–3:24 (J)   Creation of Humanity
         4b-7   Introduction; Creation and Quickening of Humanity
         8-15   The Garden; 10-14 The Four Rivers
        16-17   The Prohibition
        18-20   Creation of Animals
        21-25   Creation of Woman
        3:1-7   The Serpent and Temptation
         8-13   Discovery and Hearing
        14-19   Punishment of the Serpent, the Woman, and the Man
        20-21   Naming of the Woman; Garments
        22-24   Expulsion from the Garden
4:1-16 (J)   Cain and Abel
          1-2   Birth and Professions of Cain and Abel
         3-16   Fratricide
4:17-26 (J)   Genealogy of Cain's Descendants
5:1-32 (P)   Genealogy from Adam to Noah
6:1-4 (J)   The Sons of the Gods and the Giants
6:5–9:17 (JP)   The Flood
         5-13   Decision to Destroy and to Preserve Noah
        14-22   Command to Build the Ark

3

1:1–2:4A   THE CREATION OF THE WORLD

1:1 *In the beginning God created the heavens and the earth.*

2 *And the earth was still a desert waste, and darkness lay upon the primeval deep,*
and God's wind was moving to and fro over the surface of the waters.

3 *And God said: Let there be light! And there was light.*

4 *And God saw that the light was good.*
And God separated the light from the darkness.

5 *And God named the light day, but the darkness he named night.*
And it was evening and it was morning, one day.

6 *And God said: Let there be a firmament in the middle of the waters,*
that it may form a separation between water and water. 'And it was so.'[1]

7 *And God made the firmament and created a separation between the waters above the firmament and the waters under the firmament.*

8 *And God named the firmament heaven.*
And it was evening and it was morning, a second day.

9 *And God said: Let the water beneath the heaven gather into one place, so that dry land may appear. And it was so.*

10 *And God named the dry land earth, but the gathering of the water he named sea. And God saw that it was good.*

11 *And God said: Let the earth sprout forth fresh green:*
nlants which produce seed, 'and' fruit trees that bear fruit on the earth each of its kind, [fruit] containing its own seed. And it was so.

12 *And the earth sprouted forth fresh green: seed-bearing plants, each of its kind, and trees that produce fruit containing its own seed, each of its kind. And God saw that it was good.*

13 *And it was evening and it was morning, a third day.*

---

1. Apostrophes (' ') indicate emendations to the Hebrew text. See my commentary on Genesis for details.

14 *And God said: Let there be lights in the firmament of the heavens, to separate*
   the day and the night;
   let them serve there as signs to determine the seasons, days and years.
15 *And let them serve as lights in the firmament of the heavens,*
   so that it may be light on the earth. And it was so.
16 *And God made the two great lights:*
   the greater light to rule over the day, and the lesser light to rule over the
   night, and the stars too.
17 *And God put them in the firmament of the heavens to give light over the*
   earth,
18 *to rule over the day and the night*
   and to separate light and darkness.
   And God saw that it was good.
19 *And it was evening and it was morning, a fourth day.*
20 *And God said: Let the waters teem with living beings,*
   and let birds fly above the earth across the firmament of the heavens.
21 *And God created the great sea monsters and every living being that moves,*
   with which the waters teem, each of its kind,
   and every winged bird, each of its kind. And God saw that it was good.
22 *And God blessed them, saying:*
   Be fruitful and increase and fill the waters in the seas, and let the birds
   increase on the earth.
23 *And it was evening and it was morning, a fifth day.*
24 *And God said: Let the earth bring forth living beings, each of its kind:*
   cattle and reptiles and wild animals, each of its kind.
   And it was so.
25 *And God made the wild animals, each of its kind, and the cattle, each of its*
   kind, and all animals that creep on the ground, each of its kind.
   And God saw that it was good.
26 *And God said: Let us make human beings according to our image,*
   like ourselves. Let them rule over the fish in the sea and over the birds in the
   heavens and over the cattle and over all 'wild animals'
   and over all reptiles that move on earth.
27 *And God created the human race according to his image,*
   according to the image of God he created it, as male and female he created
   them.
28 *And God blessed them 'saying':*
   Be fruitful and increase and fill the earth
   and make it subject to you! Rule over the fish in the sea
   and the birds in the heavens and over every living being that moves on earth!
29 *And God said: I now hand over to you every seed-bearing plant over the*
   whole face of the earth and every tree,
   with fruit-bearing seed in its fruit;
   they are to serve you for food;
30 *while to every animal on the earth and to every bird in the heavens*
   and to every animal that creeps on the earth, [to everything] that has the
   breath of life in it,
   I give every sort of grass and plant for food. And it was so.

31 *And God saw everything that he had made, and it was very good.*
   And it was evening and it was morning, the sixth day.
2:1 *And so the heavens and the earth with all their host were completed.*
2   *And on the seventh day God completed his work that he had done.*
   And on the seventh day he rested from all his work that he had done.
3   *And God blessed the seventh day and made it holy;*
   because on it he rested from all his work which God had created by his action.
4   *This is the origin of the heavens and the earth, when they were created.*

OUTLINE OF 1:1–2:4a

With the Creation story (Gen. 1), the author of P begins a historical work that extends from the creation of the world through the patriarchal narratives, the exodus from Egypt, the revelation at Sinai, and the journey through the wilderness to the entrance into the promised land. In this work, whose goal is the establishment of worship in Jerusalem, P makes clear from the beginning, with the Creation story, that the God who led his people along this way also created the world and humanity, and blessed all living things. In the first chapter of the Bible, both aspects of God's work are seen in the creation of the world: his invariable creation by word in all works, and his specific acts in each of the works of creation.

God created the world by his authoritative word. The unique language of the first chapter, its solemn, rhythmic style, stems from the series of repeated phrases that appear throughout the chapter as components of the creative commands: (1) the introduction, "And God said . . ." (vv. 3, 6, 9, 11, 20, 24, 26); (2) the command in the jussive, "Let (there) be . . ." (vv. 3, 6, 9, 11, 14-15, 20, 24, [26]); (3) the report of its accomplishment, "And it was so . . ." (vv. 3, 7, 9, 11, 15, 24, 30); (4) and finally the judgment (also called the "approbation formula"), "And God saw that it was good" (vv. 4, 10, 12, 18, 25; 31

[expanded]). In addition, there is (5) the temporal statement, "And it was evening . . ." (vv. 5, 8, 13, 19, 23, 31), which P adds for the purpose of linking the Creation to the rest of his history. The chronological framework indicates the organized totality of time. For the author of this chapter, every event is due to the authoritative word of God. Each new section of his work begins with God speaking an authoritative word (to Abraham in Gen. 17, to Moses in Exod. 25, etc.).

Side by side with the invariable creation by word is the particular act of the Creator in each new work. God divides (vv. 4, 7, [9]), names (vv. 5, 8, 10), makes (vv. 7, 16, 25), puts (v. 17), creates (vv. 21, 27), blesses (vv. 22, 28). These words are distributed among the works of creation as follows: "separating" and "naming" apply to the first three (vv. 3-5, 6-8, 9-10); "making" and "putting" to the heavenly bodies (vv. 14-19); "making" to the firmament (v. 7) and the land animals (vv. 24-25, 26); "creating" and "blessing" to the animals (vv. 20-23) and the human race (vv. 26-31). Many parallels to these primitive notions of the Creation are attested both within and outside of Israel; the period of seven days associated with God's creative command appears only here.

Many anomalies can be explained by the incorporation of earlier traditions. The eight acts of creation are taken from a tradition that shows a striking similarity to the sequence of creation in the Babylonian creation epic, Enuma Elish, which derives in turn from older traditions. These eight acts of creation are so distributed over six days of creation that on the third and sixth days two acts of creation occur. Other difficulties—for instance, how the creation of light at the beginning is related to the later creation of the heavenly bodies—will be dealt with in their place.

All attempts to eliminate these difficulties by transpositions or deletions in the text are thus unnecessary. The Creation story as we read it is by nature an organic composition in which earlier and later voices coalesce.

1:1-2 IN THE BEGINNING

In the first words, P gives the Creation story a title that comprehends the creation of heaven and earth in one towering clause. These are the words used for creation in praise and in the confession of the Church. The entire chapter thus unfolds from this one clause. The Hebrew word *berēʾšît* ("in the beginning"; Greek *génesis*) has become the title of the first book of the Hebrew Bible. It means not the beginning of something, but simply The Beginning. *Everything* began with God. But "God" does not mean here a being conceived or imagined by human beings; rather, God is one who acts. Reality exists only because God acts.

God creates (the Hebrew word is used only of God's creating) "the heavens and the earth." Two words designate a single whole. The expression makes clear that here limits are set to the human intellect. We are in a position to comprehend the expanse of the universe only from the perspective of the earth. With the three clauses of the second verse, the narrator seeks to describe the opposite of creation, the "before." The Hebrew expression *tōhû wābōhû* indicates a desert waste, analogous to the Greek *cháos*; its darkness is uncanny, something like what animals experience during a solar eclipse; and "a violent wind," encountered in many cosmologies of the ancient world, intensifies the sense of chaos.

1:3-10   THREE SEPARATIONS

The world the human race inhabits emerges from three acts of separation that make it possible for creatures to live on the earth. From these three separations comes the fundamental order of time and space. The alternation of day and night (vv. 3-5) establishes the organization of time; the creation of the firmament (vv. 6-8) distinguishes "above" and "below"; the division of water and land (vv. 9-10) establishes "here" and "there." The author is not trying to describe the way Creation takes place—that is impossible. He wants to explain to his hearers their present world: it is a whole that, as God's creation, is still in his hands. By associating acts of naming with these three separations, P establishes that the fundamental organization of time and space is defined and established by God. Human beings cannot change it.

3-5   Unlike any other known description of Creation, P begins with the separation of light and darkness, thereby giving the category of time precedence over that of space. The created world is to be understood first and foremost as an event, and only then as matter. The creation of light and its separation from darkness makes possible the succession of days, the temporal order in which the world was created. It is striking that darkness is not described in the same terms as light, as being good. Here we see God's "prejudice" toward light. Of course, darkness is as indispensable as light; but only light can signify salvation. A trend is hinted at here that will shape the story of the created world.

6-8   The representation of heaven as a solid body is found worldwide; it survives into the present in the English word "firmament," which derives from the Latin translation of the Hebrew term. Its physical nature, however, was not what mattered to P, but rather what it conveyed about the separation between "above" and "below," the fundamental vertical structure. When he calls this solid body heaven, he makes it clear that heaven is a part of creation; it is no longer divine, a dwelling place of the gods.

9-10   With the division between water and land, the horizontal plane joins the vertical, making possible the distinction between "here" and "there." The judgment of both acts (vv. 6-7 and 9-10) follows here, because in both the world is created as ordered space. God saw that it was good: these separations make it possible for creatures to live on the earth.

1:11-25   THREE (FOUR) QUICKENINGS

After the first three acts have laid the foundation, the creation of living beings follows in the next three. The world is created for life, in order that living beings may spring forth from it. The coming of life takes place in three stages: plants, animals, human beings. These three stages have retained their importance even in the era of modern science, as have the steps in the evolution of life. Again, the author of P does not claim to be able to say how this happened. He was concerned to show that the present world, with its wealth of phenomena, is a single whole in the hands of its Creator, that the human race as living beings belongs to the totality of living beings, a creature among creatures.

11-13   The creation of living beings begins with plants, with vegetation. At one time the creation of plants involved different stories; here it comprehends vegetation as a totality, and part of the creation of the world. When God commands the earth to bring forth plants, we hear echoes of the ancient notion of Mother Earth. P is saying here that creation and generation are not mutually exclusive. The earth is to bring forth all kinds of plants of which only two basic varieties are known. Despite its variety, vegetation is an organic whole (compare the separation in the first three acts). Each one of the millions of plants, through its relationship to its own species, belongs to the organic whole. Here too, as with the larger stages of evolution, the description of Creation is not in conflict with scientific questions of origin. The notion of flora appearing derives from priestly lore that had been gathered and preserved for generations.

14-19   Now the creation of animals should follow. The narrator, however, consciously places the creation of the heavenly bodies between that of plants and animals. He claims that the heavenly bodies, which in the ancient Near East were gods of supreme importance, are creatures like plants and animals. Like them, they function within the created order, as the account stresses. They are called

9

lamps or lights. That is not to be degrading or derisive, but they are shown to be subject to the limitations of createdness. That the heavenly bodies are signs to determine holiday seasons, as well as days and years, is understood worldwide. In this way the regularity of the calendar (days and years) can be distinguished from particular dates. In the statement that their purpose was to "rule" (vv. 16-18), the fact that the heavenly bodies were once seen as gods shines through. Here the word has only a weak sense of "ruling," as in Psalm 136:7-9: "the sun to rule over the day. . . ." The creation of the heavenly bodies in Genesis 1:14-19 seems to contradict the creation of light in vv. 3-5. But P does not mean that the heavenly bodies were not created until after the light. In vv. 14-19 he is following tradition; in vv. 3-5 he is concerned to establish the seven-day schema of Creation as the introduction to history.

20-25 With the creation of the animals, blessing is joined to creating. The creation of the animals includes fertility, the original meaning of the blessing. The "breath of life" (= living being) comprehends both animals and humanity. The formula "Be fruitful and increase!" is not a command: it confers the ability to reproduce through generations. The blessing links the primal events (1:28; 9:1-2; 8:17) with the patriarchal history (35:11; 47:27; 28:3; 48:4) and with the history of the nation (Exod. 1:7; all P).

The creation of the terrestrial animals (Gen. 1:24-25) is distinguished from that of the fish and birds (vv. 20-23); here too the species are noted. The blessing of the terrestrial animals is not specifically mentioned; but as 8:17 makes clear, it also applies to them.

1:26-31 THE CREATION OF THE HUMAN RACE

P's solemn interpolation sets the last act of creation apart from what has gone before. It begins with a decision by God (the plural "Let us . . ." is a grammatical form characteristic of decisions). Two aspects of this act are special: its special relationship to God, and its special command. God intends to create human beings "according to our image, like ourselves." The question of what that means has been asked again and again (for an overview of the history of interpretation, see my *Genesis 1–11*, pp. 147-155). It does not mean a particular human quality; it is not an isolated assertion about human beings, but rather concerns the purpose of their creation. The Creator wants to create a being analogous to himself, to whom he can speak, who will listen and speak to him. This remains true despite all human differences; every person is created in the image of God.

Humanity is given a special task. By virtue of being created, it bears a responsibility; human dignity and responsibility are inseparable. Humanity exercises sovereignty over the rest of creation. The verb used here means "subjugate," and is used particularly of the rule of kings (e.g., 1 Kgs. 4:24; Ps. 110:2). According to the ancient view, however, there is no suggestion of exploitation; on the contrary, the king is personally responsible for the well-being and prosperity of those he rules. His rule serves the well-being of his subjects. This is what is meant here by humanity's rule over the rest of creation (in contrast to Sumerian and Babylonian creation stories, where humanity was created "to bear the yoke of the gods," that is, to serve the gods through the cult). When this is exemplified by rule over the animals (cf. Ps. 8:6), then it is because the personal element in humanity is most involved here; humanity can remain most fully human through ruling animals, as we see in passages describing the shepherd (Ps. 23; John 10).

Two conditions of human existence still need to be stated in addition to what has been said about its relationship to God and its purpose. The human race is God's creation as male and female. There can be no human existence apart from this existence in two sexes; humans are communal creatures, and all human community is based on the community of male and female. As God's creation, the human race receives a blessing. That blessing is primarily, as with the animals, fertility. Through procreation, conception, and birth the blessing produces the chain of generations that P places after the Creation story in chapter 5. The succession of generations of the human race, however, is different from that of the animals. Implicit in being created in the image of God is the capacity for language; the succession of human generations is a succession of names (as we see in Gen. 5 and 10), and in the succession of names lies the beginning of history. History grows out of the blessing conferred on the human family.

In conclusion, however (1:29-30), something else common to human beings and animals is mentioned: both are appointed their food. Throughout all of human history it remains a fact that human beings require food, and that it is allotted by the Creator. The detail that human beings like animals are assigned only plants as food reflects the ancient tradition of a "Golden Age" when killing for the sake of living was not yet necessary. This primal motif corresponds to the eschatological motif of the peaceable kingdom (e.g., Isa. 11:2-9).

Finally (Gen. 1:31), the approbation formula sums up the entire work of creation: "And he saw that it was very good." In God's sight the entire creation is good, in spite of all that seems incomprehensible, cruel, and terrible to human beings. The goodness of creation is based solely on God's authority; what it is good for, such as it is, only

God knows. But because it is good in God's sight, joy in God's creation (as it is expressed in the praise of creation in the Psalms) is set free in human beings. Moreover, this "goodness" also comprehends beauty (the Hebrew word can mean both "good" and "beautiful"); joy in God's creation contains within itself all joy in what is beautiful.

2:1-4A   THE SEVENTH DAY

In the creation narratives of many peoples the creator-god rests from his work at the end; after the conclusion of the creation, he can no longer intervene. P modifies this motif. It is because of God's rest on the seventh day that this day is holy. The holiness of the seventh day is related to the whole of the now completed work. It establishes an order for humanity that organizes time into the everyday and the holy. This separation ends the Creation that began with three separations. It comprises not only an anticipation of the Israelite Sabbath, but beyond that a gift of the Creator (he blesses it) to humanity. Through the sanctification of the seventh day, the "otherness" of the holy in the midst of the invariable march of time stands out from the flow of events, an intimation of a goal for the creature that God created to correspond to himself.

The clause that concludes the priestly account of Creation (v. 4a) is in reality its title, added to the end to recall the towering clause (1:1) of the beginning.

CONCLUSION   1:1–2:4A

The primary thrust of what is said about Creator and creation in Genesis 1:1–2:4a is reverent preservation of the mystery that is not accessible to human imagination.

Thus P does not speak of creation didactically, but in a way that confronts the hearer with its unfathomability. P knows that he does not have either the first or the last word to say about creation. He allows the voices that have gone before to speak along with him, for creation can be spoken of only in the harmony of the many voices of generations stretching through history. The account of Creation speaks its own language. The simple fact that the first page of the Bible speaks of heaven and earth, sun, moon, and stars, plants and trees, birds, fish, and animals of the field says that God is concerned with all these creatures, and not only with the human race.

An interpretation that did not grant to creation its own significance, but saw its meaning only in relation to soteriology, has inevitably caused the particular acts of God in creation to be ignored. We see today what devastating consequences this disregard has had.

The disregard in the Church and theology for what the Bible says regarding creation is due to the fact that since the beginnings of the natural sciences, the Creation story seems largely to have lost its credibility. The scientific explanation has taken its place. But according to the interpretation presented here, the P Creation story has something to say about the beginnings of the world and the human race that natural science cannot say. On the other hand, the Creation story is completely open to the scientific explanation of the origins and the beginnings of the world and the human race, and already includes it in a nutshell. An "either-or" opposition between the biblical account of creation and the scientific explanation of the world is therefore unnecessary.

A closing word about the relationship of Genesis 1 to the Bible as a whole: The history of the people of God, which begins with the patriarchs (Gen. 12–50) and the exodus from Egypt (Exodus) and extends through the history of the Israelites to Christ and his apostles, finds in Genesis 1 a framework that links this history to the beginning of time, the world, and the human race. Everything in it is based on this beginning. But as Genesis 1 already anticipates a goal for humankind, so the Bible—Old and New Testaments—tells of a final event that includes all of humanity and creation, and brings them to the goal destined by the Creator.

2:4B–3:24 CREATION AND LIMITATIONS OF THE HUMAN RACE

2:4b When the LORD God[1] made earth and the heavens—
5   there was not yet any shrub of the field on the earth
   nor had any plant of the field yet sprung up,
   for the LORD God had not yet caused rain to fall upon the earth,
   nor was there any man to till the ground;
6   and a stream of water used to rise from the earth
   and water the whole face of the ground—
7   then the LORD God formed man out of dust from the ground
   and breathed into his nostrils the breath of life;
   so the man became a living being.

8   And the LORD God planted a garden in Eden, in the east,
   and put the man that he had formed in it.
9   And the LORD God made all kinds of trees grow out of the ground,
   pleasant to look at and good to eat,
   and the tree of life in the middle of the garden,
   and the tree of the knowledge of good and evil.

1. Throughout this section of the text the combination form of the divine name *yhwh ʾelōhîm* has been rendered "the LORD God."

10 *And there is a river going out from Eden to water the garden.*
And from there it divides into branches and becomes four [separate] streams.
11 *The name of the first is Pishon;*
it is the one that flows around the whole of the land of Havilah, where there is
gold,
12 *and the gold of this land is precious.*
There is fine resin there and onyx stone.
13 *The name of the second river is Gihon;*
it is the one that flows around the whole of the land of Cush.
14 *The name of the third river is Tigris,*
that is the one that flows across from Ashur.
And the fourth river, that is the Euphrates.

15 *And the LORD God took the man*
and put him in the garden of Eden,
to till and watch over it.

16 *And the LORD God commanded the man:*
Of all the trees of the garden you may eat;
17 *but of the tree of the knowledge of good and evil*
you may not eat;
because on the day that you eat of it you must die.

18 *And the LORD God reflected:*
It is not good that the man be alone;
I will make a helper for him that is fit for him.
19 *And the LORD God formed out of earth*
every kind of animal of the field and every kind of bird of the heavens,
and he brought them to the man,
to see how he would name them;
and just as the man would name the living beings
so was that to be their name.
20 *And the man gave names to all the cattle*
and to the birds of the heavens and to all animals of the field,
yet for man, he found no helper fit for him.
21 *Then the LORD God caused a deep sleep to fall on the man,*
so that he fell asleep.
And he took one of his ribs and closed up its place with flesh.
22 *And the LORD God built the rib,*
which he had taken from the man, into a woman,
and he brought her to the man.
23 *Then the man said:*
This at last is bone of my bone
and flesh of my flesh!
This one shall be called woman, because she is taken from man!
24 *And so a man leaves his father and mother*
and stays fast by his woman, and they become one flesh.
25 *And the two of them were naked, the man and his woman,*
and they felt no shame before each other.

14

3:1   *And the serpent was more astute than all the animals of the field,*
which the Lord *God had made. And he said to the woman:*
Has God really said: you may not eat of any of the trees of the garden?

2   *The woman answered the serpent:*
Of the fruit of the trees of the garden we may eat;

3   *but of the fruit of the tree in the middle of the garden*
God said: you shall not eat of it,
and you shall not touch it, otherwise you shall die.

4   *And the serpent said to the woman:*
You will certainly not die!

5   *God knows well, that as soon as you eat of it, your eyes will be opened,*
and you will be like God, knowing what is good and evil.

6   *Then the woman saw that it would be good to eat from the tree,*
that it was pleasant to look at
and that the tree was desirable so as to become clever.
So she took some of its fruit and ate,
and she gave it to her man with her, and he ate.

7   *Then the eyes of both of them were opened,*
and they realized that they were naked,
and they sewed fig leaves together and made themselves aprons.

8   *When then they heard the* Lord *God*
moving about in the garden at the time of the day breeze,
the man and his woman hid themselves
from the presence of the Lord *God among the trees of the garden.*

9   *And the* Lord *God called to the man*
and said to him: Where are you?

10   *He answered: I heard you coming in the garden,*
and I was afraid because I am naked; and so I hid myself.

11   *He said: Who told you that you are naked?*
Is it that you have eaten from the tree
from which I forbade you to eat?

12   *The man said: The woman whom you gave me as a companion,*
she gave me of the tree, and so I ate.

13   *And the* Lord *God said to the woman: What is it you have done!*
The woman answered: The serpent induced me to eat.

14   *And the* Lord *God said to the serpent:*
Because you have done this,
cursed are you among all cattle and among all animals of the field;
on your belly shall you crawl,
and dust shall you eat your whole life long.

15   *Enmity I am putting between you and the woman,*
between your seed and her seed;
it will crush your head and you will snap at its heel.

16   *To the woman he said:*
I will increase greatly your pains in childbearing,
in pain you shall bear children.
Your longing shall be for your man, but he shall rule over you.

17   *And to the man he said:*
Because you have listened to the voice of your woman
and have eaten of the tree
of which I had forbidden you to eat:
cursed is the ground because of you;
with toil you shall eat from it your whole life long.

18   *Thorns and thistles it shall bear you,*
and you shall eat the plants of the field.

19   *In the sweat of your face you shall eat your bread*
until you return to the ground again,
because you were taken out of it.
For you are dust and to dust you shall return.

20   *And the man named his woman Eve,*[2]
because she became the mother of all living.

21   *And the* LORD *God made coats of skin for the man and his wife and clothed*
them.

22   *And the* LORD *God said:*
Now the man indeed has become like one of us,
in knowing what is good and evil.
However: let him not now stretch out his hand,
take from the tree of life, eat and live forever!

23   *So the* LORD *God sent him out of the garden*
to till the ground from which he was taken.

24   *And he expelled the man*
and at the east of the garden of Eden he stationed the cherubim
and the flickering flaming sword,
to guard the way to the tree of life.

The first chapter of the Bible deals with the creation of the human race as only one of the works of creation. The second chapter deals almost exclusively with the human race as God's creation. Scholars are virtually unanimous in regarding the second chapter as the work of an earlier scholar and theologian than the first. It is more significant, however, that the creation of the world (ch. 1) and the creation of the human race (ch. 2) were originally independent and separated by millennia. The earlier notion is that of the creation of the human race, going back to a time when humanity understood the world only from its own perspective. This notion is found primarily in primitive cultures. It required a long period of development for humanity to understand the world as an autonomous organic unity, independent of the human race, such as we encounter in Genesis 1. When the creation of the world and the creation of the human race are linked in a single nexus in the first chapter of the Bible, as also in the Apostles' Creed, behind this association lies a long trajectory whose traces still appear in the biblical Creation stories. Furthermore, chapters 2 and 3, which we read as one continuous narrative, are artfully assembled

2. The Hebrew form *ḥawwāh* resembles the Hebrew word for "life."

from two narratives. Just as chapter 1 grows out of the recognition of the intimate connection between "heaven and earth" and their entire host of created beings, so chapters 2 and 3 grow out of the recognition of the intimate connection between the human race as God's creation and the human race with its limitations of sin and death. This narrative reflects a sense of the enigma of human existence, which can be comprehended only in its polarities of birth and death, joy and pain, exaltation and abyss.

Therefore the following approach to this narrative (Gen. 2–3) is suggested: The narrator is not trying to detail what happened in the past, when God created the human race. He cannot do that; there is no witness to those events. He wishes to tell people of *his* time and future generations what it means to them that God created them, that they are God's creation.

In dealing with this long narrative, it is important to remember that a narrative can be understood only as a totality and from the perspective of the whole. When we read through the two chapters, the first thing we notice is that the story of how God created the human race ends with Genesis 2:24, but then moves on without a seam to the story involving the serpent, God, the man, and the woman, which ends with expulsion from God's garden. The second story is linked yet more closely to the first by the fact that it is already alluded to within the first narrative, in verse 9 (the tree of the knowledge of good and evil) and verses 16-17 (the prohibition).

This arrangement can be presented schematically.

2,4b-6	
7-8	
	9
15	
	16-17
18-24	
	25
	3,1-7
	8-13
	14-19
	20-24

17

2:4B-25   THE CREATION OF THE HUMAN RACE

4b-7   The creation of the human race in the beginning. Verses 4b-7 constitute the first cohesive section, comprising three parts. The first clause (v. 4b) is a transition linking chapter 1 with what follows; it summarizes all of the first chapter in the single clause, "When the LORD God made earth and the heavens." This transitional clause also reveals how a narrative of the creation of the world has been linked with a narrative of the creation of the human race. The divine name in Genesis 2–3 is always "*yhwh* Elohim"; in Genesis 1 it was "Elohim"; from Genesis 4 on (from J, the Yahwist), it is "*yhwh*." "*yhwh* Elohim" (translated "the LORD God") as a divine name in Genesis 2–3 is probably meant to form a transition between the two names.

5-6   The second part (vv. 5-6) is marked by a fixed formula that appears very frequently in creation narratives, "When . . . there was not yet." It has the function of making clear, in a naive way, that God's act of creation is to be distinguished from his work in history: it happened when there was as yet nothing at all. This part is clearly analogous to Genesis 1:2.

7   It is the third part (v. 7) that first makes the positive assertion: God created the human race. This is done by means of two acts. First, the LORD God forms man out of dust from the ground. This sentence does not, as is commonly supposed, represent the idea of the theologian who wrote down this narrative in the tenth or ninth century B.C. Rather, he has preserved in his account a very old and widespread ancestral tradition that he considers worthy of respect, a tradition that also appears elsewhere in the Old Testament (e.g., Job 10:8: "Thy hands fashioned and made me . . . ;" cf. Job 4:19; Ps. 90:3; 103:14; 104:29; 146:4; Isa. 29:16). It is found in Egypt and Babylon, and is also encountered frequently in creation narratives of primitive cultures (for details, see my *Genesis 1–11*, with bibliography). For the narrator of Genesis 2–3, this tradition presents the point he himself wishes to convey: that the human race has its existence and its form from God, and that the elements of which the human body consists all belong to our world. The fact that the man is made of "dust" already intimates that he will one day return to dust (3:19).

The second act consists in God's breathing into man the breath of life. The narrator is speaking here of the miracle of life; it is the breath of life breathed by God: "so the man became a living being." It is not that a soul is breathed into the man's body, but rather that he is made a "living soul" (to use the Hebrew expression), that is, a living being. The Bible does not say that a human being is made up of body and soul, or of body, soul, and spirit. God's creation is this man in the totality of his being. Therefore God is concerned not only with the "soul," but equally with the body. A higher regard for the spiritual or ideal than for the corporal or material has no basis in the creation-faith of Genesis.

8-15   The creation of the human race in its relationships. However, this does not complete the creation of the human race; the man is not yet fully human simply because he has been formed. In the biblical Creation narrative, humanity is considered to be God's creation in all its relationships. Integral to the creation of the man is his environment (the garden), his food (the fruits of the garden), his work (v. 15), his community (vv. 18-24), and in all of these his relationship to his Creator. God has created the human race as a totality that includes these elements of its existence; if they are disordered, humanity is disordered. If we take God seriously as Creator of the human race, we must acknowledge that God is also concerned with the environment, sustenance, work, and community. Our usual idea of "Paradise" does not come from the biblical Creation narrative. Rather, God puts the man whom he has created in the garden "to till and watch over it." It is land that needs tilling and watching. At his creation, the man is assigned a task. God entrusts the earth to the man, and therefore expects something of him. Human life without such a task, which depends on him, would not be full human existence. Work here takes on a significance that does not depend on human values. It is a commission received from the Creator.

The Hebrew word represented by "till" is like to the Latin *colere*. Both refer primarily to agriculture, but their meaning includes every kind of "work," all human labor. All human endeavor is seen here as "cultivation" or "culture" (from Latin *colere*). No distinction is made between physical and intellectual work; intellectual work is not valued more highly than physical. The word pair "till and watch over" makes it clear that tilling without watching does not fulfill the commission humanity received from its Creator. Spoliation and exploitation of the earth and its productivity show disrespect for the Creator's commission, and must in the end operate to the detriment of humanity. When humanity fouls and pollutes the earth that has been put in its charge, it destroys the environment that God has entrusted to it to watch over.

10-14   The four streams. Following the description of the garden in which God placed the human race, an ancient bit of geography has been inserted (vv. 10-14). It is an attempt to link the "information" about God's garden with geography. From the river that flows through the garden issue the streams that make the earth fruitful. Two of the streams bear the names Tigris and Euphrates; the other two names are unknown. The number four calls to mind the four quarters of the earth (cf. Zech. 1:8, 11).

16-17   The command. This command the LORD God gives to his creatures actually belongs to the narrative that begins in 3:1. It is included here to link the two narratives.

18-25   The creation of the woman. At this point, when the man is "finished" and apparently provided with all of life's necessities, the Creator pauses in his work and asks himself whether this is now the creature that he intended to create: whether the man is all right just as he is. He comes to the conclusion: No, something is still lacking. Here the narrator is emphasizing something of peculiar importance to the human creature: namely, community. The reflection of the Creator, that this is not yet the true human being that he had intended, elevates the bisexuality of the human race from something taken for granted to the realm of conscious reflection: "It is not good that the man be alone." Then he takes this reflection a step further, by engaging in the "abortive experiment" of creating the animals before creating the woman. Thus the uniqueness of the community between two human beings is contrasted with the possibility of community between man and animal.

19-20   The creation of the animals. But this is not meant to downgrade the significance to humanity of the creation of the animals. The first part of the Creator's decision, "I will make a helper for him," applies also to the animals. However, it is left to the man himself to discover how the animals can help him. Of course, he must take them just as God created them; but God brings them to him so that he can give them names, and with the names a statement of what he understands them to be. By giving the animals names, the man arranges them in his world. At the same time, language comes to play a role in the process of creation: "nomenclature" is invented. Names are given first to the animals, because as living beings they are closest to the human race. This feature of the Creation narrative receives surprising confirmation from the history of animal names. The development has been, by a millennia-long process, from *nomen proprium* to *nomen generis*, from proper noun to common noun. In primitive languages a single genus, such as cattle, will have at least a dozen names, often even more, depending on the stage of development, physical characteristics, and so forth. Observation or practical experience with animals finds expression in these names—in our terminology, the results of ethology. It is a good sign that in our time the importance for humanity of knowing and understanding the animals has finally been rediscovered.

21-25   The clause "a helper . . ." (v. 18) in God's decision reappears at the completion of the creation of the animals: "yet for the man, he found no helper fit for him." So God creates the woman, and in her the creation of the man becomes complete.

The creation of the woman from one of the man's ribs is not intended to be a factual description, and must not be so understood. The narrator wishes to ground the intimate relationship between man and woman in the process of creation itself, and to this end he employs another ancient depiction of the creation of the human race, also found elsewhere. Like the animals before, God now brings the woman to the man, and the man receives her with an "exultant welcome" (J. G. Herder). Now he has been given the helper fit for him! Here "helper" is meant in its broadest sense—not only for work or procreation, but for mutual help in all spheres of human existence. Implicit in the fact that she "suits him" or "is fit for him" is mutual self-understanding in conversation, in silence, in openness to one another. These words express the community of man and woman so simply and fundamentally that they are still relevant for us today; cf. Ecclesiastes 4:9-12, which sounds like an exposition of our passage: "Two are better than one, . . . for if they fall, one will lift up his fellow. . . ."

The words with which the man greets the woman are rhythmic because they reproduce an exclamation; rhythmic language is characteristic of exclamations. It is an outcry of joyous surprise by the man who discovers in the woman his companion.

> "This at last—
> flesh of my flesh, bone of my bone.
> She shall be called woman (ʾiššāh)
> because she is taken from man (ʾîš)."

It is deliberate that the narrative of the creation of the human race uses two basic linguistic forms: "naming" and exclamation. The newly discovered "fitness" is expressed in the naming of the woman, which the man does on his own initiative: "She shall be called woman." The Hebrew etiology (the Hebrew word for "woman" appears to be the word for "man" with a feminine ending) draws together the narrative, asserting that the creation of the human race has reached its goal in the companionship of man and woman. Verse 24 is an addition, appended to the narrative to explain the elemental power of love between man and woman, which is independent of any existing institutions. The Song of Songs also expresses the same idea: "Love is strong as death" (8:6).

The community of man and woman is understood in the Creation narrative of Genesis 2 to be a lifelong association that comprises all facets of life; it includes maturity and old age, and lasts until death. Human existence includes the man and the woman equally. This statement is more significant and more comprehensive than that which subordinates the woman to the man in Genesis 3:16b, a passage which is misleading apart from 2:21-24.

TEMPTATION AND FALL

3:1-7 The temptation. Genesis 3 was once an independent narrative. Its opening is linked to the creation of the human race by 2:9 ("the tree of the knowledge of good and evil," as in 3:5), and the command in 2:16-17. The motif of God's garden is common to the two narratives. The narrative begins with God placing the human beings, his creation, in a garden and making all its fruits available to them; they need suffer no want. He forbids them only to eat of the fruit of the tree in the middle of the garden. If they eat from it, they must die; the prohibition is intended to protect them. By giving the man the command, God expects something of him. If he trusts the one who gave the command, he will adhere to it; but he is also free to act in opposition to the command. Here the narrator is portraying the incomprehensibility of human existence—that humanity goes astray, that humanity sins. This must be said of the human beings created by God: that is the way God's creatures are.

Up to a certain point we can explain why human beings break God's command, which is meant only for their own good. There is a force that compels them; it both comes from within and approaches from without. What is prohibited is especially enticing: "pleasant to look at and good to eat from it" is the summary in 3:6, expanded by the serpent's words. The power of temptation approaches from outside: this is masterfully said in verses 1-7. The serpent is nothing more than the narrative symbol of this power of temptation, which mysteriously speaks through the mouth of one of God's creatures. The serpent does not represent either a mythical being or the devil. It does not exist as a speaking, tempting force outside this scene. The narrator wishes to make it clear to his hearers, by means of this legendary touch, that he is not entertaining them with a story from the distant past. Rather, he is speaking of his hearers themselves, of the mysterious power of enticement and temptation inherent in human existence, familiar to every human being, which marks a limitation of humanity. No ethics, religion or ideology can alter the fact that this is the way God's creatures are. "The temptation appears suddenly as something absolutely inexplicable in the midst of God's good creation. It is left a mystery" (Walther Zimmerli).[1] There is no explanation for the origin of evil.

1. *I. Mose i–xi: Die Urgeschichte*, 2nd ed. (Zurich: Zwingli, 1957).

The serpent, like every true temptation, has something to offer: "You will be like God, knowing what is good and evil." That means knowing what is helpful and harmful—knowledge in its comprehensive sense. And humanity is created with a strong desire to know, and to enhance its existence through knowledge. "The woman saw that the tree was desirable so as to become clever": this clause links the enticement with the temptation. The temptation offers an enhancement of her life: "You will become like God!" But what the tempter does not say is that by transgressing God's command, the human beings will transgress a limit set for them. With the transgression they will in fact gain knowledge; that they will at the same time lose the security God's command was intended to provide will be revealed only later.

The tempter is after both of them; it is enough, however, that he tempts the woman. The community of man and woman, which proved to be so positive in chapter 2, also has its negative sides; there is no ideal human community. Here the narrator points to another way of falling into transgression: joining in. It is human nature to avoid making a decision whenever possible: Adam Tag-along. This narrative articulates a wisdom also found in many sayings from the book of Proverbs. Here the narrator is not raising a finger in warning against temptation; he knows that would be futile. He is trying to make his hearers conscious of it, taking them seriously. He demands that his hearers consider that in the end, the tempter is right up to a point. The man eats from the forbidden fruit and does not die! His eyes are indeed opened, and he does know something that he had not known before. The transgression of one of the limits set for humanity, even one of God's commands, does enhance life and increase knowledge. Only thus can the power of temptation, the power of sin, be taken seriously. What humanity has lost in the process will not be seen for a while.

Something is recognized. The temptation scene was introduced by the words: "They were naked and they felt no shame" (2:25). But now they feel shame. They have learned something, and can also act on that knowledge: they make themselves aprons. This makes it clear that their shame is shared, specifically a sense of nakedness. The surprising thing is that shame can also be positive; "shameless" is a pejorative term. A transgression can have a positive result, insofar as repentance follows from it. The shame of the two human beings is meant in this ambivalent sense. They feel shame because something is not right; but this is how they become conscious that they have transgressed. The serpent was right, and they were wrong.

8-24 The human race in its limitations. Genesis 3:8-24 has a structure that follows universal legal process: identification or detection of the culprits, hearing or trial, defense, and sentence.

8-13 Adam, where are you? Chapter 3 belongs to the corpus of sin and punishment narratives that also includes chapter 4 and other texts of the Primal History. Verses 1-7 deal with sin, verses 14-24 with punishment; the intermediate section (vv. 8-13) has a significance that is best expressed by the question God directs to the man: "Adam, where are you?" Were God only a judge punishing transgression of his command, the punishment could follow immediately on the transgression. But because he is also the merciful God, as Psalm 103 says, he follows the man to the place where God himself has taken him. God follows the man, and so he can defend himself: the man is questioned and can respond.

Trial and judgment face-to-face with God, almost as a peer, is alien to our reality. The narrator speaks of a primal event outside this reality. Such an event occurs in the Old Testament only here and in the parallel chapter 4, and in the New Testament only in the allegory of Matthew 25, where an eschatological event parallels the primal event. A legal trial is pictured, but in the primal event there is as yet no difference between law and religion. What is said here and in chapter 4 is true not only of sins against God (ch. 3), but also of transgressions or offenses against others (ch. 4). The trial is conducted before God and the punishment is decreed by God himself; thus the legal procedure established here by God, the Creator of the human race, is valid for all of humanity. Inherent in this procedure, however, is the right of sinners or offenders to defend themselves.

The first reaction of the man when he hears God coming is to hide; he is afraid. This is also human. It is human nature to seek to avoid the consequences of a crime, to hide; the instinct of self-preservation is strong. It is not normal to commit a crime and immediately confess and face the consequences; it is normal, and always will be, to hide. And if we are apprehended and tried, we try to defend ourselves. One who is apprehended by God receives the chance to defend himself. God still grants the transgressor the freedom to say *everything* that might contribute to his defense, for only so can he finally acknowledge the justice of the verdict. He must plead "extenuating circumstances" so that they can be taken into account. What the man and the woman plead in their defense is appropriate; that must be acknowledged. When the man, conducting his defense, goes so far as to object: "The woman whom you gave me . . . ," even this implied charge against God is allowed, so that the accused may have full freedom to defend himself. This liberty does not change the indictment, but it is essential so that the judge will confront a free man when he pronounces his verdict.

Only the serpent is not interrogated. This fact points out the full significance of the man's answerability (at trial) for his own deeds: the origin of evil cannot be explained. In the face of this inexplicability, the man is responsible.

14-19   Sentences. The real sentence that should follow the trial is expulsion from the garden (vv. 20-24); this is the only punishment that fits the crime. To make this clear, we really should first read the narrative without verses 14-19, and then consider those verses as a unit. They develop and expand the punishment; they describe human existence apart from God. They are not actually punishments, but rather states that reflect the condition of separation from God. The use of the "curse formula" is noteworthy. A curse is pronounced on the serpent and the land, but not on the man and the woman. The narrator thus hints that the curse formula belongs to an earlier stage of human history. It comes from a "magical" way of thinking, in which the distinctions between things, animals, and people are not yet sharply defined. Punishment, however, is a personal transaction. The curse on the serpent preserves an early form of the curse formula, one that employs direct address. Both judgments on the serpent originate in a different context. The first explains the serpent's unique shape and means of locomotion as a curse imposed on it; the second defines the curse as perpetual enmity between this animal species and the human race. Such narratives, whose purpose is to explain animal characteristics, were once common throughout the world. They bespeak an involvement with the animals. When the narrative says that there is a curse on an animal or species, there is a presentiment of the "groaning of creation." In 2:19-20 the animals are characterized as a help to humanity; here the permanent strife between humanity and one species of animal is attributed to a curse. The inexpicability of this curse serves as an allegory for the inexplicability of the power of temptation to sin. The traditional interpretation of the clause ". . . it will crush your head and you will snap at its heel" as a protoevangelium is therefore impossible, if only because the "seed" of the woman and the serpent can mean only the generations to come, not an individual (Mary or Jesus).

The sentences on the woman (3:16) and the man (vv. 17-19) do not reflect acts of punishment; they are not appropriate to the transgression, but rather describe the limited nature of human existence in its separation from God. What is meant as simultaneous is described as cause and effect. In this way the narrator rejects a one-sided view of humanity; the human race is neither absolutely good nor absolutely bad. Even though subject to fallibility, suffering and death, it is still God's creation, intended for life and joy.

In the sentence on the woman, the difficulty and pain of pregnancy and childbirth are seen as the hardship of her life; and her longing after her man and the man's dominion over her are seen not as a change in state, but as a description of the difficulty of a woman's life as then understood. This understanding can change in the course of millennia; nevertheless, there is here an element of a woman's life that remains constant through all changes. As far as the relationship between the woman and the man is concerned, the one-sided subordination "he shall rule over you" is timebound, and it is doubtful whether it should be retained in the marriage ceremony. Genesis 2–3 has something to say on this subject; the clause in 3:16 expresses only one side of the relationship of man and woman, whereas in 2:21-24 man and woman are equals, and no trace of subordination is to be found. In contrast to the temporary subordination of the woman stands the permanent relationship between man and woman: the difference between them is a part of human existence that will always remain.

The sentence on the man has been secondarily expanded; behind it lies a simpler form:

"Cursed is the ground because of you,
thorns and thistles it shall bear you.
In the sweat of your face you shall eat your bread,
until you return to the ground again,
because you were taken out of it."

To the positive meaning of work as God's task for humanity a negative limitation is added here, preventing idealization or glorification of work (including women's work). Human labor is always linked in some way with pain and effort; every kind of work has its thistles and thorns that cannot be removed. When new technology eases the burden of labor in many respects, this is only to be welcomed; but it is typical that at a time when work has been lightened considerably, we speak more than ever of stress and strain. In all work that is done seriously and enthusiastically, worthwhile achievement presupposes toil, sweat, and thorns. When human labor is limited here by death, it is not perceived as punishment. It is the limit to the hardship of human labor. It is part of the span of life that extends from birth to death. All human achievement, whether insignificant or impressive to human eyes, meets its limit in death. This also makes it clear that human beings are more than their work, and must not be simply identified with it. No one is indispensable;

everyone will one day be taken away: "until you return to the ground again, because you were taken out of it."

20-24   Expulsion from God's garden. This is the real punishment for transgressing God's command. At the same time, the narrator is saying something that is a part of human existence, something everyone can know: Plain, simple trust in God, expressed perhaps as a prayer for protection and peace through the night, can be disturbed or threatened by transgression of one of God's commands. Just as a transgression or offense against another person necessarily means a separation, a rupture of intimacy, so too with God. Sin separates from God. But the compassion of the Creator goes into the world with his creatures, even though he removes them from his garden and thus from his presence. In the world their existence is limited by mortality, pain, and suffering ("Why art thou so far . . . ?"). That God's compassion accompanies them is the meaning of the symbolic action that follows. The first consequence of transgression was awareness of nakedness and a sense of shame. The aprons the man and woman made in response to their newly acquired knowledge were of no use when they hid from God. Now God makes clothing for them. They need no longer feel shame, either toward him or toward each other: a metaphor of forgiveness. Following this is another sign that God's compassion accompanies them. The woman becomes a mother (this clause actually belongs with the first birth, 4:1), and her man gives her the name "Life" (Eve, Hebrew *ḥawwāh*). This name is explained: "because she became the mother of all living." Even separated from God, humanity remains blessed by God.

After the sign of the "merciful punishment" (3:21), the real punishment is executed: the LORD God expells the human beings from the garden to live abroad on the earth (v. 23).

The final section, verses 21-24, is not a unity: the expulsion from the garden, for example, is narrated twice, in verses 23 and 24. Often in ancient narratives many threads come together in the final section, because the oral antecedents of a narrative had many variants. Several of the variants would be assimilated into the written form, and frequently the loose ends would be tied up at the conclusion. So it is here. Verses 22 and 24 belong to an independent motif, that of the tree of life, which is already introduced into the narrative at the beginning (2:9). It is an entirely different story, which is appended here to chapter 3. It tells of a traveler who goes on a journey in search of the fruit of the tree of life. A variant is found in the Gilgamesh epic, where Gilgamesh, stricken by his friend's death with a horror of death, sets off in search of the "plant of life" that will protect him from death. This motif is clearly recognizable in God's reflection in verse 22, which the narrator uses to link the two narratives (v. 22a and 22b): "lest he take from the tree of life, eat and live forever!" To prevent this (v. 24 follows v. 22), God has the tree of life guarded by cherubim, mythical guardian figures, probably conceived as hybrid creatures (human and animal), and by a flickering flaming sword, a weapon conceived as an independent being, also a mythical image. The narrative of the tree of life includes clearly mythical touches, which, however, are totally lacking in the narrative of the man's disobedience and expulsion from God's garden.

The narrative of "Paradise and Fall" continues to have significance for Judaism, Christianity, and Islam even today; it is also familiar almost throughout the world: everyone knows Adam and Eve. It is based on traditions about the creation of the human race common to all of humanity. In contrast to this universal significance stands a limited, dogmatic interpretation, which finds here the basis for the doctrine of "original sin," caused by the "Fall." For example, Augustine writes: "The fall of man must also be understood as a descent into an inferior state of being, so that sin must be understood not as a lack, but as a degradation that changes the quality of being." However else this statement may be supported (for example, 4 Esdras 7:118), it is not an exposition of Genesis 2–3. The Primal History portrays human existence as created existence in a sequential narrative that attempts to explain the juxtaposition of positive and negative in humanity, the potential and limitations of creatureliness. It does not speak of a "Fall." Neither, in the Bible, is sin something that can be inherited. The real tragedy in associating Genesis 2–3 with a doctrine of fall or original sin is that once we grasp this doctrine, we think we grasp the narrative, or what it intends to convey; we no longer need to hear it. The interpretation given here seeks to make just one thing clear: we must listen to this narrative if we are to understand it.

The real question informing the narrative is: Why are those created by God limited by death, pain, toil, and sin? We ask this question because we are affected by the contrast. The narrative does not provide a precise or objective answer. Instead, we are expected to notice that the threatened death penalty is not imposed; the curse does not touch the human race. Alienation from God does not mean absolute separation. Rather, in this alienation from God sin and death are the harsh realities in which we remain imprisoned, while yet remaining God's creation. His compassion accompanies us, the Creator's blessing stays with us.

What is said here holds for the entire human race, for God is the Creator of all of humanity. It is this universality that most clearly links the narrative of the creation of the human race and its transgression with the account of the life and passion of Christ in the New Testament. In both, humanity is seen in all the positive aspects of its existence, as well as in its limitations imposed by sin and death. In the story of Jesus of Nazareth, in his words and deeds, his encounters with others, the dominant feature is fundamental human nature, as in Genesis 2–3. This account deals with human beings as creatures: hungry and thirsty, sick and well. In Jesus' passion and death, the limitations imposed on humanity by sin and death are confronted. Subtly yet unmistakably there emerges the connection between what the Bible says about the human race in the beginning and what the New Testament gospels tell about Jesus of Nazareth. It is the history of the relationship between God and humanity, begun in the creation of the human race and leading to Christ and his work.

GENESIS 4   CAIN AND ABEL;
THE DESCENDANTS OF CAIN

1   *And the man knew his wife Eve,*
and she became pregnant and bore Cain.
And she said: I have acquired a man, with the LORD.
2   *And she bore again [a son], Abel, his brother.*
Abel became a keeper of flocks and Cain became a farmer.
3   *After some time Cain presented an offering to the LORD from the produce of*
the field.
4   *And Abel also presented an offering from the first-born of his flocks,*
that is from their fat portions,
and the LORD regarded Abel and his offering,
5   *but he did not regard Cain and his offering.*
So Cain was very angry and his face fell.
6   *Then the LORD said to Cain:*
Why are you angry? and why has your face fallen?
7   *Surely, if you do good, is there not a lifting up,*
and if you do not do good,
sin is there lying in wait at the door,
it is greedy for you,
but you must master it.
8   *And Cain said to his brother Abel: . . . Let us go into the field.*
And when they were in the field,
then Cain rose up against his brother Abel and killed him.
9   *And the LORD said to Cain:*
Where is your brother Abel?
And he said:
I do not know. Am I my brother's guardian?

10   *And he said:*
What have you done?
The voice of your brother's blood
is crying to me from the ground.

11   *But now: cursed are you away from the ground,*
which has opened itself to receive your brother's blood,
shed by your hand!

12   *When you till the ground,*
it will no longer give you of its vitality.
A vagrant and fugitive you shall be in the land.

13   *And Cain said to the* LORD:
My punishment is too heavy to bear.

14   *See, you have now driven me from the ground.*
And I must hide myself from you.
And I must be a vagrant and fugitive in the land.
Anyone who meets me can kill me!

15   *And the* LORD *said to him:*
Not so. Anyone who kills Cain, vengeance shall be taken on him sevenfold.
And the LORD *put a mark on Cain,*
so that anyone who might meet him might not kill him.

16   *And Cain went away from the face of the* LORD
and lived in the land of Nod, to the east of Eden.

17   *And Cain knew his wife,*
and she became pregnant and bore Enoch,
who became the builder of a city,
and he named the city after his own name, Enoch.

18   *To Enoch was born Irad,*
and Irad begot Mehujael,
and Mehijael begot Methushael,
and Methushael begot Lamech.

19   *Lamech took two wives.*
The name of the one was Ada, the name of the other Zillah.

20   *Ada bore Jabal,*
who became the father of those who live in tents and with cattle.

21   *The name of his brother was Jubal,*
who became the father of all those who play the zither and flute.

22   *But Zillah too bore, Tubal-cain,*
'the father' of all those who work bronze and iron,
and the sister of Tubal-cain was called Naamah.

23   *And Lamech said to his wives:*
Ada and Zillah, hear my voice,
Wives of Lamech, listen to my word!
A man I killed because of my wound,
a boy because of my weal.

24   *If Cain is avenged seven times, then Lamech seventy-seven times.*

25   *And Adam knew his wife again,*
and she bore a son and named him Seth.

For: God has set for me another seed,
in place of Abel, because Cain killed him.
26 *And to Seth too a son was born,*
and he named him Enosh.
It was then that people began to call on the name of the LORD.

INTRODUCTION

The fourth chapter is arranged in two parts: verses 1-16, the narrative of Cain and Abel; and verses 17-26, Cain's genealogy. More precisely, the genealogy begins in verses 1-2 and continues in verses 17-26; the narrative of Cain and Abel (vv. 2-16) has been interpolated. Thus this narrative is an expansion inserted into a genealogy, a common feature in Genesis. It grows out of a genealogical entry concerning Cain; besides his conception, birth, and naming (v. 1), it mentions only his vocation and the fact that he killed his brother (as yet nameless) and therefore was banished from the land by the LORD. The narrative in verses 2-16 is modeled closely on that in chapter 3: in both, transgression is followed by discovery, trial by God in person, and sentence. As in chapter 3, the punishment is mitigated to expulsion. A trangression against God parallels a transgression against a human brother; in both, God is judge. Chapter 3 is governed by the man-woman relationship, chapter 4 by the brother-brother relationship. Genesis 4:2 (part of the genealogy) forms the exposition; then the narrative tells of the transgression (vv. 2-8) and the punishment (vv. 9-16). In the first section, the motive (vv. 3-5) and the deed (v. 8) follow the exposition; between them is the LORD's warning to Cain. The second section continues with detection and trial (vv. 9-10), sentence (vv. 11-12), Cain's protest (vv. 13-14), God's answer (v. 15), and the execution of the punishment (v. 16).

1-2 Verses 1-2 begin a genealogy that is continued in verses 17ff. Genealogies are the earliest form of chronology. All preliterate peoples understand chronology only as the sequence of generations. The beginning of the genealogy (vv. 1-2) is also the beginning of the narrative. The woman becomes pregnant, bears a son, and names him Cain. This name probably means "smith," although it is not the usual word for smith in the Old Testament. It has been inferred from this name that the narrative explains the origin of the Kenites; but Genesis 1–11 does not deal with the history of tribes or nations, but rather with the Primal History of the human race. The mother explains the name with a cry of joy or praise: "I have acquired a man, with the LORD." The name Seth (4:25) is also interpreted as a cry of praise. The Creator has given humanity fertility, which remains even after expulsion from God's garden; so the mother can respond to the gift of a child with a cry of joy. She already sees in the child that she has borne the man he will be.

The woman bears another son, whom she names Abel. In the genealogy only one son was named; when the second one's name is given in the narrative, it is coined just for the narrative (it is not found elsewhere as a personal name): his brother's victim, he is named "Breath, Nothingness" (cf. Ps. 39:5, ". . . every man stands as a mere breath"; 144:4; Job 7:16). Abel was a keeper of flocks, Cain a farmer. This is a common, widespread introduction to narratives (cf. Jacob and Esau, Gen. 25:24-27) that compare two occupations, usually in a conflict. Here, however, it is not two callings among many, but the two basic occupations of one period of human history. With the coexistence of two brothers that begins the expansion of the human race, division of labor also begins. If work is imposed on the human race by its Creator, this includes division of labor.

3-5 Another narrative clause introduces the offering of sacrifice (vv. 3, 4a), God's regarding one offering and not the other (vv. 4b, 5a), and Cain's reaction. Cain and Abel each bring an offering from the firstfruits of their labor. Such a firstfruits offering was in many places the most important kind of sacrifice, in some the only kind.[1] It arises directly from the production of food, requiring neither a cultic site nor an altar. Gerardus van der Leeuw says of this kind of offering: "a sacrifice, above all a gift . . . is an acknowledgement of the bountiful source of the gift. . . . The intention is that the stream of blessing continue to flow."[2]

God regarded one offering and did not regard the other. God's failure to regard Cain's offering cannot be attributed to Cain's intention, to improper matter for the sacrifice, or to an incorrect way of offering it. What the language of the ancient narrative expresses is that the one experienced success in his occupation while the other did not. The experience of being accepted or rejected by God is identical to being or not being blessed, to success or failure. The narrator is saying that Cain is not to blame for the fact that his work was not blessed; that must remain unexplained. It is part of the primal experience of humanity that success and failure cannot be rationally explained; God regards the one offering and does not regard the other. Cain perceives this because his work did not prosper (not because, for example, the smoke of the two offerings ascended

---

1. Paul Wilhelm Schmidt, *Der Ursprung der Gottesidee*, IV (Münster: Aschendorff, 1933); Johannes Pedersen, *Israel, Its Life and Culture*, III-IV (London: Oxford University, 1940): 299-307.
2. *Phänomenologie der Religion*, 2nd ed. (Tübingen: J. C. B. Mohr, 1956), pp. 331-32.

differently). The narrative deals with the primal experience that given the same start and the same amount of effort, one will succeed and another will not. This is one of the universal sources of conflict between brothers. Cain is jealous, but the narrative sees this as an entirely legitimate reaction: Cain feels he has been treated unfairly. It is the one who has been unjustly injured who is concerned with justice.[3]

6-7   In verses 6-7 God gives Cain a warning. It comprises a question (v. 6) and an admonition (v. 7), and makes Cain completely responsible for the deed that then follows. The text is difficult; there is as yet no satisfactory interpretation of verses 6-7. Moreover, verse 6 rephrases the previous clause as a question, and 7b repeats a clause from 3:16, giving it a different meaning. The admonition in 4:7 says: It is entirely up to you, Cain; if you behave properly, you will be able to hold up your head, but if not. . . . The conclusion is unclear, but can be understood as: . . . sin is lying in ambush to overpower you, but you must master it. It is unlikely, however, especially in view of the borrowing from 3:16, that this clause was originally part of the narrative of Cain and Abel; neither is the language that of an early narrative. But the expression "lying in wait at the door" allows us to posit an earlier text in which Cain was cautioned not about sin, but about the consequences of his intended deed. In that case, the one lying in wait at the door would be the spirit of the slain (the Assyrian word *rabiṣūm,* which refers to a demon, corresponds to the Hebrew word for "one who lies in wait"), which would then pursue him. This is a common image; because the idea of a dead spirit later became offensive, it was replaced in the narrative by "sin." (For other proposed interpretations of this difficult passage, see my *Genesis 1–11,* pp. 300-301.)

8   The account of the deed follows, told in few words. At the beginning of verse 8, the words "And Cain said to his brother Abel" introduce a saying that has dropped out of the text. The ancient versions restored it as "Let us go into the field," and this could be the original text. He wants to have Abel where there will be no witnesses to the deed (cf. Gen. 37, also a plot to murder a brother). The two verbs "rose up against . . . killed . . ." portray the deed as deliberate and premeditated. With these few harsh words the narrator says: This is what human beings are like; brother can even murder brother.

9-16   Retribution follows the transgression. God himself, in direct address as in chapter 3, conducts the trial and executes the punishment. The sequence parallels chapter 3: 4:9-10, trial (3:9-13);

3. In this connection see Helmut Schoeck's sociological study, *Der Neid* (Freiburg: Alber, 1966).

4:11-12, sentence (3:14, 19); 4:15, mitigation (3:21); 4:16, expulsion (3:23, 24).

9-10   The trial takes the form of a question, or rather a series of questions, addressed to the murderer. The accused retains the right to answer, to defend himself: "Where is your brother Abel?" (cf. "Adam, where are you?," 3:9). With his answer, "Am I then my brother's guardian?," Cain denies his responsibility toward a fellow human being facing a mortal threat. As nearly always happens, murder is followed by a concealing lie (cf. ch. 37). God's answer exposes the lie. The conclusion of the narrative lays particular stress on God's answer: The brother's blood cries to God. Murder will out. Although no human ears hear the cry of the victim, God hears. Thus God can accuse Cain of the murder to his face: "What have you done?" (cf. 3:13). This is not a deed that can be concealed: the spilled blood cries out. The murderer cannot evade the question: "What have you done?" This holds for all of humanity, for all of human history. True, murders do occur that are not discovered and punished; but this does not change the fact that with this clause one human being is protected from another. Human community in which murder is not punished is impossible. What is done in the primal event by God himself is done in history by institutions; but what these institutions do is what God has determined for the human race, his creation.

11-12   The words "Cursed are you" introducing the sentence indicate that a more ancient concept lies behind verses 11b and 12a, according to which an evil deed automatically brings a curse. The punishment lay in the consequences of the deed: the soil that had accepted the blood of the slain denies the farmer its yield; he must leave the land and wander in misery. Adam is not cursed, but Cain is. Among human beings estranged from God, limited by sin and death, there is the peculiar possibility of living under a curse, a possibility embodied in Cain. A curse has the power to set apart; one thus set apart is taboo. Anyone who associates with him is infected. The one who is cursed is expelled. The expression "vagrant and fugitive" is found only here (vv. 12, 14) in the Old Testament; it is part of the curse formula. It means a driven, hunted existence, not a nomadic way of life (as suggested by Julius Wellhausen and many commentators).

13-15   Cain's lament protests the punishment, which seems to him too severe; his plaintive objection (v. 13) is developed in verse 14. In verse 15, God mitigates the punishment. Martin Luther has translated verse 13: "My sin is too great to be forgiven." Since H. G. A. Ewald, the verse has been understood differently: Cain is protesting the severity of his punishment. It must be remembered that the

Hebrew word ʿāwôn can mean both sin and punishment. Already implicit in Cain's lament are the three determinative complaints found in the laments of the Psalter: "You have now driven me . . ." (what God has done); "I must hide myself from you!" (what I must do); "Anyone who meets me can kill me!" (what enemies do). Cain considers the sentence of expulsion to be just as severe as the death sentence: "It is a question whether ancient man saw a distinction in degree between banishment and death."[4]

15   This conclusion (the last clause of v. 14) is negated by God's answer, which protects Cain from being killed by anyone. Its structure reflects apodictic law. Cain, who is now abroad as an outlaw, is protected by law. The intention is to prevent vendettas. No human being has the right to interfere with the execution of God's punishment. To prevent this, God "puts" a mark on him. This can refer only to an individual, not a group, and therefore cannot indicate a tribal or a universal mark of protection or a sign that someone belongs to God. It is a mark intended to protect this specific man, Cain, in this particular situation, from being killed. The form of the mark in unknown, and cannot be inferred from the narrative.

16   Finally there comes separation from God, as in chapter 3. Cain is banned from God's presence. The name of the land reflects this: Nod, where Cain now dwells, is the Land of Misery. "East of Eden" should also be understood this way: away, far from God (cf. John Steinbeck's *East of Eden*).

CONCLUSION

"Humanity" includes not only Adam and Eve, but also Cain and Abel. In Genesis 4:2-16, humanity is understood as the human brother. Traditional interpretation usually understands the relationship of 4:2-16 to chapters 2–3 as intensification. But the narrator does not see Cain's crime as an intensification of the sin that Adam and Eve began; instead, sin against a brother is here added to sin against God. Both are part of human fallibility. The traditional interpretation renders the social aspect of sin insignificant; but in the Primal History itself, sin against a brother is an essential consequence of sin against God.

Where the New Testament refers to the story of Cain and Abel (Matt. 23:35; 1 John 3:12; Heb. 11:4; 12:24), it draws on the Jewish tradition that sees it as an example of the contrast between the righteous and the sinner. Here Cain is a priori "wicked." This under-

4. P. A. H. de Boer, "Kain und Abel," *Nederlands Theologisch Tijdschrift* 31 (1942): 209.

standing is often adopted in Christian interpretation. But in the narrative itself Cain is not a priori wicked; his resentment of his rejection is seen as legitimate and human. Cain's sin begins with his decision to eliminate his brother. Thus the narrator is saying: inherent in humanity is the possibility of crime, the possibility of fratricide. For the Christian, this narrative makes it clear that the work of Christ on behalf of the human race includes even this extreme possibility.

4:17-26 THE DESCENDANTS OF CAIN

1, 17-26   Verses 1 and 17-26 comprise a genealogy that presents a primal event in the form of a sequence of generations. Beginning with the common origin of all humanity, it deals with the establishment of significant forms of civilization. The first section (vv. 1, 17-18) presents a sequence of seven generations with only two expansions, in verses 1 and 17b. The second section (vv. 19-24) presents only Lamech's generation; here the expansions dominate. In another form, verse 2, which now functions as an exposition for verses 2-16, probably belonged to the genealogy as well. Thus the expansions exhibit a clear pattern. In the first section they deal with primitive civilization: agriculture and the settlement of cities; in the second, with nomadic culture: the arts of music and metallurgy. This hints at an undersanding of cultural evolution, but at the same time demonstrates the understanding that the fundamental achievements of civilization belong to primeval times: Israel has inherited them. The structure of the Primal History makes it clear that specialization of labor and the development of civilization are inherent in the growth of the human race created by God. However, this flourishing of civilization also conceals the danger of an exaggerated sense of power (vv. 23-24), which leads into chapters 6–8.

17-18   Verse 17 reports the birth of a son to Cain in the three acts characteristic of a genealogy. The last clause of verse 17 is to be read "after his (Enoch's) name" rather than "after his son's name." The progress from agriculture to urban life is accomplished in the sequence of births; since Cain was called a farmer, he cannot be a city builder as well. The name "Enoch" probably derives from a verb meaning "dedicate." The founding of the city is presented as the beginning of civilization. It happened in the distant past; Israel did not participate in it: "great and goodly cities, which you did not build" (Deut. 6:10).

Verse 18 lists the descendants of Enoch up to Lamech, a series of five generations. With Adam and Cain, this is a series of seven.

"Mehujael" and "Mihijael" are variants of the same name; both were preserved by the tradent. "Methushael" is interpreted as "Man of the Underworld," "Lamech" as a title (*lumga*) for the god Ea as patron of song and music. Both names have Babylonian origins.

19-22   As the human race increases, so do the accomplishments of civilization. When in the final generation of the genealogy several sons and daughters are born, this also indicates the proliferation of cultural accomplishments. Behind this presentation stands a rich and varied tradition known from other ancient Near Eastern materials; only a small sample of it is incorporated here. After the settled civilization of the farmers and city dwellers (vv. 17-18) comes nomadic civilization; tent dwellers and nomads trace their origin to Jabal, musicians to Jubal, and metalworkers to Tubal-Cain (vv. 20-22). The invention of musical instruments is attributed to the nomads, as in many nations musical instruments are connected with shepherds (for example, the pipes of Pan), and the two names "Ada" and "Zillah" possibly allude to singing. In secular use, the flute and lyre (or zither) belonged together; later the stringed instrument was introduced into worship. The blacksmith's art is also traced back to the nomads (v. 22); wandering smiths are found in many places in the ancient world.

23-24   The Song of Lamech is appended here to the genealogy, but it originated as an independent song. Many such very short songs have been preserved from ancient times (for example, Exod. 15:21). The fact that the imperative to the listeners (Gen. 4:23) is addressed to Lamech's wives indicates an early origin in a family group. The song comprises three clauses; the first two form a parallelism. Verse 24 connects the song to the narrative of Cain and Abel. It could be that this verse was added when the two parts of chapter 4 were joined. In the present context it concludes the genealogy and at the same time joins it to verses 1-16. The song of Lamech magnifies one human being's ability to kill another. Detached from its present context, it was a "boasting song," with which a strong man bragged to his wives and also threatened his enemy. But the narrator of chapter 4 intends to convey more: humanity's increased skills at weaponry also make possible an increase in mutual destruction. The narrator has seen both sides of the advances of civilization: their enhancement of the quality of life, and also the way they increase the possiblity of self-assertion.

25-26   These verses attach another independent genealogy to the first: this proceeds from Adam through Seth to Enosh (to Noah, according to 5:29). It is preserved only in part. Earlier interpretation saw this as a genealogy pleasing to God, in contrast to the corrupt genealogy of Cain's descendants. But the text does not say this. The naming in verse 25 parallels that in 4:1: "God has set for me a seed" is a cry of joy over the gift of a son, and therefore progeny. "In place of Abel, because Cain killed him" is a secondary addition, intended to form a connection with verses 1-6. In verse 26 the genealogy is continued; Seth also begets a son, whom he names Enosh. There is no particular significance to the fact that here, in contrast to verse 25, the father names the son. Hebrew *'enôš* is actually a collective noun meaning "humanity"; here it becomes a name.[1]

The expansion "It was then that people began to call on the name of Yahweh" is difficult, since the origin of Yahweh worship is told of at the beginning of Exodus, and hence began with the exodus from Egypt. Since both passages derive from the same narrator (J), they cannot mean the same thing. What is meant here is that worship of God began in primeval times. In this way a clear distinction is drawn between the Israelites' worship of Yahweh and what we call religion (there is no comparable word in the Old Testament). J knows that religion is common to all known peoples. Non-Israelite sources also describe the origin of the cult as occurring in primeval times. Worship is here spoken of as "calling on God's name." This means that by means of God's name a genuine contact between humanity and God is effected. In fact, this is the basis of all forms of worship, as we still see in the Christian liturgy: "In the name of the Father. . . ."

CONCLUSION

In contrast to the myth of Prometheus, no robbery and no folk heroes are needed here to wrest the advances of civilization from the gods. They are already inherent in the blessing bestowed by God on his creation so that the human race itself may be able to achieve civilization. The development of civilization is based in God's will for his creation. Because God is *one*, the origins of civilization cannot be traced back to mythical beings; it is the human race that founded the first city, that invented metallurgy and musical instruments. The progress and development of civilization are based on God's charge to work, and in the blessing that makes growth possible. Like civilization, religion is part of human history from the very beginning. But a cultural advance can also increase the desire for power and the ability to destroy. The escalation from fratricide to a multiplied ability to kill speaks for itself.

1. Cf. Claus Westermann, "*'ādām* Mensch," cols. 42-44 in *Theologisches Handwörterbuch zum Alten Testament*, ed. Ernst Jenni and Westermann, I (Munich: Christian Kaiser, 1971).

5:1-32 THE PRIMEVAL GENEALOGY

1   *This is the list of the genealogy of Adam:*

    When God created humankind, he made it in the image of God,
2   *male and female he created them*
    and he blessed them and called them human beings
    when they were created.

3   *When Adam was 130 years old, he begot [a son]*
    in his own image, corresponding to him,
    and named him Seth.

4   *Adam's life span, after he begot Seth, came to 800 years.*
    And he begot sons and daughters.

5   *The total life span of Adam came to 930 years. Then he died.*

6   *When Seth was 105 years old, he begot Enosh.*

7   *After Seth begot Enosh*
    he lived another 807 years and begot sons and daughters.

8   *The total life span of Seth came to 912 years. Then he died.*

9   *When Enosh was 90 years old, he begot Kenan.*

10 *After Enosh begot Kenan*
    he lived another 815 years and begot sons and daughters.

11 *The total life span of Enosh came to 905 years. Then he died.*

12 *When Kenan was 70 years old, he begot Mahalalel.*

13 *After Kenan begot Mahalalel*
    he lived another 840 years and begot sons and daughters.

14 *The total life span of Kenan came to 910 years. Then he died.*

15 *When Mahalalel was 65 years old, he begot Jared.*

16 *After Mahalalel begot Jared*
    he lived another 830 years and begot sons and daughters.

17 *The total life span of Mahalalel came to 895 years. Then he died.*

18 *When Jared was 162 years old, he begot Enoch.*

19 *After Jared begot Enoch*
    he lived another 800 years and begot sons and daughters.

20 *The total life span of Jared came to 962 years. Then he died.*

21 *When Enoch was 65 years old, he begot Methuselah.*

22 *And Enoch walked with God.*
    After Enoch begot Methuselah
    he lived another 300 years.

23 *The total life span of Enoch came to 365 years.*

24 *And Enoch walked with God.*
    And he was no longer there, because God took him.

25 *When Methuselah was 187 years old, he begot Lamech.*

26 *After Methuselah begot Lamech*
    he lived another 782 years and begot sons and daughters.

27 *The total life span of Methuselah came to 969 years. Then he died.*

28 *When Lamech was 182 years old, he begot a son.*

29 *And he named him Noah, saying:*
    This one will create relief for us from our work

and from the toil of our hands from the ground
which God has cursed.

30 *After Lamech begot Noah*
he lived another 595 years and begot sons and daughters.
31 *The total life span of Lamech came to 777 years. Then he died.*
32 *When Noah was 500 years old*
Noah begot Shem, Ham, and Japheth.

INTRODUCTION

The genealogies are an essential component of the primal events. Their significance is not in spanning the time from Creation to the Deluge, as earlier interpretations suggested, but in forming a transition between the creation of the human race (vv. 1-2) and human history. Humanity is the creature that extends the power of the Creator's blessing into the realm of time. The first section (vv. 1-5) links the ten-generation genealogy from Adam to Noah with the creation of the human race. The purpose of God's creation of the human race (1:26-31) continues in this genealogy. The blessing God bestowed on his creation: "Be fruitful and increase . . . !" is realized in the succession of generations; it becomes operative in the new rhythm of generations extending into time in an unbroken sequence, in the rhythm of conception and birth, lifetime and death.

The beginning of human history in the flux of generations is presented in a unique literary form consisting of one constant and one variable element. The constant element comprises the identical clauses repeated throughout the chapter, divisions of the sequence of generations: conception (and birth), life span before and after the birth of one named son, conception of other sons and daughters, death. The variable element comprises the names and numbers. These two elements together form the basis of human history: the invariable creatureliness and its ever-changing historical expressions.

This understanding challenges the prevailing view of history, which holds that human history can be comprehended in facts and dates, that is, solely in variable elements. On the contrary, the elements that are constant, always and everywhere the same, common to humanity in every period, play a significant role in human history. Therefore a theory of history that thinks it possible to ignore these constant, creaturely elements has become questionable. It is because of such a one-sided understanding of history that traditional interpretations of chapter 5 have emphasized only the names and numbers. But this does not reflect the author's intention. He wishes to say, first and foremost, that the Creator's blessing is effected in the constant progression of human history.

THE NAMES AND NUMBERS

The first three names are the same as those of 4:25-26: Adam, Seth, Enosh. The fourth through ninth names are related to those in 4:17-18; two are identical. This shows that the series of ten is composed of two different pieces, both with an Israelite history. Previously the Old Babylonian King List, preserved by the Greek historian Berossos (then included in Eusebius' history), was considered to be a parallel to Genesis 5. This list enumerates ten kings before the Deluge; it was even thought that there were parallels to some of the biblical names. The discovery of the cuneiform original of the King List, however, revealed that the names were Sumerian. The number of kings in the older lists was eight. Since these discoveries, it is no longer possible to call the Sumerian King List a parallel to Genesis 5. The principal difference is that the Sumerian list is in the category of historical traditions, while Genesis 5 belongs to the genre of genealogy. The similarity is limited to the fact that P has added to the ancient genealogy the life spans that were not originally part of it.

P's numbering system is a secondary construction. The uncertainty of this tradition is obvious from the fact that it is preserved differently in three different texts. Most noteworthy is the length of the life spans, the longest 969 years (in the Sumerian King List, the longest reign is 72,000 years; these are mythical numbers). The long life spans in Genesis 5 are usually explained as the result of a greater life force in the primeval period, which later decreased. But this is improbable, since Isaiah 65:20, for instance, specifies the upper limit of the life span in the eschatological kingdom as 100 years. The large numbers in Genesis 5 have a different significance. They refer to the distant past of the human race in the vast expanse of prehistory, a vastness that cannot be measured by the standards of present history. Behind these numbers lies an implicit understanding that the human race is far older than can be indicated with ordinary life spans and genealogies. This is what P intends in using this genealogy with its large numbers to connect Creation (5:1-3) and known human history.

1-5   P begins by recalling the creation of the human race (1:26-31). It is the creation of humanity that is continued in the genealogy of Adam (now a proper name). In this way, P gives special emphasis to the idea of creation according to the image of God. God has created the human race to be like him, as his counterparts. This is true of all humanity, for whom God's blessing is realized in the succession of generations. The life force bestowed by God is at work in the increase and spread of humanity.

6-8   This pattern reduces human life to conception (and birth), the begetting of a child (presupposing marriage), life span, and death: this is what links all humanity, what is common to all as long as there is a human race.

24   Verse 24, the account of Enoch's removal, does not fit into this pattern. He "walked with God": he was a godly man who had a special relationship with God. Thus he did not die a natural death: "God took him." The emphasis is on the inexplicability of this removal; there is no notion of any mythical heavenly realm here.

29   This verse actually focuses on Noah the vintner (9:20-27) in the form of an etiology recalling the cultural development outlined in 4:17-22; it speaks of work and recreation. The discovery of wine provided a source of joy for hard-working humanity.

CONCLUSION

Genesis 5 represents the basic flow of history: humanity is the creature that extends into history by virtue of God's blessing. Individuals are human only as links in this chain. God's blessing includes all of humanity, from beginning to end. Although P's narrative leads up to the establishment of the temple in Jerusalem, he intends this chapter to say that God the Creator, worshipped in the Jerusalem sanctuary, is the God of all humanity. The creation and blessing of the human race begins the path that leads to the sanctuary and worship in Jerusalem. Here P exhibits a universalism that brings all humanity into a relationship with its Creator whose praises are sung in the Psalms.

The New Testament also has a genealogy at the beginning of the story of Jesus; in the New Testament as in the Old, the story of salvation is prefaced with a genealogy (Matt. 1:1-17; Luke 3:23-38). The theological significance of the genealogy at the beginning of the New Testament lies in the fact that God's saving actions in Christ are inconceivable apart from the blessing that embraces all humanity. The humanity of Jesus is a part of human history, whose beginning is portrayed in Genesis 5.

6:1-4   THE SONS OF THE GODS AND THE GIANTS

1   *And then,*
     when humankind began to increase on the face of the earth
     and daughters were born to them,
2   *then the sons of the gods saw that the daughters of humankind were*
     beautiful.
     And so they took wives for themselves from among them all,
     just as their fancy chose.

3   *And Yahweh said:*
My spirit shall not remain forever in humankind,
because indeed they are flesh.
Their life span shall cover 120 years.

4   *The giants (Hebrew nᵉpilîm) were in the land in those days,*
and afterwards too,
when the sons of the gods came to the daughters of humankind,
and they bore [children] to them;
these are the heroes, the men of renown,
who were there of old.

INTRODUCTION

Understanding this brief text is made difficult by the fact that in it two originally distinct narratives were joined, and in the process both were abridged. The two strands in the narrative can be seen most clearly at the end (this is often the case; see comments on 3:22-24), where in 6:4a the culmination is the "giants" (*nᵉpilîm*) and in verse 4b the heroes (*gibbōrîm*). The first is an etiological note that explains the origin of the giants: the sons of the gods see and take wives, who bear them children: the giants. The other is a mythical narrative. It has the same beginning: the sons of the gods see and take wives. There follows a different continuation, which is difficult to understand only in verse 3: God intervenes in the encroachment of the "sons of the gods," because through this transgression of a boundary, humanity is endangered. This motif is encountered twice in the Old Testament, although in different forms: in the Patriarchal History (Gen. 12:10-20), where Israel's mother is endangered, and in the story of David (2 Sam. 11–12). In all three narratives a strong man sees the beauty of a woman and takes her; in all three the transgression of a boundary endangers community, and God intervenes. All three texts tell how the natural human desire for beauty endangers limited humanity when it transgresses the limits set for humanity.

It is not the desire for beauty as such, but rather the transgression of limits that is the trespass against which God intervenes. From the two parallel narratives it can be inferred that an earlier form of Genesis 6:3 told of an intervention by God.

The Yahwistic narrator (J) in chapters 1–11 brought together in the narratives of crime and punishment two offenses by individuals (chapters 3 and 4) and two collective offenses (6:1-4; 11:1-9); both the latter involve the transgression of human limits. The offense in 11:1-9 is technological (the building that reaches to the heavens); in 6:1-4, it is the elevation of the *genus humanum* to a superhuman group as the result of a liaison between the "sons of the gods" and human women.

To represent the danger of transgressing limits, the narrator draws on a familiar ancient Near Eastern myth, probably of Canaanite origin. In this myth "sons of the gods" (*bᵉnê hāʾᵉlōhîm*) refers to divine beings, not "angels," as earlier interpreters assumed. Since humankind is still a homogeneous unit in these primal events, not yet broken down into political or social groups, the narrator represents the "sons of the gods" as a class superior to the human race (see my *Genesis 1–11*, pp. 365-68, 371-73).

1   The increase of the human race is found elsewhere in stories dealing with the dawn of history as an introduction to the narrative, for example in the Epic of Atrahasis: "The land became great, the people increased. . . ." Here, too, the event so introduced leads to the disastrous punishment of the Deluge.

2   In the Old Testament, beauty is primarily not an objective quality that is present but, rather, an event. Beauty is present when it is perceived, thus setting an event in motion. Genesis 2:23 also records a discovery of beauty; there it leads to enduring togetherness. Here another possibility is contrasted: that a powerful person discovers beauty and seizes it because he has the power to do so. As the parallelism shows, the narrator here is thinking of a human phenomenon, which he presents in mythological dress: an act of aggression made possible by superior force.

3   This act of aggression demanding God's intervention is presupposed by verse 3. The transition, however, is awkward. All we can be certain of is that the verse describes a sentence passed by God, imposing limits; it is not, however, passed against the "sons of the gods," who would seem to deserve punishment, but against the human race. The text is clearly out of order. The verdict setting limits to the human life span presupposes a human attempt to extend life beyond the human norm. We may speculate that there was a version of the narrative in which the "sons of the gods" who had married human wives allied themselves with humanity (like Prometheus) and strove to aggrandize the human race, an attempt the Creator had to resist (cf. 11:1-9). "My spirit" refers to the life-giving power of the Creator, which is not to remain permanently with mortals. This is further explained by the clause "because indeed they are flesh." The text is difficult. "Flesh" here has the sense "helpless earthly creature" (Hermann Gunkel). God's limiting verdict blocks the attempt to transgress human limitations by imposing a restriction on human life, similar to restriction imposed in 3:22, 24.

4   The fourth verse also presents problems. The narrative continues in verse 4b: children are born of the liaison between the sons of the gods and the human women. This can be related because God's

sentence was not destruction but restriction. In chapters 3–4, too, punishment is followed by the birth of a child.

Something more must be said about these children. Verse 4a refers to them as *nᵉpilîm*. This word is explained in Numbers 13:33 as meaning "giants": "the sons of Anak, of the race of giants." The phrase in Genesis 6:4 "and afterwards too" distinguishes the Nephilim of the Primal History from the Nephilim in the story of the spies. Originally the word referred to mythical beings, as can still be seen in Ezekiel 32. In his commentary on Ezekiel, Walther Zimmerli finds in chapter 32 a reference to Genesis 6:1-4 and cites the demigods of Babylonian and Greek mythology.[1] But there is nothing mythological about the statement in the last sentence: "These are the heroes, the men of renown, who were there of old." This shows once more that two different traditions have been combined here. The theme that human arrogance is in danger of overreaching itself appears also in Israel's prophets, for example the song in Isaiah 14 describing the fall of the King of Babylon to the underworld.

6:5–9:17, 28-29   THE FLOOD

6:5   *When Yahweh saw*
that the wickedness of humankind on earth was great,
and every planning and striving of its heart was always only wicked,

6   *then Yahweh was sorry that he had made humankind on earth,*
and he was grieved at heart.

7   *And Yahweh said:*
I will wipe out humankind whom I have created
from the face of the earth,
from humans to beasts, reptiles
and birds of heaven,
because I am sorry that I have made them.

8   *But Noah had found favor in the eyes of Yahweh.*

9   *This is the story of Noah.*
Noah was a just man.
He was blameless among his contemporaries;
Noah walked with God.

10   *And Noah had three sons: Shem, Ham, and Japheth.*

11   *But the earth was corrupt in God's eyes,*
the earth was full of violence.

12   *God looked at the earth and it was certainly corrupt,*
because all flesh had corrupted its way of life on earth.

1. *Ezekiel 2*. Hermeneia (Philadelphia: Fortress, 1983), p. 176.

13   *And God said to Noah:*
           I have decided to put an end to all flesh,
           because the earth is full of violence because of it.
           And so I will wipe it from the earth.

14   *Make an ark for yourself out of gopher wood,*
           make it with rooms,
           and coat it inside and outside with pitch.

15   *Thus shall you make it:*
           its length is to be 300 cubits,
           its width 50 cubits, and its height 30 cubits.

16   *Make a roof on the ark at the top*
           [according to the cubit you shall make it],
           and the door of the ark you are to put in the side of the ark,
           a lower second and third deck you shall make.

17   *But I am now unleashing the Flood upon the earth,*
           so as to destroy all flesh under heaven that has in it the breath of life,
           everything that is on the earth shall perish.

18   *But with you I am setting up a covenant:*
           You are to go into the ark, you and your sons
           and your wife and the wives of your sons with you.

19   *And from all that lives, from all flesh,*
           you are to bring two of each into the ark,
           to keep them alive with you;
           there is to be a male and a female of each.

20   *Of the birds according to their kind and of the animals according to their*
           kind, of everything that creeps upon the ground, two of each are to come
           to you to be kept alive.

21   *You are to take every sort of food that is eaten,*
           and store it up,
           that it may serve as food for you and them.

22   *And Noah did everything, just as God had commanded him.*

7:1   *And Yahweh said to Noah:*
      Go into the ark, you and your whole household,
      for you I have found just before me
      among this race.

2   *Of all clean animals take seven each, male and female,*
      and of the animals that are not clean, two of each,
      male and female,

3   *[and of the birds of the air seven each, male and female,]*
      to keep their kind alive on earth.

4   *For seven days from now I will bring rain upon the earth for forty days and*
    forty nights,
      and every existing thing that I have made
      I will wipe from the earth.

5   *And Noah did everything that Yahweh had commanded him.*

6   *And Noah was 600 years old,*
           when the Flood [water] came upon the earth.

7   *And Noah and his sons*
    and his wife and his sons' wives
    went into the ark to escape the waters of the Flood.
8   *Of the clean animals and of the animals that are not clean,*
    and of the birds and of all that crawls on the earth,
9   *two of each, male and female, went into the ark with Noah,*
    as God had commanded Noah.

10 *And after seven days the waters of the Flood came upon the earth.*
11   *In the six hundredth year of Noah's life, in the second month, on the*
        seventeenth day of the month.
        On this day all the fountains of the great deep burst forth,
        and the windows of heaven were opened.

12 *And rain poured upon the earth for forty days and forty nights.*
13   *On this very day Noah and his sons*
        Shem, Ham, and Japheth
        and Noah's wife and the three wives of his sons
        went into the ark,
14   *they and all wild animals according to their kinds,*
        and all cattle according to its kind,
        and all that crawls on the earth according to its kind,
        and all birds according to their kinds, all winged birds.
15   *And they went into the ark to Noah,*
        two and two of all flesh that had the breath of life in them.
16   *And those that went in*
        were male and female of all flesh,
        as God had commanded him.
    And Yahweh shut the door behind him.
17   *Then the Flood came [for forty days] upon the earth,*
    and the waters increased and lifted up the ark,
    so that it was high above the earth.
18   *And the waters mounted and increased greatly upon the earth,*
        and the ark floated upon the surface of the waters.
19   *And the waters mounted greatly upon the earth,*
        and all the high mountains under heaven's expanse were covered;
20   *15 cubits additional the waters rose,*
        so that the mountains were covered.
21   *Then all flesh perished, all that moved upon the earth,*
        birds and cattle and wild animals,
        and all that swarmed upon the earth, and all humankind.
22 *Everything that had the breath of life in its nostrils,*
    everything that lived on the dry land, all died.
23 *So he wiped out every existing thing on the face of the earth,*
    human beings and animals and crawling things and birds of heaven,
    all of them were wiped from the earth.
    Only Noah was left and what was with him in the ark.
24   *And the waters mounted over the earth for 150 days.*

47

8:1　　　*Then God thought of Noah*
　　　　and of all the wild animals and cattle
　　　　that were with him in the ark.
　　　　And God made a wind blow over the earth
　　　　so that the waters subsided.

2　　　　*And the fountains of the deep were closed*
　　　　and the windows of heaven;
　and the rain from heaven was stopped,

3　*and the waters receded gradually from the earth,*
　　　　and the waters disappeared at the end of 150 days.

4　　　　*And on the seventeenth day of the seventh month*
　　　　the ark came to rest on the mountains of Ararat.

5　　　　*And the waters continued to recede until the tenth month;*
　　　　on the first day of the tenth month the tops of the mountains became
　　　　visible.

6　*And at the end of forty days*
　Noah opened the window that he had made in the ark

7　*and he sent the raven out*
　and it flew to and fro until the water on the earth had dried up.

8　*Then he sent the dove to fly away*
　to see if the waters on the earth had subsided further.

9　*But the dove did not find any place where it could rest its foot,*
　so it came back to him in the ark,
　for there was still water over the whole earth.
　Then he put out his hand,
　and caught it and brought it back into the ark.

10　*He then waited another seven days;*
　then he sent the dove out of the ark again.

11　*And the dove returned to him in the evening,*
　and behold, it had a fresh olive leaf in its beak.
　So Noah knew that the waters had subsided from the earth.

12　*Then he waited yet another seven days,*
　and sent the dove out again,
　and this time it did not come back to him.

13　　　　*In the 601st year of Noah's life, on the first day of the first month,*
　　　　the waters of the earth had dried up.
　Then Noah removed the roof from the ark,
　and behold, the surface of the earth was dry.

14　　　　*On the twenty-seventh day of the second month, the earth was com-*
　　　　pletely dry.

15

　　　　Then God spoke to Noah and said:

16　　　　*Go out of the ark, you and your wife*
　　　　and your sons and your sons' wives with you.

17　　　　*And all the animals that are with you, all creatures,*
　　　　birds and cattle and all crawling things that swarm upon the earth,
　　　　bring them out with you, that they may breed upon the earth,
　　　　and increase and multiply upon the earth.

18   *And Noah went out*
        and his sons and his wife
        and his sons' wives with him.
19   *And all the wild animals and all the cattle,*
        all the birds and everything that crawls on the earth,
        all of them went out of the ark according to their kinds.

20 *And Noah built an altar to Yahweh*
     and took of all the clean animals and of all the clean birds
     and offered burnt offerings upon the altar.
21 *And Yahweh smelled the sweet odor and said to himself:*
     Never again
     will I curse the ground because of human beings;
     for the inclination of the human heart is evil from its youth.
     And never again
     will I slay every living creature, as I have done.
22 *While earth lasts, there shall never cease*
     seedtime and harvest, frost and heat,
     summer and winter, night and day.

9:1   *And God blessed Noah and his sons and said to them:*
     Be fruitful and increase and fill the earth.
2   *Fear and dread of you*
      shall come over all animals of the earth
      and over all birds under heaven
      and over all that creeps upon the earth
      and over all fish in the sea;
      they are given into your hand.
3   *All that moves and lives shall serve you for food,*
      as I have given you the green plants, so I give you all.
4   *Only flesh with its soul, its blood, you shall not eat.*
5   *But your own blood will I demand;*
      from all the animals will I demand it, and from humans in turn will I
      demand the life of a human being.
6   *Whoever pours out human blood,*
      by a human shall his blood be poured out;
      for in the image of God he made humans.

7   *But you, be fruitful and increase,*
      spread over the earth and rule over it.

8   *And God said to Noah and to his sons with him:*
9   *Now I, behold, I am setting up my covenant with you,*
      and with your descendants after you
10   *and with every living being that is with you,*
     with the birds, with the cattle,
     and with all wild animals with you,
     all that have come out of the ark with you.
11   *I am setting up my covenant with you,*
     that never again shall all flesh
     be wiped out by the waters of the Flood,

and that never again shall a flood come
to destroy the earth.
12 And God said:
This is the sign of the covenant
that I am establishing between myself and you
and every living being with you
for all future generations.
13 My bow I am putting in the clouds,
which shall be the sign of the covenant between me and the earth.
14 When I now form clouds over the earth,
and the bow becomes visible in the clouds,
15 then I will remember my covenant
which exists between me and you and all living beings,
and never again shall the waters become a flood
to destroy all flesh.
16 And when the bow is there in the clouds,
I will look at it so as to recall the everlasting covenant,
between God and all living beings, all flesh
that is on the earth.
17 And God said to Noah:
This is the sign of the covenant, which I am setting up
between myself and all flesh that is on the earth.

28 Noah lived another 350 years after the Flood.
29 The whole of Noah's life-span was 950 years.
Then he died.

INTRODUCTION: THE STRUCTURE OF THE FLOOD NARRATIVE

The narrative begins with God's decision to destroy the human race; it ends with God's decision never again to destroy the human race. In God's initial decision, in the ever-present possibility of human failure, the Flood narrative is related to the creation of humankind. It is a kind of complement to Creation in that it raises the possibility that the human race may be destroyed. This possibility is averted in God's concluding decision for preservation. A drama arises from the tension between the decision to destroy and the decision to preserve a single individual. The peril and destruction of the human race has its counterpart in the peril and deliverance of an individual, which makes possible the final decision to preserve the human race. The resulting structure has five parts.

1. God's decision to destroy the human race and preserve Noah.

2. Preservation, part 1: the command to build the ark and the announcement of the Flood.

3. Destruction: the coming and result of the Flood.

4. Preservation, part 2: the end of the Flood and departure from the ark.

5. God's decision to preserve the human race.

As it has come down to us, the Flood narrative is a composite of two sources or traditions: J and P. Both works contained a Flood narrative. To preserve them both, the tradents (or redactors) who shaped the Primal History of Genesis 1–11 in its present form interwove them. Both, however, include all five elements of the structure, which suggests that there was a common tradition prior to both. At this point we must deal with the prehistory of the Flood narrative outside of Israel. First, however, we shall list the most important differences between J and P in the Flood narrative. (1) There are many stylistic differences, including J's use of the divine name "Yahweh" and P's use of "Elohim." (2) P includes a continuous precise chronology, whereas J gives only a few rough estimates of the time involved. P even includes the precise day on which the Flood began and ended (7:11; 8:5), as well as precise information about the duration of its various stages and Noah's age, and the exact dimensions of the ark. (3) There are several contradictions. According to J, seven pairs of all the clean animals enter the ark and one pair each of the unclean animals (7:2-3); according to P, there was one pair of each (6:19-20; 7:15-16). According to J, after seven days rain falls for forty days (7:4); according to P, the water rises for 150 days (7:24) and recedes for 150 days (8:3). (4) The P narrative has been preserved in its entirety; from the J narrative, we are missing the announcement of the Flood, the command to build the ark, and the departure from the ark. On the other hand, J has elements not found in P: Noah's sending of the birds (8:6-12) and the sacrifice of the preserved animals (8:20-21). P diverges most from J in its conclusion (9:1-17), the blessing of Noah and the covenant with him, which have no counterpart in J. This section gives P's Flood narrative a more theological cast. (5) Despite these differences and even a few contradictions, the tradents combined J and P to create a work that tells a coherent and convincing story of the Flood.

THE FLOOD NARRATIVE OUTSIDE ISRAEL

The flood story is found throughout the world. Like the creation narrative, it is part of our basic cultural heritage. It is truly astonishing: everywhere on earth we find stories of a great primeval flood. For a long time, scholars knew of scattered flood narratives only among the high civilizations of the ancient Near East, above all the eleventh tablet of the Gilgamesh epic. New research has shown, however, a whole history of flood traditions to be surveyed throughout the Near East. Furthermore, a wealth of flood traditions among primitive civilizations has been discovered; these agree in their major features, such as the destruction of the human race and the deliverance of an individual, while exhibiting characteristic differences, so that, for example, the decision of the gods (or of a single god) to destroy the human race is found only in the flood stories of the advanced civilizations. It is impossible to treat any of these in isolation, since, for example, the flood stories of the advanced Mediterranean civilizations contain elements of stories found in primitive civilizations, and the motif of sending forth birds, found in J but not P, is amply attested in the flood stories of primitive civilizations. The details cannot be discussed here; I refer the reader to my full discussion of the religio-historical background of the Flood narrative in my *Genesis 1–11*, pp. 398-406.

6:6-8   Decision to destroy (J). This introductory passage from J contains doublets and repetitions (Yahweh is "sorry" before and after his decision). In an earlier, simpler form the narrative said only: "When Yahweh saw that the wickedness of humankind on earth was great, Yahweh said: I will wipe out humankind from the face of the earth" (vv. 5a, 7a); everything else explains or emphasizes. By means of these expansions, the narrator J introduces his own interests, just as he does in 12:1-3 at the beginning of the patriarchal narrative. Between the two clauses of the early narrative, "When God saw . . . God said," he inserts a "God was sorry . . . ," thus linking the Flood narrative with the creation of the human race, to which God looks back in retrospect—in the light of what he sees *now*. A similar role is played by the emphasis in 6:5b: *all* planning and striving is now only wicked. The elaboration suggests that J struggled with this motivation; he shrank in horror from God's decision to destroy, and therefore places so much emphasis on it. He struggles with the inexplicable incongruity between the creation of the human race and the decision to destroy it; but it was J who introduced the incongruity into the narrative! In the deluge narrative of the Gilgamesh epic (Tablet XI), the incongruity is explained simply: the god who chooses preservation is not the same god who chose destruction. But the explanation given by the polytheistic myth is not open to the narrator in Israel, for whom God is one. And so the division between gods becomes a division within God. The shift that places the division within God makes God human: "and he was grieved at heart." God suffers from his decision to destroy humanity. The same motif appears in the prophets of judgment, when God recognizes that he must intervene as judge against his own people (Isa. 1:2-3; Jer. 12:7-13). It is this paradoxical suffering of God in the face of the judgment he himself must bring that led in the history of Israel with its God to the positive significance of suffering for the salvation of the people.

5   God's "seeing" is more than mere perception; it leads to action. What God sees is "the wickedness of humankind on earth." A state of great depravity has set in; it is the basis for God's decision to destroy humanity. Human wickedness has grown so enormous that it threatens the very humanity of the human race. The narrator is not referring to a generalized sinfulness that takes concrete form in particular evil deeds; he means that on a particular occasion wickedness so gathered to a head that it perverted an entire generation. Because J understands the human race historically, he is able to grasp the significance for the entire human race of the rare concentration of evil in the depravity of a whole group. God's decision to destroy has to do solely with this phenomenon. The translation "planning and striving" expresses the parallel meaning of the two nouns. The people are "always" intent on wickedness.

6   "He was sorry" is used in the same way in 1 Samuel 15:11: "I [God] am sorry that I have made Saul king." But in the same chapter we read: "He is not a human being, to be sorry" (v. 29); cf. also Numbers 23:19. The contradiction emerges from the fact that God's actions sometimes appear contradictory to mortals. The true intent of the declarative statement "he was sorry" appears in what follows: "and he was grieved at heart." God suffers because he must judge humankind.

7   The decision to destroy does not come until verse 7. The narrator uses a particularly harsh expression ("wipe out"; also in 7:23 and Judg. 21:17). The brutality leads him to repeat the motivation.

8   The decision to destroy is met by the decision to preserve Noah. Noah is a familiar figure, who does not have to be introduced. Unlike P (v. 9), the narrator sees God's gracious favor as his reason for preserving Noah, not Noah's saintliness. Despite the judgment that God must bring upon humanity, he shows mercy toward one.

9-22   Announcement of Judgment and Command to Noah. This section is entirely from P. Although the course of events is roughly the same, the special features of P's account are clear.

9-12   The emphasis shifts to Noah and his character. The use of Noah's genealogy (vv. 9-10) to introduce the story of the Flood gives it the introduction "This is the story of Noah" (v. 9a). Three clauses emphasize Noah's righteousness. The genealogy looks forward to P's conclusion (9:1-17), which is a single long speech addressed to Noah: the story leads up to the covenant with Noah. The genealogy includes the naming of Noah's three sons (v. 10), from whom the three races will be descended after the Flood. Only now, in verses

11-12, do we come to the decision to destroy humanity and the reason for it: the earth is corrupt and full of violence. But for the sake of the one righteous man human history continues on through the catastrophe; "the world is saved on account of the righteous man" (Benno Jacob).

9   Two words are used to describe Noah's character: "just" is a social term, referring to conduct commensurate with the norms of society. "Blameless" (*tāmîm*, literally "whole, perfect") is a cultic term, describing a sacrificial animal without blemish.

11   Noah's righteousness is contrasted to the depravity of the world, which is underlined by threefold repetition. The use of "the earth" three times as subject suggests that this depravity is somehow contaminating: it affects the world in which humanity lives. But P says nothing of how this depravity came about.

12   In the background stands the experience of sudden universal corruption, such as there has always been and always will be. Here the summary expression "all flesh" means "all human beings"; the animals are not included.

13-22   This long speech addressed by God to Noah (only in P) has two sections characteristic of P: a command (vv. 13-21) and its execution (v. 22). Each of the two parts of the command—to build the ark (vv. 14-16) and to outfit it (vv. 18-21)—is introduced by the decision to destroy the human race (vv. 13 and 17). The focus, however, is entirely on the God's commandment and its execution; his decision is only the dark background against which the promise to deliver Noah, implicit in the command, stands forth.

13   The statement "I have decided to put an end to all flesh" (literally, "the end of all flesh has come before me") telescopes two different statements. The first comes from verse 12a: "God looked at the earth and it was certainly corrupt" (literally, "The corruption of the earth has come before me"); the second, "The end of all flesh has come," was borrowed by P from the prophets of judgment (cf. Amos 8:2, "The end has come upon my people Israel," which became the motif of Ezek. 7:2-3, 6-7, 10, 12). Thus P suggests the connection between God's judgment upon his people and his judgment upon humankind in the Flood.

14-16   These verses record the command to build the ark. Noah is instructed to build a "box" of given dimensions (v. 15) out of the wood of a conifer, divided into compartments and covered with pitch inside and out; it is to have three decks, a roof, and a door (v. 16). The order is conveyed in the tersest possible style and is not entirely intelligible; it is inadequate for a reconstruction. It is very similar to the order in the eleventh tablet of Gilgamesh, the Babylonian flood narrative (for a comparison of the two, see my *Genesis 1–11*, pp. 418-420). The Babylonian account differs completely, however, in that the order is followed by a detailed description of how it was carried out (lines 48-74), of which there is no trace in Genesis 6.

Because the length of a cubit varied, the dimensions are uncertain. It is commonly assumed that the length was between 130 and 150 meters, the width 22 meters, and the height about 12 meters. In Gilgamesh the dimensions are much larger.

17   Verse 17 continues verse 13, repeating it in part. This is the first time P uses the word "Flood" (*mabbûl*, "deluge"; originally the heavenly ocean), in order to contrast it directly with the word "covenant" (*berît*, literally "promise") in verse 18. In this verse, "all flesh" means "everything that lives," including animals.

18-21   This is the second part of the order: Noah is commanded to go into the ark with his family (v. 18) and to bring a pair of every kind of animal into the ark (vv. 19-20), along with food for all (v. 21).

18   The command is introduced by the clause: "But with you I am setting up a 'covenant.'" This statement anticipates the "covenant ceremony" at the end (9:9) and makes sense only from that perspective. There the word *berît* means a promise; here it obviously means an order or command. But this command implies a promise: by going into the ark, Noah and his family are saved. The two go together: God saves by commanding; what he commands brings salvation.

19-20   The animals are to be rescued along with the human race; a pair of each is enough to continue the species (contrast J in 7:2-3). As at Creation, human beings and animals go together. This is among the earliest motifs of the Flood narrative; millennia before the biblical account, human beings and animals are saved together. The detailed listing is typical of P's style; it is intended to recall the story of Creation. In both passages, human beings do not exist in isolation: their daily needs are also rescued by being brought into the ark: work, family, animals, food—God's command encompasses them all. By our reckoning, of course, Noah could not possibly have brought all the animals into the ark and fed them there; but anyone who takes this tack has failed to understand the story: man and beast were saved from catastrophe together.

22   P does not recount how God's command was carried out. For him, only one thing matters: Noah did what God had commanded. In the Babylonian narrative, the carrying out of the command is narrated in full and vivid detail, down to a list of the quantities of oil and wine provided by the master builder for the workers' celebration (lines 70-73). P's only concern is that God commands and

his commands are carried out (as in Gen. 17 [Abraham], Exod. 24:15ff. [Moses], and many other passages), just as at the beginning he spoke and it was done (Gen. 1).

7:1-9   Command and Execution (J). Here it is particularly clear that two narratives have been combined. Once again God's command to Noah is recounted (vv. 1-3) along with the announcement of the Flood (v. 4), and we are told that Noah did as commanded (v. 5; cf. 6:22). In addition, however, the carrying out of the command is described (7:7-9). Between verses 1-5 and 7-9 a statement from P (v. 6) has been inserted. J's account of the command to build the ark has been omitted in favor of P's.

1   What is said of Noah in 6:8 and 7:1 makes sense only in the context of the Flood narrative: Noah found favor in the eyes of God in the light of God's decision to destroy humankind; God found him an appropriate person through whom to preserve the human race.

2-3   J says only the necessary minimum, whereas P goes into excruciating detail. "Animals" is used here in its general, comprehensive sense; the birds were added in verse 3a by a hand seeking to be even more precise. But a distinction is made between clean and unclean animals, and the difference between J and P depends on this distinction ("seven of each" versus "two of each"). J presupposes that the distinction between clean and unclean was universal. He cannot have been thinking of the much later Israelite law. The distinction is much earlier and general: it originally distinguished the useful animals from those without any human use. Fewer of the unclean animals come into the ark, but they are included in the rescue of living creatures; they have the same right to live as the clean animals.

Verse 3b (following v. 2) concludes God's command and states its purpose: the preservation of life.

4   Next follows the announcement of the Flood, parallel to 6:13, 17 (P). In contrast to P, J ascribes it to forty days of rain—a catastrophe, but a realistic possibility. Like 6:5-7, J points out the terrifying contrast in God's action: "Every existing thing that I have made I will wipe from the earth."

5   There follows in verses 5, 7-9 the carrying out of God's command. Since, however, what is commanded in verses 1-3 is carried out in verse 7, verse 5 probably referred originally to the building of the ark, which has been omitted by J (cf. 6:22 [P]).

6   Verse 6 is P's account of the beginning of the Flood, and goes with verse 11.

7-9   Now the carrying out of the command in verses 1-3 is recounted; in verses 8-9, J (clean and unclean) and P (the numbers) have been confused. Verse 9b concludes the carrying out of God's command (like 6:22 in P).

6, 10-24   The Flood (P). P's description of the Flood is framed by chronological statements in verses 6 and 11 at the beginning and verse 24 at the end. Only a few verses from J have been included: verses 10 and 12 at the beginning, 22-23 at the end, and 16b-17 in the middle.

Structure: Beginning of the Flood (6, 11 [P]; 10, 12 [J]); entering the ark (13-16a [P]); God shuts the ark (16b [J]); the waters rise (17 [J]; 18-20 [P]); devastation (21 [P]; 22-23 [J]); conclusion (24 [P]).

6, 11a   Genesis 7:6 (P) dates the beginning of the Flood in the six hundredth year of Noah's life; verse 11a begins a precise chronology of the Flood's stages, continued in 7:24; 8:3b, 4, 5, 13, 14. Such a precise chronology appears elsewhere in the Old Testament only in Ezekiel, who is roughly contemporaneous with P; the dating follows the Babylonian calendar. The chronological system is hard to follow; in any case, the starting point is the final statement: the day the Flood ended (8:13-14) is "New Year's day."

11b   The parallelism of these two clauses has the effect of poetry: "All the fountains of the great deep burst forth / and the windows of the heavens were opened." The phrase "great deep" (*tᵉhôm rabbāh*) appears only in poetry (Isa. 51:10; Amos 7:4; Ps. 78:15). The "windows" of heaven also open in Isaiah 24:18 and Malachi 3:10; the same expression occurs in Ugaritic texts. Both clauses suggest the irruption of chaos into the order of creation; cf. Psalm 93. We may therefore assume that, in describing the Flood, P drew upon an original narrative poem about the Flood, which included Genesis 7:11b; 8:2a, and other material. The prosaic chronology added by P is clearly distinct from this poetic prototype; but P integrated his borrowed material so well that we cannot reconstruct his original. Here we see once more that the biblical Flood narrative had a long and complex prehistory—not surprising in view of the wealth of parallels.

12   The forty days and forty nights of rain is clearly a different phenomenon from the cosmic flood of verse 11b. Verse 12, like Gilgamesh XI, depicts a natural event, albeit of extraordinary magnitude; verse 11b depicts a mythological cosmic catastrophe. The two different pictures of the Flood are clearly evident here.

13-16   Noah enters the ark. The description is formal and ceremonious: P clearly attaches great importance to this section. It constitutes the heart of the Flood story, between the beginning, which emphasizes Noah's righteousness, and the conclusion, which describes the blessing and promise after Noah leaves the ark. Verses 13-16a are the high point of the narrative: in entering the ark, Noah obeys the word of God that came to him as a command, meant for his salvation.

The carefully structured syntax of these verses is dominated by the verb "they went in" (vv. 13, 15, 16); the entrance into the ark is depicted as a solemn procession.

13   The expression "on this very day" is found only in P; each time it refers to a day on which a commandment of God is carried out (Gen. 7:13; 17:23, 26; Exod. 12:41).

14, 15   P is not describing an actual event—that would be hard to imagine—but painting a scene: the entrance is like a procession. The list of all the animals appears at three crucial points in the Flood story: the entrance into the ark (7:14), the death of all living beings outside the ark (7:21), and the exit from the ark (8:19).

16a   "They went in as God had commanded them." The commandment was addressed to a single individual; it led to the procession of all living beings into the safety of the ark.

16b   A fragment from J has been inserted after verses 13-16a (P); in J, it went with verses 7-9 (parallel to 13-16a). The redactor has interpolated the scattered J material at appropriate points in P's narrative. This material probably had a different sequence when J was still an independent narrative: 7:1-5, 10, 7, 16b, 12, 17b, 22-23. Probably the redactor added the clause "and Yahweh shut the door behind him" because, despite its naive language, it beautifully expresses God's care for his creatures.

17-20   The water rises (v. 17 [J]; vv. 18-20 [P]). Verse 17a, except for the number of days, repeats verse 6b (P). Apparently it is intended as a recapitulation. The addition of "for forty days" on the basis of J is harmonizing; the LXX, following verse 12, adds "and forty nights." The function of verse 17a is uncertain. Verse 17b continues verse 12: "Rain poured . . . and the waters increased. . . ." In J's extremely terse account, this statement stands out: "And the waters increased and lifted up the ark, so that it was high above the earth." The gigantic drama of the Flood is compressed into these three acts.

18-20   P's more circumstantial account is clearly different, dramatizing the Flood by repetition and verbal emphasis. In essence, however, what is described is the new event of the rising water. The listener experiences it in four stages: the waters mounted and increased (v. 18a), the waters mounted greatly (19a), 15 cubits additional the waters rose (20a), and the waters mounted (24). A similar sequence appears in Psalm 93. The height to which the waters rose is indicated by the statement that all the mountains were covered by them (Gen. 7:19b, 20b). This, too, suggests the cosmic extent of the catastrophe.

21-23   The effect (v. 21 [P]; vv. 22-23 [J]). The destruction of all living beings is clearly recounted twice in these verses. The redactor can include both versions because the repetition adds emphasis. The echo of Genesis 1 shows that verse 21 belongs to P. "All flesh" in verse 21a includes animals (21bα) and human beings (21bβ), as in 6:17. While P emphasized the rising waters, J emphasizes the destruction of all living beings (7:22-23), corresponding to the introduction in 6:5-8. P is concerned with God's majesty, even in God's judgment upon humankind, whereas J is much more concerned with the terrible fate that befell human beings and animals. Not only is J for once more expansive here; he also adds his own comment to the neutral account to which P restricts himself (7:21): "God wiped out. . . ." How deeply moved the narrator is by what he has to record is shown by the last clause in verse 23: of all living beings, only this remnant, so tiny in comparison to all that had been wiped out, survived! As in Amos 3:12, the surviving remnant helps express the terrible scope of the destruction.

24   "And the waters mounted. . . ." This clause brings the preceding story to a wonderful conclusion. Here we see the art of the redactor who forged the two accounts into a single narrative.

8:1-9, 17   The end of the Flood. Like the beginning, the conclusion in P clearly differs from that in J. In the latter it comprises three acts: the end of the Flood (8:1-5 [omitting 2b, 3a], 13a, 14), the command to leave the ark and its carrying out (8:15-19), and blessing and covenant (9:1-17). In J, after the brief statement in 8:2b, 3a that the Flood ceased, the emphasis is on Noah's sending forth of the birds (vv. 6-12), which culminates in the drying up of the earth (v. 13b). The conclusion is Noah's sacrifice and God's promise (vv. 20-22).

1-5, 13a, 14   The retreat of the waters in these verses echoes the coming of the Flood in 7:17-21, 24. The climax in the middle is the statement in 8:1: "Then God thought. . . ." P uses the same verb in a similar context in 19:29, where it likewise introduces the deliverance of a single individual from the destruction of Sodom. The usage in 30:22 is also similar: "But God thought of Rachel and heard her prayer." This "thoughtfulness" presupposes mercy toward the threatened person and leads to God's saving act (cf. also Exod. 2:24). God's inclusion of the animals recalls the story of Creation. Two events bring about the end of the Flood: both the windows of heaven and the fountains of the deep are closed. Genesis 8:2a parallels 7:11b; like the latter, it is rhythmical and thus belongs to P's poetic source. The wind that dries the earth in 8:1b is a different matter. It made sense in a story of a less extensive flood; here it clashes with the statement of the immense height of the waters in 7:19-20.

2b, 3a   In these verses the redactor has introduced J's short statement about the Flood's retreat. When J was still an independent narrative, the chronological statement in verse 6 ("at the end of forty days") probably preceded verse 2b. J's account is much simpler than P's: the rain stopped and the waters gradually receded. This passage shows that J pictures the inundation as less than total.

3b-5   Verse 3b refers to the 150 days in 7:24; the Flood recedes when its sources are shut off. At the same time the ark comes to ground. The date is recorded to the very day. This section abounds in chronological statements (8:3b, 4, 5a, 5b, 13a, 14), which lead up to the end of the Flood in verse 13a. Probably the ark is able to come to rest immediately because the Flood reached 15 cubits above the highest peaks (7:20) and the ark, with a height of 30 cubits (6:15), had a draft of 15 cubits—an ingenious calculation.

The ark lands on Mount Ararat. This landing on a mountain is one of the earliest elements of the Flood story. A mountain can also be the place of deliverance from the Flood without additional technological means. The text does not speak of a specific mountain named Ararat; 8:4 reads, "On the mountains of [the region of] Ararat." This region (Akkadian Urartu) is the mountainous area west of the Tigris river. Where the story originated, the mountains of Ararat must have been the highest mountains known. In the Indic flood narratives, analogously, the ark lands on the Himalayas. The vague statement in verse 4 does not refer to a specific mountain.

6-12   Noah sends out the birds (J). Each of the three attempts (8:6, 8-9; 8:10-11; 8:12, 13b) comprises three acts: the sending of the bird, its return, and the conclusion drawn. The first act is the same in all three cases; tension is introduced by the seven days' wait. In the second act, the dove's actions differ in each case; in the third act, the episode reaches its climax when Noah "knows."

6   The first words of verse 6 in J originally preceded verse 2b (see above). The word "another" in verse 10 suggests that the grounding of the ark had already been reported (having been omitted on account of v. 4 [P]) and that verse 6 began with the statement that Noah waited another seven days (as in Gilgamesh XI:145).

7   Noah sends a raven. This verse introduces a variant of the thrice-repeated sending of a dove, in which Noah sends three different birds, as in Gilgamesh XI:141-45. The episode of the raven does not mesh well with the three flights of the dove.

8   The bird's mission as stated in verse 8 shows that this was originally the first sending. The bird will see what Noah, shut up in the ark, cannot.

9   The dove comes back "for there was still water over the whole earth." This is almost identical with Gilgamesh XI:151: "No resting place attracted her eye, so she returned." There follows an interpolation in Genesis 8:9b; since it is the only addition in the course of the three acts, it must have special significance. Noah puts out his hand

and the dove returns to where it knows it is safe. The narrator's point is that the relationship of trust between animal and human being is what makes the attempt possible; this relationship derives from the fact that both are God's creatures (1:16-28; 2:19-20). The compassionate description helps us feel something of this trust.

10-11 In the last clause of verse 11, the scene of the dove reaches its climax; the almost rhythmical language makes this clear. The dumb creature is able to convey a message as "a harbinger of peace" (Umberto Cassuto). This message, too, presupposes a relationship of trust between human being and animal. Now Noah knows what he had to know.

12, 13b The third flight serves only to confirm the result of Noah's experiment. By not returning, the dove tells those still shut up in the ark that they, too, can now come forth to freedom.

Verse 13b follows verse 12 directly (v. 13a belongs to P). Now the tension is resolved. Noah has learned what he wanted to learn. He looks out, and his eyes once more behold the familiar earth. Now he can act. This concludes the train of events that began in 7:10 with the coming of the Flood.

A final comment on verses 6-12: the episode of the birds is found only in J, who here clearly diverges from P. Throughout the story of the Flood, P emphasizes the majesty of God's actions; in P, a word from God (8:15) reveals to Noah what he must discover by experiment in J. Noah is more human in J than in P—he yearns impatiently for deliverance. J's account reflects a fundamental aspect of human nature, which leads Noah to conduct an experiment. Originally the experiment was a search for a way out of a desperate situation. Once again, the experiment characteristically involves not an object but a living being. The first great achievements of civilization had to do with plants and animals. Noah's experiment with the dove stands within the larger context of animal domestication. There are extra-biblical parallels: "It was an ancient custom at sea, indispensible when compasses were unknown, to bring birds along and let them loose on the high seas in order by their course to determine the direction of land."[1]

13a, 14-19 The end of the Flood and the exit from the ark (P). As is typical of P, this section is structured as order and execution; cf. 6:13-21. The command to leave the ark (8:15-17), dated by the end of the Flood in verses 13a, 14, is carried out in verses 18-19.

13a, 14 The two dates can be understood sequentially, but verse 13a makes verse 14 unnecessary; it is probably a variant calcula-

---

1. Hermann Karl Usener. *Die Sintflutsage untersucht* (Bonn: F. Cohen, 1899), p. 254.

tion (cf. 7:6 and 11 at the beginning of the Flood story). The date in 8:13a is dominated by the number "one": "In the 601st year, on the first day of the first month." The number "one" is emphasized by repetition, typical of P's style. The reference, following the Greek text, is to the 601st year of Noah's life (cf. 7:11). On this date begins a new age, the era after the Flood. This date is the climax of the whole series of dates assigned to the stages of the Flood; the day the Flood ends becomes "New Year's day." If in later times the cosmos is renewed in a cultic ceremony on New Year's day, the conclusion of the Flood story suggests the reason (like the seventh day in Gen. 2:1-4a). Thus the New Year, like the Sabbath, takes on universal significance.

15-17   The command to leave the ark given to Noah and his family in verses 15-16 is extended in verse 17 to all the animals; for them the blessing of fertility is renewed. The list turns the command to go forth into a command to form a solemn procession whose rhythm is echoed by the language. "Each particular group of creatures is accounted for in God's command" (Walther Zimmerli). The Creator's blessing is renewed for all the animals rescued from the Flood and preserved from destruction.

18-19   God's commandment means life; to obey his commandment is to choose life: Noah and his family and all living beings "according to their kinds" (literally, "with their families") go forth from the ark to live the new life vouchsafed them upon the renewed earth. They go forth "with their families," because life is life in community.

20-22   Sacrifice and promise (J). The end of J's Flood narrative has the same emphasis as its beginning (6:5-8), which it echoes. In God's promise that follows Noah's sacrifice, the Flood narrative finds fulfillment.

20   Noah's sacrifice echoes a feature found in many flood stories. Ziusudra, Utnapishtim, Deucalion, and many others offer sacrifice after the flood. In the ancient world, it is the appropriate and natural reaction when one has survived a deadly peril. The celebration of deliverance in a sacrifice offered to the deliverer contains two elements: the worshipper gives thanks for his deliverance and entrusts himself to the deliverer for the new life that is beginning. The Primal History contains the two aspects of sacrifice fundamental to all religions: the sacrifice of Cain and Abel is concerned with blessing; the sacrifice of Noah is concerned with deliverance—it is the sacrifice of someone who has been rescued from mortal danger. Sacrifice is offered to the God who delivers and blesses.

21-22   The statement "And Yahweh smelled the sweet odor" is formulaic. It appears in the same context in Gilgamesh XI:159-161 and continues as sacrificial terminology in Israel into the latest period. It means that God was pleased to accept Noah's sacrifice. The first two lines of Genesis 8:21 recall the prologue (6:5-8) and Genesis 3; in God's reversal of his decision to destroy (8:22b), J gives his final interpretation of the Flood story. The statement "Never again will I . . ." recalls 3:17; the following "for the inclination . . ." echoes 6:5. God decides to leave the human race upon his earth, not to curse it ever again despite its inclination to wickedness. He will not intervene to punish every transgression; he will patiently endure mortals as they are, with all their tendency toward evil. This is the meaning of Jesus' words in Matthew 5:45: "For he causes his sun to rise on the evil and on the good, and his rain to fall on the just and on the unjust."

22 The negatively formulated promise in verse 21b is now followed by a positive promise: God guarantees that the earth will endure "while earth lasts." The actual expression is unique: "all the days of the earth." Elsewhere the phrase "all the days" always refers to the entire lifetime of a living being. When J speaks of "all the days of the earth," he is coining a new idiom, in which he sees the cosmic event extending through the totality of time. Here for the first time, as far as we can tell, "the history of the natural world"[2] is seen as a single whole. The Flood narrative with its climax in 8:20-22 endows the created, natural world with its own history; the world existing after the great catastrophe is the world that has been preserved. It will be preserved in God's hands until the end he determines for it. This preservation takes shape in the great rhythms affecting all that lives, in the breath of life. The four pairs of words refer to the rhythmical alternations of the year (seedtime and harvest, summer and winter) and the day (frost and heat, night and day). In the Near East, "frost and heat" can also mean the alternation of day and night.

At the end of his Flood narrative, J includes the existence of time in God's decision, time that runs in cyclic rhythms. The Old Testament's understanding of time is not limited to linear history; there is a place for a cyclic understanding of time as well. Without cyclic rhythms, linear time would not exist. Just as God's work of salvation and judgment is associated with linear time, so his blessing is associated with cyclic time. In the great rhythms by which creation breathes, God blesses and sustains our earth.

9:1-17 Blessing and covenant: P's conclusion. God's concluding discourse deals solely with the significance of the Flood. Both sections of this discourse begin and end with roughly the same words (a form called "inclusio" in rhetoric): 9:1b = 9:7; 9:9 = 9:17b. As God's

2. Carl Friedrich von Weizsäcker, *The History of Nature*, trans. Fred. D. Wieck (London: Routledge and Kegan Paul, 1951).

final word ending the Flood, both sections belong together, like the two sections of 8:20-22 (J). In fact, the two parts together make a single statement: the first part renews the blessing, the second guarantees that the Flood will never come again.

1-7   Two blessings ("Be fruitful . . .") in verses 1 and 7 frame the new relationship between humankind and animals in verses 2-3, with two restrictions stated in verses 4 and 5-6. In the aeon after the Flood, there is a new aspect to God's blessing of his creatures (Gen. 1:28-29): to be human, it is now necessary to kill.

1   In Genesis 5 God's likeness was passed from Adam to his descendants; in Genesis 9, similarly, after the Flood the blessing of the Creator is passed on to Adam's descendants. The life that God has preserved and blessed continues through time. Chapter 10 will develop this theme further. The human race, saved from catastrophe, grows toward its future and spreads over the earth through the blessing of the Creator. P, too, associates the Flood closely with Creation.

2-3   Humankind was already given dominion over the animals at creation (Gen. 1:28); here that dominion is expanded to permit them to kill animals for food. The words "fear and dread" also appear, with reference to Israel's enemies, in the promise of the land of Canaan (Deut. 11:25), as does the expression "given into your hand." In contrast to Genesis 1:29, 9:3 says explicitly that people are permitted to eat meat. We may note that permission to kill animals for human food does nothing to change God's blessing of the animals as stated in verse 10. It is typical of the Primal History to state in sequential narrative aspects of the world that today are simultaneous. P is saying that the need to kill is an "afterthought" in God's creation; as Genesis 1:29-30 shows, it was not willed initially by the Creator.

4   There follows a restriction. This limitation on the permission is meant to preserve the creatures whose killing is permitted. The widespread notion that the verse prohibits the eating of blood is not quite accurate. What is involved is not blood as such, but blood as the life of an animal, the flowing blood of a living creature. This, then, is the meaning of the restriction: you must not eat the life of an animal together with its flesh.

5-6   The narrator sees a connection between the pouring out of animal blood and the pouring out of human blood. The restriction in verse 4 means also that God is still the Lord of animal life. Now P adds: God is also Lord of human life. Therefore the commandment "Thou shalt not kill" applies absolutely and unconditionally to the human race. The verse is dominated by the thrice-repeated "will I demand." The slaying of one person by another is explicitly labeled fratricide.

Verse 6 adds a punishment and its motivation. The punishment has form of an "apodictic law." There is a parallel in Matthew 26:52: "For all who take the sword will perish by the sword." The second half verse, ". . . by a human shall his blood be poured out," is not in legal style but rather in the language of the Primal History, because it holds for all humankind. God's demand for retribution on behalf of a life that has been taken is fulfilled in fact by human justice, which throughout the ancient world is executed in the name of God or the gods.

There follows the motivation: God made humans in his own image. Therefore murder is a direct attack on God's sovereignty. Murder is a sin against God (cf. Gen. 4); this holds for all humanity. The extraordinary character of this outrage is recognized even by the secular world.

7 The concluding sentence, which summarizes verses 1-2, says that only these restrictions humanize the spread and dominion of the human race.

Rabbinic theologians have derived the "Noachian laws" from Genesis 9:1-7, said to apply to all the descendants of Noah. But the purpose of the text is not to establish a collection of laws.

8-17 The covenant and its sign. This section contains an unusual number of repetitions. It falls into two parts: the setting up of the "covenant" (vv. 8-11) and the establishment of the sign of this covenant (vv. 12-17).

8-11 The first part can be reduced to two clauses: "I am setting up my covenant with you" (vv. 8-11a) so "that never again shall a flood come" (v. 11b). In solemn words, God establishes a covenant with those who have been saved in the ark, both the humans and the animals: the assurance that a flood will never again destroy the earth. In substance it is the same assurance as in J's conclusion (8:20-22). Here it is called a "covenant" (Hebrew $b^e r\hat{\imath}t$). But it is not a "covenant" in our sense of the word, in the first place because it is not mutual—nothing is said of Noah's response—and in the second place because it also includes the animals (9:11). The basic meaning of the word is "promise" or "(solemn) assurance," and that is what it means here. It can mean "covenant" when it refers to a mutual agreement, as in the covenant between God and Abraham in Genesis 17. P deliberately uses the same word in both passages in order to suggest the connection between the two. Genesis 9 and 17 both share God's assurance that promises something forever. The particular meaning here in 9:8-11 is that the continued existence of the world and all living creatures within it is based on God's word, on God's promise.

12-17 The sign of the covenant. Here the repetitions are especially noticeable. Verse 12 introduces the theme: God will establish a

sign of his covenant; verse 13 names the sign: my bow. Verses 14-15
tell how the bow is to function as a sign; verse 16 repeats the same
thing in different words. Verse 17 returns to the introductory verse
12. We may assume that P drew upon an earlier document here,
which ended the Flood story with an explanation of how the rainbow
appeared after the Flood—an etiological conclusion. P incorporates
this material but interprets the rainbow as a sign of the "covenant," a
sign confirming God's promise. Since Julius Wellhausen, the text has
been widely understood to mean the bow as a weapon set aside by
the warrior Yahweh, but this interpretation has no foothold in the
text.

In the explanation of the sign, verses 14-16 are very striking: it is
not those who see the rainbow who will be reminded of God's promise, but God himself. Here P pushes his purpose in this section to its
ultimate limit: the preservation of the human race and of all things
living is entirely in God's hands. God remembers his covenant. This
is the point of P's ending to the Flood narrative: the history of the
natural world and the history of the human race are grounded in
God's unconditional affirmation of his creation, his "Yes" to all
things living, which cannot be shaken by any catastrophe in the
course of this history or by any human transgression, depravity, or
rebellion. God's promise is set in stone "as long as earth endures."

28-29   Here follows P's genealogical conclusion, which records
Noah's life span and death.

Some concluding remarks about the Flood: The Flood narrative begins with God's decision to destroy the human race; it ends
with God's decision never again to destroy the human race. The Bible
shares with the whole ancient world the possibility of speaking of a
destructive God or gods. This possibility is grounded in the identification of reality with the work of God (or the gods). Catastrophes
are part of human experience; there is no reality without them. The
Flood story is universal because, since the earliest known stages of
human history, people have sensed that belonging to the human
race is perilous. This awareness goes hand in hand with a sense of
being a finite creature. The Creator can take back his act of creation.
This knowledge found expression in the flood stories. Undoubtedly
their individual forms are based on experiences and memories of
actual catastrophes, but their truly universal aspect is not a racial
memory of an event long past—the distances in space and time rule
out such a possibility—but the knowledge, based on real experiences and expressed by all these stories, that the human race is an
endangered species.

The specifically biblical aspects of the Flood narrative appear
only within the larger context in which it stands in the Bible. The text

deliberately presents the story as a parallel to God's judgment against his own people, proclaimed by the prophets of judgment. Like God's judgment against his people, his judgment against humankind is based on the prevalence of sin. The judgment of God against his people, announced by the prophets, is expanded to a judgment of the world announced in the apocryphal books of the Old and New Testaments. Like the Flood story, these texts are concerned with all humankind. We can see in the Bible a clear structure in which the end echoes the beginning. It is the same God who in the Primal History announces his decision to destroy humankind and then promises to preserve it "so long as the earth endures," who at the climax of his history announces judgment against his people but promises to preserve a remnant, and who in the last judgment at the end of human history will be both judge and savior of humankind. He is the *one* God, experienced as savior by Israel in its history, but also the God and Lord of all the human race from its beginning to its end.

The message of Jesus of Nazareth, the savior sent by God at the turning point of history, has its locus in the work of God the savior and judge, which extends from the beginning of the human race to its end.

9:18-27 NOAH AND HIS SONS

18 *The sons of Noah who went out of the ark*
    were Shem, Ham, and Japheth.
    And Ham it was who was the father of Canaan.
19 *These three are the sons of Noah,*
    and from them the whole earth was populated.

20 *And Noah, a tiller of the soil, began to plant vineyards.*
21 *And when he drank from the wine, he became drunk,*
    and he lay uncovered in his tent.
22 *Then Ham, the father of Canaan, saw his father's nakedness,*
    and he told his brothers outside.
23 *But Shem and Japheth took the cloak,*
    laid it on the shoulders of each of them, went backwards with it,
    and so covered their father's nakedness;
    their faces were turned away,
    so that they did not see their father's nakedness.

24 *When Noah awoke from the effects of the wine,*
    he noticed what his youngest son had done to him,
25 *and he said:*
        Cursed be Canaan!
        Slave of slaves shall he be to his brothers!

26 *And he said:*
   Blessed be Yahweh, the God of Shem,
   but Canaan shall be his slave.

27 *May God enlarge Japheth,*
   that he may dwell in the tents of Shem,
   and Canaan be his slave.

18-27 These verses, belonging to J, combine two independent units: verses 18-19 constitute the transition from the Flood narrative to J's Table of Nations; verses 20-27 are a narrative about Noah and his sons, which comprises a story of crime and punishment, a brief comment on the development of civilization, and a collection of blessings and curses. The names of Noah's three sons come from a genealogy that also includes the note about viticulture. The narrative belongs to J's series of primal crime/punishment narratives, but has gone through several stages of expansion. One can attempt to identify an earlier form of the narrative that dealt solely with the son of Noah the wine-grower and ended with the curse on this son. A special problem is raised by the name of the son: verse 22 speaks of Ham, the father of Canaan, whereas verses 25-27 speak of Canaan. The discrepancy is due to the fusing of several traditions in 9:20-27. The names of Noah's three sons—Shem, Ham, and Japheth—come from a genealogical tradition appearing in several passages, including 9:18-19 and 10:1. These three names also appear in 9:22-23, except that verse 22, like verse 18, calls Ham the "father of Canaan." The curse in verse 25, however, is directed against Canaan, and verses 25b and 27b also speak of Canaan. The fact that the name appears five times in 9:18-27 means that it is integral to the tradition and therefore certainly belonged to the original form of verse 25, where it a single name and part of the narrative. The name "Ham," on the other hand, belongs to the genealogy in verse 18. The two elements were harmonized by the addition of "Ham it was who was the father of Canaan" in verse 18 and "Ham, the father of . . ." in verse 22. Before they were combined, the genealogy (v. 18) spoke only of Ham, the narrative (vv. 20-27) only of Canaan.

18-19 God's promise after the sacrifice (8:20-22) is followed by a concluding statement that the new human race after the Flood descended from the sons of Noah. The words of 9:19 contain an implied contrast: they are just three, and from them comes the whole human race! While chapters 2–3 spoke only of "the human being" (singular), from this point on the human race is thought of as a whole: from the three sons of the man saved from the Flood springs the whole human race! The words "Ham it was who was the father of Canaan" are a later addition to harmonize "Ham" in verse 22 with "Canaan" in verse 25.

20-27 The primal history is a time of beginnings (Gen. 4:26; 6:1; 10:8; 11:6); viticulture begins with Noah. Agriculture he learned from his ancestors; to it he now adds viticulture. As in 4:17ff., the advance of civilization is presented in genealogical form. Viticulture was already alluded to as a mark of progress in 5:29: the necessary labor of agriculture is now relieved by the production of wine, a festal drink. Later the vine will be a sign of eschatological blessing (Mic. 4:4).

21 The story begins with Noah's drinking wine, becoming drunk, and lying naked in his tent. The ancient world saw nothing reprehensible in drunkenness. We are often told without any hint of disapproval that someone becomes drunk at a celebration. But the power of wine, which weakens the senses, can be dangerous: Noah lies naked, and nakedness is disgraceful.

22 It was a serious moral offense for Canaan (or Ham) not to cover up his father but instead to leave him lying naked and tell his brothers outside. In the Ugaritic Aqhat epic, helping a father returning drunk from a celebration is listed among the obligations of a son.[1]

23 In contrast to the behavior of Canaan (or Ham), the honorable conduct of Noah's other two sons is emphasized by a detailed account. It is characteristic of the narrator's technique to let the simple actions speak for themselves. This is the first mention of a contrast between honorable and dishonorable conduct on the part of sons toward their father where the sons play a role that determines the course of events.

24-27 Noah's curse and blessing. Genesis 9:20-27 differs from the other crime/punishment narratives in Genesis 2–11 in that it is not God who punishes and also in that the reward of proper behavior is described as well as the punishment. It is also noteworthy that Noah's reaction seems quite inappropriate; this suggests the composite nature of the story.

24 The curse upon Canaan makes sense if we remember what is at stake: a continuity between generations that was vital for the world. This continuity demanded an unbroken chain of tradition from one generation to the next. The chain could remain ᵕ broken only if those departing were respected by those arriving. Respect for elders was an imperative for group self-preservation. Here Noah represents the group. This is why he curses his son for disrespect.

25 The father curses the son who has dishonored him to a life of disgrace: he must live as a slave among his own brothers (cf. Gen.

1. James B. Pritchard, ed., *Ancient Near Eastern Texts*, 3rd ed. (Princeton: Princeton University, 1969), p. 150.

27:29, 40). The curse is seen primarily from the perspective of the family, where it would be scandalous for a brother to be a slave to his brothers (cf. ch. 37). There may also be secondary political overtones.

26   The abrupt "and he said" at the beginning of verse 26 suggests that the blessings upon Shem and Japheth are secondary additions. Only the curse upon Canaan is a necessary element of the narrative; the two other brothers only did was what expected of them, which required no reward; nowhere else is a special reason stated for a father to bless a son. The addition of verses 26 and 27 is due to the existence of the three sons. The style of verse 26 shows that it is very late: "Blessed be . . ." (*bārûk*) followed by a divine name is a doxology like those concluding the divisions of the Psalter. When Yahweh is called "the God of Shem," "Shem" can only mean "Israel"; but nowhere else is "Shem" so used. The identification must be ad hoc. The same is true in verses 26b (which is only a modified repetition of v. 25) and 27b.

27   The origin of the blessing on Japheth and its original meaning can no longer be determined. It may once have been an independent blessing, for it predicts a specific historical event: expansion beyond the group's own territory. But expansion into the territory of Shem is out of place in juxtaposition with a blessing on Shem. Neither can "Japheth" refer to the Philistines, who, some claim, joined with Israel in the conquest of Canaan. It is hardly conceivable that the Philistines should receive a blessing promising them expansion into the tents of Shem (Israel). The original meaning cannot be recovered.

Each of the sayings is different. Only when verses 26 and 27 are added do Noah's words suggest an allusion to national destinies. Such an interpretation would remove Genesis 9:20-27 entirely from the Primal History. Verse 25 cannot be made to yield a coherent notion of three nations or groups of nations.

Concluding remarks on 9:18-27:   In J's narratives of crime and punishment, 9:20-27 adds the relationship of parent to child to the relationship of man to wife (ch. 3) and brother to brother (4:2-16). When a son uncovers his own father's nakedness, the proper relationship between parent and child is broken. This points up a norm of conduct universally necessary for the continuity between generations on which society is based. In Israel, this norm later became the fourth commandment of the Decalogue. As generations pass, dishonor shown a father threatens the preservation of what has been achieved as well as the possibility of further progress.

28-29   P's genealogy in chapter 5 takes us from Adam to Noah; 5:32 mentions Noah's three sons. This conclusion comes only now, after the Flood; thus verses 28-29 also end P's account of the Flood. Within the Flood narrative, the genealogy was continued in 6:9, 10;

7:6; these verses are followed by 9:28, 29. With Noah's death, the tenth generation of the genealogy in chapter 5 comes to an end.

10:1-32 THE TABLE OF NATIONS

1   *These are the genealogies of the sons of Noah.*
     The sons of Noah were:
     Shem, Ham, and Japheth.
     . . . and to them sons were born after the Flood.

2   *The sons of Japheth are:*
     Gomer and Magog and Madai and Javan and Tubal and Meshech and Tiras.
3   *The sons of Gomer are: Ashkenaz and Riphath and Togarmah.*
4   *The sons of Javan are: Elishah and Tarshish, Kittim and Rhodanim.*
5   *From these the isles of the nations spread.*
     These are the sons of Japheth according to their lands,
     according to their language, according to their clans in their nations.

6   *The sons of Ham are:*
     Cush and Egypt and Put and Canaan.
7   *The sons of Cush are: Seba and Havilah and Sabtah and Ragmah and*
     Sabteka.
     The sons of Ragmah are: Sheba and Dedan.

8   *And Cush begot Nimrod.*
     He was the first man of might on earth.
9   *He was a mighty hunter before Yahweh.*
     And so it is said: A mighty hunter before Yahweh like Nimrod.
10   *The beginning of his kingdom was Babel*
     and Erech and Akkad and Kalneh in the land of Shinar.
11   *From this land he went up to Asshur*
     and built Nineveh and Rehoboth-Ir and Kalah
12   *and Resen between Nineveh and Kalah,*
     that is the great city.

13   *And Egypt begot*
     the Ludim and the Anamim and the Lehabim
14   *and the Naphtuhim and the Pathrusim*
     and the Casluhim and the Kaphtorim,
     from whom the Philistines came.

15   *And Canaan begot Sidon, his firstborn, and Heth,*
16   *and the Jebusites and the Amorites and the Girgashites*
17   *and the Hivites and the Arkites and the Sinites*
18a *and the Arvadites and the Zemarites and the Hamathites.*
18b *Afterwards the clans of the Canaanites spread abroad,*
19   *so that the territory of the Canaanites extended*
     from Sidon toward Gerar as far as Gaza
     and toward Sodom and Gomorrah
     and Admah and Zeboim as far as Lasha.

20 *These are the sons of Ham*
    according to their clans, according to their languages,
    in their lands, in their nations.

21   *To Shem also sons were born,*
        the father of all the sons of Eber, the elder brother of Japheth.

22 *The* sons of Shem *are:*
    Elam and Asshur and Arpachshad and Lud and Aram.
23 *And the sons of Aram are: Uz and Hul and Gether and Mash.*

24   *And Arpachshad begot Shelah, and Shelah begot Eber.*
25   *And to Eber two sons were born:*
        the name of one was Peleg,
        for in his days humankind divided itself,
        and the name of his brother was Joktan.
26   *And Joktan begot*
        Almodad and Sheleph and Hazarmaveth and Jerah
27   *and Hadoram and Uzal and Diklah*
28   *And Obal and Abimael and Sheba*
29   *And Ophir and Havilah and Jobab.*
        All these are the sons of Joktan.

30   *And their dwelling places are*
        from Mesha toward Sephar as far as the mountains in the east.

31 *These are the sons of Shem*
    according to their clans, according to their languages,
    in their lands, in their nations.

32 *These are the clans of the sons of Noah*
    according to their genealogies, in their nations,
    and from them the nations spread
    on the earth after the Flood.

INTRODUCTION

A glance at chapter 10 reveals two styles: one highly formalized and often repetitious, the other freer and less systematic. This shows that the "redactor" combined P and J to make up the "Table of Nations." The bulk of chapter 10 is P; the redactor inserts major sections from J in verses 8-19 and 24-30, in each case just before the words "these are the sons of Ham" (v. 20 [P]) or "Shem" (v. 31 [P]). The only other J verses are 1b and 21. The redactor (= R) thus gives us the systematically organized text of P with two supplementary sections clearly recognizable as J; they are more detailed and contain more names. By means of a genealogy, P represents the variety of nations as a single entity, like a family. The disadvantage of this presentation is that it provides no geographical or historical information about these nations. Only by interpolating from J is R able to give the impression that we have before us a history of the nations; for J describes the territories of the nations and adds notes about their histories, especially the empire of Nimrod in verses 8b-12.

Basic to the Table of Nations in Genesis 10 is the prehistoric representation of history as genealogy. J's Table of Nations grows out of the conclusion to the Flood story (9:18-19), whose last clause ("and from them the whole earth was populated") is developed in Genesis 10. This concluding motif belongs to the tradition of many flood narratives (e.g.: ". . . and begot children, from whom is descended everyone now living on the earth").[1] The J material may derive from lists kept by the commercial chancery at Jerusalem or other trade centers. The information about foreign nations in P, in the form of lists, was probably collected and preserved by the same circles that produced the P document.

Consistent with the style of P, the Table of Nations begins with the "toledoth" formula: the genealogies (Hebrew *tôlˁdōt*) of Noah's sons are to be traced, from whom the nations of the earth are descended. Verse 1b ("and to them sons were born after the Flood" [J]) follows 9:19 and is continued by 10:8-12.

2-5 The sons of Japheth. From Japheth are descended seven "sons," actually nations; from one of these sons are descended three nations, from another four, making a total of fourteen. Here the genealogy serves only to represent families of nations.

2 The name "Japheth" corresponds to the Greek "Iapetos," one of the titans, the son of Uranos and Gaia. The name is Indoeuropean. Of Japheth's seven sons, Gomer (found also in Ezek. 38:6) corresponds to the Cimmerians, cuneiform "Gimirrai," an Indoeuropean nation. Magog, appearing with the same group of nations in Ezekiel 38:2 and 39:6, is otherwise unknown. Some connection with Gyges of Libya has been suggested. "Madai" refers to the Medes and their territory (Isa. 13:17, etc.); they are an Indoeuropean nation like the Persians, with whom they are often associated. "Javan" refers to the Ionian Greeks (Ezek. 27:13; Isa. 66:19), later by extension to all the Greeks. Tubal and Meshech are almost always mentioned together (e.g., Ezek. 27:13, together with Javan). Both were located in eastern Asia Minor. Tiras, not mentioned elsewhere, is one of the Sea Peoples.

3 The sons of Gomer. In Jeremiah 51:27, Ashkenaz is one of the "foes from the north." It is mentioned in Assyrian inscriptions alongside Gomer. Many follow Herodotus in identifying Ashkenaz with the Scythians. Riphath is otherwise unknown. Togarmah (associated with Javan in Ezek. 27:13-14) appears as Tagarama (a region and city) in Hittite texts.

---

1. J. K. R. Riem, *Die Sintflut in Sage und Wissenschaft* (Hamburg: Agentur des rauhen Hauses, 1925), p. 32.

4   The sons of Javan. Elishah (Akkadian Alašia) corresponds to Cyprus, "the land of copper." It is also mentioned in texts from Mari, Nuzi, and Ugarit. At first it was the name of a city; later it was extended to the surrounding countryside and finally to all of Cyprus. Tarshish (Isa. 66:19; Jonah 1:3; 4:2; cf. the ships of Tarshish in 1 Kgs. 10:22, etc.) is often identified with Tartesos, the Phoenician colony in Spain.

"Kittim" and "Rhodanim" differ from the preceding names in being plurals; they clearly belong to a separate tradition and are secondary here. The names clearly refer to the two islands of Cyprus and Rhodes with their Greek inhabitants. Kition is a city on Cyprus (cf. Isa. 23:1, etc.). The name was extended from the city to a region and then to the entire island.

5a   The Hebrew word translated "isles" in verse 5a means both islands and coastlands, appropriate for both Javan and the "sons of Javan," to whom "from these" refers. The author is saying that the spreading has continued to his own day.

5b   The ceremonious, monotonous conclusion is repeated three times: verses 5b, 20, and 31; the style recalls chapter 1. The profusion of names culminates in what each has in common. Each of these nations is part of the human race, and as such has its own land to live in, its own language that unites those who speak it, and its own family structure to sustain the continuity of national life over generations. This is the first attempt in the history of humankind to define the basic elements that make a group a "nation" or "people." Its purpose is to show how the variety of nations and peoples constituting the human race is grounded in the Creator's will and made possible by his blessing.

Of the fourteen names mentioned, ten are clearly identifiable. The majority of them appear in Ezekiel 38, in a partially identical group of nations to the far north. They are seen from the perspective of the sixth century B.C., the time of Ezekiel and P. From the seventh century on, these nations were probably known to Israel as the nations of the far north. Therefore J could not have been familiar with the majority of them and does not mention the "sons of Japheth."

6-20   The sons of Ham (P and J).

6   Four sons of Ham are named; these are the four great nations of the south, listed from south to north. Cush is Nubia (Greek Ethiopia), the land south of Egypt (cf. Isa. 11:11). The text next names *miṣrayim*, the general Semitic term for Egypt. It was known from the earliest times (cf., for example, Gen. 12:10-20). Put (Jer. 46:9; Ezek. 30:5) is Libya (Josephus). "Canaan" refers to the lowlands west of the Jordan, above all the coastal plain, including Phoenicia. It can also mean all of Phoenicia. It is assigned to Ham in this genealogy because Canaan belonged to Egypt at an earlier period.

7   The sons of Cush. Instead of groups associated with these three great lands, there is a loose list of five "sons of Cush" and two sons of Ragmah (groups of Arabian nations). We know the location of Seba, a land in the far south (Isa. 43:3; 45:14). Havilah (cf. Gen. 2:11) is called a son of Joktan in 10:29, but is one of the sons of Keturah in 25:18; it is a region in Arabia. The identity of Sabtah is uncertain; the ancient Arabian commercial city of Sabatah in the Hadramaut has been proposed. The names of two sons of Ragmah, Sheba (Saba) and Dedan, have been added from a separate tradition. Both also appear together in Genesis 25:3 (the genealogy of the sons of Keturah) and Ezekiel 38:13. The Sabaeans, a wealthy nation in southwest Arabia, are often mentioned; 1 Kings 10:1ff. speaks of the queen of Sheba. Caravans from Dedan are mentioned in Isaiah 21:13; in Jeremiah 25:23 and 49:8 it is mentioned alongside Edom.

8-19   Here is inserted J's material on the "sons of Ham." Of the four sons mentioned in verse 6 (P), J repeats Cush (vv. 8-12), Egypt (vv. 13-14), and Canaan (vv. 15-19); then follows in verse 20 P's concluding statement about the sons of Ham.

8-12   The empire of Nimrod. These verses are very different from what has gone before; here we have a narrative instead of a mere list of names. It is harmonized with the preceding list simply by the inclusion of two series of names in verses 10 and 11-12, which are a later addition. In verses 8-12, J tells how the nations were scattered over the earth. The establishment of an empire is related in three acts: the birth of the ruler, the establishment of the empire, and its expansion.

8   In the introductory clause "And Cush begot Nimrod," both names designate individuals. This is the same kind of genealogy as that found in Genesis 4:17-26. The name "Nimrod" appears elsewhere in the Old Testament only in Micah 5:6, where Assyria is called the "land of Nimrod." The name is not attested outside the Old Testament. Here too, then, we are dealing with the figure of a founder who cannot be identified with any historical person; he is the legendary founder of an empire along the two rivers, whose name is part of the language (Gen. 10:9).

"Nimrod began to be (cf. 4:26; 9:20) a man of might on earth." The might of Nimrod's rule is looked upon as an epochal beginning.

9   The description of Nimrod as a mighty hunter is a separate tradition that has been inserted here; verse 10 should follow verse 8. The phrase "before Yahweh" has neither positive nor negative overtones; it is emphatic, a kind of superlative. The statement comes from a proverbial expression of a universal sort: the deeds or actions of a contemporary are compared to those of a famous figure from the past. In the ancient world, hunting was a sport of kings; there are many illustrations of royal hunts. In the background, however,

stands a vital function of the king in the early period of sacral kingship, when his duties included destruction of the wild animals that threatened the community (dragon slayer).

10 It was Nimrod's mighty deeds that made him king and founder of an empire; first he became overlord of Babel (cf. Gen. 11:9; Isa. 13:1), a city in the land of Shinar (the Old Testament term for Babylonia; cf. Gen. 11:2; Isa. 11:11). An added list names other cities: Erech (Babylonian Uruk), on the Euphrates; Akkad (the only mention in the Old Testament), north of Babylon, founded around 1500 B.C. by Sargon I, who made it his capital; and Kalneh, otherwise unknown.

11-12 Expansion of Nimrod's empire. Conquest is supplemented by peaceful colonization. It is suggested that Babylon, in the south, had the older civilization, which spread toward the north. Genesis 4:17 also mentions the building of cities, but in 10:11-12 it is connected with the expansion of an empire. The Assyrian city of Nineveh on the Tigris was made the royal residence by Sennacherib in the eleventh century; the book of Jonah calls it "the great city" (cf. Gen. 9:12b, referring to Nineveh). An appended list adds three additional Assyrian cities: Rehoboth-Ir (Hebrew for "city squares"); Kalah (Assyrian Kalhu), south of Nineveh; and Resen, "between Nineveh and Kalah."

13-14 The sons of Egypt are merely named in a loosely appended list of nations, still largely unexplained. Unidentified are the Ludim, Anamim, Naphtuhim, and Casluhim. Of the rest, the Lehabim are the Libyans, the Pathrusim are the inhabitants of Upper Egypt, and the Kaphtorim are the Cretans. The plural forms represent a secondary harmonization. The only relatively clear point is the association of the list with Egypt.

15-19 The sons of Canaan (J). Verses 15, 18b, 19 deal with the expansion of the Canaanites. Here J contrasts expansion through conquest (vv. 8-12) with expansion through growth and migration. The interpolated list of names, all plural, in verses 16-18a represents a separate tradition.

15 "And Canaan begot . . ." parallels verses 8 and 15, representing the development of families into nations. "Canaan" is meant in the broadest sense. Canaan is not viewed from the perspective of Israel but as a member of the family of nations. "Sidon" refers to all Phoenicia, as in 1 Kings 16:31. "Heth" refers to the Hittites; the Assyrians called Palestine "the land of the Hittites."

16-18a This section consists of two interpolated lists of names, the first of which (vv. 16-17a) comprises four Canaanite peoples. The Jebusites are the inhabitants of Jerusalem and its environs (Judg. 1:21); the Amorites are named after Amurru, the Early Babylonian term for Palestine and Syria. It is a common name, and can refer to the pre-Israelite population as a whole. Here, as in Joshua 11:3, it must designate only a subgroup. The Girgashites appear also in other lists (cf. Gen. 15:21); their location is unknown. The Hivites probably inhabited central Palestine (Josh. 11:3).

17b-18a Next we have a list of five Phoenician cities. The Arkites are the inhabitants of modern Tell ʿArqā (Greek Arkē, Assyrian Arqā) north of Tripoli. The Sinites are from a city near ʿArqā. The Arvadites come from the northernmost island city of Phoenicia; their name has come down to the present. The Zemarites are located just to the south. The Hamathites are the inhabitants of Hamath on the Orontes, the only inland city of the Phoenicians.

All the names in this list can be identified with certainty. It represents an independent tradition, recording information about a neighboring territory. The list was probably composed and preserved at the Jerusalem court.

18b-19 This passage follows verse 15, and describes the expansion of the Canaanite peoples and their territory. The geographical information is quite vague, consisting only of a few boundary points.

20 P's conclusion to the "sons of Ham" section (cf. vv. 5 and 31).

21-31 The sons of Shem (J and P). This section is a composite of J and P. The introduction (v. 21) is from J; the list of Shem's sons (vv. 22-23) is from P, concluding with verse 31. The P section frames two passages from J: the descendants of Arpachshad (vv. 24-25) and the sons of Joktan (vv. 26-30).

21 This verse contains only J's introduction to the list of Shem's sons; the following verse (P) contains the list itself. To the introductory clause "To Shem also sons were born" verse 21 appends two additions intended to give Shem special status vis-à-vis Noah's other two sons: from him is descended Eber (from whom in turn Abraham is descended), and he is the elder.

22 This verse is P's list of Shem's sons. Its structure is the same as that of the list of Ham's sons in verses 6-7 (P). Elam is the enormous country east of Babylon with Susa as its capital (cf. Gen. 14:1). Asshur is mentioned frequently in the Old Testament; its earliest location was on the middle Tigris. The name "Arpachshad" has not been explained with certainty; here it represents Babylon. Lud is generally identified as Lydia; this identification, however, is inappropriate here, since Lydia is in Asia Minor. Aram is a large group of peoples in Syria and Mesopotamia.

23 Only for Aram are four more nations added; the names "Uz," "Hul," "Gether," and "Mash" have not been explained. There is an "Uz" in Edom (Job 1:1), but it is an open question whether that is the reference here. The list of Aramaic groups in J is quite different.

24-25   These verses (J) continue verse 21 (J); something has probably dropped out between the two passages. "Arpachshad" is also mentioned by P (v. 22). The sequence from Shem through Arpachshad, Shelah, and Eber to Peleg parallels Genesis 11:10-17 (P). These are merely personal names. Verses 24-25 therefore really belong to the genealogy in 11:10-32, the line traced from Shem to Abraham. This observation is confirmed by the statement in verse 25 that "in his days humankind divided itself," which is out of place in chapter 10 but fits well with chapter 11, where it is a separate tradition of the events narrated in 11:1-9.

26-30   While verses 24-25 contain only personal names, the list appended in verses 26-30 contains only place names. Besides "Joktan," which links the two lists, there are thirteen; nine of these cannot be identified, nor can territory described in verse 30. The group as a whole can nevertheless be identified with assurance through the name "Hadramaut," here "Hazarmaveth," still used today for the southwest coast of Arabia, east of Yemen. It is also mentioned by Strabo, Pliny, and others. The name "Sheba" in verse 28 is also certainly identifiable as the name of the tribe that later developed into the Sabaean empire (cf. 10:7; 25:3). All these passages point to southern Arabia. The two names "Ophir" and "Havilah" in verse 29 are also mentioned elsewhere in the Old Testament, both as lands of gold (1 Kgs. 9:28). The locations of Sheleph and Uzal (Gen. 10:26, 27) are not known, but the names appear in the works of Arabian geographers (cf. Ezek. 27:19). The other six names are otherwise unknown.

Verse 29 concludes the list of the sons of Joktan. Verse 30 describes their territory, but the three names mentioned cannot be identified with certainty.

31-32   Verse 31 concludes verses 21-30, and verse 32 concludes chapter 10 as a whole.

CONCLUDING REMARKS ON CHAPTER 10

When we look back over the many names of nations and peoples, classified after Noah's sons as Semites, Hamites, or Japhethites, we get the impression of a very incomplete and composite attempt to survey the nations of the known world. But what is most important is neither the individual names nor the list as a whole, with all its gaps and deficiencies—these represent the very limited geographical knowledge of that era—but the conception behind them: the attempt, magnificent despite its deficiencies, to provide a survey of the nations of the earth as members of the human race. Such an attempt is really without parallel in the ancient world. This conception is nothing less than the logical consequence of what was stated in the first chapters of the Primal History: God is the Creator of *all* human-kind. God created the whole human race—this statement is spelled out in detail, as it were, by the Table of Nations at the end of the Primal History: the human race, which exists today as a multiplicity of nations, is the humanity created by God. For it is God's blessing imparted to his creatures (Gen. 1) that allows humanity to expand in the course of time (ch. 5) and fill the space of the earth (ch. 10). Some seventy nations are named here, all of which are said to have only one thing in common: they spring from the work of the Creator. As Paul says in his speech on the Areopagus (Acts 17:26): "God made from one human being every nation."

11:1-9   THE TOWER OF BABEL

1   *And (it happened) the whole world had one language*
    and one vocabulary.
2   *And as they journeyed from the east,*
    they found a plain in the land of Shinar
    and settled there.
3   *And they said to each other:*
    Come, let us make bricks and bake them thoroughly!
    And they used brick for stone and bitumen for mortar.
4   *And they said:*
    Come, let us build a city and a tower,
    with its summit touching the heavens!
    So we will make a name for ourselves,
    lest we be scattered over the face of the earth.

5   *Then Yahweh came down*
    to look at the city and the tower that the people had built.
6   *And Yahweh said:*
    See, they are one people and they have all one language,
    and this is only the beginning of what they will do.
    Henceforth nothing will be impossible for them
    in what they propose to do.
7   *Come, we will go down and confuse their language there,*
    so that no one understands the language of another.
8   *And Yahweh scattered them from there over the face of the whole earth,*
    and they left off building the city.

9   *For this reason their name is called Babel,*
    for there Yahweh confused the language of the world,
    and from there Yahweh scattered them over the whole earth.

INTRODUCTION

The narrative is framed by verses 1 and 9; it tells how the situation of today (v. 9) came to replace what had once been (v. 1). The narrative comprises two parallel sections: in verses 2-4 people speak and act; in 5-8 God speaks and acts. This structure is typical of etiological narratives, which explain how a past event accounts for a present phenomenon. But the etiological motifs and narratives in the Primal History must be distinguished from those in historical contexts (e.g., Josh. 1–9). In contrast to the latter, the prehistoric narratives are intended to account for something inexplicable in the order of the created world, such as the birth pangs women suffer. Because Genesis 11:1-9 mentions the city of Babylon, this text stands on the borderline between prehistoric and historical etiology. In addition, several originally disparate motifs have been combined here. The motif of the dispersal of the human race over the entire earth belongs originally to the Flood story. The motif of the confusion of languages is independent, as is that of the building that reaches to heaven.

A wealth of parallels to the tower story exists throughout the world, although scarcely any have been found in the immediate environment of Israel. It is significant for our knowledge of its prehistory that an African form of this story is known, which ends with the destruction of the building and says nothing of the confusion of languages or of the dispersal of humanity.[1] The extensive and complex prehistory of this material makes it easy to understand why 11:1-9 reveals a variety of strata and motifs, from which the text gradually emerged. They all, however, belong to the preliterary stage; in its written form, the narrative is a unit. Attempts to analyze it into two written recensions (Hermann Gunkel: city recension and tower recension) have been unsuccessful.

The narrative cannot possibly have originated in Babylon; neither can it refer to a specific tower. It came into being in Israel, where the enormous buildings of Babylon were well known. Since the subject of the story is "people" in general, it belongs to the Primal History; it was set in Babylon because of the huge buildings there. The basic motifs of the story are found throughout the world; the narrative must have been shaped over an extensive period.

1 "Once upon a time" (Heb. *way^ehî*), ages ago, we are told that all people spoke the same language. This statement has no basis in experience within reach of human memory; it expresses the feeling that the present confusion of languages is abnormal. The back-

---

1. Hermann Baumann, *Schöpfung und Urzeit des Menschen im Mythos der afrikanischen Völker* (1936; repr. Berlin: D. Reimer, 1964).

ground must involve events in limited area—in an upheaval, for example, that brought people into constant contact with others speaking a different language. This statement has no bearing on attempts to seek a protolanguage spoken by all humanity.

2   The story that follows is told to explain the present situation. It begins with a journey, but we are not told by whom or from where. The form of verse 2, an itinerary, marks the transition from prehistory to history. After the Flood, the human race begins to spread abroad. In contrast to chapter 10, however, 11:1-9 understands the dispersal and linguistic confusion brought about by this spread as diminishing the quality of human life. The itinerary in verse 2 suggests the transition from nomadic to settled life. The people come "from the east," without further specification. But the scene that follows is set in "the land of Shinar" (cf. 10:10). The itinerary moves from the mists of prehistoric time to the bright beginnings of history. The group on the move is in search of an unknown goal. Now they find a lowland plain that makes it possible for them to stay: it offers water, food, and safety. Only at the end (11:9) are we told that this is the plain where the city of Babylon is located.

3-4   Now that they have found what they were looking for, they decide to build a city with a tower. In verse 3, the decision involves only the preparations; it reads literally: "Let us 'brick' bricks and fire the fire." In Enuma Elish VI:60-62, the building of Esagila is described in similar terms.[2] There we also find the motif introduced in Genesis 11:4b: "They raised high the head of Esagila toward Apsu." Verse 3b adds an explanatory note about building materials; the narrator is knowledgeable about building techniques and contrasts the foreign use of bricks and bitumen to the familiar use of stone and mortar. The use of baked bricks for building was an important invention because it meant that a quarry nearby was no longer needed. The decision culminates in the size of the building: ". . . with its summit touching the heavens!" For the narrator, the enormous buildings found in the valley of the great rivers express precisely what he wants his story to say about the greatness mortals achieve by their own devices in order to make themselves a name. "Name" is used here in the sense of "fame"—fame among contemporaries and fame among generations to come. The narrator does not condemn these efforts as such, but says that they risk hubris and the transgression of limits it leads to.

A further motivating factor is added in verse 4b to introduce the motif of dispersal in verses 8 and 9b.

5-9   The second section recounts God's intervention. It involves

2. James B. Pritchard, ed., *Ancient Near Eastern Texts*, 3rd ed. (Princeton: Princeton University, 1969), pp. 68-69.

less action than reflection. Verse 5, which tells of God's coming down, is followed in verse 7 by a repetition of the decision to come down; this difficulty is due to the combination of several once separate motifs. But the structure is clear: God sees—God considers—God decides—God intervenes—the effects of the intervention.

5   God's coming down in verses 5 and 7 is meant as an element of his punitive intervention. In contrast to chapters 2–3, 4, and 6–9, this section presupposes that God comes down from heaven. But his coming does not take place in the form of a revelation, as will be the case from Genesis 12 on. The Primal History depicts God's coming in such a way that, although he comes from heaven, he moves within the space inhabited by mortals. Heaven is not yet the "beyond."

6   When God sees what the people have accomplished, he reflects, picking up the statement of verse 1 and asking what will come of this project: "This is only the beginning of what they will do." God intervenes, says verse 5b, to prevent something worse from happening. God is afraid that the building will lead to human autonomy; such a development would call into question human finitude, which is inherent in being created by God. It is to be feared that mortals might become like God (cf. 3:5). Job 42:2 uses the same verbs to describe God's being. Against such hubris God must intervene—for the sake of humanity.

7-8   God therefore decides to confuse human language ("go down" and "confuse" are to be understood as an hendiadys; on the plural, see the discussion of Gen. 1:26 and 3:22). We should expect to hear God's decision to put an end to the human undertaking; that is how earlier forms of the story run. Instead, we have here the confusion of language, which is a consequence of God's intervention to prevent completion of the building, as presupposed by verse 8b. Therefore the decision (v. 7) and its execution (v. 8) do not agree. Even the scattering of the people (v. 8a) is itself not God's doing but a consequence of his intervention, as in the earlier form of the story. The two consequences have here replaced the primary motif: God's intervention to prevent the building from being finished. In the earlier form, the sequence was: God intervenes to prevent completion of the building—the builders give up their undertaking—they are scattered.

9   Etiological conclusion. The narrator adds a conclusion that connects what took place at the dawn of history with a phenomenon of the present, the name of the city Babylon. But the connection is only a distant echo: the verb *bālal*, "confuse," is used to explain the name *bābel*. This conclusion is a secondary addition. Even without it, the narrative is etiological, explaining the scattering of humanity over the earth and the confusion of language.

CONCLUSION

This building of a city with towers differs from the building of a city in 4:17 in that here the great city is to represent the very essence of greatness: "With its summit touching the heavens." The same motif of a great work of human hands reaching to heaven reappears in prophecy, in an oracle of judgment against Babylon (Isa. 14:13-14):

> You said in your heart:
> I will ascend to heaven, above the stars of God
> I will set my throne on high. . . .
> I will ascend above the heights of the clouds,
> I will make myself like the Most High.

At the beginning (Gen. 3:5, referring to Adam) and at the end (11:4) of the Primal History, the narrator is saying that the greatest danger facing mortals left to themselves by their Creator is the endeavor to break through the limits imposed by their finitude. The can fulfill their humanity only within the boundaries imposed. The impulse to break out can originate with either an individual (3:5) or a group (11:1). It is an astute observation that the notion of human greatness came into being with the great achievements of civilization. It is not the striving for greatness as such or the undertaking of great projects as such that is rejected here; the narrator points rather to the danger of hubris that threatens the very humanity of mortals. The basic theme of Genesis 11:1-9 anticipates the possibility of a development that was not realized until the age of technology.

There are also two secondary themes. The scattering of the human race over the face of the earth makes sense only in the context of the primary theme. It is addressed only as an aspect of this event. The narrator pursues the old motif of the scattering of humanity, seeing the danger it would face from a dehumanizing unity. God's intervention saves the human race from this danger (v. 6b). Therefore this story does not contradict chapter 10. A multiplicity of nations with the wealth of opportunities for development open to each is seen as fitting the human condition and protective of humanity. But multiplicity of nations means multiplicity of languages. This, too, is a worldwide motif. If it is seen here as a limitation and diminution of the quality of life, this estimate chimes with early experience. With all the wealth and variety offered by multiplicity of languages, the language barrier is experienced repeatedly as an obstacle; this feeling is illustrated by the hope for a mode of understanding that will transcend linguistic boundaries, as in Zephaniah 3:5-11 and the story of Pentecost in Acts 2.

11:10-26   THE GENEALOGY OF SHEM

10   *This is the genealogy of Shem: When* Shem *was 100 years old,*
     he begot Arpachshad, two years after the Flood.
11   *After Shem begot Arpachshad,*
     he lived another 500 years, and begot sons and daughters.
12   *When* Arpachshad *was 35 years old,*
     he begot Shelah.
13   *After Arpachshad begot Shelah,*
     he lived another 403 years, and begot sons and daughters.
14   *When* Shelah *was 30 years old, he begot Eber.*
15   *After Shelah begot Eber,*
     he lived another 403 years, and begot sons and daughters.
16   *When* Eber *was 34 years old, he begot Peleg.*
17   *After Eber begot Peleg,*
     he lived another 430 years, and begot sons and daughters.
18   *When Peleg was 30 years old, he begot Reu.*
19   *After he begot Reu,*
     he lived another 209 years, and begot sons and daughters.
20   *When Reu was 32 years old, he begot Serug.*
21   *After Reu begot Serug,*
     he lived another 207 years, and begot sons and daughters.
22   *When Serug was 30 years old, he begot Nahor.*
23   *After Serug begot Nahor,*
     he lived another 200 years, and begot sons and daughters.
24   *When Nahor was 29 years old, he begot Terah.*
25   *After Nahor begot Terah,*
     he lived another 119 years, and begot sons and daughters.
26   *When Terah was 70 years old,*
     he begot Abram, Nahor, and Haran.

The genealogy of Shem goes through nine generations from Shem to
the three sons of Terah. The patriarchal history begins in Genesis
11:27 with the appended genealogy of Terah. The genealogy in
11:10-26 is similar to chapter 5 (both P); it has only nine generations
because the tenth introduces the Patriarchal History. Moving into
the latter, it continues a single branch of the total human genealogy,
the branch that leads from one of the sons of Noah to Abraham. This
shows how the story of Abraham emerges from the general history of
the human race.

The numbers differ widely in the texts and the ancient versions;
like the numbers in chapter 5, they are based on an uncertain tradition. It is impossible to say that one is right and another wrong; they
are all secondary inventions. P composed the genealogy in 11:10-26
from many sources as a transition to the Patriarchal History.

10-17   These names have all appeared previously.

18-23   The new names here are Reu and Serug. The name "Reu" appears only here and has not been explained. "Serug" represents Sarugi, near Haran; the place still exists (Seruj).

24-26   The name "Nahor" corresponds to the Akkadian toponym *Til Naḥiri*, near Haran. A form identical with the biblical name is found in the Mari texts. The name "Terah" corresponds to Akkadian *Til ša Turaḥi*, north of Haran. The three names "Serug," "Nahor," and "Terah" are thus all attested as place names, all in the vicinity of Haran. This observation confirms the composite character of the sequence in 11:10-26. Place names probably became identified with personal names as the result of a gradual process.

A group of three names brings the genealogical sequence to an end in 11:26, like the group at the end of chapter 5. A series of ancestors leads up to a group of contemporaries. Here it is a group descended from Terah and his ancestors. This group dominates the entire Patriarchal History, as we see especially in chapter 24 and 27:43. In the genealogy in 11:10-26, P shows that even Abraham's forebears, who "served other gods" (Josh. 24:2), lived by the blessing of the God who created all humanity.

CONCLUDING REMARKS ON THE PRIMAL HISTORY

The Primal History establishes a relationship between God and all that is. These chapters are more than an introduction to the history of the people of God that begins with chapter 12; Genesis 1–11 puts this history in a perspective that embraces everything that exists, from the stars and clouds of heaven to the grass and flowers, from the single person whom God asks, "Where are you?" to the most remote nations of the known world. The message of the Primal History can be heard only if it is heard in its entirety. There is no justification for overemphasizing chapters 1–3, as though "Creation and Fall" were all that mattered. The narrative texts in Genesis 1–11 are of a piece with the lists; Creation and the Flood are complementary; the offense against God in chapter 3 is matched by the offense against a brother in chapter 4.

The Primal History speaks of God in such a way that his acts affect the entire world and the entire human race, transcending all differences and disparities. The meaning of the Primal History is this: what takes places in these chapters lies at the heart of *every* event, wherever located in space and time. The themes of the Primal History therefore are universal; they are found throughout the world. God is not dealing here with a specific people or a specific religion, but with the totality of the world and the totality of the human race, from the beginning to the end. The fundamental tone is that of an all-encompassing approach to reality. For this reason it would also be wrong to understand the Primal History as a fragment of early history; it is misguided to ask about the "historicity" of these events. The statements about the world and the human race as a whole are not related to the present as historical facts. The appropriate thing to ask about what these chapters say of humankind is not: "Did that really happen that way?" but: "Is that the nature of humankind?"

It is in the story of Creation that the world and the human race are first understood as a whole. To speak of the Creator means to speak of the whole. We cannot experience humankind or the world as a whole; we understand them as such only from the perspective of their origin, their creation. The Priestly writer (P) emphasizes the representation of the world as a totality—in the categories of space and time, in living beings belonging to species that constitute a single whole. And there is always the possibility that the whole may be destroyed (Gen. 6–9). Genesis 5 and 10 describe the spread of the whole human race through space and time. The Yahwist (J) emphasizes the totality of the human race: its relationship to God as his creation, the mutual relationship between creature and Creator, intimately associated with the environment in which humankind exists, territory and food, work and society. In truth, the concept of "humankind" arises from an understanding of human beings as creatures in the most universal sense. For J, however, the finitude of death and sin are also inherent in humanity. Crime and punishment are part of human life, as we are told in Genesis 3; 4; 6:1-4; 9; 11. J sees the greatest danger facing humankind in the desire "to be like God." Without these limitations, humanity would not be human.

With profound insight, the redactor has combined these two perspectives into our text of chapters 1–11. In this combination, the Primal History of the Bible has influenced the ages. From the perspective of the present, we see in the presence of these two facets the fundamental division of knowledge into the natural sciences and the humanities. What the Bible says about the events of the Primal History is addressed to all generations in their own age. What links the Primal History to any present is the blessing vouchsafed by God. God blesses his creatures; by virtue of his blessing they grow and multiply (chs. 1; 5; 10 [P]); and, after the Flood, the Creator gives his promise that the human world will be preserved in the great rhythms of blessing (8:20-22 [J]) "as long as earth endures." God's blessing is universal. The Creator holds the world in his hands; he preserves the human race generation after generation even through catastrophes: the God who blesses is also the God who saves.

The placement of the Primal History before the history of God's people incorporates what the latter says about God into the whole. The God whom Israel encountered in its history as savior is also the God who created heaven and earth. He is the God who works with the whole and preserves the whole, even during the era of his special history with his people. At the end, God's special way with his people and his way with all humanity and creation come together. The promise after the Flood already points to an end of the world (8:22); the end of the world is again the subject of the apocalypses in the Old and New Testaments, which speak of the end of the world and of humankind. The end is in God's hands, like the beginning. No one but God can bring about the end of the world and of humankind. Therefore, in the midst of time, between the beginning and the end, God placed the work of Christ.

THE PATRIARCHAL HISTORY   12–36

THE SIGNIFICANCE OF THE PATRIARCHAL HISTORY

In telling the story of the patriarchs, the Patriarchal History deals with the elementary foundations of human society: the relationship between parents and children primarily in the story of Abraham (Gen. 12–25), the relationship between brothers primarily in the story of Jacob and Esau (Gen. 25–36), the relationships among several members of a family in the Joseph story (Gen. 37–50). These narratives lent expression to the fundamental importance of the family for all other forms of society in the period when the tribes were developing into a people and a state. These basic forms of human society, however, are discussed in theological terms; the narratives cannot speak of them without speaking also of God. The sequence of generations and social cohesion (peace and blessing) within a family cannot exist apart from the words and acts of God. Family relationships are established and maintained by God's activity. This remained true in all stages of Israel's religion.

The incorporation of the Patriarchal History into the Pentateuch derives from an historical schema dating from the period of the Early Monarchy, which identified three stages that led up to and laid the groundwork for the Monarchy: the story of the patriarchs leading up to enslavement in Egypt, the deliverance from Egypt together with the period of desert wandering leading up the occupation of Canaan, and the period from the occupation to the beginning of the Monarchy. This schema appears, for example, in the parallel between the exodus of Abraham (Gen. 12:1-4a) and the exodus from Egypt (Exod. 1–15); both begin with a promise. When the Patriarchal History became part of the Pentateuch, the promises of that narrative found fulfillment in the history of the people.

Formally, the Patriarchal History is the story of a family through three generations. It is not, however, a biography in the modern sense; we are told about the patriarchs because they are ancestors, and in the stories about them their descendants find their own identity. Human life is still experienced so much in the succession of generations that our concept of the individual still does not exist. But the link with the patriarchs exists only when their story is told. It is generally true, as here, that memories of ancestors are limited to three generations. The names of the patriarchs and the fact of three generations belong to the earliest stage of the tradition. The tripartite structure itself indicates the form the story will eventually take, above all in the emphasis on the three basic types of family relationship in the three sections, as well as the suggestion of internal development within each part. The Abraham stories (chs. 12–25) deal primarily with fundamental events; they are often concerned with matters of life and death. In the Jacob and Esau narratives (chs. 25–36), institutions extending beyond the family begin to play a role; we are told of property law, covenants, legal practices, holy places, sacred acts. In Genesis 37–50 the subject of family versus monarchy is also included: this section deals with the fundamental phenomenon of kingship, "ruling over brothers."

These three acts outline a history: from families and clans through tribes to state and monarchy. The fundamental conception is probably that of the Yahwist, since such a conception is not possible until the end of the third act. From the perspective of these three stages, we can give a positive response to the question of whether the patriarchs and the patriarchal period are historical.

THE ORIGINS OF THE PATRIARCHAL HISTORY

Literary Stage

The conclusions of literary criticism remain valid for the written stage in the development of Genesis 12–36 insofar as these chapters clearly contain several recognizable literary strata, from which they were composed. But literary criticism is less important now than it was in the classic period when sources were analyzed, because more importance is now attached to the oral tradition of the patriarchal stories, which came before the literary stage. In particular, it is now clear that each of the three sections had its own distinct prehistory. The differences between them cannot be explained by assigning them to different sources. The composers of the literary sources were thus more tradents than authors in the modern sense. For each text, we must ask whether the author (J or P) is speaking for himself or handing on something said by someone before him. These authors are more recognizable in the overall conceptions of their works, in introductions and conclusions, in transitions and bridge passages, than in the individual narratives. None of the narratives in Genesis 12–36 was made up by the author; all of them go back to earlier traditions, albeit in very different ways. Furthermore, what the narratives say about

God does not simply reflect the theology of the Yahwist, for example, as was previously assumed. We must instead reckon with the possibility that what the narratives say about God goes back to the religion of the patriarchs. The interpretation of the patriarchal stories has altered fundamentally from that practiced in the classic period of source analysis: their texts can no longer be traced to the author of a literary work (J or P); the whole prior and subsequent development of the tradition must be taken into account. The earlier theory that an independent Elohistic (E) document could be found in the Patriarchal History alongside the Yahwist (J) and the Priestly Document (P) has turned out to be very dubious. The texts ascribed to this source are better accounted for as later expansions of the Yahwist's work.

Oral Stage

If texts in the Patriarchal History, even just motifs or fragments from them, go back to the period of the patriarchs (that is, in any case, the period before the exodus from Egypt), scholars must consider as much as possible the course taken by these traditions from the patriarchal period to the time the literary works were composed. This is naturally very difficult, because the course is primarily one of oral tradition. We must start with the observation that the individual texts of the patriarchal stories are extremely varied. Not all are narratives; some are lists (as in Gen. 1–11). Besides genealogies, as in Genesis 1–11, we find itineraries. Promises, which represent an independent form of tradition, constitute a third group. And among the narratives themselves we find a variety of mutually distinct types and groups, each of which demands separate investigation. One important distinction is that between family narratives and narratives of sanctuaries and divine encounters. There are other differences of both form and subject matter. The different types of narrative can be recognized only when the circles that produced them are taken into account.

As a group, the texts of the Patriarchal History exhibit signs of a gradual development extending over centuries. It is particularly important to note the changes undergone by these traditions as social and economic forms changed, to the extent that traces of the change remain. We must also remember that every text in Genesis 12–36 can have undergone alteration in the course of its transmission. Such changes are normal for a tradition that extends over centuries; they are illustrated by parallel texts like Genesis 12; 20; 26. It is impossible to identify an "original" text—all we can do is ask which text belongs to an earlier stage and which to a later. During the oral stage, all the patriarchal stories existed in a variety of forms; usually only one is extant. The only texts that can be considered candidates for a patriarchal period origin are those that reflect a way of life prior to permanent settlement and are not at odds with what archaeological discoveries say about this area and period. This singles out explanations that presuppose a social structure based solely on the family and a seminomadic way of life. These texts, too, may have changed in the course of time to reflect the circumstances of a later age. It is especially clear that, although the promises go back in their beginnings to the patriarchal period, their extensions and expansions belong to a later period. Faced with the possibility that texts from Genesis 12–36 go back to the patriarchal period, the exegete must examine much more intensively than heretofore the rhetorical forms of present-day preliterate societies, which are being studied by ethnologists and anthropologists.

Against this background, we can identify—albeit with great caution—stages in the development of the Patriarchal History. The conceptions informing the History as a whole belong to the latest period. The Priestly Document (P), exegetes generally agree, came into being during the Exile or shortly afterward. The Yahwist's history is a product of the Early Monarchy, probably the time of David or Solomon. Recently this dating has been disputed. Many scholars propose a later origin for the Yahwist's history, during the exilic period; but this thesis does not yet have sufficient evidence to support it. It is clear in any case that the patriarchal narrative of P is later than that of J. Into J's document, however, have been incorporated a large number of secondary additions, including above all passages formerly regarded as belonging to an Elohistic document (E); some of these additions are very late. These additions to J presuppose that the patriarchal stories continued to be transmitted and developed orally even after having been reduced to written form.

Narrative and Its Forms

A narrative recounts an event from an initial conflict to its resolution. The narrative trajectory from conflict to resolution gives the narrative its unity and establishes the form in which it can be handed down. The events involved in a conflict arise from and return to the plain of everyday life. In the patriarchal stories, this plain is usually the listing of genealogies and itineraries. In the preliterary period, all narrative referred to events. Storytellers recounted what took place, what they observed, in order to share it with others. Storytelling is the predecessor of all history. It appears at the beginning of both Greek historiography (Herodotus) and Old Testament historiography, as we see in the historical narratives of Judges, Samuel, and Kings. The original purpose of the stories was to allow new generations to share in the experiences and knowledge of their ancestors. This is not the place to discuss in detail the various narrative genres: folk story, tale, legend, myth, epic. The characteristic form of the patriarchal stories is family narrative, which echoes the family-based structure of the society in which they originated.

Setting and Date of the Patriarchal History

A new phase in the study of the patriarchal stories began when the results of archaeological exploration of the ancient Near East were extended to these stories and brought to bear upon them. The American scholar William Foxwell Albright spoke of an "archaeological revolution."[1] The primary aim of this new approach was to demonstrate the historicity of the patriarchal stories and figures by citing parallels. A limitation of this approach is the fact that such parallels relate almost without exception to isolated elements in the patriarchal narratives, not the narratives as a whole (in contrast to chs. 1–11). Its primary significance consists in the astonishing light it has shed on the world of the patriarchs. Scholars have attempted to connect the journeyings of Abraham, Isaac, and Jacob with large-scale migrations of peoples in the first half of the second millennium B.C., but the stories do not contain any evidence suggesting a relationship to any of these movements. Nevertheless, ancient Near Eastern archaeology and philology have illuminated the historical, sociological, economic, linguistic, and religious background of the patriarchal stories. Despite increased knowledge of the patriarchal world in the second millennium, it has not been possible to date the patriarchal period more precisely, because the stories do not contain clear references to historical events. Proposed dates have ranged from 2200 to 1200.[2] We can safely say, however, that study of the world of the patriarchs has demonstrated the possibility they could have lived and journeyed in the period before the Exodus and the settlement of the tribes in Canaan. It is also clear that the way of life and economic base of the patriarchs was that of nomads herding sheep and goats. This conclusion is fully compatible with the occasional mention of cattle as well as sporadic agriculture.

The Religion of the Patriarchs

The patriarchal stories bear witness to a religion that can be dated by religio-historical criteria before the settlement of the tribes in Canaan

---

1. *From the Stone Age to Christianity*, 2nd ed. (Garden City: Doubleday, 1957).

2. See the chart in Claus Westermann, *Genesis 12–50*. Erträge der Forschung 7 (Darmstadt: Wissenschaftliche Buchgesellschaft, 1975), p. 73.

and before the exodus from Egypt. Characteristic of this patriarchal religion is a close relationship between persons and the deity. This is illustrated by the form of personal names, by the expression "the God of my father," and above all by the stories themselves. This religion is prepolitical; the God of the patriarchs has nothing to do with war. It is also noteworthy that there is almost no trace of a relationship between sin and punishment; there are no announcements of judgment as counterparts to the promises. The patriarchs exhibit no knowledge of a large-scale cult with sacred space, sacred time, and sacred persons. In the patriarchal stories, worship is not yet a realm set apart from the rest of life; it is fully integrated into the way of life of the nomadic group. The sanctuary is not yet a structure made by human hands, but a mountain, a stone, a tree, a spring; the patriarchs themselves perform priestly functions. All transactions between God and human beings are direct, requiring no mediator.

GENESIS 12–25: ABRAHAM

Behind the text of Genesis 12–25 in its present form stands the conception of a redactor working with both the J and P documents, as well as separate Abraham traditions from which the literary works were composed. The entire complex is framed by genealogies; the unit as a whole thus deals with a succession of generations. The statement in 11:30 that Sarah was barren introduces a thread that leads to the birth and marriage of Isaac. This theme is concerned with the survival of a family into the next generation. A variety of dangers threatening this survival contribute tension in the individual narratives. The promise of a son is therefore a necessary element in the sequence of themes; it is the start of the promise motif in the patriarchal stories. This motif then expands and takes on the new function of linking the Patriarchal History with the history of the nation (12:1-3). The promises are distributed throughout the entire complex of chapters 12–25, but are concentrated in the central section (chs. 15 and 17).

A second thread linking several narratives is the theme of Abraham and Lot; they constitute a nexus. This series of narratives is framed by itineraries. Between the preliminary conclusion (21:1-7, Isaac's birth) and the final conclusion (25:7-10, Abraham's death), the redactor has added a group of Abraham narratives that illustrate the further development of the Abraham tradition (chs. 22, 23, and 24).

11:27-32   THE TRANSITION TO THE STORY OF ABRAHAM

27 *This is the history of Terah:*
    Terah begot Abram, Nahor, and Haran; Haran begot Lot.

28 *But Haran died before his father Terah in the land of his kindred, Ur-Kasdim.*

29 *Abram and Nahor took wives.*
    Abram's wife was called Sarai,
    Nahor's wife was called Milcah, the daughter of Haran,
    the father of Milcah and Iscah.

30   *But Sarai was barren; she had no children.*

31   *And Terah took his son Abram and Lot the son of Haran,*
      his grandson, and Sarai, his daughter-in-law,
      the wife of his son Abram.
      And they set out with them from Ur-Kasdim,
      to go to the land of Canaan.
      They came to Haran and settled there.

32   *And Terah was 205 years old when he died in Haran.*

27-32   Genesis 11:27-32 is intended to mark the place in the succession of generations where the events that follow take place and also to introduce the family of Abraham. According to P, they came from Ur in Chaldea; according to J, they came from Haran. The genealogical statements in verses 27 and 32 follow the *tôlᵉḏōṯ* of the Primal History in 11:10-26. The text has two parts: the genealogy in verses 27b-30 and the itinerary in verse 31 (without 31b); verses 27 and 32 constitute the framework. The Patriarchal History begins with 11:27; 11:27-32 lays its groundwork. It is a composite text, with elements of both J and P, although precise differentiation in every clause is impossible. In contrast to what is stated in the second introduction (12:1-4a), the departure of Terah from Ur and the departure from Haran are not responses to a command from God, nor is there a promise. As in Deuteronomy 6, this establishes a dividing line separating Abraham's religion from the pagan religion of his ancestors; Ur-Kasdim is intended to represent the pagan world from which Abraham's family came.

27   Verse 27 is a new beginning; the *tôlᵉḏōṯ* formula introduces the history of Terah—that is, the history that begins with Terah: it cannot end with Terah's death in verse 32. "The heading belongs to the whole subsequent story of Abraham" (Franz Delitzsch).

28   The father must experience the death of his son; Haran died in the land where his kindred lived.

29   In verse 29 the genealogy is expanded in the direction of narrative. The description of Haran "father of Milcah and Iscah" even though Iscah is not mentioned again points to an ancient tradition that told of both. Nahor married Milcah; marriage between uncle and niece is permitted in the Old Testament and is frequently encountered. The names "Sarah" and "Milcah" mean "princess" and "queen" (cf. Babylonian *šarratu*, "queen," and *malkātu*, "princess." Both names are in fact titles; they are associated with the cult of the moon, which had a special place in both Ur and Haran.

30   An expansion of the genealogy suggests a narrative; Sarah's barrenness is mentioned frequently (chs. 15, 16, 17, 18). The statement serves as an introduction to the narrative and achieves a certain emphasis through parallelism.

31   This verse has the form of an itinerary: preparations—departure—destination—stopping place. The huge distances show that the itinerary is secondary. P used this form to show that Abraham's ancestors came to Canaan from distant, pagan lands. Ur, on the lower Euphrates river, was a flourishing city in the third millennium, especially under the Third Dynasty of Ur. Haran is a famous ancient city on the Balîkh, a tributary of the Euphrates. The majority of scholars assume that northern Mesopotamia was the region from which Abraham's ancestors came. Genesis 24 speaks of Haran as the city of Nahor, Laban, and Rebekah. Its appearance here as a stopping place on the route from Ur to Canaan is probably due to the combination of two traditions.

32   The genealogical statement of Terah's death at Haran assumes that he spent his entire life there. Through his father Terah, Abraham is linked with the history of the human race presented in chapters 1–11; as the son of Terah, he is a human being, one of God's creatures.

12:1-9 PROMISE TO ABRAHAM AND MIGRATION

1   *Yahweh said to Abram:*
     Go from your land and from your kindred
     and from the house of your father to the land
     that I will show you.
2   *I will make you into a great nation*
     and will bless you and make your name great
     so that you will be a blessing.
3   *I will bless those who bless you*
     and those who curse you I will execrate.
     And in you all the families of the earth are to bless themselves.

4   *And Abram went as Yahweh had told him,*
     and Lot went with him.
          Abram was 75 years old when he left Haran.
5   *And Abram took Sarai his wife*
          and Lot his nephew and all their possessions that they had acquired,
          and the people that they had acquired in Haran,
          and they set out to go to the land of Canaan,
          and they arrived in the land of Canaan.
6   *And Abram continued on through the land to the place at Shechem,*
     to the oracle terebinth. At that time the Canaanites were in the land.
7   *And Yahweh appeared to Abram and said:*
     To your seed I will give this land.

> And he built there an altar for Yahweh,
> who had appeared to him.
> 8 And he set out from there to the hill country,
> east of Bethel, and he pitched his tent,
> Bethel to the west and Ai to the east,
> and he built an altar there to Yahweh,
> and he called on the name of Yahweh.
> 9 Then Abram journeyed on toward the Negeb.

Following the transitional 11:27-32, 12:1-3(4a) is the actual introduction to the story of Abraham. Verses 4b-5 continue the genealogy of P, and verses 6-9 (J) recount Abraham's journeys; verse 9 constitutes a transition to the narrative in verses 10-20. Genesis 12:1-3 is a command to depart accompanied by a promise. The promise recorded by J is framed so as to provide a transition from the Primal History to the Patriarchal History but at the same time point forward to the history of the nation Israel. It is the theological introit to the Patriarchal History. Following Hermann Gunkel, Gerhard von Rad considers 12:1-4a a free composition of the Yahwist. The parallels in 26:1-3; 46:1-5a (cf. also 31:3; 32:9), however, reveal a set structure: God's command to depart—continued travel or stopping associated with a promise—obedience to the command. This sequence reflects the way of life of the patriarchs and their relationship to God. Therefore 12:1-4a may be based on an earlier version having this structure and going back to the patriarchal period. If so, J built on an earlier tradition already in being.

1   The story of Abraham began with the genealogy in 11:27-32 (J and P). The statement "Yahweh said to Abram" (12:1a) follows 11:30 (J); the genealogy issues in an event, which begins with a command to Abraham from God. Abraham is dwelling in the vicinity of Haran; God orders him to depart and go to a land that he will show him. In the patriarchal period, such a command had the force of a directive in a crisis from the patriarchal God, ordering the group to set out for a different territory to save it from disaster. If we look at this directive in a larger context, it clearly echoes the command to depart at the beginning of Exodus. The history of the nation, too, begins with a command to set out for an unknown land. With the emphatic listing of the three circles that God calls on Abraham to leave, the narrator reminds his audience, now settled, of the patriarchs' migratory way of life, which began with a call to set forth into the unknown.

2-3   The significance of the promise associated with this command also goes far beyond Abraham. It has three parts, each of which elaborates the blessing promised Abraham, which will extend from Abraham (v. 3) to the circle of those among whom he lives (v. 3a) and finally to "all the families of the earth" (v. 3b).

2   In the promise "I will bless you" everything else is comprehended. The word "bless," "blessing" (Hebrew *bārak̲, berākāh*) actually refers to the power of fertility.[1] God's blessing does not come in
isolated acts but in a constant process. The blessing is essentially
outside history; this point is made with special force by chapter 27.
The formulation "I will bless you," which unites the blessing with a
promise, is a new creation on the part of the Yahwist. Here he links
the blessing with history by linking the Patriarchal History with the
history of the nation. Abraham will become a great nation; the nation
descended from Abraham will have a great name. In both cases, the
Yahwist means the politically organized nation of the Monarchy (the
meaning of Hebrew *goy*): a great and famous nation. This consists
best with the period of David and Solomon, the Early Monarchy, the
period of the Yahwist. A "great name" is an attribute of kings (cf.
2 Sam. 7:9; 8:13; 1 Kgs. 1:47).

The last clause of Genesis 12:2, "be a blessing," echoes the initial
"I will bless you." The virtue of the blessing passes from the one who
is blessed to those around him.

3   This effect on others is developed in the two parts of verse 3.
Depending on how those around Abraham act towards him, they
will be blessed or cursed. Here J has incorporated an earlier traditional saying (cf. Gen. 27:29 and Num. 24:9). This is also a promise of
protection for the one who is blessed. The last clause expands the
effective radius of the blessing even further: it will include "all the
families of the earth."

It has long been a matter of debate whether the correct translation here is "bless themselves" (reflexive), "receive a blessing" (receptive), or "be blessed" (passive). The reflexive translation is lin-
guistically more likely (cf. Ps. 72:17) and also more concrete; it is
therefore preferred. This translation, "in you [they] are to bless themselves," says no less than the receptive or passive. If the "families of
the earth" wish to be blessed by naming the name of Abraham, this
translation implies, they will indeed receive a blessing. The blessing
of God announced in the promise to Abraham does not achieve its
purpose until it encompasses all the families of the earth.

4a   The statement that concludes the introit still speaks of Abraham only as a single individual. Abraham obeys God's command,
beginning the journey of a nomadic shepherd; this journey gives no
hint of future greatness and fame. That Abraham should obey God's
command is normal and natural; not to have done so would have

---

1. See Johannes Pedersen, *Israel, Its Life and Culture*, I-II (London: Oxford
University, 1926); Claus Westermann, *Blessing in the Bible and the Life of the
Church*, trans. Keith Crim (Philadelphia: Fortress, 1968); Gerhard Wehmeier,
"The Theme 'Blessing for the Nations' in the Promises to the Patriarchs and in
Prophetical Literature," *Bangalore Theological Forum* 6/2 (1974): 1-13.

been fraught with danger. The mention of Lot here—"And Lot went with him"—lays the groundwork for the narrative in Genesis 13:5-13.

4b-5   An interpolation from P gives Abraham's age when he left Haran (at the same time localizing vv. 1-4a) and repeats the account of his departure in the language of P. The itinerary form allows verses 4b-5 to fit smoothly into the context of J; the passage appears more supplementary than repetitious.

6-9   Chapter 12 contains several rhetorical forms typical of the Patriarchal History: narrative (vv. 10-20), promise (vv. 1-3[4a]), and itinerary (vv. 4b-5 [P] and 6-9 [J]). Unlike a narrative, both itinerary and genealogy are factual. The form of an itinerary depends on the group that is traveling; the itineraries of the Patriarchal History therefore differ from those of the period in the desert. The itineraries of the Patriarchal History have a simple form: they list only a few places where the nomads stopped with their flocks, short distances apart, often with a brief statement of what took place at one of them. Genesis 12:6-9 is a good example.

6   Using a summary statement as a transition, the redactor appends what had once been an independent itinerary to what has gone before; the "land" referred to is Canaan, mentioned in verse 5 (P). The land God promised to show to Abraham (v. 1) does not become his; he remains a nomadic shepherd. His route takes him to the "place at Shechem" in the heart of the region, between Ebal and Gerizim. Excavations at Tell Balâṭah, east of Nablus, have brought to light the remains of the city. It was settled as early as the fourth millennium B.C. and flourished in the seventeenth century, long before the Israelite city. In the course of his travels, Abraham comes to a holy place or sanctuary—the text reads only "the place"; the word "holy" has not yet been used in the Patriarchal History—in the vicinity of Shechem. It was already a holy place when Abraham arrived there; the text does not say that he founded it. His route brings him "to the oracle terebinth," a reference to a tree used to obtain oracles. Such trees are found among many peoples and in many religions. They are representative of the early type of sanctuary, not made by human hands, such as are typical of the patriarchal way of life. Tree sanctuaries later came under a cloud in Israel because they were associated with Canaanite religion; this change can even be seen in the textual history of our passage.

Verse 6 ends with the statement: "At that time the Canaanites were in the land." These words are a valuable witness to the accurate preservation of a tradition associated with the dim past for an audience in the period of the Monarchy. They come from the pen of a narrator who wants to suggest how remote the time of the patriarchs is; he is saying: this took place in the distant past, long before the Israelite tribes entered into Canaan.

7   Verse 7 is a small independent unit belonging to the complex that records the history of the promise of the land. Verse 8 clearly follows verse 6; since verse 7 is a separate unit, it would be wrong to connect it with verse 6 or verses 6-8 and call the resulting unit a cult legend. The tripartite text of verse 7 is focused on its center, the promise of the land. This promise is introduced in verse 7a and ratified in 7c. The framework turns it into an episode (cf. 13:14-17). The introductory phrase "And Yahweh appeared to . . ." is late and formulaic in all the passages where it is found (18:1; 26:2, 24; 35:9). In the concluding sentence, Abraham ratifies the promise made to him. This promise will not be fulfilled until long after Abraham's death, when Israel becomes a nation. It links the Patriarchal History with the history of the nation.[2]

8-9   Verses 8-9 continue the itinerary. The departure (the verb "continue on" also appears in an itinerary in 26:22) and direction of travel are given. Then Abraham encamps. Departure and halt determine the rhythm of nomadic life. The migratory group encamps in open country between two towns, "Bethel to the west and Ai to the east." The stop would naturally include a religious ceremony. A sign is erected, a simple altar made of earth or heaped-up stones (Exod. 20:24), a temporary structure. At the same time, Abraham "called on the name of Yahweh"—a term for worship (cf. Gen. 4:26; the combination also appears in 13:4 and 26:25). Even in this simplest of forms, worship includes both word and action. In this early form, the patriarchs themselves are responsible for the worship; there are as yet no priests.

Verse 9 continues the itinerary. The Negeb ("southland"), toward which Abraham is journeying, is "the territory where Abraham really lived out his life" (Martin Noth). It extends from the hill country of Judah to the wilderness of Sin.

12:10-20   THE ANCESTRAL MOTHER IN DANGER

10   *A famine struck the land.*
So Abram went down to Egypt
to live there as an alien,
because the famine was severe in the land.

2. For a full discussion of the promise of the land, see Westermann, *Die Verheissungen an die Väter* (Göttingen: Vandenhoeck & Ruprecht, 1976), pp. 123-138.

11   *When he was approaching the Egyptian border,*
     he said to Sarai his wife:
     Behold, I know that you are a beautiful woman.
12   *When the Egyptians see you,*
     they will say: That is his wife!
     Then they will kill me, but let you live.
13   *Please say that you are my sister,*
     so that it may go well with me on your account,
     and my life may be spared because of you.
14   *And when Abram arrived in Egypt,*
     the Egyptians saw that the woman was very beautiful.
15   *The Pharaoh's courtiers saw her*
     and praised her to Pharaoh,
     and the woman was taken into Pharaoh's palace.
16   *But with Abram, all went well because of her.*
     He acquired sheep and cattle and asses,
     male and female servants, she-asses and camels.
17   *Then Yahweh struck Pharaoh [and his house] with severe plagues*
     because of Abram's wife, Sarai.
18   *But Pharaoh summoned Abram and said:*
     What have you done to me! Why did you not tell me
     that she is your wife?
19   *Why did you say: she is my sister,*
     so that I took her as a wife?
     Here is your wife, then! Take her and go!
20   *And Pharaoh ordered an escort for him*
     and sent him and his wife away
     with all they had.

This narrative appears in three variants: chapters 12, 20, and 26. Their interrelationship has been the subject of much debate; it can now be considered certain that, of the three, Genesis 12:10-20 is the earliest. The narrative is determined by the introductory statement: "A famine struck the land" (v. 10a); it sets up the journey to Egypt (v. 10b) and the return (v. 20), which frame the story. The chain of events is triggered (vv. 11-13) and concluded (vv. 18-19) by dialogues. The events themselves are recounted with extreme succinctness: Abraham's expectations are fulfilled (vv. 14-16) and Yahweh intervenes against Pharaoh (v. 17). In the overall design, the emphasis is on the dialogues.

   The origin of this narrative as an oral tale is shown by the existence of three variants. It derives from the experience of small groups of nomadic shepherds, for whom such an escape from starvation was often the only chance, however perilous. It belongs to the larger group of narratives dealing with deliverance from famine. The narrative here combines the two groups of motifs that dominate Genesis

12–25: the danger of famine, and preservation of the family when the mother is in danger.

10   The Old Testament often speaks of famine: it is a primary theme of the Joseph story (Gen. 41; 43:1; 47:4); the book of Ruth begins in 1:1 with a famine; famines are also mentioned in 2 Samuel 21:1; 2 Kings 4:38; 8:1, in communal laments during drought, and in the prophets' announcements of judgment. Famine is one of the fundamental experiences of human misery, extending from the earliest traces of human history to the present day. Throughout the world, narratives and tales speak of it as a matter of life and death. Egyptian inscriptions and illustrations show that others, too, sought relief from starvation in Egypt.

11-13   The first episode is Abraham's dialogue with Sarah at the border. After the introduction in verse 11a, Abraham points out to his wife the danger facing them in Egypt (vv. 11b-12) and suggests how she can save their lives (v. 13). Sarah's silence is sufficient answer. They approach the Egyptian border. Abraham, who has left in order to escape death from starvation, is once more staring death in the face. In view of this danger, he comes to a decision. He is entering the domain of a superior power, where he has no rights and no protection. Joseph's brothers felt exactly the same way on their way to Egypt. An insignificant man at the mercy of the powerful has only his wits for a weapon; this is true throughout the ancient world. The ruse Abraham intends to employ is based on experience with the mighty: by virtue of their power or wealth they can get any beautiful woman they desire. This theme appears three times in the Old Testament, in different contexts: in the Primal History (6:1-4), where the sons of the gods take the daughters of mortals; in chapters 12, 20 and 26 of the Patriarchal History; and in the story of David and Bathsheba (2 Samuel 11–12) in the Court History. This experience must have made a deep impression. Because Abraham is familiar with it, he must assume that his wife's beauty will bring him into deadly danger. He can escape this danger if he pretends that Sarah is his sister and she agrees. Abraham knows that he will incur a heavy burden of guilt by sacrificing his wife, but he can see no other possibility. He does not think of divine intervention—here he is not a man of faith.

14-16   The next episode takes place at the Egyptian court. Abraham's fears are realized, but the trick succeeds. Sarah's beauty attracts attention among the Egyptians (v. 14b), among the courtiers (v. 15a), and in the eyes of Pharaoh (v. 15b); Abraham's wife is taken into Pharaoh's palace (v. 15b). His wife's beauty had brought him into mortal danger; now the beauty of his supposed sister brings him favor and reward; the gifts are to compensate the brother for the loss of his sister. The ruse has succeeded, but the family is destroyed.

17-19   The third episode (vv. 17-19) begins with Abraham alive but at his wits end. Now Yahweh intervenes. He afflicts Pharaoh cruelly, even though the latter had acted in good faith and had indemnified Abraham. But in the ancient, originally magical conception of how an evil deed incurs disaster, Pharaoh has violated Abraham's marriage, albeit unwittingly. In contrast, the later conception envisions a God who intervenes personally on behalf of this protege, restoring his wife to him. From this perspective, Yahweh's treatment of Pharaoh must appear unjust. But the narrator is able to reconcile the contradiction convincingly by means of Pharaoh's words to Abraham in verses 18-19. Here Pharaoh does not address Abraham from a position of exalted power but humanly, on Abraham's own level; and Abraham is put to shame. The result is totally different from what he had expected. With all the power at his disposal, Pharaoh does nothing more than summon Abraham and speak to him. Pharaoh's accusation carries weight for the narrative as a whole. In it, the narrator shows clearly that he disapproves of Abraham's conduct toward Pharaoh and believes that Pharaoh has a clear conscience. Pharaoh's charge is justified, and it puts Abraham to shame; he can only listen in silence. Pharaoh does not speak as a king; his are the words of a man who has been deceived: "What have you done to me!" (cf. Gen. 20:9; 29:25; Num. 23:11; Luke 2:48). This is the climax of the narrative. Abraham had not considered that even Pharaoh is only human, thereby forgetting God, who can strike both Abraham and Pharaoh. Thus Abraham is put to shame and can only keep silent. He is summarily dismissed.

20   Pharaoh has Abraham escorted to the border. Abraham escapes with his wife and possessions, but humiliated. Faced with mortal danger from two sides, he could see no other course than to sacrifice his wife. He was right in estimating that this sacrifice could save both their lives temporarily.

What should be the response of persons facing mortal danger who are convinced they can save their lives only by sacrificing something that they could not possibly sacrifice apart from this danger? This question is still asked today; it will always be asked. The narrative says that possibilities are open to God that are not visible to the human eye. Thus the narrator suggests that, in such a perilous situation, a person can choose not to sacrifice something in order to buy life, not to submit to violence. But human beings usually do submit to violence. So does Abraham. To conquer fear of death through confidence that God knows a way out has always been the extraordinary course, and will continue to be so. God nevertheless condescends to the man who has submitted to violence and helps him out of the impasse to which his trickery has brought him. God punishes him, but the punishment is his shame.

13:1-18   ABRAHAM AND LOT ON THE WAY

1 *And Abram went up from Egypt, he and his wife*
and all that he had, and Lot with him, to the Negeb.
2 *And Abram was very rich in cattle and silver and gold.*
3 *He journeyed by stages,*
from the Negeb as far as Bethel, to the place
where he had pitched his tent at the beginning,
between Bethel and Ai,
4 *the place where he had previously built the altar,*
and Abram there invoked the name of Yahweh.
5 *And Lot, who had journeyed with Abram,*
also had sheep, cattle, and tents.
6a   *And the land could not support their living together,*
for their possessions were great,
6b *and they could not live side by side.*
7 *Thus there arose a quarrel between the shepherds*
over Abram's cattle and the shepherds over Lot's cattle.
At that time the Canaanites and Perizzites were living in the land.
8 *And Abram said to Lot:*
Let there be no quarrel between me and you,
between my shepherds and your shepherds,
for we are brothers.
9 *Is not the whole country open to you? Part company with me!*
If you go left, I will go right;
if you go right, I will go left.

10 *And Lot raised his eyes and saw*
that the whole plain of Jordan was well watered—
this was before Yahweh destroyed Sodom and Gomorrah—
like a garden of God, like the land of Egypt, as far as Zoar.
11a *So Lot chose the whole of the Jordan plain*
and Lot went eastward
12b *and pitched his tent as far as Sodom.*
11b   *So they parted company;*
12a   *Abram settled in the land of Canaan,*
Lot settled in the cities of the plain.

13 *But the people of Sodom were wicked and sinned greatly against Yahweh.*

14 *And Yahweh said to Abram, after Lot had parted company from him:*
Lift up your eyes and look, from the place
where you are standing, to the north and to the south,
to the east and to the west.

15 *The whole land that you see I will give to you*
    and your descendants for ever.
16 *And your seed I will make like the dust of the earth;*
    only if one can count the dust of the earth
    can he count your seed.
17 *Up, walk through the length and breadth of the land,*
    for I am giving it to you.
18 *And Abram set out with his tents and went*
    and settled by the terebinth of Mamre,
    and he built there an altar to Yahweh.

Chapter 13 comprises an itinerary (vv. 1-4[5]), the narrative of how
Abraham and Lot went separate ways (vv. 5-13, 18), and the interpolated promise to Abraham (vv. 14-17).

1-5 The itinerary. Every clause in verses 1-5 has its function as
part of an itinerary: Abraham's journey (vv. 1a, 3a) and the state of
who went with him (1b, 5a), the destination (3b, 4a), the invocation of
Yahweh at the stopping place (4b). The information about the wealth
of Abraham (v. 2) and Lot (v. 5) is a secondary expansion; it constitutes the beginning of the narrative in verses 5-13. Verse 1 is not the
conclusion to the narrative in 12:10-20; the itinerary in verses 1-5 is an
independent form. Both narratives (12:10-20 and 13:5-13) grow out of
and lead into itineraries.

1-2 Abraham goes up from Egypt into the southland (Negeb)
with his wife and possessions; Lot goes with him.

3-4 These verses continue the itinerary: "He journeyed from
. . . to . . . ," an awkward sentence with several additions; it is
characteristic of the itinerary style to consist of short statements.
Typical are the two clauses that refer to an earlier stopping place,
verses 3b-4a. Such references serve to define the stages of the journey and thus preserve it in peoples' memories.

5-13, 18 With verse 5, the itinerary passes into narrative. The
latter consists of three sections: a quarrel (vv. [5], 7a), Abraham's
proposal for conciliation (vv. 8-9), Lot's acceptance of the proposal
(vv. 10-11a). Then Lot (v. 11b) and Abraham (v. 18) go their separate
ways. With verse 18, the narrative passes once more into itinerary.
The narrative concerns a territorial conflict (cf. the narratives about
conflict over wells in chs. 21 and 26). It is noteworthy that the central
point is not mentioned: the resolution of the quarrel. We are only told
its cause and its conclusion. An earlier form of the narrative in oral
tradition must have recounted also its occasion and development.
Later these specific details faded out of sight. The well narratives are
similar.

5-7 The list of Lot's possessions singles out "tents." A "tent" is the nomadic dwelling unit, including its inhabitants; the reference is to the families of the shepherds mentioned in verse 7. Both groups include several families traveling together as shepherds, some twenty to thirty people. The increase in possessions of both groups leads to a quarrel between their shepherds (v. 7). Verse 6 gives a somewhat different reason for the separation: because their possessions were great, the land could not support both groups together. The word for possessions (Hebrew *rᵉkûš*) is characteristic of P. Since this parallel account is continued in verses 11b and 12a, the narrative of J has been expanded by the insertion in verses 6, 11b, 12a of P's account of the same event, which differs from J's in omitting the quarrel; P exhibits the same tendency in Genesis 36:7.

The meaning of the quarrel in verse 7 and in the other quarrel narratives of the Patriarchal History can be understood only when we realize that the small nomadic groups described here did not wage war; for them, the quarrel plays the role played among larger groups by battle or war. Both quarrels and wars are fought for territory and food—the survival of the group. In 13:7b, a passing comment points out once again (cf. 12:6b) that these events lie in the distant past. The Perizzites are mentioned here together with the Canaanites; they have not been precisely identified.

8-9   Abraham proposes a way of mediating the quarrel, appealing to the fact that they are related.

8   As one member of a family to another, Abraham suggests that Lot may choose what direction to go if they part peacefully. It is not the narrator's purpose to emphasize Abraham's magnanimity; Abraham is responsible for his family and his people, and must watch out for their interests. He reaches a decision with his eye on the welfare of both groups, through which he makes it possible for Lot to leave in peace. In this case, responsibility for a brother can find expression in peaceful parting.

10-11   "And Lot raised his eyes. . . ." The narrator does not say a word about what is going through Lot's mind. Lot's raising his eyes signals his decision; the audience sees what Lot sees and understands him. In Lot's view of the well-watered Jordan plain—like a garden of God!—the narrative reaches it climax. What he sees convinces him to accept the proposal made by Abraham, thus ending the quarrel.

10   Verse 10 includes several additions. The explanatory gloss "this was before Yahweh destroyed Sodom and Gomorrah" was necessary when chapter 13 became separated from chapters 18 and 19. The addition of "like the land of Egypt" actually weakens the comparison to a "garden of God." The phrase "as far as Zoar" is also unnecessary detail. Lot's decision for the Jordan plain ends the quar-

rel; with the statement ". . . and Lot went eastward," (v. 11a) "and pitched his tent as far as Sodom" (v. 12b), the narrative once more turns into itinerary. We would expect to find here a statement about Abraham's departure in the opposite direction; this statement does not come until verse 18, following a variety of interpolations.

11b-12a   P's rather different description, which belongs after verse 6, has been inserted. It is typical of P that the separation of Abraham and Lot leads to their settling, whereas in J they continue their nomadic life.

13   This verse begins a new narrative, triggered by the mention of Sodom in the second part of verse 12b in the itinerary. The groundwork is laid here for the story of Sodom and Gomorrah, into which verse 13 leads, but the narrative itself does not come until chapters 18 and 19.

14-17   This section, like chapter 15, is a promise reshaped as an episode. It can be recognized as an interpolation by its position between the two parts of the conclusion to the quarrel narrative (vv. 12bβ, 18). The transitional verse 14a is followed by the promise of the land (v. 15), framed by two imperatives (vv. 14b, 17a). God's command to Abraham: "Lift up your eyes . . . walk through . . ." is couched in elevated language. Abraham is addressed as the father of the nation; he is called upon to survey the entire expanse of what is to be the land of Israel and take possession of it symbolically. This image will make an indelible impression on later generations: our land was promised to our father Abraham by God; its possession was assured "for ever." The scene is conceived from a point northeast of Bethel, which provides an extensive view from the coastal plain to the Jordan. Walking the length and breadth of the land, as Abraham is commanded to do in verse 17, recalls a legal custom through which a piece of land is symbolically taken into possession. In contrast to 12:4a, however, this order is not carried out. It is later generations (". . . and your descendants") that will actually take possession of this land. This shows that verses 14-17 are a symbolic description of the promise of the land.

The promise of descendants in verse 16 was added because territory and descendants frequently go together. The promise of many descendants, "like the dust of the earth," does not consist well with a narrative in which Abraham and Lot part because their groups can survive only if they remain small.

18   This verse is an itinerary recounting how Abraham sets out and journeys further; it should actually follow verses 11a and 12b, which say much the same about Lot. The two passages together constitute the conclusion of the narrative, in which it once again turns into an itinerary. This is a typical conclusion to a narrative: "At

the beginning the cast of characters is brought together, and at the end they go their separate ways,"[1] as in Genesis 18:33; 33:16-17; 1 Samuel 24:22. Abraham sets out and stops once again at a sanctuary outside a town, here the terebinth of Mamre, two miles north of Hebron. Mamre was a sacred site for many centuries, as excavations have demonstrated.

The narrative in Genesis 13:1-18 describes the resolution of a conflict between Abraham and Lot without resort to violence. The story of the patriarch Abraham, who resolved a quarrel peacefully by giving up his own claims, was preserved until the postexilic period, when, following political collapse, promises of a kingdom of peace ruled by a king of peace began to be heard. The memory of the patriarchs, who had never waged war, was not forgotten.

14:1-24   ABRAHAM AND THE KINGS

1   *It was in the time of Amraphel king of Shinar,*
    when war was waged by Arioch, king of Ellasar,
    Chedorlaomer, king of Elam, and Tidal, king of Goiim,
2   *with Bera, king of Sodom,*
    and Birsha, king of Gomorrah, Shinab, king of Admah,
    and Shemeber, king of Zeboiim,
    and the king of Bela, that is, Zoar.
3   *All these joined together and proceeded to the valley of Siddim,*
    that is, the Salt Sea.
4   *For twelve years they had been subject to Chedorlaomer,*
    but in the thirteenth they revolted.
5   *In the fourteenth year came Chedorlaomer and the kings*
    in union with him,
    and defeated the Rephaim in Ashteroth-karnaim,
    the Zuzim in Ham, and the Emim
    in Shaveh-kiriathaim,
6   *and the Horites in the hill country of Seir as far as El-paran on the edge of the*
    desert.
7   *Then they turned and came back to En-mishpat,*
    that is, Kadesh, and they conquered the whole territory
    of the Amalekites as well as that of the Amorites who live in Hazazon-tamar.
8   *Then the king of Sodom marched out and the king of Gomorrah*
    and the king of Amah and the king of Zeboiim
    and the king of Bela, that is, Zoar, and they drew up
    in battle over against them in the Valley of Siddim.

1. Isaac L. Seeligmann, "Hebräische Erzählung und biblische Geschichtsschreibung," *Theologische Zeitschrift* 18 (1962): 308.

9   *Chedorlaomer, king of Elam, Tidal, king of Goiim,*
       Amraphel, king of Shinar, and Arioch, king of Ellasar,
       four kings against five.

10   *And the Valley of Siddim was full of bitumen pits,*
       and the kings of Sodom and Gomorrah fled
       and fell into them, and the rest escaped to the mountains.

11   *Then they took all the possession of Sodom and Gomorrah*
       and all the provisions and went away.

12   *They also took Lot and his possessions (Abraham's nephew)*
       and went away (he was living in Sodom then).

13   *But a fugitive came and told [it] to Abram, the Hebrew,*
       who was dwelling by the terebinth of Mamre, the Amorite,
       the brother of Eshcol and Aner, who were confederates of Abram.

14   *When Abram heard that his brother had been taken prisoner,*
       he mustered his retainers, men born in his household,
       318 men, and pursued as far as Dan.

15   *Then he attacked them by night, he and his servants,*
       and defeated them and pursued them as far as Hobah,
       which is north of Damascus.

16   *And he brought back all the possessions as well as Lot,*
       his brother, and his possessions,
       together with the women and the captives.

17   *Then the king of Sodom when out to meet him,*
       when he came back from the defeat of Chedorlaomer and the kings in union with him,
       in the Valley of Shaveh, that is, the Valley of the Kings.

18   *And Melchizedek, king of Salem,*
          brought out bread and wine; and he was priest
          of El-Elyon.

19   *And he blessed him and said:*
          "Blessed be Abram by El-Elyon,
          the creator of heaven and earth.

20   *And blessed be El-Elyon,*
          who delivered your enemy into your hand."
          And he gave him a tithe of all the booty.

21   *And the king of Sodom said to Abram:*
       "Give me the people, you take the property."

22   *And Abram said to the king of Sodom:*
       "I raise my hand to Yahweh,
       El-Elyon, the creator of heaven and earth;

23   *not a thread, not a shoestring, nothing at all*
       of what is yours will I take, lest
       you should be able to say, I made Abram rich.

24   *Except for what the people have eaten*
       and the share of the men who went out with me;
       Aner, Eshcol, and Mamre shall have their share."

Genesis 14 is a composite of three parts: (A) a report of a military campaign (vv. 1-11[12]); (B) a deliverance narrative (vv. 12-17, 21-24); and (C) the Melchizedek episode (vv. 18-20). Part A describes an event of world history; parts B and C are limited to the small territory of Canaan. Only in them are Abraham and Lot mentioned. Part C (vv. 18-20) is an originally independent unit that has been interpolated into part B (vv. 12-24). Part A (vv. 1-11) is a campaign report into which several lists have been incorporated. It deals with the campaign of a world power against rebellious vassals. There are several Babylonian and Assyrian parallels, especially in royal inscriptions. Part B (vv. 12-24) is a narrative similar to deliverance narratives from the period of the judges (cf. 1 Sam. 30).[1] Its association with Abraham dates from a late period, when the patriarchs came to be pictured as heroes and savior figures. Part C (Gen. 14:18-20) is an episode interpolated into the narrative of part B, a cultic etiology. The incident involving Abraham and Melchizedek is intended to legitimate a later liturgical institution by associating it with an event in the patriarchal period.

In its present form, the composition as a whole is determined by the large-scale setting established in verses 1-11. Its purpose is to depict Abraham as a great and mighty prince, victorious over the mighty kings of the East. The desire to represent Abraham in this light is understandable from the perspective of the late postexilic period, in the context of other efforts to give the early patriarchs a significant role on the stage of world politics (cf. the books of Daniel and Judith). Only in this late period is the bizarre collocation of such diverse elements conceivable. Against the background of this late period, it is also possible to understand the pedantic incorporation of the lists in verses 1-11 as a kind of midrash.

1-11   The war of the kings (A). Verses 1-11 constitute a short, self-contained report: In the time of . . . war was waged by . . . (vv. 1-2); they went forth . . . (v. 3) because . . . (v. 4); they went forth and conquered . . . (vv. 5-7); their enemies went forth in battle order . . . (vv. 8-9; "they conquered" is missing); their opponents fled (v. 10); the victors withdrew (v. 11). This report has been fleshed out in verses 12 and 8-9 by lists of the hostile kings (with some discrepancies), and in verses 5b-7 by a list of conquered nations, which has been harmonized with the campaign account. The awkward inclusion of these lists has made the campaign account obscure. In verses

1. See R. Ficker, "*mal'āk* Bote," cols. 900-908 in *Theologisches Handwörterbuch zum Alten Testament,* ed. Ernst Jenni and Claus Westermann, I (Munich: Christian Kaiser, 1976).

4, 5, and 9, Chedorlaomer is the leader, whereas in verse 1 he stands third. The repeated list in verses 8-9 is unnecessary. "All these" in verse 3 does not refer to the kings listed in verse 2 but to the kings of the East in verse 1; not until verse 8 is the attack of the vassal kings mentioned.

The account of the campaign in verses 4-5a is clear. The sequence vassalage—rebellion—punitive campaign is well attested (cf. 2 Kgs. 18:7; 24:1, 20). The listing of numbers is consistent with the style of royal inscriptions. The interlude in Genesis 14:5b-7 consists almost entirely of a list of conquered nations, probably from a different source; this detour on the route to the places named in verse 2 makes little sense. The secondary nature of the composition is also clear from the observation that the first three nations—Rephaim, Zuzim, and Emim—are legendary, whereas the others—Horites, Amalekites, and Amorites—are familiar historical nations. Only the single clause in verse 7a lends this interlude the character of a military campaign; it appears abruptly in the middle of the list.

Verses 8-11 continue the report of the campaign. Verse 8 follows verse 5a. The battle itself is not reported, only the flight of the Canaanite kings and the withdrawal of the kings of the East. The note in verse 10 about the place where the battle took place is geographically accurate. The discrepancy between the campaign account and its associated lists is illustrated by the fact that only two hostile kings are named, not five, as in verses 2 and 8. At the end we would expect a statement that the vassalage was reestablished, but nothing of the kind is reported.

A few remarks on the names in verses 1-11 are in order: first the four great kings, the kings of the East. Amraphel of Shinar (vv. 1, 9) was formerly identified with Hammurabi; this is impossible, however, primarily for philological reasons. The name remains unidentified. "Shinar" refers to the Babylonia. The name "Arioch," also found in Daniel 2:14, 15, 24, 25, has not been identified with certainty, nor has the land of Ellasar (Larsa?). Concerning Chedorlaomer of Elam, the kingdom of Elam, east of Babylon, is mentioned elsewhere in the Old Testament (Gen. 10:22). Both parts of his name appear in Elamite personal names (*kūdūr*, "protector"; *lagamar* is a divine name). The name "Tidal" is found five times as the name of a Hittite king. The toponym "Goiim" is puzzling and has not been explained. Of the kings of the East, only Tidal, a king of the Hittites, has been identified; of the kingdoms, only Elam and Babylon.

The kings of the five cities in 15:2 and 8 are named only in verse 2, not in verse 8. The names are unexplained; none appears outside this passage. Only here are the five cities mentioned as a group. The first four appear in Deuteronomy 29:23 and Genesis 10:19; Admah and

Zeboiim are mentioned in Hosea 11:8. The toponym "Bela" is found only here. The account of the war mentions only Sodom and Gomorrah. These ruined cities were probably located at the southern end of the Dead Sea. The Valley of Siddim (Gen. 14:3) appears only here.

12-24 Abraham the deliverer. Verses 13-16 describe Abraham's rescue of Lot; verses 17, 21-24, his encounter with the king of Sodom. Verse 12 is transitional, verses 18-20 a secondary episode.

12 This verse shifts somewhat awkwardly from the account of the campaign to another realm, that of family history. The verse constitutes a seam between two originally independent units. Here the small nomadic groups are in the process of settling amongst the Canaanite city-states. Family ties are still strong: Abraham comes to the aid of a relative.

13-14 Here, as often in the ancient world, a fugitive from battle serves as messenger (cf. 2 Sam. 15:13). Only now is Abraham introduced by name and place of residence; he is anachronistically called a "Hebrew." Three associates are also named; they appear again in verse 24 at the end of the narrative. Their names have not been identified. The rescue begins in verse 14 and ends with verse 16. The purpose is the rescue of Abraham's brother—"brother" in an extended sense, which also includes nephews. His men were born in his household and are therefore called trustworthy slaves, "retainers," literally "dedicated men"; they number 318. Of this number, Walther Zimmerli says in his commentary: "Abraham therefore must have had a household of at least a thousand men." This might be possible for one of the charismatic leaders of the period of the judges, but not for the nomadic shepherd Abraham of the early narratives. An enterprise like that described here is certainly conceivable with some 300 men; it resembles the one described in Judges 7:16-22.

15 The rescuer and his men separated into groups and attacked the enemy—literally, "he divided himself upon them by night." The narrative climaxes in Abraham's victory over vastly superior forces; the pursuit, in which he captures the booty, is part of this climax. Then the victor returns (v. 16) with his rescued nephew and the booty.

17, 21-24 Now the narrator must record what was done with the booty. This question was important during the period of the judges in Israel: can the deliverer use the fruits of his victory to build up his own strength? This narrative passionately rejects the possibility. The king of Sodom, representing the kings of the Canaanite city-states, emerges from his gate and approaches Abraham; nothing is said here of a coalition of five kings. Verse 17b is a secondary bridge linking verses 12-24 with 1-11. The king of Sodom (v. 21 follows v. 17 directly) presumes that, as victor, Abraham is entitled to the booty.

Abraham, however, asserts under oath his refusal to exercise this right. The added phrase "El-Elyon, the creator of heaven and earth" links the episode in verses 18-20 with this narrative. The oath says: "I will take nothing that belongs to you." A further reason is also stated: the king of Sodom could otherwise boast that he had made Abraham rich; this would impugn the honor of the deliverer (v. 23). For the charismatic leader, personal wealth and power are unimportant; the deliverers of Israel do not need private resources. But Abraham must look after his troops (v. 24); he claims only what they need.

All the details of this narrative in verses 12-24 represent Abraham as one of Israel's deliverers; it belongs to the period of the judges, and was later associated with Abraham. In the period of the judges, stories were told about Abraham that pictured him as one of Israel's deliverers.

18-20 Abraham and Melchizedek. These verses constitute an independent, self-contained episode. The language is explicitly cultic; it reflects the cult of a settled people, including priests and institutions not associated with the worship of the patriarchs.

Like the king of Sodom in verse 17, the king of Salem comes out of his city (v. 18) to meet Abraham. The name "Melchizedek" means "my god is salvation." "Adoni-zedek" (Josh. 10:1), the name of another Canaanite king of Jerusalem, is formed in exactly the same way. "Salem" probably means Jerusalem; Psalm 76:2 uses it in parallel with "Zion." Melchizedek is called "priest of El-Elyon." "El" is a very ancient and widespread Semitic term for god. "Elyon" (found frequently) may be the name of a god or a divine predicate, meaning "most high." It appears frequently as such a predicate, especially in the late period; Psalm 78:35 speaks of "El-Elyon." Here in Genesis 14:18 it refers to the god of a Canaanite shrine; but this god is spoken of in such a way that Abraham, too, can acknowledge him. Later, this divine predicate is especially common in the Jerusalem cult (Ps. 46:4; 48:1; 78:54). Melchizedek is called both king and priest, as is appropriate for a sacral king. The king of Sodom, too, is both; but only his role as king is emphasized, and only Melchizedek's role as priest. As Abraham returns from his campaign of deliverance, Melchizedek brings him bread and wine. Here sacred and secular are still one. He brings the exhausted warrior food and drink, thus receiving him into the protection of his citadel; but his hands are the hands of a priest, bringing bread and wine and with them the blessing of his god.

19-20 The blessing is formal and solemn; its structure is dominated by the use of Hebrew bārûk, "blessed," at the beginning of both stichs. In verse 19b "Blessed be Abram" reflects the movement of blessing from God to a human person; in verse 20a the same word expresses the praise that a human person offers to God. The verb, whose basic meaning is "endow with power," can mean both. In blessing and praise, Melchizedek's words combine the psalmody of worship with the blessing of a priest; both, however, point to a later form of worship. The cultic blessing dispensed at a sanctuary by a priest is still foreign to the patriarchal period. The divine predicate "creator of heaven and earth" is also a fixed cultic formula; it appears also in Ugaritic texts. It, too, is foreign to the religion of the patriarchs. It could not have been adopted in Israel before the period of the Monarchy, and is probably associated with the Jerusalem cult. The blessing is followed by praise: "And blessed by El-Elyon, who. . . ." The God who brought deliverance from the enemy is praised. In Exodus 18:10, the priest Jethro, Moses' father-in-law, similarly gives voice to his joy over the deliverance of Israel.

Abraham accepts the blessing and gifts at the hands of the priest-king Melchizedek, thus acknowledging him as priest and also recognizing his sanctuary. He expresses his recognition by offering a tithe. Here we see a slight inconsistency with respect to the meaning and purpose of this episode. A tithe is by its very nature a regular offering of regular yield; it is never tribute from booty taken in battle. In fact the episode reflects the offering of tithes to the Jerusalem priesthood in the period of the Monarchy. This offering is traced back to and legitimated by an event in the distant past: the blessing of Abraham by the priest of this very sanctuary and Abraham's offering of a tithe in recognition of this blessing. The narrative also honors the blessing that proceeds from the sanctuary by suggesting that it continues into the present the blessing given Abraham.

CONCLUDING REMARKS ON CHAPTER 14

In this chapter, a late addition to the early Abraham narratives, we obtain a vital insight into how the figure of Abraham survived through the centuries following the patriarchal period. It consists of three sections, each of different origin, which reflect three stages in the development of the figure of Abraham. In verses 12-17, 21-24, a narrative from the period of the judges, a battle for deliverance like those in the book of Judges is associated with Abraham. The memory of the patriarch was preserved by assimilating him to the deliverer figures of this period. This does not mean that Abraham was seen only as such a figure; the process of assimilation itself presupposes that the early narratives of Abraham lived on. Into this narrative has been inserted an episode that makes sense only in the context of the Early Monarchy, verses 18-20. This episode of Abraham and Melchizedek is intended to lay a foundation in the ancient traditions of the patriarchal period for the new form of worship, especially at the

Jerusalem temple. The narrator does not hesitate to have Abraham receive a blessing from the priest-king of a Canaanite sanctuary and offer him a tithe. All that matters to the narrator is to establish a patriarchal basis for the present form of worship. It echoes a universalistic element of patriarchal religion; in this sense, the typological interpretation of the figure of Melchizedek in the New Testament (Heb. 7) is still significant. The universal nature of Christ's work of salvation reflects the universal scope of the blessing of God Most High, which Abraham receives from Melchizedek. In the late postexilic period, when Judah was only a small province in a great and powerful empire, the author placed the campaign report in Genesis 14:1-11 at the beginning of the chapter in order to give the patriarch Abraham a role on the stage of world history, making him victor over four kings of great empires. In lending Abraham historic greatness, he was also including the nation whose father Abraham was. He was trying to bring to life for his people a glorious past that would open broader horizons for a humiliating present. But the figure of Abraham here has hardly anything in common with the Abraham of the ancient narratives.

15:1-21 THE PROMISE TO ABRAHAM

1   *After these events, a word of Yahweh came to Abram in a vision:*
        Do not be afraid, Abram.
        I am your shield; your reward will be very great.
2   *And Abram said:*
        Lord Yahweh, what will you give me?
        I must pass on childless.
        And the son of Meshek (that is, Damascus), Eliezer,
        the son of my house will be my heir.
3   *And Abram said:*
        Behold, you have given me no children,
        and behold, a son of my house will be my heir.
4   *And then a word of Yahweh came to him:*
        No, he shall not be your heir,
        but the one who comes from your own body,
        he will be your heir.
5   *And he took him out in the open and said:*
        Look up at the heavens and count the stars,
        if you can count them.
    And he said to him:
        So will your seed be.
6   *And he believed Yahweh, and he accounted it to him as righteousness.*

7   *And he said to him:*
     I am Yahweh, who led you out
     from Ur of the Chaldees, to give you this land
     to take possession of it.
8   *And he said:*
     Lord Yahweh, how am I to know
     that I shall possess it?
9   *And he commanded him:*
     Bring me a three-year-old heifer, a three-year-old she-goat,
     and a three-year-old ram, a turtledove,
     and a young dove.
10   *And he brought him all of these.*
     And he cut them down the middle and put each part opposite its counterpart,
     but he did not cut the birds.
11   *Then vultures swooped down upon the carcasses,*
     but Abram scared them away.
12   *And as the sun was going down, a deep sleep fell upon Abram,*
     and behold, a great terror came upon him.
13   *And he said to Abram: You must know*
         that your descendants will be aliens
         in a land that is not theirs,
         and they will be slaves there, and they will be oppressed for four hun-
         dred years.
14   *However, I will pass judgment on the nation that they serve.*
         After that they will go out with great possessions.
15   *But you will go to your fathers in peace,*
         and be buried in ripe old age.
16   *Only the fourth generation will return here,*
         for the wickedness of the Amorites has not yet reached full measure.
17   *But when the sun had gone down*
     and it had become quite dark, behold:
     a smoking fire pot and a flaming torch,
     they passed between the carcasses.
18   *On that day Yahweh gave Abram the solemn assurance:*
         To your descendants I am giving this land,
         from the river of Egypt to the great river, the Euphrates;
19   *the Kenites, the Kenizzites, and the Kadmonites,*
20   *the Hittites, the Perizzites, and the Rephaim,*
21   *the Amorites, the Canaanites, the Girgashites, and the Jebusites.*

Chapter 15 combines two promise narratives: the promise of the land and the promise of descendants. They have been placed deliberately in the middle of the Abraham cycle. Two independent, self-contained narratives are involved, verses 1-6 and 7-21; both, however, have approximately the same structure. A redactor combined them into a single narrative by means of a minor alteration, changing "And Yahweh said to Abram" to "And he said to him" at the beginning of verse 7, thereby making verses 7-21 the continuation of verses 1-6. In both texts, a promise has been cast in the form of a narrative; the fundamental structural elements are the promises to the patriarchs. Both texts belong to the complex recording the history of the patriarchal promises and reflect a relatively late stage in its development: in verses 1-6, the promise of a son has been combined with the promise of many descendants; and in verses 7-11, the oath indicates a later stage than the simple promise of the land. The narratives probably came into being at a time when possession of the land (vv. 7-21) and survival of the nation (vv. 1-6) were at risk; the ancient promises to the fathers were brought to life in order to remind Israel of God's promise in a time of peril.

1-6 Like the stars of heaven. Abraham responds to God's promise at the beginning of verse 1 with a protest in the form of a lament (vv. 2-3). God counters this protest in verses 4-5; now Abraham believes God, and his faith is recognized (v. 6).

1 The expression "after these events" is intended to link what is about to be told with what has gone before after some time has elapsed (cf. Gen. 22:1, 20). It presupposes the existence of a coherent story of Abraham. It is noteworthy that what follows is couched in prophetic language: "A word of Yahweh came to. . . ." This formula appears often in later narratives of the period of the Monarchy (for example, 1 Kgs. 12:22), in which the institution of prophecy is presupposed. Here the expression is formulaic. The fact that it appears in the Pentateuch only in Genesis 15:1-6 (twice) suggests a date in the late period of the Monarchy. The word of God that comes to Abraham has the form of an oracle of salvation, consisting of the reassurance formula "Do not be afraid" and its motivation. This form is especially common in Deutero-Isaiah (for example, Isa. 41:10, 14; 43:1, 5). It is reminiscent of royal oracles such as appear often in Babylonian texts.

2-3 Abraham's response in verses 2-3 has two parts; both are the lament of a childless man. The author's purpose was to preserve two traditional versions of the lament of childless Abraham. Both can go back to an ancient narrative tradition. The lament in verse 2 is introduced as a prayer: "O Lord Yahweh. . . ." The following words of the lament, "What will you give me? I must pass on childless," refer to the promise in verse 1. Abraham demurs, asking, "What good will your promise do me?" (cf. Judg. 15:18). He adds: ". . . if a stranger is my heir." Abraham's response in Genesis 15:2 introduces all three elements of a lament: God, the speaker, the others. The words are probably based on an ancient lament like those found in narratives of the early period, the lament of the childless. Similar laments are found in Ugaritic epics. Verse 3 is likewise a lament, in its context also a protest responding to verse 1. Verse 3a is a complaint addressed to God, verse 3b the conclusion that follows from it, corresponding to the second part of verse 2b. The laments in verses 2 and 3 are identical in substance and can go back to the patriarchal period; a social group that exists only in the form of a family has a future only when the chain of parents and children remains unbroken. A life without children cannot be a whole and blessed life. The use of "inheritance," however, to represent the succession of fathers and children comes from a later period after permanent settlement, when property took on vital importance.

4-5   God responds to Abraham's lament by promising a son of his own body, reinforcing this promise with a sign; in fact, however, the sign, the countless stars, is an extension of the promise of a son to include the promise of many descendants; it presupposes the combination of the two. It is precisely the promise of many descendants, cast in this lovely form, that is meant to speak to the Israelites in their days of peril. It is a revitalization of the promise of increase, which has set its indelible stamp on the endangered nation. Thus the ancient promise to Abraham lives on in a changed situation. There is a clear echo of Deutero-Isaiah's message during the Exile (Isa. 40:26): he also calls on his hearers to look up at the stars. In both passages, it is an awareness of the broad arena within which the Creator works that is contrasted to oppressive suffering.

6   The promise is met by Abraham's believing faith, and God recognizes this faith. This is stated in a sophisticated theological language typical of the period of the author who framed this scene; it is a late, theologically sophisticated interpretation. It presupposes the understanding of faith shaped by Isaiah. Isaiah made the discovery that even a king, Yahweh's anointed, might not believe a word addressed to him (Isa. 7). Thus the concept of belief or faith took on for him a new and important significance. In the early period, it was natural and expected that a word from God should be believed; in this period, therefore, the word "believe" often appears with a negative. In this late promise narrative, the word "believe" in Genesis 15:6 alludes to the author's generation, when the promises that the nation would endure began to crumble. The language and thought of a later period are even clearer in what follows: "He accounted it to him as righteousness," which presupposes a cultic language: the expression referred originally to a priest's recognition that a sacrifice was acceptable. Its usage was then extended to mean that someone's conduct was acceptable before God (Deut. 24:13). This usage appears first in Deuteronomy. The usage in Psalm 106:31 (a late psalm) parallels Genesis 15:6: "It was accounted to him [Phinehas] as righteousness."

Note: This verse is the most frequently quoted passage from the story of Abraham, because it has ties with the New Testament and is even cited by Paul in Romans 4. On its basis, Abraham is often called "the father of faith." Our statement here that we are dealing with a late theological interpretation, which cannot go back to the patriarchal period, will disappoint many. This note is addressed to them. Many parts of the Bible, and especially the stories of the patriarchs, were not composed like modern books, but came into being through a long, gradual process of development, including both oral and written stages. During this long process, a word or an entire narrative might change. All the texts of the Patriarchal History are known to us only in their final form; there is no "original" text. It is natural and normal that much should change in this long process of development. When we read the stories of the patriarchs as they have come down to us, we are participating in the process of development, the history of the tradition; we can sometimes recognize late passages. One fact must be clearly noted: later generations, long after the time of the patriarchs, attempted to interpret the old stories and the old promises in ways congenial to their own, often very different, thought processes; their interpretations have often been woven into the narratives and promises. What mattered to them was what these stories and promises meant in their own day. In other words, what we consider two different things, text and interpretation, are often inseparably linked in the text. When we read these ancient stories today, we, too, are participating in the history of their interpretation. When we are fully aware of this fact, it enriches our reading; we participate not only in the words but in their echo through later generations, not only in the ancient narratives but also in the process that leads from them through these later generations to us.

7-21 Confirmation of the promise. God promises Abraham to give him "this land to take possession of it" (v. 7). The text ends with the solemn confirmation of this promise in verse 18. As in verses 1-6, Abraham does not accept this promise immediately but asks for a sign to confirm it (v. 8). The granting of this request takes place in a ritual oath (vv. 9-18), which consists of preparations (vv. 9-10) and the actual ceremony (vv. 17-18); verses 12-16 and 19-21 are secondary additions. This structure is based on confirmation of the promise of the land (found in Gen. 24:7; 50:24 and frequently in Deuteronomy, for example, Deut. 7:8, 12, 13; 8:1, 18; etc.), here formulated as an episode.

7 A promise in general terms (v. 7) is followed by Abraham's demurral, as in verses 1-6. The words "I am Yahweh, who . . . ," an expanded "self-presentation formula" (Walther Zimmerli), resemble Exodus 20:2; Deuteronomy 5:6; and especially Leviticus 25:38. A ste-

reotyped formula recalling the exodus from Egypt is here transferred to Abraham's exodus from Ur of the Chaldees. In both cases, the formula is associated with the promise of the land. Genesis 15:7 thus presupposes the Deuteronomic idiom.

8-11 Abraham's request for a confirmatory sign (v. 8) is answered by a command from God (v. 9), with which Abraham complies (v. 10). This lays the groundwork for the ritual oath (vv. 17-18). Here it takes the form of a conditional self-execration: the one who passes between the divided halves of the animals asks to be struck dead if he breaks his oath. God is here made to perform such an oath ceremony. This action presupposes the confirmation by oath of the promise of the land; otherwise it could not be transferred to God. In verses 9-10, the action associated with the oath has been confused with a sacrificial ceremony: all sacrificial animals are named, whereas only a single animal is necessary for the oath ceremony. The thrice-repeated "three-year-old" also reflects sacrificial practice. Probably a tradent was offended by the notion of God's undertaking a ritual oath—by whom could God swear?—and therefore sought to change it into a sacrifice.

11 In a very strange and peculiar intermezzo, Abraham scares the vultures away. Most exegetes interpret the descent of the vultures as an evil omen, which Abraham averts. In this case, verse 11 would be a bridge to the interpolation in verses 12-16.

12-16 Verse 12 introduces the prediction by characterizing it as a mysterious revelation; the words "deep sleep" and "terror" have the same function in Job 4:12-15, where they likewise introduce a word from God that needs to be interpreted. Genesis 15:13-16 is a secondary interpretation of history under the guise of a prediction. Its *ex post facto* origin is shown by the introductory "You must know . . ." (cf. Josh. 23:13). The prediction concerns Israel in Genesis 15:13, 14, 16; only in verse 15 does it concern Abraham. The purpose of this interpolation is to interpret history: God's righteousness and justice are demonstrated by his passing judgment on the oppressors of the Israelites (v. 14a), as well as on the Amorites (as in Deut. 9:4-5) when the measure of their wickedness is full (Gen. 15:16b). The God who works in Israel's history also guides the history of other nations, a universalistic note. Such historical reflection is understandable in a period when the patriarchal promises took on new life and meaning for the present. The long delay between promise and fulfillment created difficulties, which these verses attempt to explain. In the middle comes the promise of a peaceful death for Abraham (v. 15; cf. Gen. 25:8; Job 5:26). This verse is a classic example of a good and peaceful death.

17-18 The ceremony proper (vv. 17-18) follows the preparations

(vv. 9-10). It is a ritual oath, which Abraham is fully conscious to experience (v. 12 goes with vv. 13-16). It takes place in total darkness, for no mortal can see God (Exod. 33:20). Fire and smoke are symbols representing God; they indicate a theophany, as at Sinai (Exod. 19). Jeremiah 34:18-19 also mentions a ritual oath; there it is a solemn mutual obligation undertaken by groups of people.

Verse 18 is interpreted commonly to mean that God made a covenant with Abraham; but the text differs considerably from Genesis 17 (P), which also refers to a covenant. Genesis 15:18 brings to a close the ceremony described in verses 9, 10, and 17, which is the confirmation of an oath. This is also suggested by the stylistic feature of inclusio: the conclusion in verse 18 echoes the beginning in verse 7. Verse 7, however, speaks not of a covenant but of the promise of the land; the Hebrew expression *kāraṯ bᵉrîṯ* here can refer only to the confirmation of this promise. The word *bᵉrîṯ* can also have the extended sense of "solemn obligation." The legal aspect of this commitment includes definition of borders: "from the river of Egypt to the great river, the Euphrates." The rhythmic language reflects the formal conveyance. These borders are meant to define the furthest possible limits of the land of the Israelites; no particular period is intended. The Euphrates is also mentioned as a boundary in Deuteronomy 11:24 and Joshua 1:4.

19-21   An addition describes the territory by listing the peoples inhabiting Canaan. Such lists appear frequently (for example, Exod. 3:8; Deut. 7:1). Usually they name six or seven peoples; here there are thirteen. The fullest list is probably also the latest.

16:1-16   SARAH AND HAGAR

1   *Now Sarai, Abram's wife, had borne him no children.*
    She had an Egyptian maidservant whose name was Hagar.
2   *And Sarai said to Abram:*
    Behold now, Yahweh has denied me children.
    Go then to my maidservant; perhaps I can get a child through her. And Abram listened to what Sarai said.
3   *And Sarai, Abram's wife, took Hagar, the Egyptian,*
            her maidservant, after Abram had lived ten years
            in the land of Canaan,
                and gave her to her husband as wife.
4   *And he went to Hagar, and she became pregnant.*
    But when she became aware that she was pregnant,
    she looked down upon her mistress.

5   *Then Sarai said to Abram: The injustice done to me*
be upon you! It was I who gave my maidservant into your arms.
Now that she is aware she is pregnant,
she looks down upon me!
Let Yahweh judge between me and you.

6   *Then Abram said to Sarai:*
Behold, your maidservant is in your power;
do with her what you think right.
When Sarai treated her harshly, she fled from her.

7   *Then a messenger of Yahweh found her by a spring of water*
in the desert on the way to Shur,

8   *and he said: Hagar, maidservant of Sarai, where have you come from*
and where are you going? And she answered:
I am fleeing from Sarai my mistress.

9   *And the messenger of Yahweh said to her: Return to your mistress*
and submit to her power.

10   *And the messenger of Yahweh said to her:*
Behold, I will richly multiply your seed,
so that it cannot be numbered for multitude.

11   *And the messenger of Yahweh said to her:*
Behold, you are pregnant and will bear a son,
and you will call him Ishmael,
because Yahweh has heard your cry.

12   *He shall be a man like a wild ass,*
his hand against all and the hand of all against him,
and he shall set himself before the face of all his brothers.

13   *And she called the name of the God who had spoken to her:*
You are the God who sees me.
For she said: Truly I have seen God,
after he saw me.

14   *Therefore the spring is called Lahai-roi;*
it lies between Kadesh and Bered.

15   *And Hagar bore Abram a son.*
And Abram named the son whom Hagar bore him Ishmael.

16   *Abraham was eighty-six years old when Hagar bore him Ishmael.*

The first section, verses 1-6, takes Sarah's childlessness as its point of departure; she gives her maidservant to Abraham as a second wife. The maidservant's pregnancy leads to conflict between the two women. In the second section, verses 7-14, Hagar, who has fled to the desert, meets a messenger of God, who promises her a son. This narrative (J) is framed by a genealogical outline (P) in verses 1a (common to J and P), 3, and 15-16. Both sections may have been independent narratives; the failure to resolve the conflict between the women in verses 1-6 makes it possible for them to be presented as a single narrative.

1-16   The narrative of the quarrel between the women goes back in oral tradition to the time of the patriarchs. In this period, a quarrel is a substantial element in the life of the social group. Men quarrel over territory and food (cf. Gen. 13); women quarrel over social position. The starting point of the narrative is Sarah's childlessness; this takes up once more the theme of Genesis 11:30. Childlessness is a great, overwhelming disaster (cf. 15:2, 3). Grasping at an expedient, she gives her maidservant to Abraham as a second wife. The Hebrew word for "maidservant," *šiphāh*, does not mean a slave but a servant of a married woman, to whom alone she is responsible. In many cases, she was a girl parents had given their daughter when she married (24:59, 61).

2   Sarah gives her husband a command, preceded by its motivation and followed by its purpose. This single sentence encompasses an aspect of the marriage between Sarah and Abraham that led to this decision. Nothing is said of the pain and bitterness accompanying it (cf. 1 Sam. 1); these overtones are heard in Sarah's "Behold now, . . .": God has closed Sarah's womb. The joys and sorrows experienced by the patriarchs and their families were determined by God's actions; the steps now taken are also dependent on God. Sarah's command to her husband, "Go then to my maidservant," is not limited to sexual intercourse; she means that he is to spend part of his time with her, that a familiar relationship will develop between them, that Sarah must now share her husband with another woman. She can do this because now there is hope: "Perhaps I can be built up through her." This is an eloquent expression of the notion that a woman's life is whole, "built up," only if she presents her husband with children. Such expedients were common. There are many references to the husband of a childless wife taking her maidservant as a concubine.

3   This verse belongs to P; where J narrates, P lists facts. The narrative turns into genealogy once more. As always in P, there is a chronological reference.

4-6   Now comes a complication. As soon as Hagar notices that she is pregnant, her attitude toward her mistress changes. She looks down on her—the translation "despised" would be too strong—because a woman's status rises when she is pregnant. Natural maternal pride now finds expression, and Sarah is offended. That this happened frequently in the world of the patriarchs is shown by §146 of the Code of Hammurabi, which deals with the problem (cf. also Prov. 30:21-23). The narrator wishes to describe a conflict that occurred repeatedly and was almost unavoidable. When Sarah describes Hagar's conduct toward her as "violence" (Hebrew *ḥāmās*), it is the subjective language of the injured woman. Sarah turns to Abraham as the only tribunal that can effect a change. Within the realm of the family, the father is judge; a quarrel can take the form of a legal action. Sarah's charge (Gen. 16:5) contains an accusation, its grounds, and a demand for justice. Sarah accuses Abraham because he permits injustice to be done her and thereby infringes on their marriage. She accordingly demands a decision between her and Abraham, so that Abraham here becomes both the judge and the accused. The sentence "Let Yahweh judge between me and you" (cf. 31:53) presupposes that Abraham's decision will be an expression of God's judgment. In his decision (16:6), Abraham accedes to Sarah's plea and gives her total freedom in her treatment of Hagar. Sarah takes immediate advantage of this freedom and "treats her harshly." The one who was oppressed is freed to become the oppressor! Conflicts of this sort are only human and are inevitable. Here we are told that they begin within the family itself. Usually a solution is possible only if the parties separate. The last sentence in verse 6 says it: "She fled from her." Hagar refuses to put up with her treatment at the hands of Sarah; her only recourse is to flee. She emancipates herself, frees herself from Sarah's hand (= "power"), fully realizing that she is putting her own life in danger. The event is recounted in the next section.

7-14 After the introduction in verse 7, everything in verses 7-13 is dialogue. The first exchange comes in verse 8: the brief address of the messenger and Hagar's brief response. While fleeing through the desert, Hagar encounters a person; the introduction in verse 7 says unmistakably that we are not dealing with a vision; the salutation in verse 8 makes it clear that the person is not a supernatural being. The salutation is a question; Hagar's answer is possible only if she recognizes the person she has encountered as a human being. God's messenger (Hebrew *malak yhwh*) appears on earth only in the form of a human being, meeting someone as he or she travels or is at work (cf. Judg. 13, etc.).[1]

The encounter takes place at a well "on the way to Shur," near the Egyptian border. The salutation in Genesis 16:8 has special significance for the narrative. It is found only in narratives involving a small circle of characters. In it contact is made and an existing sense of solidarity is preserved; rejection of the salutation means rejection of this solidarity. In the desert, far from human habitation, this meaning is especially evident.

9-12 The words of the messenger. It is striking that verses 9, 10, and 11 all begin with the same introduction: "And the messenger of Yahweh said to her." This mechanical repetition would be impossi-

---

1. See R. Ficker, *"mal'āk* Bote," cols. 900-908 in *Theologisches Handwörterbuch zum Alten Testament*, ed. Ernst Jenni and Claus Westermann, I (Munich: Christian Kaiser, 1976).

ble in an ancient narrative. We may assume that it originally introduced only one speech by the messenger and that the two others are
later additions. The most appropriate to the situation is the promise
of a son (v. 11). It exhibits a stereotyped structure found in a series of
parallels extending all the way to Luke 1:28-32 (cf. also Judg. 13:3-5;
Isa. 7:14-17, and other texts). This fixed sequence for the announcement of a son (pregnancy—birth—naming and reason for the name)
remains astonishingly constant from the time of the patriarchs to the
New Testament. The name "Ishmael" presupposes that an earlier
form of the narrative used the divine name "El." The mother's naming of the child consists with earlier practice. The announcement of
the birth of a son often includes a prediction of his later destiny or
importance: he will be a great man, a deliverer, a king (cf. Judg. 13;
Luke 1). According to Genesis 16:12, his descendants will be a proud
and mighty tribe; the verse really is a clan oracle like 9:25-27, and so
forth. These oracles do not date from the patriarchal period but from
the period when the tribes were coming into being (cf. Gen. 49).

The two speeches of the messenger in Genesis 16:9 and 10 are
secondary additions. Verse 10 is a promise of increase; it is quite
abrupt in this context and was added later. A promise of increase was
often associated with the promise of a son (cf. 15:4, 5). The command
to Hagar in 16:9 to return to Sarah contradicts verse 11, which affirms
Hagar's flight. Verse 9 is a harmonizing insertion by a redactor, who
found it necessary because chapter 21 presupposes the presence of
Hagar and Ishmael with Abraham and Sarah. The messenger's
charge brings Hagar back there.

13-14   The conclusion, in which several lines converge, appears
overloaded. Verses 13 and 14 are distinct etiological conclusions; the
text is difficult. Since the naming of the spring agrees with the naming of the mountain in Genesis 22:14, 16:14 was probably the original
conclusion; the naming of the God in verse 13 would then be a variant. Hagar names the God whom she encountered in the messenger
"God of my seeing," that is, the God who saw me (in my distress)
(v. 13a). This would be a satisfactory conclusion, but verse 13b adds
another explanation, whose text is obscure: "God have I seen, after
he saw me." This is not intended to suggest a vision, but rather
means: "I encountered God after he saw me [in my misery]." A
different reading, based on an emendation proposed by Julius Wellhausen, would be: "God have I seen, and I live after having seen
him!"

Verse 14 adds an explanation of the name of the spring Lahoi-roi
on the basis of this episode ("therefore it is called"). The name itself is
not explained; its meaning can only be hazarded, something like
"Well of the living one who sees me." But this would be only a vague

echo of an already existing name for the well. Its location is unknown.

15-16 The narrative is followed by the genealogy from P (which began it in vv. 1a, 3). P includes two pieces of chronological information: the date of Abraham's marriage with Hagar and the date of Ishmael's birth. In P, unlike J, it is the father who names the child.

Chapter 16 consists of a single narrative made up of two: the rise to its climax is a quarrel narrative, the descent to its resolution describes an encounter with a messenger of God. The narrative unites a conflict arising from the disaster of childlessness with a promise of a son spoken by a messenger of God. The central message about God conveyed by the narrative is contained in the name "Ishmael": "God hears," a name expressing praise and thanksgiving. The form of address "You are the God who sees me" says substantially the same thing. Both echo the same reaction to an encounter with a messenger from God in Luke 1: "For he has seen the lowliness of his maidservant."

Of all the modes of divine revelation in the Old Testament, the revelation of God in a messenger comes closest to the New Testament self-revelation of God in the person of Jesus. The fact that Jesus, in human form, brings a message from God, that he speaks the words of God and performs the acts of God, has an Old Testament parallel in the "messenger of Yahweh." The credal formula "truly God and truly human" can be understood after this analogy from the Old Testament narratives of God's messenger.

17:1-27 THE COVENANT WITH ABRAHAM

1   *When Abram was ninety-nine years old,*
    Yahweh appeared to Abram and said to him:
    I am God Almighty [El Shaddai];
    walk before me and be perfect.
2   *I will set up my covenant between me and you,*
    and I will multiply you exceedingly.
3a *Then Abram fell down on his face.*
3b *And God spoke with him and said:*
4   *Behold, this is my covenant with you:*
    You shall be the father of many nations.
5   *You will no longer be called Abram;*
    Abraham shall be your name,
    for I will make you father of many nations.
6   *I will make you exceedingly fruitful;*
    I will make nations out of you,
    and kings will go forth from you.

7   *I am setting up my covenant between me and you*
and your descendants after you according to their generations
as an eternal covenant,
that I will be your God and the God of your descendants.

8   *And I am giving you and your descendants the land*
where you are now aliens,
the whole land of Canaan as an eternal possession,
and I will be God to them.

9   *And God spoke to Abraham:*
Now you, you are to keep my covenant,
you and your descendants after you according to their generations.

10   *This is my covenant between me and you*
and your descendants after you that you shall keep:
every male among you is to be circumcised.

11   *You shall circumcise the flesh of your foreskin.*
That shall be the sign of the covenant between me and you.

12   *At the age of eight days, every male among you*
shall be circumcised, generation after generation;
also those born in your house and any slave bought with money from
strangers,
who is not of your offspring.

13   *Circumcise those born in your house*
and slaves bought with money.
That shall be my covenant in your flesh, an eternal covenant.

14   *Any uncircumcised man, however,*
males who have not been circumcised in the flesh of their foreskin,
his life shall be cut off from his people.
He has broken my covenant.

15   *And God spoke to Abraham:*
Your wife Sarai you shall no longer call Sarai,
but Sarah shall be her name.

16   *I will bless her,*
and by her, too, I will give you a son.
I will bless her, and she shall become nations,
and kings of nations shall come forth from her.

17   *Then Abraham fell down on his face and he laughed.*
He thought to himself:
Can a son be born to a man a hundred years old,
and can Sarah, ninety years old, bear a child?

18   *And Abraham said to God:*
If only Ishmael may live out his life before you!

19   *And God said: No, Sarah your wife*
shall bear you a son, and you shall call him Isaac.
And I will set up my covenant with him
as an eternal covenant, that I will be God to him
and to his descendants.

20   *But for Ishmael, too, I have heard your prayer.*
Behold, I will bless him and make him fruitful,

and multiply him exceedingly.
Twelve princes shall he beget,
and I will make him into a great nation.

21 *But my covenant I will set up with Isaac,*
whom Sarah will bear to you at this time next year.

22 *And God finished speaking with Abraham*
and went up in his presence.

23 *Then Abraham took his son Ishmael and all the slaves,*
those born in his house
and those bought with money,
all males among the people of the house of Abraham,
and circumcised the flesh of their foreskin
that very day, as God had commanded him.

24 *Abraham was ninety-nine years old*
when he was circumcised in the flesh of his foreskin.

25 *His son Ishmael was thirteen years old*
when he was circumcised in the flesh of his foreskin.

26 *On the same day Abraham and his son Ishmael were circumcised,*

27 *and all the men of his house, the slaves born in his house*
and those bought from strangers with money,
were circumcised by him.

Chapter 17 is a promise narrative, similar to chapter 15, but entirely dominated by the theology of the P document: P's purpose here is to summarize God's promise to Abraham and at the same time to associate with it the commandment requiring circumcision. The chapter is therefore central to P's presentation of the Patriarchal History. His purpose is to bring the promise to the fathers to life for his contemporaries.

Structure: The words spoken by God are framed by God's appearance (v. 1a) and departure (v. 22); they comprise a proem (vv. 1b-3a) and the discourse proper. The proem consists only of a succinct command coupled with a promise and Abraham's response (as in 12:1-4a). The discourse in 17:3b-21 has three parts: promise (vv. 3b-8), command (vv. 9-14), and promise (vv. 15-21). This shows that the promise is primary; the command is based on the promise. The discourse is followed by a conclusion (vv. 23-27) in which the command is carried out. The word "covenant" (Hebrew *berît*) is a leitmotif in the structure of this chapter. It appears thirteen times: once in the prologue, three times in each of the two parts of the promise discourse, and six times in the commandment section. This uniform distribution confirms that the author of P deliberately imposed a systematic structure on the chapter.

1-3a   In contrast to the discourse, the proem exhibits lapidary brevity; P here records a promise to Abraham such as he knows from tradition. He is therefore fully aware of the difference between this tradition and the interpretative discourse he composes. This conclusion is confirmed by the close resemblance of 17:1-3a to 12:1-4a.

The statement that Abraham was ninety-nine years old (cf. the preceding genealogical note in 16:3, 16 and the same figure in 11:10) and 17:24-25 constitute the genealogical framework. P uses the name "Yahweh" (which he usually avoids) because he is recording a traditional patriarchal promise. P uses the divine name "El Shaddai" ("God Almighty"?) only in the Patriarchal History and only in crucial passages: 17:1; 28:3; 35:11; 43:14; 48:3; cf. Exodus 6:3. It is an ancient term for God of uncertain meaning. It is clearly associated, however, with the religion of the patriarchs, especially in the context of blessing and increase. The words addressed to Abraham are a promise associated with a directive. Unlike the specific and limited directives of the early patriarchal stories, it governs the totality of life. Both parts of the directive have the same meaning: life in the presence of God, in which every step ("walk before me") is taken with an awareness of God's presence. The words "be perfect" aim at total and unconditional dependence on God. Here the promise of increase is primary; it dominates the entire chapter. It is associated with the word "covenant" (Hebrew *berît*) used here in its fundamental meaning of "solemn assurance," roughly synonymous with "promise." Abraham's reaction is a gesture, unaccompanied by words. For P, falling down before God says all that can be said.

3b-8　The first part of God's discourse begins with the promise of increase, solemnly introduced by "Behold, I . . ." (v. 4a; cf. v. 1b). As in verse 2, it is called a *berît* in the sense of "promise." Verse 4a could be translated: "This is the solemn promise I make to you." The promise of increase in verse 4b expands on the promise in verse 2; it is developed throughout the chapter in verses 2b, 4b, 5b, 6ab, 16b, 20ab. Only here is it developed so elaborately, a fact that demonstrates its central importance in chapter 17. Abraham, the father of a family in the early narratives, here becomes the father of nations. This expansion finds expression in a change of name: Abram becomes Abraham. The word *hāmôn*, "multitude" (represented in the translation by "many"), plays on the final syllable. The new name is analogous to the throne name given a king at his enthronement. Abraham is thus elevated to a new status: he is father of Israel and father of nations.

6　This verse continues the promise of increase, using the same verbs as Genesis 1:28. The pairing of "nations" and "kings" appears in oracles of salvation beginning with the exilic period: Isaiah 41:2; 45:1; 60:3. Genesis 17:7 adds a promise found only in P. Here *berît* clearly means "covenant"; it is set up or established with Abraham, but Abraham represents all Israel. It becomes an institution that is to endure forever. The same Hebrew word *berît* can refer both to the act (the binding assurance) and to the enduring state brought about by this act (the covenant). This institution means the relationship between God and Israel, grounded in God's promise and enduring forever. The formula "that I will be your God" is found only in P (Gen. 17:7-8; Exod. 29:45; Lev. 11:45; 22:33; 25:38; 26:45; Num. 15:41). The setting up of the covenant is solely an act of God; therefore we find here only one half of the "covenant formula," "I will be your God and you shall be my people," although even in P the covenant is mutual, as the rest of the chapter shows. Genesis 17:8b repeats the promise of "being your God" yet again; together with verse 7 it frames the promise of the land in verse 7, which appears only in this verse. Thus P gives the promise of increase primacy over the promise of the land. Even in the Exile it remains in force; but the vital point is that God maintains his relationship with his nation even when it is exiled from its own land.

9-14 The ordinance of circumcision. Verses 9-14 comprise the circumcision command (vv. 10b-11a) and instructions detailing how it is to be carried out (vv. 12ab, 13a, 14a). All the other passages (vv. 9, 10a, 11b, 13b, 14b) are meant to associate the circumcision ordinance with the "covenant." If these are omitted, verses 10b, 11a, 12ab, 13a, 14a constitute a coherent unit: a legal text dealing with circumcision, imposing it on the entire nation. This requirement came into being when political collapse and exile made circumcision a sign of membership in the people of Yahweh, a confessional sign. It is P's purpose to give circumcision the status and dignity of a divine ordinance; he therefore appends the divine discourse addressed to Abraham to the commandment and makes it a "sign of the covenant." This commandment and its observance make the covenant a mutual transaction between God and his people.

Circumcision is actually a ritual having nothing to do with the cult. It was common in the ancient world and is found in the Near East, Africa, America, and Australia, but not among the Indoeuropeans and Mongols. It is a very ancient custom, as is shown by the use of flint knives (Exod. 4:25). There are so many explanations and motivations for the ritual that its original meaning cannot be determined. The Israelites adopted it when they entered the land of Canaan (Josh. 5:2-9) and began to establish permanent settlements. On the whole, circumcision did not set Israel apart from its neighbors; when it was adopted, therefore, it could not have had a specifically religious meaning. Neither is it referred to in any of the early law codes. Only when the state ceased to exist did circumcision take on the significance given it in Genesis 17. Only then does rejection of the "sign of the covenant" mean breaking the covenant (v. 14).

15-21   The second part of the promise discourse adds the promise of a son to the promise of increase (v. 16), thus including Sarah in the promise; she, too, receives a new name. No reason is given; the meaning of the name, "princess," is explanation enough. The promise to Sarah is introduced by "I will bless her." In verse 16a this verb introduces the promise of a son, in verse 16b the promise of increase; the parallel illustrates the harmonization of the two promises (cf. 15:1-6). Blessing and increase are commonly linked by Deuteronomy (for example, Deut. 7:13).

17-18   The promise discourse is interrupted by Abraham's doubting reaction. Abraham falls down—but he laughs! This seems strange, almost bizarre, in the context of P. Here P clearly has in mind Genesis 18:10-15; but he changes the scene so that it is Abraham, not Sarah, who laughs. Nevertheless, the gesture of falling down in reverence is Abraham's first and most important reaction. His "laughing" plays on the name of the son, but in a different way than in chapter 18, where (in contrast to 11:30) the reason for laughing is Sarah's advanced age. Abraham's doubts are also expressed in his prayer for Ishmael (17:18), as well as in the gesture of reverence. P is saying that God goes his majestic way in bringing to pass what he has promised; he is not dependent on Abraham's faith. What he requires of Abraham is humble obedience, even when he cannot believe the promise. For P, Abraham is not the "father of faith," as in Genesis 15:6. What God has promised he will bring to pass, regardless of human response. This is P's interpretation of the name "Isaac."

19-21   God's response in verses 19-21 first (v. 19a) repeats the promise that Sarah will bear a son and states his name. No explicit explanation of the name is given; it is implicit in the preceding verses. The name "Isaac" (Hebrew *yiṣḥāq*) can be an abbreviated theophorous name ("El laughs," "El rejoices") or a situation name ("He laughs"— the father or the child). The various explanations in chapters 17, 18, and 21 originated with the narratives and are really only allusions, not explanations. They can therefore differ.

There follows in 17:19-21 a differentiation between Isaac and Ishmael. The latter, as Abraham's son, receives the promise of increase as requested by Abraham in verse 18; it is Isaac, however, in whom the "covenant" of God with Abraham is to be continued. The promise for Ishmael contains the same combination of blessing and increase as in verse 16, as well as a clear reference to Ishmael's history: "Twelve princes shall he beget"—a proleptic reference to the genealogy of Ishmael in Genesis 25:12-18. Again we see here the universalistic side of P: God's blessing extends beyond Israel to other nations.

God's discourse, which began with the covenant between God and Abraham, ends in 17:21 with the continuation of the covenant in and through Isaac, Abraham's son. The chronological statement at the end indirectly records the year of Isaac's birth; it echoes 18:10, 14 almost word for word. The end of God's discourse is recognized explicitly in 17:22; God's departure balances his appearance (v. 1).

23-27 The conclusion reports how the command in verses 9-14 was carried out. Abraham did what God had commanded. It is explicitly stated who must be circumcised (v. 23a); the statement is repeated in verses 23b and 27. The carrying out of the command is also described in great detail (v. 23b). In both cases, precise fulfillment of the commandment is stressed. The statement of Abraham's and Ishmael's ages belongs to the genealogical frame of the chapter.

P's purpose in chapter 17 is to use the ordinance of circumcision to associate the patriarchal promise, which actually concerns all Israel, firmly with the family. P sees in the history of the patriarchs the basis for the three precultic rituals that, in his view, guarantee the continuation of families as the basic units of the people of Israel after the disappearance of the state: circumcision (ch. 17), marriage within one's own people (chs. 27–28), and burial in one's own land (ch. 23).

18:1-16A   ABRAHAM AND THE THREE GUESTS

1   *And Yahweh appeared to him by the terebinth of Mamre*
    while he was sitting at the entrance to his tent
    in the heat of the day.
2   *Now as he raised his eyes and looked about,*
    behold, there were three men standing before him.
    When he saw them, he ran to them from the entrance to his tent
    and bowed low toward the ground,
3   *and said:*
    Sir, if I have found favor in your eyes,
    please do not pass your servant by.
4   *Let a little water be brought*
    that you may wash your feet,
    then rest under the tree.
5   *In the meantime I will bring a little bread,*
    that you may refresh yourself; then you can go on.
    Why else has your journey brought you your servant's way?
    They said: Do as you have said.
6   *Then Abraham hurried to the tent to Sarah and said:*
    Quickly, take three measures of flour, knead it,
    and make some cakes.
7   *Then Abraham ran to the cattle,*
    took a nice tender calf and gave it to the servant,
    who made haste to prepare it.

8   *Then he took curds and milk and the calf*
that he had prepared and set it before them;
he himself waited on them under the tree while they ate.

9   *Then they asked him: Where is Sarah your wife?*
He replied: Inside the tent.

10   *Then he said: I will certainly come back to you*
this time next year.
Sarah then will have a son.
But Sarah was listening at the entrance to the tent behind him.

11   *Now Abraham and Sarah were old, advanced in years,*
and Sarah no longer experienced the cycle of women.

12   *Then Sarah laughed to herself and thought:*
Now that I am used up, should I still have sexual pleasure?
And my husband is old.

13   *Then Yahweh said to Abraham: Why is Sarah laughing and saying:*
Am I really to bear a child now that I am old?

14   *Is anything too difficult for Yahweh?*
At this time next year I will come back to you,
and Sarah will have a son.

15   *But Sarah denied it, saying: I did not laugh,*
because she was afraid.
But he said: No, you did laugh.

16   *Then the three men rose and left.*

Chapter 18 begins a large narrative complex embracing chapters 18–19 as well as 21:1-7. Its sections were once independent narratives, as was 18:1-16a. The adaptation to the larger context can be seen in the fact that the real point of departure, the childlessness of Abraham and Sarah, is not mentioned at the beginning but inserted parenthetically in verse 11, and that the natural conclusion, the birth of the child, is not recounted until 21:1-7. An additional peculiarity is the development of the introduction in 18:1-8, which is so circumstantial that it seems like an independent narrative. This can be explained if two narratives have been combined in 18:1-16a: the promise of a child to a childless couple to deliver them from their distress, and the visit of a messenger of God (or several messengers), who rewards friendliness and hospitality with a gift, the promise of a son. There are many parallels to both narratives, which in fact lead up to the same conclusion: the promise of a child.

    1-8   The visit. A masterful description of a visit—arrival, invitation, hospitality. It brings us amazingly close to the world and way of life of the patriarchs. The scene opens with the unexpected arrival of a group of strangers at Abraham's tent. The great importance of hospitality in the life of nomads is also common among early settled cultures. The visit of a stranger could have vital significance; strangers come from another world and can tell about it. In many narra-

tives, a chain of events is triggered by the arrival of someone from far away. This is the reason given for the exhortation to hospitality in Hebrews 13:2: "thereby some have entertained angels unawares." Such stories are based on real experience.

1-2   The first words, "And Yahweh appeared to him," interpret what follows from a much later perspective, as a theophany; but the Patriarchal History describes theophanies differently. In an earlier form, the narrative probably began something like this: "When Abraham was sitting under . . . , there came. . . ." The strangers arrive in the midday heat, a time when travelers turn in to find rest and shade. They come unexpectedly and stand facing Abraham—the equivalent of knocking. They require hospitality, and Abraham hastens to ask them in. He bows before them; he does not know who they are, and they may be persons of dignity. He addresses one of the three as "Sir" (literally, "My lord"). In what follows, the story alternates between a single visitor and three; the simplest explanation is that two narratives have been joined, one dealing with three visitors, the other dealing with one visitor who promises a son.

4-5   The following sentences develop the invitation. Abraham offers them the chance to wash the dust off their feet (as in Luke 7:44), relax in the shade, and enjoy a meal. The understatement is the language of polite discourse. In measured and restrained words, the three men accept the invitation.

6-8   Hospitality. The vivid description helps us share in Abraham's enthusiasm, which extends to Sarah and the servant; we can see him standing opposite his guests, alert to wait on them. Anyone who listens attentively to this wonderful story must sense that it illustrates a unique culture of hospitality, now lost to us.

9-16   In the second section, verses 9-16, Abraham scarcely appears. In an earlier, independent narrative, the promise was spoken to the mother, as in most parallels. The visit leads up to the promise that Sarah will have a son (cf. Gen. 11:30; 15:2-4; 16:11; 18:10-14; 21:1-7; also 17:15, 16, 19, 21 [P]). We also find the promise of a son in Judges 13:2-5; 1 Samuel 1:17; 2 Kings 4:8-17; Luke 1–2. That we are dealing with a stereotyped narrative form is shown, for example, by the phrase "at this time next year," which appears in exactly the same words in 2 Kings 4:16, 17. A similar promise of a son appears in the Ugaritic epics.

10b-12   Since the promise is addressed to Abraham in this narrative, Sarah is skillfully introduced by having her overhear the conversation and laugh because she finds it so incredible. Here (v. 11) is finally inserted into the introduction to the narrative, which motivates Sarah's laughter. In Genesis 11:30 the reason for Sarah's childlessness was infertility; here it is the couple's advanced age.

This may be a variant, possibly to heighten the effect. The interplay that follows involves Sarah and the visitors. Genesis 18:12 states explicitly Sarah's reason for laughing; it is a natural reaction (cf. 2 Kgs. 4:16).

13-15 Surprisingly, the response is introduced by the words "Then Yahweh said to Abraham." Verse 14a explains why the messenger is so referred to: "Is anything too difficult for Yahweh?" In other words, the messenger represents the one who sent him; the messenger has been commissioned to deliver the promise, which comes from one for whom nothing is too difficult. Thus the messenger counters the unbelief expressed in Sarah's laughter, indicating that he is a messenger from God. Now Sarah is frightened; her fear takes the form of trying to deny that she laughed. Now that she realizes what she has done, she would like to undo it. The messenger responds: you cannot undo what is done. This statement must be heard in the context of what has gone before: "At this time next year. . . ." Then Sarah will remember having laughed. And the memory of the messenger's visit will endure in the name of her child.

18:16B-33 ABRAHAM QUERIES THE DESTRUCTION OF SODOM

16b *But Abraham went with them to see them on their way.*
And already they were looking down on Sodom.
17 *But Yahweh reflected: Shall I hide from Abraham*
what I am to do?
18 *Yet Abraham is to become a great and powerful nation,*
and all the nations of the earth shall bless themselves in him.
19 *For I have chosen him, that he may charge his sons*
and his house after him
to observe the way of Yahweh and to do what is just and right,
so that Yahweh may bring upon him what he promised him.
20 *And Yahweh said: The outcry over Sodom and Gomorrah—*
it is great, and their sin, it is grave.
21 *I will go down and see if what they have done*
accords with the outcry that has come to me,
and if not I must know.
22 *Thereupon the men turned from there*
and went in the direction of Sodom.
But Abraham remained standing before Yahweh.
23 *Abraham approached Yahweh and said:*
Will you really sweep away the just with the wicked?
24 *Perhaps there are fifty just in the city;*
will you sweep them away and not pardon the place
for the sake of the fifty just who are in it?

25 *Far be it from you to do such a thing,*
   to kill the just with the wicked,
   to treat the just as the wicked,
   far be it from you!
   Should not the judge of the whole world do what is just?
26 *Then Yahweh said: If I find fifty just*
   in the city, for their sake
   I will pardon the whole place.
27 *Then Abraham answered and said:*
   Behold, I presume to speak to my Lord,
   though I am dust and ashes.
28 *Perhaps there are five less than fifty just;*
   will you destroy the whole city for want of five?
   He said: If I find forty-five there,
   I will not destroy it.
29 *And he spoke once more to him and said:*
   Perhaps only forty will be found there.
   He said: I will not do it for the sake of forty.
30 *And he said: Let my Lord not be angry if I speak again!*
   Perhaps only thirty will be found there. And he said:
   I will not do it if I find thirty there.
31 *And he said: Behold, I presume*
   to speak to my Lord:
   Perhaps twenty will be found there.
   And he said: I will not destroy it for the sake of twenty.
32 *And he said: Let my Lord not be angry if I speak again!*
   Perhaps only ten will be found there.
   And he said: I will not destroy it for the sake of ten.

33 *Then Yahweh went away, when he had finished speaking with Abraham.*
   But Abraham went back to his place.

Between the departure of the men in 18:16a and their arrival at the gate of Sodom in 19:1, an episode consisting of a dialogue between Abraham and Yahweh has been introduced. It has two sections: the announcement to Abraham of the destruction of Sodom (which follows 13:13) in 18:17-21 and Abraham's questions in verses 23-32. The whole episode is a theological inquiry disguised as a dialogue; the text does not narrate a train of events, but is the product of theological reflection. The subject matter is the justice of God's actions in history. Concern for God's justice is especially evident in the great complex of material in the book of Proverbs that deals with the fate of the righteous and the wicked. These proverbs date from the postexilic period. This background helps us understand the concern for God's justice in Genesis 18. The debate between Job and his friends belongs in the same context. Certain exilic and postexilic texts in the prophets are also especially concerned with the justice of God's actions in history: Ezekiel 14:12-20, which closely resembles Genesis 18;

Jeremiah 18:7-10; and Jonah 3–4, dealing with the destruction of the people of Nineveh. This question could not arise in Israel until after 587 B.C.; all these texts date from after the fall of Jerusalem. For the theologian who inserted Genesis 18:16b-33 here, the destruction of Sodom was a good illustration of his question; enabling him to associate it with the patriarchal promise. The situation is similar in the case of 15:13-16, which also seeks to explain God's justice in his governance of history ("You must know . . ."). Both passages may well date from about the same period.

16b-22   After a transitional passage (v. 16b), Yahweh informs Abraham of his decision to destroy Sodom (vv. 20-21), on the basis of his reflections in verses 17-19. Verse 16b takes Abraham and the men to a place where they can look down on Sodom. Yahweh's internal debate (vv. 17-19: "But Yahweh reflected") is a decision disguised as a question. God wishes to inform Abraham of his decision, if he is worthy of the promise that has been given him. The promise is that of increase (v. 18), formulated in terms that recall chapter 17 (P). The importance bestowed upon him in the promise is developed in 18:19 with respect to Abraham's significance for Israel. Here we see the late stage in the history of the promises, in which they serve to exalt the patriarch Abraham; he is vouchsafed a share in God's own plans (cf. Amos 3:7). His importance to the Israel of the author's day consists in his teaching his descendants to go in the "way of Yahweh" (a common term for the late religion of devotion to the law), practicing "what is just and right." Here, too, Abraham is not the father of faith but the father of "righteousness and justice," that is, devout adherence to the law. This is the language of the postexilic period among those who identified religion ("the way of Yahweh") with the practice of righteousness and justice. This view is here traced back to Abraham; the last clause of Genesis 18:19 says expressly that observing the way of Yahweh and doing what is just and right is the necessary condition if the promises made to Abraham are to be fulfilled. Only with Deuteronomy are the promises, originally unconditional, made conditional upon obedience (cf. also 22:15-18; 26:5).

Now follows in 18:20-21 God's communication to Abraham of his decision to destroy Sodom and Gomorrah. These verses sound like the beginning of a narrative dealing with the destruction of a sinful city. They might follow the statement in 13:13 that "the people of Sodom were wicked and sinned greatly against Yahweh." These sentences from the old narrative were incorporated by the author of 18:16b-33. After Yahweh's decision in verses 20-21 the narrative had him set out at once for Sodom. But here the author of verses 16b-33 has inserted the dialogue, using verse 22 as a transition: two men go their way (there are two in Gen. 19), but Abraham remains standing before Yahweh in order to question him.

23-32   The dialogue comprises two parts: verses 23-26 and 27-32. Most exegetes have interpreted it as intercession by Abraham on behalf of Sodom. But wherever we find a clear example of intercession (for example, Amos 7–9; Jer. 11; 15–16), it has a fixed structure that clearly marks it as a prayer, a plea addressed to God. That is not true here. Genesis 18:23-32 has nothing in common with the language of prayer. The structural form is question and answer, not plea and response. It is clear to Abraham from the beginning, even as he asks his questions, that God will carry out the judgment against Sodom he has determined.

23   The first question asked by Abraham, "Will you really sweep away the just with the wicked?" does not dispute God's right to destroy; but such destruction can be just only if it strikes solely the wicked. The following verses (vv. 24-26) serve to emphasize what has already been said: the righteous must not be allowed to suffer like the wicked! This is the heart of Abraham's concern. Surely "the judge of all the world" must be just (v. 23)! The author recalls the psalms that extol God as judge of the world (cf. Ps. 94:2; Job 34:17). God's answer in Genesis 18:26 agrees with Abraham: if there are fifty just in Sodom, he will not destroy the city.

27-32   The second section serves only to sharpen the question; no new arguments are introduced. Abraham ventures onward in verses 27-32, albeit deferentially. Behind his insistence lies the question of God's justice. He must push to the utmost limit the question of whether a judgment that destroys is a just judgment. God's answer never changes: a monotonous no, no, no. God's justice is confirmed from his own mouth. Abraham stops with ten because ten constitute the smallest group. Were there fewer, they could be saved individually.

The theologian who interpolated 18:16b-33 into the ancient story of Abraham was drawing on the narrative of how Sodom was destroyed by divine judgment; he was bound to this story. His purpose is to show that God's judgment was just. His argument is so framed as to dispel all doubts. When the fate of individuals was at issue, the distinction between the devout and the wicked was easy; the problem arose when cities or nations faced God's judgment. It was vital to demonstrate the justice of God's actions in history in an age when one's relationship with God was determined by "righteousness and justice." Therefore the author has righteous Abraham, who is just, stand up before God in the name of justice; God confirms that he does not destroy the just with the wicked. This interpolation makes sense only from the perspective of an age in which the mutual relationship between human beings and God was determined by the concept of righteousness and justice.

19:1-29   THE DESTRUCTION OF SODOM AND THE RESCUE OF LOT

1   *And the two messengers arrived at Sodom in the evening,*
    as Lot was sitting at the gate of Sodom.
    And Lot saw them, rose, went to meet them,
    bowed with his face to the ground,

2   *and said: Please, my lords, turn aside into the house*
    of your servant to stay the night. Wash your feet.
    Tomorrow morning you can go your way.
    But they said: No, we will pass the night in the street.

3   *But when he pressed them strongly, they turned aside*
    and went into his house, and he prepared a meal for them,
    baked unleavened bread, and they ate.

4   *But before they lay down,*
    the men of the city, the men of Sodom, surrounded the house,
    young and old, all the people from far and near.

5   *They cried out to Lot and said: Where are the men*
    who came to you this evening?
    Bring them out to us that we may know them.

6   *Then Lot went out to them before the door and shut it behind him*

7   *and said: Please, my brothers, do nothing wicked.*

8   *Behold, I have two daughters who have not known a man;*
    I will bring them out to you.
    Do with them as you please,
    only do nothing to these men, for they are harbored
    under the shelter of my roof.

9   *But they cried out: Away with you! And they also said:*
    This man has come as an alien
    and wants to play the judge.
    Now we will deal worse with you than with them.
    Then they surged forward against the man, against Lot,
    and moved to break down the door.

10 *But the men stretched out their hands and pulled Lot*
    into the house and shut the door.

11 *But the people outside the door they struck with blindness,*
    small and great, so that they wearied themselves in vain
    to find the door.

12 *Then the men said to Lot: Do you have anyone else here?*
    Your sons and daughters and whoever in the city belongs to you,
    take them away from this place.

13 *For we are going to destroy this place, because the outcry*
   over it before Yahweh is great,
   and so Yahweh has sent us to destroy it.

14 *So Lot went out and spoke to his sons-in-law,*
   who were to marry his daughters, and said:
   Away, leave this place;
   for Yahweh is going to destroy the city.
   But his sons-in-law thought he was joking.

15 *But when dawn broke, the messengers urged*
   Lot to hurry, saying: Up, take your wife
   and your two daughters here,
   lest you be swept away in the punishment of the city.

16 *But when he lingered, the men seized him and his wife*
   and his two daughters by the hand,
   because Yahweh wanted to spare them, brought him out,
   and set him outside the city.

17 *When they had brought them out, he said:*
   Save yourself! Flee for you life! Do not look behind;
   do not stop anywhere in the valley.
   Flee to the mountains, lest you be swept away!

18 *But Lot said to them: No, my lord!*

19 *Behold, your servant has found favor in your eyes,*
   and you have shown me great mercy
   in saving my life.
   But to the mountains I cannot flee;
   disaster might reach me and I might die.

20 *Behold, that city there is near enough*
   to flee to; it is so small!
   I might flee there—it is so small!—
   and save my life.

21 *And he said to him: Behold, even this matter*
   I will grant you, and the city of which you speak
   I will not destroy.

22 *Flee there in haste, for I can do nothing*
   until you arrive there.
   Therefore the city is called Zoar.

23 *The sun had just risen over the land*
   and Lot had just come to Zoar,

24 *when Yahweh rained brimstone and fire upon Sodom and Gomorrah,*
   from Yahweh in the heavens,

25 *and so destroyed those cities and the whole plain*
   and all the inhabitants of the cities and the produce of the fields.

26 *But when his wife looked behind her, she became a pillar of salt.*

27 *But early in the morning Abraham betook himself to the place*
   where he had stood in the presence of Yahweh.

28 *And when he gazed down upon the territory of Sodom and Gomorrah*
   and upon all the region of the plain,

> *he saw smoke rising from the land*
> *like the smoke of a furnace.*

29 *When God destroyed the cities of the plain,*
  then God remembered Abraham,
  and delivered Lot from the destruction,
  when he destroyed the cities in which Lot had lived.

Narratives concerning the destruction of a city are basically the out-growth of a catastrophic experience. It is the terror of those who have escaped (Lot) or the witnesses (Abraham in vv. 27-28) that shapes the story of the catastrophe. Such narratives can be transformed or trans-ferred; they can give rise to variants and attract a variety of other themes. The memory could live on as a mere historical datum, as in the many references to the judgment upon Sodom and Gomorrah in the Old and New Testaments (for example, Isa. 1:9-10; 13:19; Jer. 49:18; 50:40; Ezek. 16:46-50, 53-56; Amos 4:11; Matt. 10:15; 11:23-24; Luke 10:12; 17:29). An example is Deuteronomy 29:23: "an overthrow like that of Sodom and Gomorrah, Admah and Zeboiim." No other incident from Genesis is cited as often in the Old or New Testament. These references need not all go back to Genesis 19; the tradition was handed down in many variants. The destruction of other cities was also recounted as an example of divine judgment, as is shown by a comparison of Genesis 19 to Judges 19:15-25 (Gibeah). The narratives have a family resemblance but exhibit substantial differences. There are also many extrabiblical narratives with the structure of Genesis 19 (sin—judgment—preservation of a single individual); they also share the theme that the sin consists in a violation of hospitality, and that the one who is saved is the one who welcomed the deity. A familiar example is the story of Philemon and Baucis from Ovid's *Metamorphoses*; there is also a very similar parallel from India.

Structure: Verses 1-3, arrival of the men and Lot's welcome; verses 4-11, attack and defense; 12-17 and 18-22, command to leave the city; 23-25(26), destruction of the city; 27-28, connection with Abra-ham; 29, a parallel account from P. The first section, verses 1-11, as its parallel in Judges 19:15-25 shows, is relatively independent; the sec-ond section, Genesis 19:12-17 and 24-25, belongs in the context of narratives describing primordial catastrophes, as can be seen from the parallels in Genesis 6–9.

1-3 Arrival of the men and Lot's welcome. These verses follow 18:22(23), where the destination, Sodom, has already been named. The statement that it was "in the evening" is picked up by 19:15a and 23a; an event taking place at night is described. The site of the city has been the subject of much discussion, but the geographical details point to the Dead Sea, and more specifically, despite opinions to the contrary, its southern end. The invitation and welcome resemble 18:1-8, except that here the messengers are welcomed into a house inside a city, as the mention of the gate in 19:1 makes clear. Lot has become a city dweller; the gate where he sits at evening represents the city.

4-11 Attack and defense. The wickedness of Sodom was already mentioned in 18:20-21; now the messengers who were to investigate (18:21) experience its enormity personally. Crime is common throughout the world; throughout the world it disrupts human society. Here the crime is unnatural lust together with a particularly repulsive violation of a guest's right to protection. It is emphasized that "young and old" participate in the attack, from throughout the whole city, "from one end to the other." The whole city is indeed depraved.

Lot had offered the men the protection of his house; the "shadow of his roof" lent them security. Violation of this sanctuary was a terrible crime. And so Lot does his utmost to protect his guests. He boldly confronts the mob, warns them not to commit this crime, and even offers to hand over his daughters, an offer born of desperation. But the threats of the advancing mob make the offer pointless; they even threaten Lot himself. He and his guests are now in extreme danger. Now the strangers intervene and effect a rescue. They seize Lot and drag him into the house; the mob outside retreats. Those within perceive this as a miracle of deliverance and say: "They have been struck with blindness!" As in our language, this idiom refers not to blindness in the literal sense but to temporary failure of sight. The word, which appears only here and (in the same context) in 2 Kings 6:18, suggests an ancient narrative in which this idiom appeared.

12-17 Two narrative strands converge in verses 12-17: (a) the preservation of Lot and his family from destruction, based on (b) the announcement of Yahweh's decision to destroy the city and the deliverance of a single individual (cf. Gen. 6–9). The composite nature of the narrative explains some minor discrepancies. The deliverance takes the form of measures (injunction to leave the city, insistence on haste) within the bounds of human ability. The refusal of Lot's sons-in-law to listen (19:14) underscores the severity of God's judgment and is presupposed in 19:30-38.

The chronological statement in verse 15 begins a new section. It effectively says: "It is high time!" The next chronological statement comes in verse 23, which speaks of the dawn. What takes place between dawn and sunrise demands utmost haste, expressed in the series of imperatives in verses 13-17. At the last minute, however, Lot hesitates (v. 16a), so that the men have to seize him and force him to move. Lot has chosen settled life in a city (ch. 13); now he cannot break away. The men leave him outside the city (19:16), warning him once more to hurry: "Flee to the mountains!" This command is underlined by the command not to look back: mortals may not look upon God's destroying judgment, a common theme. Verses 23-26, the conclusion, must be read immediately following verse 17.

23-26 The destruction of Sodom. At dawn catastrophe strikes Sodom. It is now related in lapidary style in just two sentences (vv. 24-25), probably an old account from a source used by the narrator of chapter 19 and linked with the preceding narrative by the chronological statement in verse 23a and the statement of Lot's arrival at Zoar. The destruction of the cities (v. 24) was brought about by a rain of fire and brimstone, a traditional stereotyped formula for an annihilating act of divine judgment (cf. Deut. 29:23; Isa. 30:33; 34:9; Ezek. 38:22; Ps. 11:6). Deposits of asphalt and sulfur are still found near the shore of the Dead Sea. Genesis 19:25 describes the effects. The word used here and in verse 21 to describe the destruction (Hebrew *hāpak̠*, "turn over," equivalent to "catastrophe") is inconsistent with the rain of brimstone. The catastrophe affects the city itself and the plain around it, destroying human beings and vegetation. Thus the narrative comes to its violent conclusion. Verse 26 is an independent episode, a traditional element belonging to the narrative of Lot's deliverance (vv. 12-17); it presupposes the command in verse 17. The brief statement records the tripartite sequence prohibition—transgression—punishment, an ancient and widespread narrative theme rooted in magical thought. The real point is the power of a taboo; the etiological explanation of a rock formation is a secondary element. It reflects local geography: there are salt pillars that resemble human figures on the shore of the Dead Sea. This motif appears frequently in Greek legends (cf. Ovid's *Metamorphoses*); in the Old Testament, metamorphosis of a human being is found only here. In its present context, the episode says that Lot's deliverance was a deliverance at the brink of the abyss.

27-29 In these last sentences the narrative comes to a majestic conclusion. They link the story of Sodom's destruction with Abraham and bring the great narrative complex of chapters 13; 18–19 to a close. Abraham, coming to the place and looking down on the scene of the catastrophe, silently and reverentially acknowledges it as God's judgment. We do not need to be told that he recognizes God as judge. Here we have the counterpart to Genesis 12:1-4: the fact that all the families of the earth will bless themselves in Abraham does not mean that God's only activity is blessing. It is the human race, threatened and often visited by catastrophes and acts of divine judgment, that nevertheless receives that promise of blessing. The God who blesses is also the God who judges. Abraham looks down in silence upon the scene of destruction.

29   A brief account (P) of the destruction of the cities is appended. It consists of four clauses, the central one being the statement: "Then God remembered Abraham" (cf. Gen. 8:1: "Then God remembered Noah"). All that matters to an author of the later period is the relationship of God to Abraham, which makes it possible for him to save his kinsman Lot from catastrophe. His generation must be told the significance of God's promise to Abraham: I will be your God.

19:30-38   LOT'S DAUGHTERS

30   *But Lot went up from Zoar and dwelt in the mountains*
      with his two daughters,
      for he was afraid to dwell in Zoar;
      he lived in the cave, he and his two daughters.
31   *Then the elder daughter said to the younger: Our father is old,*
      and there is no man left in the land
      who might come to us in accordance with the custom of the world.
32   *Come, let us make our father drunk with wine*
      and lie with him, and thus through our father
      have descendants.
33   *So in that night they made their father drunk with wine,*
      and the elder went and lay with her father,
      who was not aware of her lying
      or of her rising.
34   *But the next morning the elder said to the younger:*
      Behold, I slept last evening with my father.
      Let us make him drunk with wine again tonight.
      Then you go and lie with him, that through our father
      we may have descendants.
35   *And so that night, too, they made their father*
      drunk with wine. Then the younger arose
      and lay with him, but he was not aware
      of her lying or of her rising.
36   *Thus the two daughters of Lot were pregnant by their father.*
37   *The elder gave birth to a son and called him Moab;*
      he is the father of the Moabites to this day.
38   *The younger, too, gave birth to a son and called him Ben-Ammi;*
      he is the father of the Ammonites to this day.

Genesis 19:30-38 is a report expanded to form a narrative; its nucleus is an itinerary (v. 30) coupled with genealogical information (vv.

145

36-38). It has been expanded by the interpolation of an episode telling how the daughters of Lot came to bear their sons (vv. 31-35). This brings the story of Lot to a close.

The elements of this text come from three different realms. The motif of new life after annihilating judgment belongs to the realm of the Primal History; in the narrative of the destruction of Sodom, Lot, who escapes from destruction, is the counterpart of Noah in Genesis 6–9. This is illustrated by 19:31, which could also be translated: "There is no man left upon earth." The realm of tribal oracle is the background to the etiological explanation of the origin of Moab and Ammon, neighboring tribes to Israel: the sons of Lot's daughters become the fathers of two tribes or nations; intermediate generations are omitted for brevity. The etiological conclusion in verses 37 and 38 cannot antedate the tribal period. The third realm is the composition of the Abraham-Lot cycle, in which 19:30-38 became the conclusion of the story of Lot. A thematic harmonization with the Abraham cycle is also evident in having the continuity of generations preserved through the birth of a child (vv. 32, 34).

30   Verses 30 and 36-38 constitute a framework in the form of a report. Verse 30 is a typical itinerary passage; it follows the itinerary statements in 13:11-12. The reason stated in 19:30b ("for he was afraid . . .") provides the link with 19:12-26, from which we learn that Lot's two daughters are without husbands. "The cave" probably refers to a cave known to the audience.

31-36   The suggestion Lot's elder daughter makes to her younger sister has two motivations, both based on their hopeless situation: they must die without offspring. Their lives, although spared, can be meaningful only if these lives are continued through children. It is therefore truly a "decision born of desperation" (Franz Delitzsch). For this reason, moral judgment is inappropriate, whether it labels the decision "reprehensible" (August Dillmann) or "heroic" (Hermann Gunkel). Verses 33-35 tell how the plan succeeded; verse 36 states in conclusion that for both women it resulted in the birth of a son, thus leading into the concluding genealogy in verses 37-38.

37-38   The conclusion consists in an explanation of how Moab and Ammon came to be; "to this day" means that they are still Israel's neighbors. The report of the sons' birth also records their naming; the meaning of the names is only vaguely implied. The purpose of the verses is to trace the distant relationship of Israel to Moab and Ammon through their descent from Lot, Abraham's nephew. Originally, the names of the children must have been simple personal names; they have been changed to fit the etiology.

It is characteristic of the Abraham cycle that Abraham should be not only the father of Israel but also the father of nations; therefore the lineage of his nephew Lot, traced to its conclusion in verses 30-38, is also important. When the later conclusion (vv. 37-38) speaks of Moab and Ammon as distant relatives of Israel, a positive relationship is implied, as in Deuteronomy 2:9, 19. The subsequent hostility of Israel toward both (Deut. 23:3-6) may have led later exegetes to interpret the text as denigrating both peoples.

Central to the text is the desperate action of Lot's anonymous daughters. Such rebellious acts on the part of women are also told of Hagar (Genesis 16), Rebekah (Genesis 27), and Tamar (Genesis 38). They all have the same purpose: to bear a child of their own, the only future possible for women. Women were more important in the patriarchal period than later.

20:1-18   ABRAHAM AND ABIMELECH

1   *Abraham journeyed from there to the Negeb*
     and settled between Kadesh and Shur.
     While he was living as an alien in Gerar,
2   *Abraham said of his wife Sarah: She is my sister.*
     But Abimelech, the king of Gerar,
     sent him to fetch Sarah.
3   *Then God came to Abimelech in a dream by night*
     and said to him: Truly, you are a dead man because of the woman
     you have taken; she is a married woman.
4   *But Abimelech had not yet touched her, and he said:*
     Lord, will you really kill the innocent?
5   *Did he not say to me: She is my sister?*
     And did she not say: He is my brother?
     In integrity of heart and with pure hands
     have I done this.
6   *And God said to him in a dream: I, too, know*
     that you have done this in integrity of heart,
     and I myself have kept you
     from sinning against me;
     therefore I did not allow you to touch her.
7   *But now give back the man's wife,*
     for he is a prophet, and he will pray on your behalf
     that you remain alive.
     If you do not give her back, know
     that all you and yours must die.
8   *Early the next morning, Abimelech called all his servants*
     together and repeated all these words before them;
     but the men were much afraid.
9   *Then Abimelech summoned Abraham and said to him:*

> *What have you done to us? How have I sinned against you,*
> *that you have brought upon me and my kingdom so great a sin?*
> *You have done to me what ought not to be done.*

10 *And Abimelech said to Abraham: What had you in mind*
> *that you did such a thing?*

11 *Abraham answered: Indeed, I thought*
> *that there was no fear of God at all in this place,*
> *and that they would kill me because of my wife.*

12 *And in fact she is my sister,*
> *she is the daughter of my father, but not the daughter*
> *of my mother, and so she could be my wife.*

13 *And so when God called me to go from my father's house*
> *to a foreign land, I said to her:*
> *This favor you must do me*
> *everywhere we go: say on my behalf that I am your brother.*

14 *Then Abimelech took sheep and oxen, male and female servants,*
> *and he presented them to Abraham,*
> *and returned his wife Sarah to him.*

15 *And Abimelech said: See, my land is before you,*
> *settle where you please.*

16 *And to Sarah he said: Behold, I am giving your brother*
> *a thousand pieces of silver; that shall be a vindication of your honor*
> *before all of yours—*
> *thus you are entirely vindicated.*

17 *Then Abraham prayed to God,*
> *and God healed Abimelech, his wife, and his maidservants,*
> *that they might have children once more.*

18 *For Yahweh had closed every womb*
> *in the house of Abimelech because of Sarah, Abraham's wife.*

Contrary to what is usually held, Genesis 20:1-18 is not a parallel narrative to Genesis 12:10-20 and 26:6-11; it is not a narrative in the strict sense at all. Although it remains within a narrative framework, it is really a reflection on the narrative in 12:10-20, on which it is based. The core of the text, 20:3-13, consists of dialogue; the action (vv. 1-2 and 14-18) is peripheral. The text is rather a search for answers to questions raised by the ancient narrative. Both dialogues in verses 3-13 deal with accusation and defense: who is in the right, who is in the wrong? This question is debated in charge and countercharge. The facts as such are not important; they take on meaning only in the context of the debate. The old narrative is retold from a new perspective: to define who is a fault. This question determines the source and setting of Genesis 20; it is the motive for the retelling.

1-2   The narrative framework begins with an itinerary (cf. Gen. 13:1); Abraham's route takes him to the Negeb (cf. 12:9; 13:1). As usual, the itinerary records a departure and a stopping place. Abraham settles between Kadesh (14:7) and Shur (16:7)—at the extreme southern end of the Negeb.

Neither statement in 20:2—Abraham's claim that Sarah is his sister and the statement that the king of Gerar has Sarah summoned—makes sense without Genesis 12. No reason is given for either until later in the passage. Genesis 20:2, therefore, is not really the beginning of a narrative but an introduction to the dialogue in verses 3-13. This is clearer if verse 2 is reformulated as a subordinate clause: "When Abraham . . . , then God came in a dream. . . ." Here, in contrast to 12:10-20, the king is king of the Canaanite city Gerar.

3-13 The dialogue constitutes the heart of the passage. Verses 3-7 inquire into the guilt of Abimelech, verses 9-13 the guilt of Abraham.

3-7 These verses are introduced (in v. 3a and again in 6a) and concluded as a revelation to Abimelech in a dream; but the material introduced is inconsistent with the framework: it is a legal action comprising accusation, sentence (v. 3) and defense (vv. 4-5), and a review of the sentence (vv. 6-7). God's speaking to Abimelech is a literary fiction making possible the dialogue about Abimelech's guilt. Genesis 31:24 and Numbers 22:9, 30 use the same technique of introducing a passage by having God speak in a dream; in each case, God speaks to a non-Israelite. The sentence (Gen. 20:3b) is pronounced in the language of secular law (cf. Isa. 38:1). It is imposed for a crime against property, as we see from the added clause "She is a married woman": it was widely accepted in the ancient world that a wife was the property of her husband. To take a married woman is universally held to infringe a divinely sanctioned right.

4-5 In verses 4-5 the accused states his case; the action runs its prescribed course. The question of the accused, "Lord, will you really kill the innocent?" constitutes the heart of verses 3-8: like 18:25, it questions the justice of God. In 20:5, Abimelech bases his question on the impossibility of knowing that Sarah is Abraham's wife; both said that she was his sister. Thus he shifts the blame to Abraham and solemnly declares his innocence: ". . . in integrity of heart and with pure hands . . ."; cf. Psalm 24:4.

God's response in Genesis 20:6-7 consists in a modification of the sentence subject to a condition stated in verse 7; thus he recognizes Abimelech's defense and confirms the propriety of his conduct. In verse 6b he states his reason for having afflicted Abimelech, although this point has not yet been mentioned; it is addressed later in verses 17-18. Familiarity with the story in Genesis 12:10-20 is presumed. The affliction that befell Abimelech (12:17) was not God's punishment; its purpose was to prevent actual adultery. God demonstrates his justice toward the innocent. Acquittal, however, is conditional upon the king's giving Abraham back his wife (v. 7). Here we still find an echo of the ancient view that even unintentional adultery is an outrage. Therefore the sentence of death imposed in verse 3b is reinstated if the condition is not fulfilled, for the woman belongs to another man. The use of "prophet" to describe Abraham reflects a later age, when the word took on the general meaning "man of God." As such, he can intercede for the king. This more general sense of "prophet" presupposes the historical development of prophecy.

8-13 Verse 8 is a bridge using the style of a dream narrative: upon awakening, the king assembles his court (like Pharaoh in Gen. 41:8). The court shares the king's fear of God; Abraham was wrong to think (20:11) there was no fear of God in the place! The second section is a dialogue between Abimelech and Abraham. It, too, deals with the question of guilt. Now Abimelech accuses Abraham (vv. 9-10) and Abraham defends himself (vv. 11-13); there is no mention of Abraham's acquittal. In emotional language, the king charges Abraham with having deceived him (v. 9); the question "What have you done to us?" appears in all three versions (cf. 12:18; 26:10). The second sentence is in the form of a reproach found throughout the world: "What have I done to you?" The third sentence adds for emphasis: "That was wrong." Then Abimelech interrogates Abraham as to why he did what he did; only now can Abraham reply (20:11-13). In his defense, he says in verses 11 and 13 why he claimed that Sarah was his sister. His explanation presupposes an admission of guilt. He can only appeal to extenuating circumstances. As so often, his apology begins: "Indeed, I thought. . . ." It presupposes Genesis 12:11-12 and adds: "I thought that there was no fear of God at all in this place." On this very point, however, he is confounded. "Fear of God" here means conduct that observes the basic ordinances governing human society, even with respect to strangers. The further explanation in 20:13 does nothing to improve Abraham's position. In the introductory clause, "When God called me to go from my father's house . . . ," the author of chapter 20 alludes to 12:1-5, thus presupposing 12:10-20 as the continuation of 12:1-3. This is further evidence that the present chapter is a retelling of the story. The extra statement Abraham inserts (20:12) is only a further expression of his embarrassment. Abraham can explain why he did what he did, but he cannot deny his guilt. Therefore we find no acquittal as in the case of Abimelech (vv. 6-7).

14-18 In this concluding section, Abimelech makes amends by giving Sarah back (vv. 14-16); in response to Abraham's intercession, God makes amends to Abimelech (vv. 17-18). The king not only gives Abraham back his wife but presents him with generous gifts as well (v. 14), including freedom of movement throughout the entire land.

He hands over to Abraham a large sum of money for Sarah as an "eye covering," that is, a vindication of her honor, lest others treat her with disrespect. The last three words of the Hebrew text are incomprehensible; a minor emendation makes them consistent with what has gone before: "Thus you are entirely vindicated." The point is that Abimelech generously does everything he can to compensate for the damage, even though he is not guilty in any sense. He does so out of a fear of God that puts Abraham to shame.

17-18 In response to Abraham's intercession, God lifts the affliction he has imposed on Abimelech and his family, so that they can once again bear children. Only here are we finally told about this affliction, alluded to in verse 6b; this explains the awkward position of verse 18. Its natural place would be between verses 2b and 3— unintentional and therefore all the more important evidence that the narrator of chapter 20 attached more importance to the dialogue in verses 3-16 than to the events recorded.

The astonishing thing about this retelling is primarily the fact that the Canaanite king is largely absolved of guilt; he is acquitted, but not Abraham. The theologian of a later period, reflecting on the old narrative, seeks to say to his generation that "fear of God" is quite possible outside of Israel. He silently lets Abraham's lame excuse serve as a warning against an attitude that causes people to act out of fear that others are wicked. At the same time, he says to his generation that God's treatment of his own far transcends what their pusillanimity expects of him. Abraham's blame for the damage done is not whitewashed. But it cannot stand in the way of God's mercy. This Abraham learns, to his deep shame. Furthermore, even though he is guilty, he can intercede for others; despite his limitations and deficiencies, he can be an agent of God's healing power. In this fashion, then, the stories of the patriarchs lived on. Reflection on questions raised by the old stories took the form of their retelling in ways that dealt with questions of the present. This includes the universalistic notion that reverence and fear of God may also be found in a Canaanite king.

21:1-7 THE BIRTH OF ISAAC

1 *But Yahweh visited Sarah, as he had said,*
and Yahweh did to Sarah as he had spoken:
2 *Sarah became pregnant and bore Abraham a son*
in his old age at the time that God had said to him.
3   *And Abraham called the son born to him,*
whom Sarah had borne to him, Isaac.

4	*And Abraham circumcised Isaac his son*
	at the age of eight days, as God had commanded him.
5	*But Abraham was one hundred years old*
	when his son Isaac was born to him.
6a	*And Sarah said: Laughter has God prepared for me.*
7	*And she said: Who would have announced to Abraham,*
	Sarah suckles a child! Because I have borne him a son
	in his old age,
6b	*everyone who hears it will laugh for me.*

The account of Isaac's birth brings to a close the chain of events that began with the statement that Sarah was childless (Gen. 11:30). Like the beginning in 11:27-32, this conclusion in 21:1-7 is the work of a redactor combining elements of J and P; it, too, is nevertheless a single homogeneous literary unit. It recounts the birth of a child, referring back to earlier predictions, especially in chapters 17 and 18. Sarah had been childless; now she receives a son, as had been promised her. The central verses (21:3-5) are from P; verses 1-2 are common to J and P; verses 6-7 are from J. Verse 1 brings the two narratives in chapters 17 and 18 to a conclusion, for in both Sarah was promised a son. Verse 1a might have more to do with chapter 18, verse 1b with chapter 17; apart from this, however, the parallelism of the two synonymous statements emphasizes God's favor and intervention, as in Luke 1:68. In Genesis 21:2, the narrative issues in a genealogical conclusion; but it alludes once again to the promise (17:21; 18:10, 14) and thus in context to Sarah and Abraham's advanced age (17:17, 24; 18:11-14). This conclusion, therefore, is intended deliberately to encompass both narratives recording the promise of a son.

In 21:3-5, a passage from P has been incorporated without change. Naming comes with pregnancy and birth; as always in P, it is the father who names the child. The name had been enjoined in 17:19: ". . . and you shall call him Isaac." Circumcision follows, as commanded in 17:12. As elsewhere in P (16:16; 17:24), Abraham's age is stated in 21:5. Verse 6 follows verse 2; here the mother names the child, with the explanation of the name coming in verse 6. In verse 3 (P), the father gives the name. Here it is clear that verses 1-6 are a composite of two versions, but they have been combined so skillfully that there is no apparent discontinuity. The explanation "Laughter has God prepared for me" interprets the name as a cry of praise. "Laughter" is here synonymous with joy. Verse 6b says that others share in the joy: ". . . everyone who hears it will laugh for me."

Verse 7 is a further expression of the mother's joy at the birth of her child; it comprises two rhythmic clauses. The exclamation means: "Who would ever have thought that I would have a child!" But the "who would have thought" is presented as an event: the father receives a message that his wife has borne him a child (cf. Jer. 20:15; Job 3:3). This is the traditional form taken by this message of the birth of a child. It has survived the centuries, with different emphases. During the monarchy, the birth of a child was important for the continuation of the dynasty; it thus became a message of rejoicing for the entire nation. After the fall of the monarchy, the ancient form was used to announce the birth of the savior king: "A child is born to us, a son is given to us!" (Isa. 9:6). It comes to life once more in the announcement of the savior in Luke 2: "For to you is born this day the Savior."

21:8-21   HAGAR AND HER CHILD

8   *The child grew and was weaned.*
And on the day that Isaac was weaned,
Abraham held a great feast.
9   *But when Sarah saw the son of Hagar the Egyptian,*
whom she had borne to Abraham,
playing with her son Isaac, she said to Abraham:
10   *Drive out this servant woman with her son!*
For the son of this servant woman shall not be heir
with my son, with Isaac!
11   *This troubled Abraham very much because of his son.*
12   *Then God said to Abraham: Do not be troubled*
because of the boy and your maidservant;
in all that Sarah says to you, do as she says.
For your descendants shall be called after Isaac.
13   *And moreover I will make the son of the maidservant*
into a great nation, for he is a descendant of yours.
14   *The next morning, Abraham took bread*
and a skin of water and gave them to Hagar,
and lifted the child onto her shoulder
and bade her farewell. But she went
and wandered in the desert of Beer-sheba.
15   *Now when the water in the skin was finished,*
she cast the child under a bush
16   *and went and sat over against him,*
about a bow's shot away; for she thought:
I cannot watch the death of the child.
So she sat over against him.
But the child raised his voice and cried.
17   *But God heard the voice of the boy,*
and the messenger of God called to Hagar from heaven
and said to her: What is the matter, Hagar? Do not be afraid,
for God has heard the boy's voice.

18 *Get up, take the boy where he is lying*
    and hold him by the hand,
    for I will make him into a great nation.
19 *And God opened her eyes and she saw a well of water.*
    And she went and filled the skin with water
    and gave the boy a drink.
20 *And God was with the boy.*
    And he grew and lived in the desert,
    and he became a bowman.
21 *And he lived in the desert of Paran,*
    and his mother took a wife for him from the land of Egypt.

We are told how the peaceful existence of Abraham's family was disrupted by a harsh demand made by Sarah (vv. 9-13). Hagar is forced to leave (vv. 14-16), but God averts disaster (vv. 17-19). This episode concludes with stability restored (vv. 20-21). The two dominant themes of conflict within the family and peril while traveling in the desert are appropriate to the patriarchal period, as is the genealogical framework (vv. 8, 20-21). Genesis 21:8-21 is a parallel to Genesis 16. Because it parallels a narrative belonging to J and uses "Elohim" throughout where J has "Yahweh," the written form of 21:8-21 must come from another hand. Since it follows the conclusion in verses 1-7, it goes back to an interpolator.

8 Genealogies include information about births, marriages, and deaths. Other material may be added, especially when a genealogy introduces a narrative. This happens here with the mention of a weaning feast, a practice unique to this passage. Children were usually weaned at the age of three; the feast concludes the first stage of life and can be called a rite of passage. It should be viewed in the light of the high infant mortality among primitive peoples. It was celebrated because the child had survived this first, especially vulnerable, stage of development.

9-13 The action is introduced in typical fashion: "And Sarah saw. . . ." Nothing is said about what she thought; that is clear from what she does. She sees the two children playing together; the listener can guess what she is thinking. The scene is followed by her harsh demand in verse 10. A woman's only future lies in her own son; Sarah intervenes ruthlessly on behalf of her son because her future is at stake. The other son must leave. A struggle for existence is being played within the family. The situation here differs from that in chapter 16. There Hagar is Sarah's personal servant; here she is Abraham's maidservant, and as such his concubine. Sarah has no relationship with the Hagar of chapter 21. Sarah's demand provokes a serious conflict; Abraham is deeply disturbed (v. 11). The conflict itself is not described; it probably lasted a considerable period. It is ended by God's directive to Abraham to accede to his wife Sarah's demand (vv. 12-13). The directive is based on an implicit promise: "You do not have to worry about Hagar and your son" (v. 12a). This says all that is necessary to the situation. The promise has been extrapolated into the future in the last clause of verse 12 and in verse 13, which speak of the descendants of Isaac and Ishmael. Only to Isaac shall the nation of Israel trace its beginnings, but Ishmael shall also become a great nation. This extension closely resembles Genesis 17:19-21 (P). In both cases, the point is the line dividing the descendants of Isaac from the descendants of Ishmael.

14-16 In the account that follows, only the bare minimum is related; but the silence accompanying the action is eloquent. Here Ishmael is still a child, although according to Genesis 17:25 (P) he would already be sixteen years old. Hagar sets out with the child early in the morning (cf. 19:27; 22:3). Abraham sees to the necessary provisions, which cannot amount to much. Abraham's gesture of placing the child in Hagar's arms speaks for itself. The following verb means literally "and he dismissed them." There is deliberately no mention of the blessing pronounced by Abraham at their departure. Abraham sends his concubine and his child out into the desert of Beer-sheba, the southern part of the Negeb. Hagar wanders about in the desert, a woman alone with a small child. The water runs out, and both face death from lack of water. Of the agony of the following hours, only a single moment is described: the child is on the point of death, and Hagar casts him under a bush; she herself sits down at the distance of a bowshot, awaiting the death of her child. The scene ends with the child's crying.

17-19 God hears the voice of the crying child, and that means his rescue. Thus the narrative reaches its goal. It tells of deliverance from death, a theme later sung by so many psalms: ". . . for he has heard the voice of my crying." This can be understood only by those who rejoice with those who have been delivered and join them in giving thanks to their deliverer. The old narrative continued the statement of verse 17a "But God heard . . ." with verse 19: "And God opened her eyes. . . ." In between has been inserted a speech by an angel (vv. 17b-18), a variant that gives the impression of being composite. A messenger from God comes to Hagar, asks: "What is the matter, Hagar?" and promises that her prayer will be heard by speaking the reassurance formula "Do not be afraid." He tells Hagar to take the boy by the hand; in other words, the messenger of God will show her the way to the life-saving well. The promise from verse 13 has been added in the last clause. In the earlier form of the narrative, verse 19 follows 17a directly; God intervenes as soon as he hears the boy's crying. Now Hagar sees the well she could not see before.

20-21 The tension is resolved; the child is saved, as is his mother. The narrative returns to stability with the statement: "God was with the boy." In his act of deliverance as well as his act of blessing, the God of Abraham remains with Ishmael, the son of the serving maid, who has been expelled from Abraham's family. He lives in the desert and becomes a bowman. This is the first and almost only time a weapon is mentioned in the Patriarchal History. Hagar, herself an Egyptian, finds an Egyptian girl to be his wife. A tribe both related to Israel and foreign to Israel comes into being.

God allowed Sarah, who cast out her rival, to have her way; but the rejected woman experiences the miracle of deliverance. Ishmael is "the son of the serving maid," but God heard the crying of a child dying of thirst. The history of the nation of Israel also begins with the experience of deliverance; here, too, it is "outcasts" who share this experience. The Bible can speak of Christ as Savior only through the experience of those who have encountered the Savior in mortal peril.

21:22-34 DISPUTE AND TREATY WITH ABIMELECH

22 *Now at that time Abimelech and Phicol, the commander of his army, said to Abraham:*
God is with you in all that you do.

23 *Now then swear to me by God that you will not deal falsely with me*
or my children or my children's children.
As I have shown favor to you, so do you to me
and the land in which you live as an alien.

24 *Then Abraham said: I swear.*

25 *But Abraham remonstrated with Abimelech*
about a well of water, which the servants of Abimelech had seized.

26 *Abimelech replied: I do not know*
who has done this. You have said nothing about it to me,
and I have heard nothing of it until today.

27 *Then Abraham took sheep and cattle and gave them to Abimelech,*
and the two of them made a treaty.

28 *And Abraham set seven ewe lambs apart.*

29 *Then Abimelech asked Abraham: What is the meaning of these seven lambs*
that you have set apart?

30 *He answered: The seven lambs you must accept from me*
so that they may be a witness
that I dug this well.

31 *Therefore the place is called Beer-sheba,*
because there they pledged themselves.

32 *So they made a treaty in Beer-sheba.*
Then Abimelech and Phicol, the commander of his army, departed
and returned to the land of the Philistines.

33 *But Abraham planted a tamarisk in Beer-sheba,*
and there he called upon the name of Yahweh, God eternal.

34 *And Abraham lived a long time as an alien*
in the land of the Philistines.

A late addition to the story of Abraham, which resembles the Isaac tradition in chapter 26, deals with a quarrel over a well. The right to wells was a vital matter for the nomadic patriarchs and their flocks. The theme therefore undoubtedly goes back to the patriarchal period. These narratives have preserved the memory that the very existence of the patriarchal families depended on the wells along their routes. In a later period these narratives were altered; the text of chapter 21 exalts Abraham by having a king make a treaty with Abraham and ask for his favor in a quarrel over a well.

22-24, 27   The scene is introduced by a linking formula, "at that time," which presupposes a continuous story of Abraham (cf. Gen. 15:1; 38:1). In fact, the scene should be introduced by Abimelech's coming to Abraham, which is echoed by his departure in 21:32; but such an introduction is lacking. Abimelech addresses Abraham, recognizing his power and making a request. A king asks a nomadic shepherd to swear always to treat him fairly. These words can only date from a time when people no longer had a clear idea of the patriarchal period but wanted to exalt the father of the nation: a king begs him for a favor! Abraham accedes to the request (v. 24). The parallel in chapter 26 shows, however, that a formal treaty, mutually binding, was agreed to. This is only alluded to in 21:27. The animals Abraham gives to Abimelech are in preparation for the ceremony. The treaty in verse 27b is a mutual nonaggression pact.

25-26, 28-32   A new episode begins with verse 25, for Abraham can hardly remonstrate with Abimelech immediately after an oath of loyalty. In Genesis 26:27, too, Isaac remonstrates with Abimelech, but under more reasonable circumstances. Our passage records a quarrel over a well; as in chapter 26, it leads to the etymology of a toponym. Chapter 21 does more to emphasize the superiority of Abraham than does chapter 26. Genesis 21:28-30 continues verses 25-26. In verse 26 Abimelech's answer was conciliatory; now we are told how Abraham tricks Abimelech into recognizing his right to the well. He sets seven ewe lambs aside; the catchword "seven" leads up to the meaning of the well's name. Abimelech asks what this action means. Abraham says that they are a present and urges Abimelech to accept them. In this case, rejection of the gift would also have denied

157

Abraham's right to the well. Because acceptance of the gift takes place before witnesses, it becomes an attestation (Hebrew ʿēḏāh); here the gift has binding force. Abraham has emerged victorious from the conflict. This event lent the place its name: "Beer-sheba" means "well of seven" (v. 31a). On the basis of verse 24, however, verse 31b adds another explanation: "well of the oath." Verse 32a follows upon verse 27b. The conclusion (v. 32b) reports Abimelech's departure with his commander.

33-34   All narratives of quarrels over wells are set along routes of migration; they are framed by itineraries. Genesis 21:33, too, belongs to an itinerary, like Genesis 12:6. Only in the present passage is it recorded that Abraham planted a tree at a stopping place on his travels. This does not refer to the founding of a cult. The tree is intended as a landmark; they will come upon it again in the course of the next migration that brings them to this place. As Abraham does everywhere he stops, he calls upon the name of God (cf. 12:8). Only here in the Patriarchal History is God referred to as El Olam, "God eternal." The Hebrew word ʿôlām does not mean an eternity beyond all time, but an immeasurably long stretch of time. Genesis 21:34 is a redactional conclusion to verses 22-33.

22:1-19   ABRAHAM'S SACRIFICE

1   *Now it happened after these events*
    that God tested Abraham. He said to him: Abraham!
    He answered: Here I am.
2   *And he said: Take your son, your only son,*
    whom you love, Isaac,
    and go forth to the land of Moriah and offer him there
    as a burnt offering on one of the mountains
    that I will tell you.

3   *And Abraham rose early in the morning,*
    saddled his donkey, and took his two servants
    and his son Isaac with him.
    He had split wood for the burnt offering.
    And he set out and went to the place
    that God had told him.

4   *On the third day, Abraham raised his eyes*
    and saw the place from a distance.
5   *And Abraham said to his servants:*
    Stay here with the donkey;
    I and the boy want to go there and worship.
    Then we will come back to you.

6   *Then Abraham took wood for the burnt offering*
       and laid it upon his son Isaac.
       He himself took the fire and the knife.

       So the two went on together.
7   *Then Isaac said to his father Abraham: Father!*
       And he said: Yes, my son.
       And he said: Behold, fire is here and wood is here,
       but where is the animal for the sacrifice?
8   *And Abraham said:*
       God will provide an animal for the burnt offering, my son.
       So the two went on together.
9   *And they came to the place that God had told them.*
       And Abraham built the altar there,
       and arranged the wood on it;
       then he bound his son Isaac
       and laid him on the altar, on top of the wood.
10   *And Abraham stretched out his hand and took the knife*
       to slaughter his son.
11   *Then the angel of Yahweh cried to him from heaven and said:*
       Abraham! Abraham! And he said: Here I am.
12   *And he said: Do not put your hand on the boy*
       and do him no harm.
       For now I know that you fear God,
       because you have not refused me your son, your only son.
13   *And Abraham raised his eyes and looked, and behold,*
       there was a ram entangled in the bushes by its horns.
       And Abraham went and took the ram
       and offered it in sacrifice in place of his son.
14   *And Abraham gave this place the name "Yahweh sees,"*
       of which one still says today:
       On the mountain Yahweh makes himself seen.

15   *And the angel of Yahweh cried out to Abraham a second time from heaven:*
16   *I swear by myself—an oracle of Yahweh—*
       because you have done this and have not withheld from me your son, your
       only son,
17   *therefore I will bless you and make your seed prosper*
       like the stars in the heavens
       and like the sand on the seashore,
       and your posterity will possess the gate of their enemies.
18   *And through your seed all the nations of the earth shall bless themselves,*
       because you have listened to my voice.

19   *Then Abraham went back to his servants,*
       and they set out and went together to Beer-sheba,
       and Abraham stayed in Beer-sheba.

This narrative begins with a statement of its theme (v. 1a): God tests Abraham. The structure of the text reflects the elements of the test. In verses 1b-2, the task is imposed; in verses 3-10, Abraham carries out the task up to a certain point; in verses 11-12a, he is exempted from completing the task. Verse 12b recognizes that the test has been passed and substitutes a different conclusion; verse 13 records Abraham's reaction; verses 14 and 19 conclude the narrative with Abraham's return. Verses 15-18 are a later addition.

Genesis 22 is one of the most beautiful narratives in the Old Testament; here it is especially important that exegesis should make it possible to hear the text itself.

1-2   The introductory statement makes it clear that Genesis 22 is a theological narrative. God's "testing" is a secondary interpretation of an event, not the event itself. The verb "test" is characteristic of Deuteronomic interpretation of history: God tested his people on their journey through the desert (Deut. 8:2). The notion that God tests his people is older than the idea of testing a single individual (Job 1). The theological narrative of Genesis 22 must therefore be relatively late. God speaks to Abraham as one human being to another (v. 1b); contact is established immediately (cf. vv. 7 and 11). The command, terrible as it is, is spoken from this shared intimacy. (Immanuel Kant, abstracting the content of the spoken word from the word as a form of address, concludes that God could not have spoken these words.) The command comprises a series of three imperatives. The need for Abraham to seek out a distant place for the sacrifice is the idea of a late period. The formulation of the directive is similar to Genesis 12:1; possibly the echo of the beginning is deliberate. The words "your only son, whom you love" are directed at the audience of the narrative. They are intended to underline the harshness of God's demand. The destination is described only as a land, the "land of Moriah"; the name appears elsewhere only in 2 Chronicles 3:1, where "the mountain Moriah" refers to the temple mountain of Jerusalem. Perhaps the name was changed at a later date to reflect this identification. The Samaritans claim Mount Gerizim as the mountain of sacrifice.

The third imperative orders Abraham to sacrifice his child. Human sacrifice, especially child sacrifice, is attested frequently in the history of religions; it was practiced by Israel's neighbors. It is hardly known in primitive religions. It appears to have existed only during limited periods; the substitution of animal sacrifice for human sacrifice is also widely attested. In the Old Testament, sacrifice of a firstborn son is commanded by Exodus 22:29 (34:19), but redemption of the sacrifice is also commanded by Exodus 34:20 and 13:13. It is later forbidden on penalty of death (Lev. 18:21; 20:2-5). Everywhere child sacrifice is mentioned in the Old Testament it is condemned.

3-10   The command is followed by an account of how Abraham carries it out. Verse 3 records the preparations in detail; of the journey, all that is described is the moment when Abraham sees the mountain in the distance (v. 4). At this moment begins the drama, in which the father and his son will be the only actors. Abraham must now leave behind the two servants, who represent his household. Father and son alone together on their journey constitutes the setting of verses 6-8. It is emphasized by the statement: "So the two went on together." Their dialogue (vv. 7-8) is organized around five repetitions (in the Hebrew) of "And he said," the monotony of which increases the tension. It begins with a moment of human contact: from the silence in which each is alone, it establishes the bond that makes conversation possible. But the father does not answer his son's question directly; he conceals his task from his son. His answer, however, "God will provide an animal for the burnt offering," points to God as the one who will answer the question. What for him, the father, has been a settled fact ever since God's command he represents to his son as an open possibility for God. The meaning of his answer will be confirmed subsequently in the name Abraham gives the mountain.

Isaac does not pursue his question. He has sensed that his father cannot tell him more. The conversation must remain open—that is what the concluding statement means. Abraham must carry out God's command; verses 9-10 follow verse 4. The description of the sacrifice is consistent with the patriarchal period in that the father himself performs the sacrifice and first must build the altar. Furthermore, he does not use sacral implements but items he has brought from home. Up to the final moment he does not waver from carrying out God's command.

11-12 When Abraham stretches out his hand to kill his son, the turning point comes (vv. 11-12). Abraham hears a voice that countermands the order to kill his son, on the grounds that Abraham has passed the test (v. 1). When God's word intervenes in the midst of a chain of actions, the patriarchal stories refer to a messenger of God. In this late narrative, however, it is no longer an earthly messenger as in chapter 16 but a being "from heaven." The repeated cry of Abraham's name (22:11a; cf. 1b, 7) is the loudest word in the narrative and marks its turning point. In it we already hear the joy of the good news to come. This command, too, comprises two clauses. "Do him no harm" means that nothing will happen to the child; this was God's intent from the beginning. At its high points, the narrative often takes on poetic form.

13-14 The sacrificial action interrupted by the angel's cry in verses 11-12 must be completed; only then will the sacrifice of the child cease to be necessary. Abraham's seeing the ram at this moment is to be understood as a directive from God. Now Abraham knows that he is doing God's will when he sacrifices the ram instead of his son. At this point we hear an echo of the substitution of animal sacrifice for human sacrifice. Only now can we hear Abraham's reaction to what has taken place (v. 14). It is contained in the name he gives the place where this has happened: "Yahweh sees [= 'takes note']." This name is an expression of deliverance from desperate need, an expression of joy, praise of God. It reflects the answer Abraham gave his son in their darkest hour. As a name permanently attached to this place, it will continue to bear witness to what took place here, to the God who "sees his own," the God who sees the anguish of those in the depths. Verse 14b is a different and secondary etymology of the name: "Yahweh appears." The sanctuary on the mountain is named for a manifestation of God.

15-18   Verses 15-18 are a secondary addition, recognizable as such from the words "a second time" that link them with what has gone before and from their different style. These verses do not narrate events but rather extend the promise. Following the bridge in verse 15, verse 16a introduces the promise as an oath spoken by God (as in ch. 15). God's swearing by himself is found elsewhere only in Exodus 32:13, in the same context; in both passages, God confirms the promise of increase by his oath. This reinforcement of the promise belongs to a late period, as do the phrase "oracle of Yahweh," which presupposes the development of prophecy, and the description of the promise as a reward for human conduct (Gen. 22:16b and 18b), which presupposes Deuteronomic theology. The promises of the patriarchal period are unconditional. Verses 17-18a promise Abraham blessing and increase, like the stars and the sand by the sea, as well as victories (cf. 24:60) and the extension of the blessing to the nations (22:18a). The promise is made with Israel in mind. All its individual clauses are also found elsewhere.

19   Verse 19 should be read immediately following verse 14a. Once the tension is resolved, the narrative returns to a stable situation. Abraham returns with Isaac to his servants, and together they go back to Beer-sheba. In the final clause, the narrative merges into an itinerary; in an earlier version, this itinerary with its mention of Beer-sheba probably also began the narrative.

To read this narrative as glorifying a person is to misunderstand it; panegyrics on Abraham (Søren Kierkegaard) miss its significance. Those who participate in this narrative know what it means to sacrifice a child. "One can only suffer with [Abraham] in helpless silence" (Ephraim A. Speiser). The point of the narrative is not to extol a human being but to praise God, who has seen suffering. In Romans

8:32, Paul is thinking of Genesis 22. In this verse he places the suffering of Christ in the larger context of the suffering of God. The narrative is interpreted very differently in Hebrews 11 and James 2:21-23. What matters, however, is not the variety of interpretations but the continued vitality of the story.

22:20-24   THE DESCENDANTS OF NAHOR

20   *It happened after these events*
that Abraham received the news:
Milcah, too, has borne children to your brother Nahor.
21   *Uz his firstborn, and Buz his brother,*
and Kemuel the father of Aram,
22   *Chesed, Hazo, Pildash, Jidlaph, and Bethuel.*
23   *Bethuel begot Rebekah.*
These eight Milcah bore to Nahor, Abraham's brother.
24   *And his second wife, whose name was Reumah, gave birth also:*
Tebah, Gaham, Tahash, and Maacah.

Just as a genealogy of Abraham's family introduces the Abraham cycle (Gen. 11:1-32), so too such a genealogy concludes it, listing the sons of Nahor by Milcah (22:21-23) and his second wife Reumah (v. 24): eight sons by the former and four by the latter, like the sons of Jacob. The names of the two wives and most of the sons are personal names. This genealogy is the outgrowth of a family history; only later did it come to reflect a group of tribes (cf. the number twelve).

20   Verse 20 is a bridge in the form of a message to the father (cf. 21:7). The "too" with Milcah refers back to Sarah in Gen. 21:2-3. Sarah and Milcah are mentioned together in 11:29; probably at one time 22:20-24 followed 21:1-8.

21-23   Of Milcah's sons, six have names that are personal names only; the names of the two oldest, Uz and Buz, are also place names (cf. Jer. 25:20-23; also Job 1:1-3; 32:2). According to Gen. 36:28, Uz was located in northern Edom; Buz was probably close by. A secondary addition mentions Rebekah as the daughter of Bethuel (22:23), looking forward to chapter 24.

24   Three of Nahor's sons by Reumah have purely personal names, which occur only here. "Maacah" is also the name of a region near Mount Hermon (Josh. 12:5).

Like Genesis 11:27-32, the purpose of the genealogy of Nahor's descendants is to point out the relationship of the father of the Israelite nation with a group of other nations.

23:1-20 SARAH'S DEATH AND THE PURCHASE OF THE BURIAL CAVE

1   Sarah lived 127 years,
2   then Sarah died at Kiriath-arba, that is, Hebron,
    in the land of Canaan. And Abraham went
    to mourn for Sarah and to weep for her.
3   Then Abraham arose from before his dead wife
    and said to the Hittites:
4   As an alien and sojourner I am among you;
    give me land for burial among you,
    that I may bring out my dead and bury her.
5   Then the Hittites answered Abraham:
6   Please listen to us, my lord.
    You are a godly prince in our midst;
    bury your dead in the best grave we have.
    None of us will refuse you his grave
    to bury your dead.
7   Then Abraham arose and bowed low before the people of the land, before the
    Hittites.
8   And he said to them: If it is then your will
    that I should bring out my dead and bury her,
    then listen to me and intercede for me with Ephron,
    the son of Zohar,
9   that he may give me the cave of Machpelah, which he owns,
    which is at the end of his property; at the full current price
    let him give it to me in your presence to possess as a burial place.
10   But Ephron was sitting among the Hittites; and Ephron the Hittite
    answered Abraham before the Hittites, before all
    who had come into the gate of the city, as follows:
11   But please listen to me, my lord!
    The piece of property—I make a gift of it to you; the cave upon it
    I also give to you. Before the eyes of my people
    I give it to you. Bury your dead.
12   Then Abraham bowed low before the people of the land
13   and said to Ephron, so that the people of the land could hear:
    But please, if you will, listen to me!
    I will pay the price of the property; take it from me,
    that I may bury my dead.
14   But Ephron answered Abraham:
15   Please listen to me, my lord!
    a piece of land worth four hundred shekels of silver—
    what is that between you and me! Now bury your dead.
16   And Abraham came to an agreement with Ephron, and Abraham weighed
    out for Ephron the sum that he had named in the presence of the Hittites,
    four hundred shekels of silver at the current merchants' rate.
17   Thus the property of Ephron at Machpelah,

opposite Mamre, the property together with the cave,
with all the trees upon the property and in the whole area surrounding it,
18 *was made over to Abraham as owner before the eyes of the Hittites,*
all who had come into the gate of the city.

19 *Afterwards Abraham buried his wife Sarah in the cave*
on the property of Machpelah, opposite Mamre,
that is, Hebron, in the land of Canaan.
20 *Thus the property together with the cave upon it was made over by the*
Hittites into Abraham's possession as a burial place.

The account of Sarah's death in 23:1-2, 19 concludes the story of
Abraham in P. It has been expanded by the addition of an account of
how Abraham purchased her grave (vv. 3-18, 20), which is in turn to
be Abraham's grave. This expansion describes in detail the purchase
of the cave of Machpelah as a burial place in a series of three inter-
changes (vv. 3-6, 7-11, 12-18). The purpose of the purchase runs
through the whole account as a leitmotif: "to bury [Abraham's] dead"
(vv. 4, 6, 8, 11, 13, 15). There are many ancient Near Eastern parallels
illustrating the sale and purchase of a piece of land—in Neo-Babylo-
nian dialogue contracts, for example. There is no evidence, however,
to indicate that the author was using specific sources; the procedure
was a matter of general knowledge. The chapter as a whole was
composed by P.

1-2 The report of Sarah's death follows 21:2-3 (P); she died at
Hebron, 22 miles south of Jerusalem at the intersection of four
routes. The graves of the patriarchs were localized east of Hebron,
under the great mosque.

Abraham performs the ritual of mourning, going outside to lament the dead (cf. Ezek. 24:15-23).

3-6 When the mourning is finished, burial must take place
(v. 19); Abraham wishes to purchase a site from the local inhabitants.
Here they are called "Hittites," a late term for the pre-Israelite inhabitants of Palestine, usually called Canaanites. Such a purchase concerns the entire community, before whose representatives the transaction takes place. Abraham requests a burial place for "[his] dead"
(v. 4); his request is granted with polite formality. As an "alien and
sojourner" he can acquire property only with the appro. : of the
community. The response of the citizens (vv. 5-6) shows respect for
Abraham: the speaker addresses him as "lord" and calls him a "godly
prince"; the honorific title is probably intended to suggest that Abraham is under divine protection. The citizens generously give him
free choice; none will refuse him a burial site.

7-11 The second interchange begins with Abraham's bow to
express his gratitude (v. 7). He accepts their offer and voices his
desire for a specific burial site, asking the representatives of the

community to support his request before Ephron, the site's owner, and expressing his willingness to purchase the site for its full commercial value (vv. 8-9). The owner of the property thereupon offers him all of it, including the cave, as a gift; the rest of the citizenry are witnesses to this offer (vv. 10-11). Of course everyone understands this generous gesture; how "generous" the offer is will be shown by the purchase price named in verse 15.

12-18   Again Abraham bows (cf. v. 7). The sale of a piece of property is here a social transaction of utmost significance; it is carried out according to fixed forms, which reveal a cultural structure that prevented buying and selling from being reduced to a mere commercial transaction. Abraham expresses his thanks for the gift, but reacts in the expected way by repeating his offer to purchase the property (vv. 12-13). Now Ephron can name his price, which is extremely high: four hundred shekels of silver! He skillfully maintains the appearance of generosity by suggesting that the price is trivial: "What is that between you and me!" His words "Bury your dead" are made to sound like a favor he is granting Abraham. This subtle humor is also part of the culture of buying and selling.

Abraham agrees to accept the price, although he knows that it is much too high. For him, what matters is the significance of this purchase. The acquisition of the burial site is so important to Abraham that he will pay any price for it. He completes the transaction by weighing out the sum in pieces of silver before the eyes of the citizens, who thus become witnesses to the change of ownership (v. 16). The result of the transaction is then restated in precise detail, including a description of the property acquired. It is emphasized once more that the agreement was struck before witnesses; the witnesses vouch for its validity, rather than a written bill of sale.

19-20   Only now can the narrative recount Sarah's burial. This report will later be followed by that of other burials: Abraham (Gen. 25:9); Isaac, Rebekah, and Leah (49:30-32); and Jacob (50:13). The concluding sentence (23:20) links the burial (v. 19) with the purchase (vv. 17-18): Sarah is buried on the property acquired by Abraham.

The reason this genealogical report was expanded to include a detailed description of the purchase appears in the repeated leitmotif. The property that has been acquired is not a small, representative piece of the promised land, but simply a site for a grave. Such a transaction is of course improbable in the patriarchal period; it seems out of character with the life of nomads herding sheep and goats, and it is not attested elsewhere. It makes sense, however, from the perspective of the Exile and the exilic period, when the people banished from their land wanted at least a burial place for "their dead" to call their own. This is the real background to the leitmotif in chapter 23.

This observation makes it even clearer that, in the three sections of the Patriarchal History where P becomes more discursive, he is establishing the three most important family rituals antedating the cult: birth (chapter 17), marriage (chapter 26), and death (chapter 23). In the exilic period, the family became the primary vehicle for the survival of the people and their religion.

24:1-67   THE WOOING OF REBEKAH

1   *Abraham was now old and advanced in years,*
     and Yahweh had blessed Abraham in everything.

2   *Then Abraham spoke to his servant, the oldest of his household,*
     who administered all that he had:
     Now put your hand under my thigh!

3   *I will have you swear by Yahweh,*
     the God of heaven and earth, that for my son
     you will not take a wife from the daughters of the Canaanites,
     among whom I live.

4   *Rather you shall go to my own land and to my own kinsmen*
     to take a wife for my son Isaac.

5   *And the servant said to him: Perhaps the woman will not want to follow me*
     to this land; shall I then bring your son back to the land whence you came?

6   *And Abraham answered him: Take care*
     that you do not bring my son back there.

7   *Yahweh, the God of heaven, who brought me from my father's house*
     and from the land of my kinsmen,
     who spoke to me and swore to me:
     To your posterity I will give this land—
     he will send his angel before you
     so that you will be able to take a wife for my son from there.

8   *But if the woman is not willing to follow you,*
     then you are free from this oath to me;
     but you must not bring my son back there.

9   *The servant then put his hand under the thigh of Abraham,*
     his master, and swore to him to act according to these words.

10   *Then the servant took ten of his master's camels*
     and all sorts of goods from his master,
     and set out and went to Aram Naharaim, to the city of Nahor.

11   *Then he made the camels kneel down outside the city*
     at the well, toward evening, at the time
     when the women come out to draw water.

12   *And he said: Yahweh, God of my master Abraham,*
     grant me success
     and show favor to my master Abraham.

13 *Behold, I am standing here at the well*
    where the daughters of the inhabitants of the city come out
    to draw water.

14 *Now the girl to whom I say: Please lower your jar*
    that I may drink, and who answers: Drink,
    and I will water your camels, too—let her be the one
    you have destined for your servant Isaac, and by this
    I will know that you have shown favor to my master.

15 *And even before he had finished speaking, behold, Rebekah came out,*
    the daughter of Bethuel the son of Milcah,
    the wife of Nahor the brother of Abraham;
    she was carrying her jar on her shoulder.

16 *She was a girl of very beautiful appearance, a virgin,*
    no man had touched her. She went down to the well,
    filled her jar, and came up again.

17 *Then the servant ran to meet her and said:*
    Please let me drink a little from your jar.

18 *She said: Drink, sir. And quickly she lowered her jar to her hand and gave*
    him a drink.

19 *When she had given him enough to drink, she said:*
    I will also draw water for your camels,
    until they have had enough to drink.

20 *And quickly she emptied her jar into the water trough,*
    and she drew water for all his camels.

21 *But the man gazed at her silently, to know*
    whether Yahweh would make his journey successful or not.

22 *Now when the camels had drunk enough, the man took a golden nose ring*
    weighing half a shekel
    and put it on her face, and two bracelets on her arms,
    each weighing ten gold shekels.

23 *And he said: Tell me, please, whose daughter are you?*
    Will we find room in your father's house to pass the night?

24 *She said to him: I am the daughter of Bethuel*
    the son of Milcah, whom she bore to Nahor.

25 *And she also said to him: We have plenty of straw and fodder, and room to*
    pass the night with us.

26 *Then the man bowed and prostrated himself before Yahweh,*

27 *and he said: Blessed be Yahweh, God of my master Abraham,*
    who has not withdrawn his steadfast love and fidelity from my master.
    As for me, Yahweh has truly led me safely along the way to the house of my
    master's brother.

28 *But the girl ran and related everything in the house of her mother.*

29 *But Rebekah had a brother, who name was Laban.*

30 *Now when he saw the nose ring and the bracelets on the arms of his sister,*
    and when he heard what his sister Rebekah had to tell: The man spoke thus
    and so to me, Laban ran out to the man at the well. And when he came to the
    man, behold, he was still standing with his camels at the well.

31 *And he said to him: Come in, blessed of Yahweh!*
Why are you standing outside? I have prepared the house and made room for the camels.
32 *Then the man came into the house, and Laban unloaded the camels and gave them straw and fodder,*
but to him and those with him water to wash their feet.
33 *Then he laid food before him, but he said:*
I will not eat until I have carried out my commission.
He replied: Speak!
34 *Now he said: I am the servant of Abraham.*
35 *Yahweh has blessed my master so that he has become very rich.*
He has given him sheep and cattle, silver and gold,
servants and maidservants, camels and asses.
36 *And Sarah, my master's wife, has borne him a son in her old age; to him he has given all that he has.*
37 *Now my master made me swear, saying: You must not take a wife for my son from the daughters of the Canaanites,*
in whose land I dwell.
38 *Rather you must go to the house of my father and to my family to take a wife for my son.*
39 *I answered my master: Perhaps the woman will not follow me.*
40 *Then he said to me: Yahweh, before whose face I have walked, will send his angel with you and will make your journey successful, so that you will bring back a wife for my son from my family and from the house of my father.*
41 *Then you will be free from the oath for me: if you go to my family and they do not give her to you,*
then you will be free from the oath for me.
42 *Now when I came to the well today, I said:*
Yahweh, God of my master Abraham, if you are really making the journey I undertake successful,
43 *behold, I am standing at the well; now the girl who comes out to draw water, and I say to her:*
Please give me a little water to drink from your jar,
44 *and she says: Drink, and I will water your camels, too—let her be the wife that Yahweh has destined for the son of my master.*
45 *And even before I had finished speaking to myself,*
behold, Rebekah came out with her jar on her shoulder, went down to the well, and drew water. And I said to her: Please give me a drink.
46 *Then quickly she lowered her jar and said: Drink, and I will water your camels, too.*
So I drank, and she also watered the camels.
47 *And I asked her: Whose daughter are you?*
And she answered: The daughter of Bethuel the son of Nahor, whom Milcah bore to him. Then I put the ring on her nose and the bracelets on her arms.
48 *And I bowed and prostrated myself before Yahweh and blessed Yahweh, the God of my master Abraham, who had led me the right way to take the daughter of my master's brother for his son.*

49   *And now, if you are disposed to show grace and fidelity toward my master,*
    so tell me, and if not, so tell me,
    that I may turn to the right or to the left.

50   *Then Laban and Bethuel answered: This has been arranged by Yahweh!*
    There is nothing we can say, pro or con.

51   *Here is Rebekah; take her and go, that she may be the wife of your master's*
    son, as Yahweh has destined.

52   *When Abraham's servant heard these words, he prostrated himself on the*
    ground before Yahweh.

53   *The servant then brought out ornaments of silver and gold*
    and garments and gave them to Rebekah,
    and also he gave costly gifts to her brother and to her mother.

54   *Then they ate and drank, he and the men with him, and spent the night. But*
    when they rose in the morning, he said: Let me go back to my master.

55   *But her brother and her mother said:*
    Let the girl stay with us some days, say ten days,
    then you may go.

56   *But he answered them: Do not detain me.*
    Since Yahweh has made my journey successful,
    allow me to go back to my master.

57   *Then they said: Let us call the girl herself and ask her.*

58   *So they called Rebekah and said to her: Will you go with this man? She*
    answered: I will go.

59   *So they said farewell to their sister Rebekah and her nurse and Abraham's*
    servant and his men.

60   *And they blessed Rebekah and said to her:*
        You, our sister, become thousands of thousands,
        may your posterity gain the gate of their enemies!

61   *Then Rebekah and her maid arose,*
    they mounted the camels and followed the man.
    And the servant took Rebekah and went.

62   *And Isaac had come from . . . to Beer-lahai-roi,*
    and was living in the region of the Negeb.

63   *When Isaac one evening went out into the field*
    for a stroll, he raised his eyes
    and saw camels coming.

64   *And when Rebekah raised her eyes and saw Isaac,*
    she dismounted from the camel

65   *and said to the servant: Who is this man,*
    who is coming across the field to meet us?
    The servant answered: That is my master.
    Then she took her veil and covered herself.

66   *But the servant told Isaac everything that he had accomplished.*

67   *Then Isaac led Rebekah to the tent of Sarah, his mother,*
    and he took Rebekah as his wife and loved her.
    So Isaac was consoled after his father's death.

Chapter 24 is the longest narrative in Genesis, recounted in un-
paralleled detail. But the story related is itself quite simple: Abraham

commissions his servant to fetch a wife for his son from his far-off family (vv. 1-9). The servant carries out his commission (vv. 10-66) and tells his master (now Isaac) that he has fulfilled it (v. 67). All this is to tell how Isaac acquired a wife. In essence, we are dealing with a genealogical notice; tension is created by uncertainty as to whether the project will succeed. At the same time, God's governance becomes a primary element in the story: everything depends on whether God will allow the successful performance of the commission.

The entire narrative is an artful literary composition based on a simple genealogical statement. It belongs in the context of the supplements following the provisional conclusion of the story of Abraham (21:1-7). Nevertheless, the section of the narrative describing the meeting at the well that leads to marriage has clear parallels in Genesis 29:1-14 (Jacob) and Exodus 2:15b-22 (Moses), which shows that this section is based on an earlier narrative that was once handed down by oral tradition. How this early narrative has been reshaped can be seen from the fact that nothing Genesis 24 says about God's miraculous guidance appears in the parallels. A family narrative based on a genealogical notice has been reshaped and expanded so as to illustrate God's guidance. At the beginning, Abraham promises his servant God's aid; at the critical moment, the servant prays for this assistance through a sign; the servant's thanksgiving confirms that the sign has been given and acknowledged by Laban. As its language shows, this reediting is substantially later than the ancient family narrative; compare, for example, verse 7 with Psalm 91:11.

1-9   Abraham has arrived at a ripe old age (v. 1); now he has but one wish. It is so important to him that, to see it fulfilled, he gives his servant a mandate in the form of an oath (vv. 2-4). The duties of the servant, whose importance is underscored by a triple introduction, correspond roughly to those of a steward. His name is not mentioned. As in Genesis 47:29, the oath involves the ritual of touching the generative organ; here, too, we are dealing with a last will prior to death (24:2). The servant is to swear "by Yahweh, the God of heaven and earth." The divine predicate here is similar to that in Genesis 14:19-20 and suggests the language of a late period (24:3a). Only now does Abraham state his request: his son is to take a wife from among his family, to whom the servant is to travel (vv. 3b-4). The servant merely clarifies one point; it goes without saying that he is ready to undertake the commission of his master (v. 5). Abraham answers his servant's question (vv. 6-8) by forbidding him expressly to take Isaac back to his homeland. This is because God has brought him forth from there (12:1-3) and promised him the land (12:7; 15:7, 18); this motivation presupposes a continuous story of Abraham. The promise of the land in the form of an oath is Deuteronomic language. At the same time, Abraham's answer introduces the leitmotif: the servant can be confident of God's guidance (24:7b). The "angel going before you" also appears in Exodus 23:20 with reference to the people and in Psalm 91:11 with reference to an individual. The servant swears the requested oath (Gen. 24:9, following up v. 2).

10-12   Only the beginning and end of the journey are recorded (vv. 10-11). The servant comes to the "city of Nahor" and stops to rest with his camels at the well outside the city. The well is a place of assembly for women and girls. The servant knows that the moment of decision is at hand; he prays to God that he may be successful in his mission and also asks for a sign by which he may recognize the right woman (vv. 12-14). Characteristic is the reshaping of what was once an omen, which really belongs to the realm of magic, into a prayer addressed to God; the sign will confirm God's guidance. The prayer is answered at once. A girl whose beauty and virginity are extolled comes to the well—she is the one! (vv. 15-16). As predicted by the sign, she gives the servant a drink of water at his request and also waters his camels (vv. 17-20). "But the man gazed at her silently . . .": with this statement the narrator succeeds in freezing the lovely picture by the well. In the servant's gaze, the commonplace event takes on profound significance in the context that dominates the narrative as a whole: ". . . to know whether Yahweh would make his journey successful" (v. 21; cf. v. 7).

22-27   Before the servant asks the crucial question, he rewards the girl with extravagant generosity simply for treating him and his animals so kindly (v. 22). Only then does he ask about her family and request accommodations. The servant hears the familiar names and receives the hoped-for invitation (vv. 23-25). Now he can breathe easier. This relaxation of tension, this joy over success finds expression in his prayer of thanksgiving. The spontaneous exclamation "God has led me here!" is thus placed in a solemn liturgical context (vv. 26-27) that recalls the Psalms. In this prayer the narrative reaches its first climax; the sentence in the middle of the prayer states the meaning of the narrative as such: "God has led me." It is a naive, childlike spirituality that speaks here, but what it says is fundamental to any relationship with God.

28-32   With verse 28, the scene shifts from the well to the house of Nahor, who is clearly dead; Laban is the head of the house (v. 31). "In the house of her mother," Rebekah recounts what has happened to her (v. 28). Laban invites the servant ("blessed of Yahweh"; cf. vv. 1b and 27) in and accommodates both him and his animals in the house.

33   Now follows the second part of the narrative, which recounts how the servant carries out the mandate he had received from his master Abraham. He refuses the invitation to eat, which is an

element of hospitality, until he has carried out his commission. The meal does not come until verse 54. But the servant asks first to have his message heard; his request is granted, and now he can say what is on his mind (vv. 34-49).

34-48   He introduces himself as Abraham's servant; everything he says relates to Abraham, not himself (vv. 34-36). This brings him to his commission, which he recounts in great detail (vv. 37-41), together with the events that have brought him into Laban's house (vv. 42-48). Verses 37-41 repeat verses 2-9, and verses 42-48 repeat verses 11-27. The detailed repetition has a clear purpose: if the listeners, and Laban in particular, share personally in the servant's story, they will be convinced that everything has been arranged by God, exactly the point made in verse 50. But the readers of the narrative also share personally in the experience of how a series of events turns into a narrative that itself plays a role in the train of events. That this narrative should undergo some variation when repeated is natural and springs from the situation to which it is addressed. Thus Genesis 24 is a parade example of how the stories of the patriarchs came into being: as oral narratives, they all had a function in the society in which they originated; then, as they were recounted to later generations, they took on their own life independent of their original situation.

49-52   With the servant's question, the narrative now arrives at its second climax (v. 49). Once again, the servant himself recedes entirely into the background; the answer is addressed to Abraham. Laban's response—the words "and Bethuel" are a later addition to show that the answer is also spoken in the name of Rebekah's father—is joyful and wholehearted assent. He has been persuaded: "This has been arranged by Yahweh!" In Laban's answer we hear the voice of the narrator—so wondrously has God acted in the lives of our ancestors! Yahweh has destined Rebekah to be Isaac's wife (v. 51). The servant's bow pronounces his Amen (v. 52).

53-58   The tension is relaxed. Now the servant brings out his gifts, and he and his retinue can sit down to a meal; he has carried out his commission. But the very next morning he asks permission to depart. Not even the customary friendly request to stay a while longer can detain him. He has an urgent desire to tell his master that his mission has been successful. Perhaps he is afraid that Abraham might die before his return. Once again we hear the leitmotif: "God has made my journey successful!" The girl, asked to decide for herself, agrees (vv. 57-58). She agrees not only to leave at once but also to journey to a foreign land and marry a man whom she does not yet know. She, too, has been persuaded that this is her appointed way.

59-61   And so the camel train can set out. Farewells are spoken, and those staying behind give their departing sister and daughter a blessing for her journey to a foreign land (v. 60). Here we see the earliest function of a blessing: it is given at departure, when a member of a family leaves its company. It is an effectual word, intended to influence the future of the one who leaves. A wish for increase is combined with a wish for victory. Probably the former originated as a nuptial blessing; the latter is an expansion relating to the tribe into which the family was to develop.

The caravan sets out (v. 61). First Rebekah and her maidservant make ready; then they are picked up by the servant and his retinue, and all set out.

62-65   Again departure is followed immediately by arrival. The meeting of Isaac and Rebekah is told with great restraint. Isaac is now dwelling in a different place, at Beer-lahai-roi in the Negeb (v. 62). He sees the caravan in the distance; Rebekah sees Isaac, learns who he is, and puts on her veil (vv. 63-65). There is only this delicate allusion; there is no need to say more. The meeting has been reduced to its absolute minimum, a single gesture by the girl. She wishes to show the customary respect to the man who will be her husband. The veil is not worn permanently, but a bride meets the bridegroom veiled.

66-67   The servant reports his fulfillment of Abraham's commission. The fact that he addresses Isaac presupposes that Abraham has died in the interim. He we see another function of narrative: reporting. Those who heard this report then continued to tell how Abraham's servant acquired a bride for Isaac. Thus the narrative came to life and was handed on.

The long narrative ends with a marriage (v. 67; cf. Ruth 4:13), thus merging once more into the genealogical account that constitutes the core of the narrative. But the marriage itself cannot be the last word here. What God has arranged through the success of the journey necessarily includes the blossoming of love between man and wife, who had been strangers to each other. This growth of love is profoundly related to the concluding statement: "So Isaac was consoled after his father's death" (the reading "mother's" is incorrect). Grief over death gives way to joy over new companionship. For Abraham to begin a history, not only must a child be born (Gen. 18), but two people must find each other in love.

This narrative is important for the history of prayer in the Old Testament because it shows that prayer is a reaction to events and that spontaneous petitions and thanksgivings addressed to God reflecting these events are a natural expression of life with God.

25:1-18 ABRAHAM'S DEATH AND HIS SONS' DESCENDANTS

1   *Abraham took another wife, whose name was Keturah.*
2   *She bore him Zimran and Jokshan, Medan and Midian, Ishbak and Shuah.*
3   *Jokshan begot Sheba and Dedan, and the sons of Dedan were the Asshurim, the Letushim, and the Leummim.*
4   *And the sons of Midian: Ephah, Epher, Hanoch, Abida, and Eldaah. All these are the descendants of Keturah.*
5   *But Abraham gave all his property to Isaac.*
6   *But to the sons of the other wives that Abraham had he gave presents and while he was still alive sent them away from his son Isaac eastward, to the eastern country.*

7   *This is the length of Abraham's life span that he lived: 175 years.*
8   *Then he expired. Abraham died at a ripe age, old and full of years, and was gathered to his people.*
9   *His sons Isaac and Ishmael buried him in the cave at Machpelah in the field of Ephron, the son of Zohar the Hittite, opposite Mamre,*
10   *the field that Abraham had bought from the Hittites. There Abraham and his wife Sarah were buried.*
11   *And after the death of Abraham, God blessed his son Isaac, and Isaac lived at Beer-lahai-roi.*

12   *This is the genealogy of Ishmael, the son of Abraham, whom Hagar the Egyptian, Sarah's maidservant, bore to Abraham.*
13   *And these are the names of the sons of Ishmael, according to their names and according to their birth order: Nebaioth, the firstborn of Ishmael,*
14   *then Kedar, Adbeel and Mibsam, Mishma, Dumah and Massah,*
15   *Hadad and Tema, Jetur, Naphish, and Kedemah.*
16   *These are the sons of Ishmael, and these are their names in their settlements and encampments; twelve princes according to their tribes.*
17   *And this is the life span of Ishmael: 137 years. Then he expired and died and was gathered to his people.*
18   *They lived from Havilah to Shur, east of Egypt, toward Assyria. He set himself before the face of all his brothers.*

The conclusion of the story of Abraham in Genesis 25:1-18 is a composite of various texts. The account of Abraham's death in verses 7-10 (P) is sandwiched between two genealogies tracing collateral lines descended from Abraham: the genealogy of the sons of Keturah (vv. 1-6) and the genealogy of Ishmael (vv. 12-18 [P]). The Priestly Document (P) ends its story of Abraham with 25:7-18; verses 1-6 are a secondary addition.

1-6   The genealogy of Keturah's sons in verses 2-4 is introduced in verse 1 by the statement that Abraham took another wife. Her name, "Keturah," which is not found elsewhere, means "incense"; it suggests the territory in which these tribes dwell: Arabia is the land of incense. Of the sixteen names in verses 2-4, a few (such as "Midian" and "Sheba") are attested as names of places or tribes in the Syroarabian desert. The ending *-an*, which occurs six times, points to the same area. Verses 1 and 5-6 constitute the framework; they guarantee that Isaac's inheritance will not be reduced.

7-11   Abraham's death is described in the fashion typical of the Patriarchal History, by telling how long he lived (v. 7). He died "at a ripe [literally 'good'] age," i.e., his death was not untimely. The idiom "old and full of years" says the same thing (cf. Gen. 35:28-29 [P]). Death is looked upon as the necessary and meaningful end of a human life, what we would call "a full life." At his death he "was gathered to his people." This does not refer to a state in which one might imagine the deceased, but to their significance for those still living: they are among the departed ancestors, whose memory is preserved. A peaceful death also requires burial, which is now described (25:9-10). These verses echo chapter 23: Abraham possesses a place where he can be buried. His sons bury him in peaceful harmony; P ignores the expulsion of Hagar and Ishmael. Genesis 25:11 would be more appropriate at the end of chapter 24, where it would tie in with 24:1 and also echo the statement of Isaac's dwelling place in 24:62. Possibly 25:11 has been transferred from the end of chapter 24 to its present position.

12-18   Verses 12-18 combine the *tôlᵉḏōt* of Ishmael (of which only the beginning [v. 12] and the end [v. 17] have been preserved) with a list of Ishmaelite tribes (vv. 13-16, 18). The information in verse 12 comes from chapters 16 and 21. A new introduction ("These are the names . . .") in 25:13a indicates that what follows is a list: verses 13b-15 record the twelve names, a group of Arabic tribes; verse 16 is a caption concluding the list. The double phrase "in their settlements and in their encampments" points to a culture in part nomadic and in part settled. Verse 18 continues verse 16; the territory occupied by the tribes is defined by two boundary points. Verse 18b adds a description of these tribes almost identical with Genesis 16:12b. It is typical of tribal oracles. Both 25:2-4 and 13-16, 18 deal with groups of Arabic tribes, tracing them back to Ishmael or another wife of Abraham. Verses 1-6 might be a secondary expansion of verses 12-18.

These genealogies at the end of the story of Abraham are meant to express that the blood relationship of these tribes to Abraham is more important than the political divisions and enmities of later ages. It is more deeply rooted. Abraham is the father of the religion of both Israel and Islam.

CONCLUDING REMARKS ON THE STORY OF ABRAHAM

We may summarize the development of Genesis 12–25 by saying that a redactor combined two existing stories of Abraham, one from the Yahwist (J) and one from the Priestly Document (P). We see the hand of the redactor (R) especially in his introduction (11:27-32) and conclusion (21:1-7). This work then continued to grow by accretion, because the oral tradition of the Abraham stories continued after the written documents had taken shape. We cannot name an author of these later texts; neither do they belong to a single literary work. They were instead added individually to the extant Abraham traditions. Several kinds of text were added. First are the promise texts, which constitute an independent tradition. Promises are added to narratives (Gen. 16:10, 12; 13:14-17; 22:15-18), independent promise narratives are composed (15:1-6; 15:7-21; 17), and Abraham's importance is grounded in the promises he received (18:18; 24:7). Then come the narratives that developed out of theological reflection (18:18b-33; 20:1-18; 22; 24), and finally chapter 14, a very late composite of different themes.

The Yahwist's work and the Priestly Document have conceptions of the story of Abraham that reflect their own periods. In the case of the Yahwist, the crucial point is the firm link he forges connecting Abraham, the patriarch from the dim past, with the history of Israel: Yahweh becomes the father of the nation Israel. This relationship is so firm that Yahweh becomes the God of Abraham. P borrows this conception and adapts it to his own situation. Because the continued existence of Israel itself is in danger, for P the heart of the Abraham story is the covenant between Abraham and God in chapter 17, the guarantee of Israel's existence grounded in its relationship with God, in worship and the law.

What the early narratives say about Abraham must be distinguished from these conceptions. The common element in these early texts is suggested by the word "father." The Abraham stories focus on the birth of a child, the preservation of its life and that of its parents in the face of mortal danger, and the continuation of Abraham's family into the next generation. This simple continuation of human life from one generation to the next has priority over all other areas of human existence. For Abraham, the future depends on the birth of a child. God speaks to him in the promise of a son, and God acts to preserve the son and his family. Everything that takes place in these texts is a transaction between Abraham and God, between God and Abraham. This relationship with God is the basic determinant of Abraham's existence.

JACOB AND ESAU   25:19–36:43

The conception behind chapters 25–36 as a whole is easy to see. At its heart is the conflict between Jacob and Esau (chapters 26–33), into which has been inserted the narrative of Jacob's sojourn with Laban (chapters 29–31), framed by the theophanies in chapters 28 and 32. The birth and naming of Jacob's sons (29:31-30:24) is an insertion within the insertion. The introduction (25:19-34) and conclusion (chapters 35–36) are essentially genealogical; they serve to make chapters 25–36 into a family history. The itineraries differ somewhat from those in chapters 12–25. They are dominated by the theme of "flight and return," introduced in chapter 27 and resolved in chapter 33. This marks the transition from brief narrative to larger narrative complex. The theme of this complex is the conflict between two brothers, Jacob and Esau; inserted into it is the conflict between Jacob and Laban, and into that conflict the conflict between Leah and Rachel. While chapters 12–25 are concerned with the continuity of generations over time, chapters 25–36 deal with concurrent struggles for existence and rank. Genesis 29–31 and 29:21–30:24 are variants on the conflict theme; in the former (between nephew and uncle), what is at stake is food; in the latter (between two women), it is social rank and status. The theophany and sanctuary narratives in chapters 28, 32, and 35 were originally independent narratives of a very different nature; they have been skillfully woven into the complex.

Chapters 26 and 34 have nothing to do with the story of Jacob and Esau; chapter 26 belongs to the Isaac tradition, and chapter 34 is an episode from the time of the judges.

In contrast to chapters 12–25, the promises play a minor role in 25–36. Here the typical promise is the promise of God's presence; this consists with the dominant role played by blessing in 25–36. In addition, there is less emphasis than in 12–25 on God's direct intervention and direct conversation with God. Instead, more importance is attached to institutions such as treaties, legal procedures, and cultic sites. All in all, we see here a stage of development that is later in many respects than in chapters 12–25.

GENESIS 25–36: JACOB AND ESAU

25:19-34　THE BIRTH OF ESAU AND JACOB; THE POT OF LENTIL SOUP

19　　　*This is the story of Isaac, the son of Abraham.*
　　　　Abraham begot Isaac.
20　　　*And Isaac was forty years old when he took as his wife Rebekah,*
　　　　the daughter of Bethuel the Aramean of Paddan-aram,
　　　　the sister of Laban the Aramean.
21　*But Isaac prayed to Yahweh on behalf of his wife, for she was barren.*
　And Yahweh heard his prayer,
　and Rebekah his wife became pregnant.
22　*And when the children were crushing each other in her womb,*
　she said: If this is so with me, then why do I live?
23　*And she went to inquire of Yahweh. And Yahweh said to her:*
　Two nations are in your body
　and two tribes [are separating themselves] in your womb.
　One tribe is stronger than the other,
　and the elder shall serve the younger.
24　*Now when the time came for her to give birth,*
　behold, there were twins in her womb.
25　*The first to come out was ruddy,*
　like a cloak of hair all over, and he was called Esau.
26　*Then his brother came out, his hand grasping Esau's heel, and he was called*
　Jacob.
　　　　But Isaac was sixty years old when they born.
27　*Now when the boys grew up, Esau became a man*
　expert in hunting, a man of the open field,
　but Jacob was a quiet man, who dwelt in tents.
28　*Isaac preferred Esau, because he liked to eat game,*
　but Jacob was the favorite of Rebekah.

29　*Once when Jacob was boiling a soup,*
　Esau came in from the field exhausted.
30　*And Esau said to Jacob: Let me swallow*
　some of that red stuff, of that red stuff there, for I am exhausted!
　Therefore he is called Edom.
31　*But Jacob said: First sell me your right as firstborn.*
32　*Then Esau replied: I am almost dying of hunger,*
　what use to me is my right as firstborn!
33　*Then Jacob said: First swear to me.*
　And he swore to him and thus sold
　to Jacob his right as firstborn.
34　*Then Jacob gave Esau bread and the bowl of lentil soup.*
　He ate and drank, rose up, and went.
　Thus Esau disdained his right as firstborn.

19-26   The introduction to the story of Jacob and Esau is a composite
put together by the redactor (R) using J (vv. 19-20) and P (v. 26b), like
Genesis 11:27-32. It is an expanded genealogy; the unusual feature is
the birth of twins. The story to follow deals with the hostility between these twins. Everything reported here has to do with events
within the family; only 25:22-23 speaks of the destiny of nations. This
saying is an interpolation; verse 24 follows verse 21.

19-20   In P these verses follow the death and burial of Abraham
in 25:7-10. Now begins the story of Isaac, or rather the story of his
family. "Abraham begot Isaac" is probably a gloss. Verse 20 records
the descent of Rebekah in great detail, echoing the narrative in chapter 24. The toponym "Paddan-aram" appears only in P.

21-24   These verses come from J; the juncture is awkward. Verse
21 is a brief summary of a narrative: "Isaac prayed to Yahweh on
behalf of his wife, and Yahweh heard his prayer." We may assume
that the narrative began with some such statement as Genesis 11:30.
It dates from the patriarchal period, because the father intercedes
personally for his wife. Genesis 25:24 also belongs to this period.

22-23   These verses constitute an independent episode, relating
to a theme from the patriarchal period, which has been inserted here.
In Rebekah's twin sons, later generations saw the tribal ancestors of
Israel and Edom. Stories were told of how the children fought while
still in the womb, which the mother took as an evil omen. This theme
can go back to the patriarchal period. The mother's lament, "If so,
then why do I live?" is the primordial question Why, a universal
expression of suffering found throughout human civilization (cf.
Gen. 27:46; Jer. 20:18, etc.). The following statement, however, presupposes the existence of oracles, an institution of the sedentary
period. The texts that use the expression "inquire of Yahweh" date
overwhelmingly from the period of the Monarchy. God's answer
points to the same period. A rhythmic oracle like Genesis 9:25-27;
27:27-29, and resembling the tribal oracles, it predicts the subjugation of an ancient people by an upstart smaller people. In it we hear
the victor's pride; it is a *vaticinium ex eventu,* which may have originated at the court of David in celebration of the victory over Edom.
The poetic power with which this oracle bridges an historical chasm
is astonishing. The generation of the Early Monarchy sees in an event
from the distant patriarchal age a reference to its own present experience. The parallels in Genesis 27:29, 40 are similarly powerful. This
period also saw the origin of the Yahwist's history, which associated
the history of the patriarchs with the history of the nation.

24-26   A genealogical statement has been expanded into a narrative. When Rebekah gives birth, she is discovered to have twins. In
Genesis 38:27-30, too, the birth of twins raises a special question:

which is the firstborn? As is often the case, the names of the twins are related to the circumstances of their birth. We are told that "the first to come out was ruddy"; the Hebrew word *ʾdmônî*, "ruddy," "reddish brown," would lead us to expect the name "Edom"; instead we are given a second description: "like a cloak of hair" (cf. the cloak of Elijah in 2 Kgs. 2 and the cloak of John the Baptist in Matt. 3:4). Here we would expect the name "Seir," corresponding to Hebrew *śēʿār* "hair" (cf. the hill country of Seir in the land of Edom [Gen. 36:8, 9]). But instead we are told that he was called Esau, a name that has nothing to do with either description. The explanation may be that 25:26 required the etymology of the name here; and, the etymology of "Esau" being unknown, two suggestions were introduced: the familiar identification of Esau with Edom and Seir with the land of Edom. Both suggestions would then have originated elsewhere. In 1 Sam. 16:12 and 17:42, the word "ruddy" is used to describe a handsome youth; in the Gilgamesh epic, Enkidu is described as being "hairy," like a wild man. Genesis 25:26 says that the other twin grasped his twin brother's heel, a birth omen open to a variety of explanations; he is accordingly named Jacob (Hebrew *yaʿᵃqamaob*; cf. *ʿāqēb*, "heel"). This was originally a theophorous name meaning "May God protect." The statement of Isaac's age in verse 26b is from P.

27-28 These verses are still part of the genealogy, like Genesis 21:20, but they lead into 25:29-34. Describing the different occupations of two brothers is a common way to begin a narrative (cf. Gen. 4:2). Such narratives usually reflect the coexistence or hostility of different cultures, the conflicts and competition between them. The theme includes the question of whose favorites they are, as we see from 25:28, which clearly leads up to chapter 27.

29-34 Here a brief narrative of hunter and herdsman, once independent, has been inserted. As in verses 22-23, the younger gets the better of the elder. The introduction to the action in verse 29 presupposes the exposition in verse 27. The purpose of the action is to illustrate the superiority of the younger brother, who is astute and farsighted. Esau's words and actions are a deliberate caricature: he is uncouth, coarse, and stupid. Jacob, on the contrary, is farsighted; he thinks of the future and is determined to rise in the world. And so he tricks his brother out of his right as firstborn—easily, because his brother disdains it. Jacob is cautious and sees that the transaction is confirmed by oath. Esau stupidly agrees, eats his lentils, and goes away. The narrator sums up: thus Esau disdained his birthright!

The narrative here associated with Jacob and Esau originally dealt with a herdsman who gets the better of a hunter; it may have originated in the Transjordan, where conditions were ripe for such a cultural transition. The "Esau" of this narrative has nothing to do with the Esau of chapter 27 or 33, which depict him quite differently. The description does not caricature an individual but a type. The narrative has to do with class rivalry; we hear the triumph and mockery of the upstart shepherd making sport of the uncouth and stupid hunter. This is the self-assertive voice of a rising culture. It is the only historical passage in the Patriarchal History that looks back from the perspective of nomadic herdsmen to the earlier civilization of hunters and gatherers, a primitive stage of civilization that can be found throughout the world.

26:1-35   ISAAC AND ABIMELECH

1   *There came a famine in the land, over and above the earlier famine in Abraham's time; so Isaac went to Gerar, to Abimelech the Philistine.*

2   *And Yahweh appeared to him and said:*
Do not go down to Egypt;
stay in the land that I will tell you.

3   *Sojourn in this land;*
I will be with you and will bless you,
for to you and your descendants I will give all these lands
and so fulfill the oath I swore to your father Abraham.

4   *And I will make your seed as numerous*
as the stars of heaven. And to your seed
I will give all these lands, and in your name shall
all the nations of the earth bless themselves,

5   *because Abraham harkened to my word*
and kept what I ordered him to keep:
my commandments, statutes, and laws.

6   *And Isaac remained in Gerar.*

7   *Now when the men of the place asked about his wife,*
he said: She is my sister;
for he was afraid to say: She is my wife.
Otherwise [he thought] the men of the place might kill me
because of Rebekah, for she is very beautiful.

8   *Now when he had been there a considerable time,*
Abimelech, king of the Philistines, looked out of his window
and saw Isaac caressing his wife Rebekah.

9   *Then Abimelech summoned Isaac and said:*
Well, she is your wife then! How could you say:
She is my sister! And Isaac said to him:
I thought I would die because of her.

10   *Then Abimelech replied: What have you done to us!*
How easily one of the people might have lain with your wife,
and you would thus have brought guilt upon us.

11   *Then Abimelech issued a command to the whole people:*
      Whoever touches this man or his wife shall be put to death.

12   *But Isaac sowed in that land, and he reaped*
      in that year a hundredfold.

13   *And Yahweh blessed him, and the man became wealthier*
      and wealthier, until he was exceedingly wealthy.

14   *He had flocks of sheep and herds of cattle*
      and a large household; therefore the Philistines envied him.

15   *But all the wells that the servants of his father had dug in the days of his father Abraham*
      the Philistines had blocked up and filled with earth.

16   *Then Abimelech said to Isaac: Depart from among us,*
      you have become too powerful for us.

17   *So Isaac left the place*
      and encamped in the valley of Gerar and stayed there.

18   *And Isaac dug again the wells*
      that the servants of his father Abraham
      had dug in the days of Abraham,
      which the Philistines had stopped after the death of Abraham,
      and he gave them the same names
      that his father had given them.

19   *And when Isaac's servants dug in the valley,*
      they found a well and a spring of water.

20   *And the shepherds of Gerar came into conflict*
      with the shepherds of Isaac; they claimed:
      The water belongs to us. So he named the well Esek,
      because they had disputed the matter with him.

21   *Then they dug another well*
      and again came into conflict over it;
      therefore he named it Sitnah [Quarrel].

22   *Then he moved on from there and dug another well.*
      Over it there was no conflict.
      Then he called it Rehoboth [Broad Place] and said:
      Now Yahweh has made room for us
      so that we can spread out in the land.

23   *And from there he went up to Beer-sheba.*

24   *And Yahweh appeared to him that night and said:*
      I am the God of Abraham your father; do not be afraid,
      for I am with you. I will bless you
      and increase your descendants for the sake of Abraham my servant.

25   *And he built an altar there and called on the name of Yahweh.*
      And Isaac pitched his tent there,
      and Isaac's servants dug a well there.

26   *And Abimelech came to him from Gerar with his adviser Ahuzzath and Phicol, the commander of his army.*

27   *And Isaac said to him: Why have you come to me,*

since you are my enemies
and sent me away from you?

28 *But they said: We have seen clearly*
that Yahweh is with you; therefore we thought:
There should be a treaty sworn between us,
between us and you,
and we wish to make a pact with you

29 *that you will do us no harm, just as we*
have not touched you and have done you only good
and let you go in peace;
You are now indeed blessed by Yahweh.

30 *Then he prepared them a meal, and they ate and drank.*

31 *And early on the following morning they swore an oath.*
And Isaac bade them farewell and they departed in peace.

32 *The same day, Isaac's servants came and brought him news about the well*
they had dug.
And they said to him: We have found water.

33 *Then he called it Shibah [Oath].*
Therefore the city is called Beer-sheba to this day.

34 *When Esau was forty years old, he took as wife Judith,*
the daughter of Beeri the Hittite,
and also Basemath, the daughter of Elon the Hittite;

35 *They were a source of bitter grief for Isaac and Rebekah.*

In chapter 26 the few extant Isaac traditions are recorded. It is a self-contained literary composition that has been inserted here, as we see from 25:28, which leads into chapter 27. The author, therefore, cannot be J; he is a tradent who assembled the Isaac tradition to preserve it. The chapter as a whole is a composite of several traditional units, but it is a deliberate composition. At its core is an itinerary (26:17, 22a, 23, 25b) with notes about wells (vv. 15, 18, 19-25, 32-33); these are framed by a story concerning Isaac and Abimelech, a Philistine king (vv. 12-14, 16-17 and 26-31). These notes are the earliest sections of the chapter, an ancient tradition preserved by incorporation within a later frame. The introduction (vv. 1-11) has the purpose of showing, in the context of the earlier narrative in chapters 12 and 20, how Isaac came to the territory of Abimelech.

1-11   These verses are not an originally independent narrative but a literary imitation of Genesis 12:10-20, which also incorporates elements of 20:1-18. The explanations given by these two texts are presupposed. Genesis 26:1 conflates 12:10 and 20:1. The words of Abimelech in 26:9-10 correspond to 12:19 and 20:9a. There are awkward transitions (26:8a) and afterthoughts (v. 7). In verses 2-5, a promise to Isaac has been inserted, which is intended to parallel the initial promise to Abraham. Its new features are the promise, "I will be with you and will bless you," and the statement declaring Isaac

186

the heir of the promise given to Abraham. Abraham, however, is a model of obedience to the law (as in Gen. 22:15-18); the promise is God's reward for this obedience.

Genesis 26:6-7 continues the narrative. Verse 6 follows verse 1; these verses presuppose Genesis 12:11-15. In 26:7 the question asked by the men of the place bears no relationship to the king's discovery; also omitted is the important element of the king's desire to have the woman for himself. Verses 9-10 have been toned down with respect to chapters 12 and 20: the king merely fears that the inhabitants of Gerar might commit adultery. The king's accusation (v. 10) is followed without motivation by his edict concerning anyone who touches Isaac or Rebekah, an edict that honors them highly. At the same time, this statement explains how Isaac comes to prosper in the land of the Philistines.

12-17 The second section, verses 12-17 (omitting v. 15), describes this prosperity. Yahweh blesses Isaac (cf. v. 3a), so that he becomes "exceedingly" wealthy. The description of wealth in verses 12-14 is inconsistent with the patriarchal period, reflecting the wealth of a large-scale farmer of the sedentary period; it is as anachronistic as the comparison to the king of the Philistines in verses 26-31. Thus Isaac becomes a great man (repeated three times in v. 13) in the land of the Philistines. This notion, too, is out of place in the patriarchal period. The patriarchs were not "great." This whole description is possible only long after the patriarchal period. Isaac's wealth arouses the envy of the Philistines (v. 14b), and conflict threatens. Now follows Isaac's fall (vv. 16-17; v. 15 goes with v. 18), with no more explanation than his rise. Abimelech ejects him on the spot (cf. Gen. 12:19). As a result, Isaac must once again lead the life of a nomadic herdsman, as we learn from the itinerary clause in 26:17b. The only function of this ejection in the chapter is to forge a link between the Isaac-Abimelech narrative and the well material. The tradent who combined the two did not reflect that return to a nomadic way of life would spell disaster for the greatness of Isaac described in verses 12-14.

15, 18-25 This section transports us to another world. Verse 15, which goes with verse 18, has been interwoven with the Abimelech narrative to ease the transition; the same phenomenon occurs again in verses 30-33. This central section of chapter 26 contains a very ancient tradition, going back to the patriarchal period, in which accounts of wells are set in an itinerary. The writer who assembled chapter 26 out of various traditions had before him an itinerary with information about wells, which made sense only against the nomadic background of the patriarchs. The lives of the people and their flocks depended on these wells. It was therefore necessary to preserve the locations and names of the wells along the route for the next migration; such itineraries were handed down by exchange with other groups. A newly dug or newly acquired well was given a name, often associated with an event that took place when the well was discovered (vv. 32-33) or a quarrel between the herdsmen of two groups for a source of water (vv. 15-20 and 21; also indirectly v. 22). When wells stopped up by hostile groups were redug, they were given their old names (vv. 15, 18). The fact that two wells are named "Quarrel" (vv. 20, 21) and one bears witness to avoidance of a quarrel (v. 22: Hebrew *reḥōḇōt*, "breadth," interpreted as meaning "Now Yahweh has made room for us") illustrates the major importance of the quarrel in this way of life—a bloodless precursor of war.

In verses 24-25 another theophany (cf. vv. 2-5) with a promise has been appended. Here, too, Isaac receives the promise for the sake of Abraham.

26-31 These verses continue and conclude the story of Isaac and Abimelech. The situation cannot be left with Abimelech's ejection of Isaac. And so Abimelech, the king, seeks out Isaac; the outcome is a treaty that does Isaac honor. King Abimelech comes as a petitioner to Isaac (vv. 26-27), together with his commander Phicol and his adviser Ahuzzath; the presence of a counselor and a military officer lends weight to the proceedings. Isaac is thus presented as equal in dignity to a king; it is he who opens the negotiations with a question. Abimelech introduces and concludes his request (vv. 28-29) with a recognition that Isaac is "blessed by Yahweh." Because he realizes this, Abimelech asks Isaac to enter into a treaty with him, which resembles a nonaggression pact. This offer from the king of a Philistine city to the nomadic herdsman Isaac (as the well material depicts him) makes sense only if we realize that this narrative is telling the generation of a much later period that the promise given to the patriarchs promised greatness to the nation of Israel; Isaac here represents this nation, which even the kings of the nations (cf. 1 Kgs. 10) must recognize as being blessed by Yahweh.

Isaac accepts the offer; again he is the one who takes the initiative in making the pact (vv. 30-31), which is sealed by a shared meal and mutual oaths. Again Isaac is depicted as the king's equal; mutual oaths are exchanged only between people of equal rank. And at the end it is Isaac who brings the scene to a close by sending his guests away in peace (v. 31b). The pact does not annul the ejection; the oath is limited to agreement that neither party will injure the other. Peace between two groups does not necessarily lead to friendship or intimacy; it can also mean that one lets the other depart in peace.

32-33 The final note about a well actually goes with verses 15, 18-25; here, because the well is named "Oath," it serves to link the two sections; cf. above on verse 15. It is possible that the author changed the original name of the well (translated *Abundantia,* "abundance, profusion," by the Vulgate) to fit the context. The brief account of the event—"We have found . . ."—suggests something of what the discovery of a well meant to nomadic herdsmen. The concluding etymology, which seeks to explain the name "Beer-sheba" through association with this event, is part of the link; it really belongs to the pact between Isaac and Abimelech.

34-35   These verses, from P, connect a genealogical notice concerning Esau's marriage with a narrative that does not resume until 27:46–28:9.

27:1-45   THE FIRSTBORN CHEATED
OF HIS BLESSING

1   *When Isaac had grown old and his eyes were so dim*
    that he could no longer see,
    he summoned his elder son Esau. And he said to him:
    My son! And he answered: Here I am.
2   *He said: Behold, I have grown old*
    and do not know when I shall die.
3   *So take your weapons, your quiver and bow;*
    go into the fields and hunt me some game.
4   *Then prepare me a savory dish, such as I like,*
    and bring it in to me so that I may eat,
    that my soul may bless you before I die.
5   *But Rebekah had been listening*
    when Isaac was speaking to his son Esau. Now when Esau went into the
    fields to hunt game for his father,
6   *then Rebekah said to her son Jacob: Behold, I heard*
    how your father said to your brother Esau:
7   *Bring me some game and prepare a savory dish,*
    that I may eat and bless you in the presence of Yahweh before I die.
8   *And now, my son, listen to what I say and do as I order you.*
9   *Go to the flock and get me two fine young goats,*
    so that I may prepare them as a savory dish for your father,
    such as he likes.
10 *Take that in to your father,*
    that he may eat and bless you before he dies.
11 *But Jacob said to his mother Rebekah: Consider!*
    My brother Esau is a hairy man, but I am smooth.
12 *Perhaps my father will touch me, then I would stand before him*
    as one mocking him, and I would bring
    a curse upon myself instead of a blessing.
13 *But his mother said to him: Upon me be the curse,*
    my son! Now do as I say; go and bring me the goats.

189

14 Then he went and got them and brought them to his mother,
and his mother made a savory dish,
such as his father liked.

15 Then Rebekah took the festal garments of Esau, her elder son,
which she had with her in the house,
and put them on her younger son Jacob.

16 But she put the skins of the goats
on his arms and on his neck.

17 Then she put the savory dish that she had prepared
and bread into the hands of her son Jacob.

18 He went in to his father and said:
My father! He answered: Here I am.
Who are you, my son?

19 And Jacob said to his father: I am Esau,
your firstborn. I have done as you told me.
Sit up and eat of the game
so that your soul may bless me.

20 Then Isaac said to his son: How did you find it so quickly, my son?
He answered: Yahweh your God put it in my way.

21 Then Isaac said to Jacob: Come close, my son,
that I may touch you and see if you are really my son Esau or not.

22 And Jacob came close to his father, and he touched him
and said: The voice is the voice of Jacob,
but the arms are the arms of Esau.

23 And he did not recognize him, for his arms were hairy,
like the arms of his brother Esau. And so he blessed him.

24 And he said to him: Are you my son Esau?
And he answered: I am.

25 Then he said: Bring it to me,
so that I may eat of the game of my son,
that my soul may bless you.
Then he brought it to him and he ate. And he also brought him wine, and he
drank.

26 Then Isaac his father said to him:
Come close to me, my son, and kiss me.

27 And he came close and kissed him. And he smelled the smell of his clothes,
and he blessed him, and said:
    Behold, the smell of my son, like the smell of the field which Yahweh has
    blessed.

28   May God give you of the dew of the heavens and of the fat of the earth
    and grain and wine in plenty.

29   Peoples shall serve you and nations shall bow before you.
    Be lord over your brothers;
        may your mother's sons bow before you.
    Cursed who curses you, and blessed who blesses you!

30 Just when Isaac had finished his blessing over Jacob,
and Jacob had scarcely left the presence of his father Isaac,
his brother Esau came back from the hunt.

31   He, too, prepared a savory dish and brought it in to his father;
      and he said to his father:
      Let my father sit up and eat of the game
      of his son, that his soul may bless me.

32   But Isaac his father said to him: Who are you?
      He answered: I am your son, your firstborn, Esau.

33   Then Isaac trembled violently all over and said:
      Who was it then who hunted the game
      and brought it in to me? Now I finished eating
      before you came. I have already blessed him,
      and he will remain blessed.

34   When Esau heard these words of his father,
      he uttered a loud and bitter cry.
      And he said to his father:
      Bless me, too, my father.

35   But he said: Your brother came deceitfully
      and took your blessing.

36   Then he said: Indeed, he is rightly called Jacob;
      this is the second time he has supplanted me.
      He took my birthright, and now
      he has also taken my blessing. And he asked:
      Have you not kept a blessing for me?

37   Then Isaac answered and said to Esau:
      Behold, I have made him lord over you
      and have given him all his brothers as servants;
      grain and wine I have bestowed on him;
      what is left for you, my son?

38   And Esau said to his father:
      Have you just one blessing, father?
      And Esau lifted up his voice and wept loudly.

39   Then his father Isaac answered and said to him:
          Behold, far from the fat of the earth shall be your dwelling,
          and far from the dew of heaven above.

40   By your sword you shall live and your brother you shall serve.
          But it shall come to pass, when you tear yourself free,
          you will break his yoke from your neck.

41   But Esau bore a grudge against Jacob because of the blessing
      with which his father had blessed him,
      and Esau made up his mind:
      The days of mourning for my father are approaching.
      Then I will kill my brother Jacob.

42   But when Rebekah was told the words of her elder son Esau, she sent for her
      younger son Jacob. And she said to him:
      Behold, your brother Esau will take vengeance on you;
      he will kill you.

43   Now listen to me, my son. Up and flee to Haran, to my brother Laban,

44   and stay with him a while
      until your brother's fury abates,

45 *until your brother's anger turns away from you*
and he forgets what you have done to him.
Then I will send for you
and bring you back.
Why should I lose both of you in one day?

Genesis 27 is among the narratives that recount a regularly recurring event (in this case a ritual event) made unique by outside intervention. This narrative depicts a father's blessing in great detail and thus records for us its individual elements: summons by the father and/or request by the son, identification, food and drink to strengthen the father, approach and touch, formula of blessing. In contrast to the Abraham narratives, the tension is not brought about by an elemental crisis such as famine or infertility, but by a human act that interrupts the normal course of the blessing. The issue is competition between brothers. Rebekah wants to guarantee the right of primogeniture for her younger son. Since only one can be blessed, a drama ensues.

This narrative was originally a family story, recounted orally. It developed through several stages of tradition. Its milieu is no longer that of nomadic herdsmen, but points to a later stage of settled life; an earlier form has been altered to fit these circumstances. The blessing formulas in verses 27b-29 and 39-40 are even later, since they presuppose the historical development of the tribes and the nation.

1-17   The narrative begins with Isaac's instructions to Esau (vv. 1-4). In the light of his approaching death, he asks his elder son to make the preparations for receiving a blessing. The brief exposition in verse 1a follows 25:27-28, a bridge between chapters 25 and 27. This bridge shows that in chapters 25–36 the larger thematic context (flight and return) takes priority over the individual narratives.

The original *Sitz im Leben* of blessing is a farewell (cf. Gen. 24:60); in a blessing, the one who is departing passes on vital energy to the one who will continue on in life. In this process, there is no distinction between a spiritual aspect, represented by the spoken word, and a corporeal aspect, represented by physical action. Once transmitted, the vital energy cannot be taken back or altered retroactively. In this regard, Genesis 27 illustrates the earliest understanding of blessing. The fact that only one son can be blessed is likewise a primitive feature. A later stage is illustrated by Genesis 49, where all twelve sons of Jacob receive a blessing. Chapter 27 also illustrates another development of the blessing form: the original locus of the blessing was the family (cf. also ch. 24); later its meaning changed and it could pertain to tribes or entire nations, as the sayings in 27:27-29, 39-40 show. Eventually blessing took on a permanent role in the context of worship.

The father orders his son to hunt some game and prepare a meal (vv. 3-4) such as he likes (cf. 25:28). Bow and arrow hunting (25:27) is characteristic of Edom, where the bow became the symbol of a deity; it was a land of hunters. The preparatory meal is intended to fortify the one who is to give his blessing "that my soul may bless you before I die" (27:4). The word "soul" (Heb. *nepeš*) means "vital energy" in all its aspects, as in Genesis 2:7: "living being." Esau does as he is told (27:5b, 31), but now Rebekah intervenes (v. 5a) and gives Jacob a counter-order (vv. 6-10). She has been listening and tells Jacob what she has heard. The phrase "before Yahweh" in her account, which does not appear in verse 4, was probably added to harmonize the narrative, in which it is Isaac who blesses, with the blessing formulas, in which it is Yahweh who blesses. She tells Jacob to bring her two young goats from the flock, "that he may eat and bless *you* before he dies." Jacob objects (vv. 11-12), but only because he is not sure his mother's plan will work. His mother counters his objection by taking personal responsibility for the consequences (v. 13). Jacob agrees and does as his mother tells him. The text is laconic: "Then he went and got them and brought them. . . ." But his mother herself takes care of the most important preparations (vv. 14b-17). It is the narrator's clear intent to point up Rebekah's purposeful motivation. The initiative is with Rebekah, not Jacob. The mother rebels against what she feels is a social injustice: the exclusive privilege of the eldest son, which is especially dubious in the case of twins. She is attacking a privilege of one who is "great" that excludes one who is "small."

18-29   The action of blessing is now recounted; it apparently includes all five elements of the traditional ritual (see above). Verses 18-19 introduce the blessing with Jacob's entrance and his father's question: "Who are you?" When he answers "I am Esau," Jacob irrevocably accepts the role Rebekah has assigned him. As Esau he asks for his father's blessing. But the sequence of the ritual is interrupted by his father's doubts (vv. 20-30); finally the old man succumbs to the deception, "and so he blessed him" (v. 23b). The ritual of blessing then begins in verse 24 with the formal question of identity. The meal follows (v. 25). The third element of the ritual is physical contact (vv. 26-27a) in the form of an embrace or kiss. It is necessary for the transmission of the vital energy. The transitional "and he blessed him and said" introduces the formula of blessing (vv. 27b-29). The preceding "and he smelled the smell of his clothes" marks the transition from action to words, as in Numbers 24:5: what is perceived by the senses lends reality to the vision of the future.

The transition statement in verse 27a is followed by a blessing, in poetic form, bestowing fertility and victory. Verse 27b resembles a simile: the smell of his son that Isaac smells is like that of a field blessed by Yahweh. Both this blessing and the blessing that follows in verse 28 refer to the period after settlement; they constitute a typical blessing associated with agricultural civilization, similar to that in Genesis 49:25, as the identical Ugaritic parallels show. The pairing of "heavens" and "earth" first appears among those who know their lives are dependent on the gifts of the heavens and of the earth. Genesis 27:29 adds to the fertility blessing a blessing of dominion, as in 24:60 or 48:15-19. This combination, too, is best explained in the context of settlement with its intertribal rivalries, which are referred to in the second and third lines. The statement that "peoples" and "nations" shall serve the recipient of the blessing can refer only to the nation of Israel after the birth of the state. This parallelism is found especially in the later prophets; the parallelism "serve // bow down" is typical of Deuteronomic language. The first clause is not mentioned when the content of the blessing is repeated in 27:37. The second clause is like Numbers 24:9b; cf. Genesis 12:3. The composite nature of the blessing formula in 27:27b-29 and the parallels from very different periods to each of its clauses illustrate how a blessing formula referring to the future could develop and change.

30-40 Discovery of the trick, and the blessing of Esau. No sooner has Jacob gone out than Esau returns from the hunt (v. 30). By such a change of scenes, the narrator manages to have only two persons speaking to each other. Such "single strand" narratives are typical of early storytelling; here conversation is still identical with dialogue. With verse 31 the narrative returns to the blessing ritual; verse 31a is the second part of Esau's fulfillment of his father's wishes, and continues verse 5b. Verses 31-32 are almost identical with verses 18-19; then discovery of the trick interrupts the ritual sequence. The father's horror (v. 33) and the outcry of the tricked brother (v. 34a) constitute the climax of the narrative. The conversation between father and son (vv. 35-37) reveals the deceptions, but also shows that nothing can undo its success. The father's answer (vv. 35, 37) expresses the ancient, almost material notion of a blessing, which makes it possible to steal it away. Esau's lament is followed by his pathetic question (last clause of verse 36; the play on the name "Jacob" is a late insertion): "Have you not kept a blessing for me?" Isaac's answer (v. 37) also echoes the ancient notion of a blessing, treating it as an effectual word spoken by the father: "Behold, I have . . ."; the later formulation in verses 28-29 is different. The repetition of Esau's question (v. 38), "Have you just one blessing, father?" brings us face to face with what has happened here. According to the ancient view, a blessing is "all or nothing"; now Esau must realize this, as his deceived father explains to him: I have given away everything. This is just the point against which Rebekah rebelled.

She fights at the risk of her own life (v. 13) against an existing right that she finds unjust. The scene suggests that the ancient notion of a blessing is undergoing a crisis. This is even clearer, finally, in Genesis 33:3, when the recipient of the blessing bows before the one who remained unblessed. But when Esau repeats his plea (27:38) and his father finally does give him a blessing in spite of what he has just said, the narrator is suggesting that a father's blessing must be more that what law and custom have made it. And so Esau, too, receives a blessing (vv. 39-40). Crucial to this understanding are the words "You shall live." Esau is to have a hard life, but he will live. The fertile land, watered by rain and dew, is denied him (v. 39b); but life is possible even far from agricultural land ("you shall dwell"). The prediction that Esau will live by his sword resembles the tribal oracles. Verse 40b is an expansion anticipating the history of two nations, Israel and Edom, through an historical *vaticinium ex eventu*. Edom must serve his brother (Israel), but in a later age Edom will shake off the domination of Israel (2 Kgs. 8:20-22).

27:41-45 The conclusion in verses 41-45 also provides a transition to what follows. Jacob has turned his brother into an enemy, indeed a mortal enemy, for Esau decides to kill his brother. But he cannot do this deed while his father is alive. He will wait for his father's death and the period of mourning. This gives Rebekah a chance to intervene. Once more it is she who espouses Jacob's cause. She knows that she has achieved nothing through her plan; in averting its consequences, it is again she who frames a plan. This plan, which Jacob follows, determines the structure of the whole next section, chapters 28–33: flight and return. Thus chapter 27 is also included in this complex, because it establishes the reason for flight.

Rebekah's exclamation in verse 45, "Why should I lose both of you in one day?" reveals her devastation. Her plan has failed. She did not consider that a father's blessing could not help Jacob against his brother's enmity, because a blessing can succeed only within a healthy community (cf. Gen. 37–50). This conclusion, too, suggests that the notion of a blessing is undergoing a crisis and a change.

Genesis 27 is concerned with "transmission" in an early form of society, in which there is as yet no distinction between what is spiritual and what is corporeal: in a blessing, a father transmits his vital energy to his son. The narrative presupposes that this transmission from generation to generation is a major source of conflict and rivalry. It gives rise to conflict between those who are privileged and those who are not. Here it is the mother who attacks the exclusive privilege of the eldest son. She is attacking a petrified right that works injustice. When Malachi 1:2-5 interprets this chapter to mean that God chose Jacob and rejected Esau (an interpretation borrowed and cited in Rom. 9:13), the reference is to the nations of Israel and Edom, not the two brothers, the sons of Isaac, as individuals.

27:46–28:9   THE WIVES OF JACOB AND ESAU

27:46 *And Rebekah said to Isaac:*
I am wearied to death of the Hittite women!
If Jacob takes a wife from the Hittite women, like these, from the daughters of the land,
what's the use of life?

28:1 *Then Isaac called Jacob and blessed him.*
And he charged him and said to him:
Do not take a wife from the Canaanite women.

2 *Up, go to Paddan-aram,*
to the house of Bethuel, your mother's father,
and take a wife there from the daughters of Laban,
your mother's brother.

3 *May God Almighty bless you and make you fruitful*
and multiply you, that you may become a host of nations.

4 *And may he give you the blessing of Abraham,*
you and your descendants with you,
so that you may take possession of the land of your sojourning,
which God gave to Abraham.

5 *So Isaac dismissed Jacob. He set out*
to Paddan-aram, to Laban, the son of Bethuel the Aramean,
the brother of Rebekah, the mother of Jacob and Esau.

6 *Now when Esau saw that Isaac had blessed Jacob*
and sent him to Paddan-aram,
to take a wife there, by blessing him
and charging him: Do not take a wife
from the Canaanite women,

7 *and that Jacob had obeyed his father and his mother*
and had gone to Paddan-aram,

8 *then Esau saw that his father Isaac*
did not like the Canaanite women.

9 *Therefore Esau went to Ishmael and took as wife Mahalath,*
the daughter of Ishmael, the son of Abraham,
the sister of Nebaioth, in addition to the wives
that he already had.

This is one of three extensive texts from P in the Patriarchal History. Just as Genesis 17 follows the account of a birth and Genesis 23 follows the account of a death, so Genesis 27:46–28:9 follows the account of a marriage (26:34-35). In these three texts from the Patriarchal History, P establishes the three precultic family rituals associated with birth, marriage, and death (cf. the commentary on chapters 17 and 23). It is consistent with P's theology that each of these rites of passage is associated with a commandment: here, in the case of marriage, with the charge to take a wife from one's own people. In 27:46, which follows 26:34-35, the command is based on a narrative restatement of the genealogical information contained in P's sources concerning the wives of Esau and Jacob. In addition to this genealogical material, P uses themes from chapter 27. Here it becomes especially clear that P is writing in the period of the Exile. He is familiar with the ancient narratives of J, but can reshape them on the basis of his own conceptions.

The text is governed by the command in 28:1 and 6, which should be understood in the context of P's own period. P nevertheless feels bound by the traditional genealogical material in his sources.

27:46 Rebekah's lament presupposes the statement of Genesis 26:34-35 that Esau married two Hittite (that is, Canaanite; cf. 28:1) women. They are a source of bitter grief for Isaac and Rebekah (26:35), a grief expressed in Rebekah's lament in this verse, with the added fear that Jacob might do the same thing. Formally, Rebekah's lament resembles that in 25:22; but its content has been changed to reflect P's concerns.

28:1-5 Isaac's response to his wife's lament is the command he gives his son Jacob together with the blessing he gives him for his journey to Paddan-aram. The father's charge to his son in verses 1-2 recalls 24:2-4, which it presupposes. The prohibition in 28:1b is formally similar to the prohibitions of the Decalogue. The strict prohibition against marrying a Canaanite woman is understandable from the perspective of a time when mixed marriages threatened the purity of the community and the existence of the people. The command associated with this prohibition, in which Jacob's father orders him to go to Paddan-aram and take one of Laban's daughters as his wife, is markedly at variance with the reason for Jacob's flight to Paddan-aram stated in 27:41-45. There follows in 28:3-4 the blessing the father gives his departing son. The understanding of blessing is also fundamentally different from that illustrated by chapter 27. The blessing is no longer an effectual word spoken by the father; it has been changed into an optative: God is the one who blesses. There is no longer any trace of a ritual; there is not even any mention of physical contact. The blessing has become a promise: the promise of increase in 28:3, the promise of the land in verse 4 (cf. 17:1-22). Isaac passes on to Jacob the promise made to Abraham.

The command is followed in 28:5 by its execution (cf. ch. 17). Jacob sets out to go to Laban and his family, the family of his mother.

6-9 The fact that verse 5 ends with the two names "Jacob" and

"Esau" shows that even for P the ancient tradition still involved both Jacob and Esau, even though the rivalry between them has faded into the background—so much so that Esau can take Jacob as an example! Esau's thoughts with respect to what his father said to Jacob show that P cannot evade the issue of Esau's marriage with two Canaanite women. But they also show that P is concerned to present Esau in a favorable light: he strives to please his parents by marrying yet another wife, this time from the family, a daughter of Ishmael. When P traces the prohibition against marrying a foreigner to the patriarchal period, his description is inaccurate as it stands; but one point he makes is historically accurate, namely that the history of the patriarchs established and preserved the high importance of the family for Israel and its religion.

28:10-22   JACOB'S DREAM AND VOW AT BETHEL

10   *Jacob set out from Beer-sheba*
     and went on his way to Haran.
11   *Then he came to a place and he spent the night there*
     because the sun had already set.
     And he took one of the stones of the place,
     put it behind his head, and lay down
     to sleep in that place.
12   *Then he dreamed there was a stairway set on the ground*
     and its top reached to heaven.
     And behold, angels of God were going up and coming down.
13   *And behold, Yahweh stood before him, and he said:*
     I am Yahweh, the God of Abraham your father,
     and the God of Isaac. The land on which you are lying
     I give it to you and your descendants.
14   *And your seed shall be like the dust of the earth,*
     and you shall expand west and east,
     south and north, and in you [and your seed]
     all the families of the earth shall bless themselves.
15   *Behold, I am with you and will protect you everywhere you go, and I will*
     bring you back to this land.
     For I will not leave you
     until I have done all that I have promised you.
16   *When Jacob awoke from his sleep, he said:*
     Truly Yahweh is in this place and I did not know it.
17   *And he was afraid and said:*
     How awesome is this place! Here is none other
     than the house of God, here is the gate of heaven!

18 *Early the next morning Jacob took the stone*
that he had put behind his head, set it up as a sacred pillar, and anointed the
top of it with oil.
19 *And he gave this place the name Bethel.*
But earlier the name of the city had been Luz.
20 *The Jacob made a vow and said:*
If God is with me and protects me on the journey
I am now making, if he gives me bread to eat
and clothes to wear,
21 *and I return safely to my father's house,*
then Yahweh shall be my God,
22 *and this stone, which I have set up as a sacred pillar,*
shall be a house of God,
and of all that you give me,
I will assuredly give a tenth to you.

Genesis 28:10-22 belongs to a group of narratives dealing with sanctuaries and encounters with the deity: 28:10-22; 32:1-2; 32:22-32; 35:1-15. It develops out of the itinerary in 28:10. The action begins in verse 11 and culminates in verse 19 with the naming of the site. It is actually a report expanded into a narrative; tension is introduced by the event that surprises Jacob. Genesis 32:1-2 is a close parallel. The narrative features two mutually complementary aspects. The first has to do with the origin of a sanctuary and concludes with its being named; the other is the experience of a person in flight who discovers this holy place. The first aspect points to an originally independent narrative explaining the origin of the sanctuary at Bethel, a "cultic etiology." The other aspect, however, derives from the context of chapters 27 and 29–31. The promise in 28:15 is also related to this larger context: the promise of God's presence is characteristic of the Jacob-Esau cycle. It has undergone secondary expansion by the addition of verses 13-14; verses 20-22 are also secondary. The narrative in verses 10-12, 16-19 is a single unit; there were three stages in the growth of the present text. J found in his sources a narrative describing the origin of the sanctuary at Bethel, where it had been preserved. He gave it new meaning by interpolating it into the story of Jacob and Esau: it is Jacob, fleeing from Esau, who discovers the holy place. The expansions in verses 13b-14 and 20-22 mark a third stage. It includes the history of Israel through the addition of the promise in 13b-14, which relates to this history, the history of worship in Israel through the establishment of two cultic practices, vows and tithes, in verses 20-22.

10-12 These verses follow 27:41-45; Jacob obeys his mother's instructions in 27:43 and sets out from Beer-sheba to Haran, some 75 miles distant. On this journey he has a remarkable experience.

Nightfall takes the traveler by surprise, and he has to spend the night out of doors. As the sun is setting, he finds a suitable spot. The definite article suggests the double meaning of the Hebrew word *māqôm*, "place": it can also mean "sacred place." But at this point there is nothing to suggest its sacredness. Jacob lies down to sleep there, placing a stone behind his head for protection (cf. 1 Sam. 19:13). During the night he has a dream (Gen. 28:12); this is the first dream narrative in the Old Testament. It belongs to the group of dreams consisting only of a single image; both clauses in verse 12 are circumstantial. He sees a stairway (not a ladder) connecting heaven and earth. The word is found only here; the verb from which it derives suggests a heap of piled-up stones or a ramp reaching from earth to heaven; a similar conception lies behind Babylonian temple towers. The second clause explains the function of the stairway: he sees heavenly beings (*mal'ªkê 'ªlōhîm;* cf. Job 1:6; 2:1) going up and coming down, emphasizing the connection between heaven and earth.

13-15 The repeated "And behold . . ." introduces the promise in verses 13-15 as a theophany distinct from the preceding vision: "Yahweh stood before him." He makes himself known to Jacob as the God of his fathers, Abraham and Isaac. Like Isaac in 26:3-4, Jacob, too, is an heir of the promise, which again includes both the land and descendants; the relative clause ("the land on which you are lying") connects the promise of the land with the present situation. Both promises are meant for Jacob's descendants, as 28:13 and 14 explicitly state; the promise of expansion in all directions has in mind the nation of Israel. The verb for "expand" occurs in the same sense in Isaiah 54:3. The extension of the blessing to all peoples at the conclusion of Genesis 28:14 appears also in 12:3; 18:18; 22:18; 26:4. In contrast to 28:13-14, which are clearly a secondary interpolation, the promise of God's continuing presence in verse 15 is appropriate to the situation; it consists with the way of life of the patriarchs. This promise is especially common in the Jacob-Esau cycle: 26:3, 24; 28:15; 31:3; 32:9; 46:3; 48:15, 21; 50:24. The narrative of the discovery of a holy place does not include a promise; it belongs to the second aspect, through which J turns the discovery into an episode during Jacob's flight. Jacob will experience God's help as defense against perils of the road during his flight. The special situation of Jacob is alluded to in the next clause, which follows 27:41-45: "I will bring you back." The concluding statement in verse 15b, however, includes the promise of help with the other promises in verses 13-14 ("all that I have promised you") and looks forward to fulfillment of the promise; cf. Isaiah 46:10-11.

16-19 These verses record Jacob's reaction to his dream vision. The initial verb of verse 16 ("he awoke") could follow verse 12 directly; it continues the verb in verse 11 ("he lay down to sleep"). The following exclamation ("in this place") also presupposes verse 11. It reflects the fear of a man who has come from far away, whose dream has shown him that Yahweh, the God of his fathers, is present in this place. Verse 17, however, reflects more the immediate reaction of a man who has discovered a holy place through a revelation in a dream: he is terrified of what he has seen. This narrative is a classic example of the discovery of a holy place, a discovery that initially arouses fear: "How awesome is this place!" It is found in many religions.[1]

Jacob's immediate response in verse 17a is distinct from the two explanatory designations he gives to the place, which are secondary and were associated with the original tradition. The term "house of God" is ambiguous; in context, it refers not to the stone but to the place: "This place is a dwelling place of God"; it is off limits to mortals, because God dwells there. This agrees with the original meaning of *temenos* or *templum*, a circumscribed area out of doors. The other term, "gate of heaven" (found elsewhere in the Old Testament in Ps. 78:23), designates the boundary between the divine realm and the human; there is a point of contact, but also a boundary. The notion of a holy place (house, stairway, gate) inspiring fear and awe appears in the Old Testament for the first time in this passage. It is a universal religious phenomenon not typical of patriarchal religion; here it marks the transition from the patriarchal period to a sedentary culture and its associated cult.

In Genesis 38:18 Jacob's reaction to the dream leads to an action. It, too, reflects Jacob's dread in the presence of the holy place, but it cannot take place until morning. By setting up a stone (v. 18b), Jacob marks the place so that it will be recognized as holy. The stone was near him during his dream (v. 11b) and was witness to the dream that revealed to him the holiness of the place; as such, it now becomes a monument (Hebrew *maṣṣēāh*) to alert those passing by to the holiness of the place. Insofar as this stone itself is called *bêṭ-ʾēl*, "house of God," the designation reflects an earlier stage in the cult of stones, for which the stone itself is the locus of a divine being or power. The two concepts must be kept distinct: the narrative of Genesis 28 does not belong in the context of the cult of stones, of which only a faint echo may be heard here.

The concluding statement that Jacob anointed the stone with oil is an expansion that presupposes a regular ritual of anointing a massebah. Oil, an agricultural product, points to the time of settlement.

---

1. Friedrich Heiler, *Erscheinungsformen und Wesen der Religion* (Stuttgart: Kohlhammer, 1961).

There is considerable evidence for the practice; originally it was not thought of as a sacrifice but as a means of conveying power to the sacred object. The naming of the holy place, recorded in verse 19, is an integral part of its discovery. It is not the stone that is named but the site whose holiness it attests. The earlier name of the site, Luz, is also given. Probably "Luz" ("almond tree") was originally the name of the city, which later became named for the nearby sanctuary. In this name, the story of an event marking a remote origin is brought into the present.

20-22   Comparison with other vows mentioned in the Old Testament (Num. 21:2; Judg. 11:30-31; 1 Sam. 1:11; 2 Sam. 15:7-9)[2] shows that these verses are secondary. The substance of a promise (Gen. 28:15) can hardly be simultaneously the substance of a vow in the very same text. The purpose of this addition is clear: since the sanctuary at Bethel is traced back to Jacob, the important cultic rituals of vows and tithes are also said to have been established by him.

The first sentence of verse 20 is an introductory formula common to all vows. It indicates a fixed ritual, attested from the early period of the Monarchy. All vows are undertaken at a sanctuary, which presupposes a sedentary cult. The vow has a single condition, God's presence ("I will be with you"), which is expanded in several clauses; the promise "Then Yahweh shall be my God" (cf. 17:7 [P]) refers to the cultic worship of God; the name "Yahweh" is used because that is the cultic name. In this context, the statement "And this stone . . . shall be a house of God" cannot mean that the stone Jacob has set up is to be the locus of a god but rather that it is to become a sanctuary at which Yahweh will be worshipped.

The oath concerning tithes in 28:22b is formulated as direct address, clearly reflecting a fixed idiom of liturgical language, as in a sacrificial formula. The reference is to the offering of a tithe of the harvest, a regular practice at the sanctuary of Bethel after the settlement in Palestine (cf. Gen. 14:20).

In some ways, Genesis 28 parallels Exodus 19: in both passages, for a nomadic group the cult associated with a particular place begins with the discovery of a holy place. The difference is that in Genesis 28 the discovery is made by an itinerant individual, whereas in Exodus 19 it is an itinerant group. The narrative in Genesis 28 has preserved the ancient feature that the initial reaction to the discovery is terror: the place of God is out of bounds to mortals. Later in the growth of this ancient narrative, addition of the promise to this experience of the numinous combined the two fundamental religious phenomena

---

2. Wolfgang Richter, "Das Gelübde als theologische Rahmung der Jakobsaumuberlieferungen," *Biblische Zeitschrift* 11 (1967): 21-52.

that from this point on determine the way of God's people: history and worship. The same combination appears in the phrase coined by the prophet Isaiah: "The Holy One of Israel."

29:1-30: JACOB AND LABAN; LEAH AND RACHEL

1   *Then Jacob continued his journey*
    and came to the land of the peoples of the east.
2   *And when he looked up, he saw a well out in the field,*
    and lying beside it were three flocks of sheep,
    for the flocks were watered from the well;
    and a large stone lay over the mouth of the well.
3   *And when all the flocks had gathered there,*
    they would roll the stone away from the mouth of the well and water the
    sheep; then they would lay the stone back in place over the mouth of the well.
4   *And Jacob said to them: Where are you from, my brothers?*
    And they answered: We are from Haran.
5   *And he said to them: Do you know Laban, the son of Nahor?*
    And they answered: We know him.
6   *And he asked them: Is he well?*
    And they answered: Yes, he is well. But behold,
    here comes his daughter Rachel with the sheep.
7   *He said: The sun is still high and it is not yet time to gather the flocks*
    together; nevertheless, water the sheep
    and go and pasture them.
8   *They replied: We cannot until all the flocks are gathered together; then the*
    stone is rolled away from the mouth of the well and we water the sheep.
9   *While he was still speaking with them, Rachel came with her father's sheep,*
    for she looked after them.
10 *But when Jacob saw Rachel, the daughter of his mother's brother Laban,*
    and the sheep of his mother's brother Laban,
    then Jacob went and rolled away the stone
    from the mouth of the well
    and watered the sheep of his mother's brother Laban.
11 *And Jacob kissed Rachel and wept aloud.*
12 *Then he told Rachel*
    that he was a relative, a son of Rebekah.
    So she ran and told her father.
13 *But when Laban heard the news of Jacob, his sister's son, he ran to meet him,*
    embraced him and kissed him, and brought him to his house.
    And he told Laban his whole story.
14 *And Laban said to him: Indeed, you are of my flesh and blood. And he stayed*
    with him a month.

15 Then Laban said to Jacob: Yes, you are indeed my relative;
    should you serve me without pay?
    Tell me what your wage should be.
16 Now Laban had two daughters,
    the elder called Leah, the younger Rachel.
17 Leah had dull eyes, but Rachel was of beautiful form and appearance.
18 And Jacob loved Rachel; so he said:
    Seven years I will serve you for Rachel,
    your younger daughter.
19 And Laban answered: It is better to give her to you
    than to any other man. Stay with me.
20 So Jacob served seven years for Rachel,
    and they seemed to him but a day—he loved her so much.
21 Then Jacob said to Laban: Now give me my wife,
    for the time is up that I should go to her.
22 Then Laban invited all the people of the place
    and gave a feast.
23 But in the evening he took his daughter Leah
    and brought her to Jacob and he went to her.
24   And Laban gave to his daughter Leah
        his maid Zilpah to be her maid.
25 And in the morning—behold, it was Leah!
    Then Jacob said to Laban: What is this you have done to me?
    Did I not serve you for Rachel?
    Why have you deceived me?
26 Laban replied: It is not the custom among us
    to give the younger before the elder.
27 Complete the week of feasting with this one
    and then we will give you the other for the service
    that you will do me for seven more years.
28 Jacob did so and completed the week of feasting.
    Then he gave him his daughter Rachel as wife.
29   And Laban gave to his daughter Rachel
        his maid Bilhah to be her maid.
30 Then he also went to Rachel, and he loved Rachel more than Leah, and he
    served him for another seven years.

Chapters 29–31 deal with Jacob and Laban, including the birth of
Jacob's sons (29:31–30:24). Verses 1-14 of chapter 29 describe Jacob's
journey to Laban and the meeting at the well; verses 15-30 tell how he
got Leah and Rachel as his wives. These two sections go back to
independent narratives: the encounter at the well parallels 24:11-33
and Exodus 2:15-22; Genesis 29:15-30 develops the universal theme of
the substitute bride. The same narrator J who put together chapters
29–31 as a single narrative unit depicting flight and return combined
the two themes into a single narrative in 29:1-30.

1-14   The brief itinerary in verse 1 records Jacob's departure (cf.

28:10) and his destination, the peoples of the east. The latter expression (literally, "sons of the east") refers to the tribes of the Syroarabian desert northeast of Canaan (Gen. 25:6; Judg. 6:3, 33). As in so many other cases, arrival follows departure immediately: Jacob sees a well surrounded by flocks of sheep. A well is a natural gathering place; here he can get information. He begins a conversation with the herdsmen in which he inquires about Laban's family (Gen. 29:4-6); he learns at the same time how sheep are watered at this well (vv. 7-8). Both lay the groundwork for what follows: while he is talking, Rachel is approaching with her father's sheep (vv. 6b, 9). The series of questions about Jacob's relatives ends with a question about their well-being (Hebrew šālôm). This important word refers to the healthy state of the community, which will be the subject of the narrative to follow, after Jacob is received into the šālôm of Laban's house. Will this state continue? The description of the encounter with Rachel presupposes that in that period daughters helped with the work and could go about out of doors freely and unveiled.

The statement of the herdsmen in verse 8 has put an idea into Jacob's head; his elated excitement enables him to remove the stone from the well by himself. Thus he helps his relative water her sheep. Only then does he tell the girl who he is, greeting her with a kiss, as is customary among relatives (vv. 9-12). After this encounter, Rachel runs home in excitement; she can leave the flock in Jacob's protection. Laban runs to meet his nephew (cf. Gen. 24:28-30), greets him with a kiss and an embrace, and brings him into the house (29:13). Now, however, there is an important interlude before Jacob is finally accepted into the family: "And he told Laban his whole story," as in Genesis 24. Jacob is a stranger to them; only through what he narrates does he legitimate himself as the relative he claims to be. Laban expressly confirms the relationship: "Indeed, you are of my flesh and blood." Now he is accepted and can remain.

15-30   The first section, verses 1-14, could have concluded naturally with a marriage between Jacob and Rachel (as in Gen. 24 and Exod. 2). Now, however, the narrative is expanded by the deception through which Laban has Leah become Jacob's first wife, which also makes enemies of Jacob and Laban. At the outset (Gen. 29:15-20), the peace established in verses 13-14 still obtains. They reach an agreement the terms of which Jacob himself is able to set. In contrast to the wooing of Rebekah, Jacob has come empty-handed; it is natural that he should offer his services to his stepfather (v. 18). His love for Rachel makes the lengthy period of hard work (described in 31:38-40) seem short. Laban accepts Jacob's terms (29:19); he considers a cousin the ideal suitor, according to accepted custom. The service Jacob obligates himself to perform is limited service to a relative, determined by the circumstances, not the service of a slave or laborer. The narrator seeks to show that transactions within a family can lead to new relationships in which work, performance, and reward take on increased significance. In Laban's case, what had been conduct governed by the ethics of family relationships turns into that of a man pursuing his own advantage, whose only purpose is to get maximum benefit from Jacob's labor. He uses a ruse that will gain him an additional seven years of this labor, staging a magnificent wedding but presenting Leah to the bridegroom. This deception is possible because the bride is veiled when brought to the bridegroom. Laban justifies the deception by appealing to the custom that the elder daughter is given in marriage before the younger.

Verses 21-30 constitute an outstanding example of Hebrew narrative art. What transpires here between the two men who are relatives and now become enemies, what goes on within each of them and within each of the women, is presented with the utmost intensity and at the same time with utmost restraint. The narrator's purpose is to allow his listeners to participate in his story, so that they continue to think out the lines he merely suggests. Laban strikes us here as the model of the clever businessman, telling himself that he must first look after his own interests and those of his family. He is a Babbitt; he does "the right thing," he is conservative and observes all the proprieties. But whenever he can he makes a little profit for himself. And here he sees his chance. Jacob is in the weaker position; he does not have the support of his family, while Laban knows that he has behind him the townspeople, whom he has entertained lavishly at the wedding. Jacob knows that he is the weaker party. From the moment he says: "Now give me my wife" (v. 21) to the moment he surrenders to the inevitable ("Jacob did so" [v. 28]), all we hear from Jacob's mouth is his indictment of his father-in-law: "What is this you have done to me? Why have you deceived me?" (v. 25). The sequence of events, reduced to the absolute minimum, describes with astonishing clarity and breadth of vision how someone who is strong exploits for personal gain the labor of someone who is weak, while remaining a man of honor and a respected citizen. The weaker party is forced by circumstances to acquiesce. But even after having been deceived, Jacob still keeps one thing no one can take away from him: his love for another (vv. 20, 30). The narrator has perceived with absolute clarity the connection between the callousness introduced into human relationships by the appearance of economic competition and enrichment on the one hand and the intensification of the personal and private sphere on the other. The passing comment that Jacob loved Rachel more than Leah says that Laban, despite all his machinations, has been unable to change this love; at the same time, it lays the groundwork for the conflicts that are bound to arise between the two women, which are then detailed in 29:31–30:24.

This is the first time the Patriarchal History has dealt with the relationship of employment. Initially the work is done gladly, because it is done for a beloved friend. Then, however, economic and social interests in the person of Laban gain the upper hand. On the way from patriarchs to nation, social, economic, and personal conflicts are inevitable, conflicts in which one party seeks advantage at another's expense.

29:31-30:24   LEAH AND RACHEL; THE BIRTH AND NAMING OF JACOB'S SONS

29:31 *When Yahweh saw that Leah was unloved,*
he opened her womb, but Rachel remained childless.

32 *And Leah became pregnant and bore a son,*
whom she named Reuben. *For, as she said:*
Yahweh has looked upon my humiliation;
now my husband will love me.

33 *And she became pregnant again and bore a son.*
And she said: Yahweh has heard me, that I am unloved,
and so he has given me this son also.
And she named him Simeon.

34 *And she became pregnant again and bore a son.*
And she said: Now finally my husband will be united with me,
for I have borne him three sons.
And so she named him Levi.

35 *And she became pregnant again and bore a son.*
And she said: Now I will praise Yahweh!
And so she named him Judah.
Then she stopped bearing.

30:1 *Now when Rachel realized that she bore Jacob no children,*
she became jealous of her sister,
and she said to Jacob: Give me sons;
if not I shall die.

2 *Then Jacob became angry with Rachel and said:*
Am I in the place of God, who has denied you the fruit of the womb?

3 *Then she said: Here you have my maid Bilhah;*
go to her, that she may bear upon my knees,
and that I may come to children through her.

4 *And she gave him her maid Bilhah as wife.*
And Jacob went to her.

5 *And Bilhah became pregnant and bore Jacob a son.*

6 *And Rachel said: God has given judgment for me,*

he has also listened to me and given me a son.
And so she named him Dan.

7   *And Bilhah, Rachel's maid, became pregnant again*
and bore Jacob a second son.

8   *And Rachel said: I have struggled like God*
with my sister and have prevailed.
And so she named him Naphtali.

9   *And Leah found out that she had stopped bearing;*
then she took her maid Zilpah and gave her to Jacob as wife.

10   *And Zilpah, Leah's maid, bore Jacob a son.*

11   *And Leah said: Good fortune! and called him* Gad.

12   *And Zilpah, Leah's maid, bore Jacob a second son.*

13   *And Leah said: Happy am I, for young women will call me happy! And she*
named him Asher.

14   *In the days of the wheat harvest, Reuben went into the field and found some*
mandrakes there and brought them to Leah his mother. Then Rachel said to
Leah:
Give me some of your son's mandrakes.

15   *She answered her: Is it not enough for you that you have taken my husband?*
Now you want to take my son's mandrakes!
Then Rachel replied: Well then, let him lie with you tonight
in exchange for your son's mandrakes.

16   *And when Jacob came in from the field in the evening, Leah went out to meet*
him and said: You are to come to me,
for I have hired you with my son's mandrakes.
And he went to her that night.

17   *And God heard Leah and she became pregnant.*
And she bore Jacob a fifth son.

18   *And Leah said: God has rewarded me*
because I gave my maid to my husband.
And so she called him Issachar.

19   *Then Leah became pregnant again,*
and she bore Jacob a sixth son.

20   *And Leah said: God has given me a fine gift.*
Now at last my husband will honor me,
for I have borne him six sons.
And so she named him Zebulun.

21   *After this she bore a daughter and called her Dinah.*

22   *And God remembered Rachel.*
God heard her and opened her womb.

23   *And she became pregnant and bore a son.*
And she said: God has taken away my humiliation.

24   *And she named him* Joseph *and said:*
May Yahweh add to me another son!

To the quarrel between Jacob and Laban is now added a quarrel
between Leah and Rachel, Jacob's wives (29:31–30:24). Literarily, this

passage is highly peculiar; the entire text is actually a genealogy recording the birth and naming of Jacob's twelve children. This genealogy, however, is associated with a narrative of the rivalry between Jacob's wives. What transpires between them is reflected in the names of the children or in their etymology. An earlier stratum, a narrative in several episodes of the rivalry between Leah and Rachel (29:31-32; 30:1-6, 14-18, 22-24), can be distinguished from a later genealogy recording the birth and naming of Jacob's children. The earlier narrative has been expanded by a later hand into a secondary genealogy on the basis of the existing tradition of Jacob's twelve sons; this author's purpose was to emphasize God's action in the birth of Jacob's children (29:33-35; 30:4-13, 19-24, plus some smaller additions). The basic narrative comes from J; the reviser has changed it in a few places and probably also abbreviated it. The list of the twelve sons of Jacob as recorded in Genesis 49 was given by his sources.

29:31-35   The birth of Leah's four sons Reuben, Simeon, Levi, and Judah (vv. 31-35) is an introductory passage linking the narrative with 29:15-30. In this context, the statement "When Yahweh saw . . ." introduces a new episode. God looks with mercy upon Leah's suffering and intervenes on her behalf (cf. Exod. 3:7-8): he causes her to become pregnant and bear a son. The interpolated noun clause "But Rachel remained childless" (Gen. 29:31b) paves the way for 30:1-6. The whole passage is dominated by two themes: the unloved woman and the childless woman. The clearly psalmic language in the etymology of the name "Reuben" (29:32b) suggest that it comes from the hand of the reviser; it is inconsistent with the name itself (Hebrew *re'ûbēn*), which simply means "Behold, a son!"

In verses 33-35, the reviser introduces three more births and namings. The name "Simeon" (probably an animal name: "hyena"?) is explained as meaning "Yahweh has heard me" (parallel to "has looked upon" in v. 32) and given her a second son. The hand of the reviser is revealed by the awkwardly abrupt association of the quotation from Psalms with the situation: "For Yahweh has heard that I am unloved." The etymology of "Levi" remains unknown; the text explains it not as a direct reference to an act of God but as a reference to its consequence: her husband will "be united" with her (from the Hebrew verb *lāwāh*, found only in late passages like Zech. 2:11). It would be wrong to call this style of naming popular etymology; we are dealing instead with literary fictions through which the names are harmonized artificially with the context. The reviser is also responsible for the numbering of the sons: Levi is the third (Gen. 29:34). The name of the fourth son, "Judah" (perhaps originally a toponym), is explained as a vow of praise spoken by the mother at the birth of her fourth son: "Now I will praise Yahweh!" (v. 35). The echo of the verb form (*'ôḏeh*) in the name "Judah" is very faint, but the interpretation is appropriate to the situation; once again, it recalls the language of the Psalms. The etymology of the name in Genesis 49:8 is different but involves the same verb.

30:1-6   This section continues the narrative begun in 29:31-32. Only this latter passage makes sense of verses 1-2, confirming once more that 29:33-35 is a secondary addition. Both women are mentioned in 29:31; the conflict hinted at there breaks into the open in 30:1-2. In the impossible demand Rachel makes of Jacob we hear the agony of the childless woman. Her outburst is even more moving against the background of the tender love story in 29:1-20. Rachel's suffering is increased by having to see Leah and her sons every day. Ablaze with jealousy, she directs her pain and anger at them. When she bursts out: "If not I shall die," she means it literally. Without children she has no future, nothing to expect out of life. But the anger with which Jacob responds to this outburst is also natural. What can he do about it! Rachel is demanding the impossible—that is the meaning of the question "Am I in the place of God?" (cf. 2 Kgs. 5:7). Because no one can help her, Rachel finds a solution (Gen. 30:3-4; cf. Sarah in 16:2): she gives Jacob her maid Bilhah as wife. Their son will be counted as the son of Bilhah's mistress, as is expressed by the ritual of giving birth upon the knees of the mistress (30:3-4). The mistress then gives the child its name (vv. 5-6), calling him "Dan" and explaining the name as meaning "God has given judgment for me" (Hebrew *dānann 'elōhîm*). This explanation fits the name precisely, as well as the situation of rivalry between Leah and Rachel (v. 1). In verse 6b the reviser adds an interpretation that is more devout but also more general and not really appropriate, as in 29:33.

7-13   The narrative will pick up again in verse 14; verses 7-13 have been added by the reviser to make up the number twelve.

7-8   Bilhah bears her mistress a second son, whom Rachel names "Naphtali" (etymology unknown). She gives an interpretation of the name based on her rivalry with her sister. When she says that she has struggled "like God," she means that she has struggled mightily; as in many other passages, Hebrew *'elōhîm* is to be treated as an adjective. This explanation differs markedly from the others supplied by the reviser; probably he had it before him in the narrative, of which it would then be a fragment.

9-13   These verses were added by the reviser, who is following the narrative closely. Leah, too, gives Jacob her maid as concubine and receives children through her. The two names "Gad" and "Asher" were originally divine names. Gad is a god of happiness, mentioned also in Isaiah 65:11. The exclamation "Good fortune" means literally "With (the help of) Gad." The word "Asher" (Hebrew *'āšēr*) also means "happiness" or "good fortune," and may be associated with the divine name "Asherah" (or, according to others, with the god Ashur). Leah's exclamation "Happy am I!" (literally, "I am in good fortune"), cited to explain the name, resembles her exclamation in Genesis 30:11. A second explanation has been loosely appended: "Young women [literally, 'daughters'] will call me happy!" (cf. Luke 1:48).

14-18 These verses, which follow verses 1-6, recount a new episode in the quarrel between Leah and Rachel. It takes place "at the time of the wheat harvest" (v. 14a), and in verse 16 Jacob returns from the field. Leah's son Reuben, about six years old, finds some "love apples," the fruit of the mandrake, in the field; mandrake is often considered an aphrodisiac able to promote fertility (Cant. 7:13). Rachel asks for some of the fruit, and Leah angrily refuses. Then they agree to a proposal on the part of Rachel, which leads to Leah's getting a son. On the basis of this transaction (Gen. 30:15-16), in the old narrative Leah calls him 'îš śākār, "man of hire." Here, however, the reviser has made a change, replacing this simple explanation with a double theological explanation of the name. The first part, "God heard Leah," is inappropriate here; the second part, "God has rewarded me because . . . ," is an artificial explanation based on the narrative context, which gives the word śākār the sense of "reward" instead of "hire."

19-21 The next three births were also added by the reviser. The name "Zebulun" (etymology unknown) once again is given a double explanation, based on its phonetic similarity to two different verbs, one meaning "give a gift," the other "endure"; both are dubious and are not found elsewhere. The reviser also adds the birth of Dinah, probably to make up the full twelve. No explanation of her name is given. Perhaps this verse is meant to pave the way for chapter 34.

22-24 The birth of Joseph constitutes the conclusion. It originally followed verses 14-18 of the narrative: in accordance with the mutual agreement in verse 15, we should be told that the "love apples" resulted in the birth of a child to Rachel. The reviser has omitted this element, replacing it with a theological explanation of the name "Joseph" in verses 23-24. In remarkably awkward language he gives two explanations for the name. In verse 23, it is derived from the verb 'āsap, "take away"; an imperfect form is cited to explain a perfect, "has taken away." In the second explanation (v. 24), the name is explained as an optative from a different verb meaning "add, do something again": "May he add." The latter is the philologically correct explanation.

The narrator's purpose in recounting this interlude is to show that in the time of the patriarchs quarrels between women were as important as quarrels between men. They had to do with social rank and status. In this case, there is a profound conflict between recognition as mother and recognition based on personal attraction. Here it is the woman who defends the interests of the individual against overemphasis on the interests of society. The reviser, for whom this conflict was no longer real or no longer important, gave the entire section a theological tinge in the liturgical language of his day.

30:25-43 JACOB OUTWITS LABAN

25 *After Rachel had borne Joseph, Jacob said to Laban:*
Let me go, so that I may return to my own house and land.
26 *Give me my wives and my children,*
for whom I have served you, that I may go.
You yourself know how I have served you.
27 *Laban answered: If I have found favor in your eyes, I have learned [by divination] that Yahweh has blessed me because of you.*
28 *And he continued: Name the wages that you demand of me and I will give them to you.*
29 *He replied: You yourself know well how I have served you and what has become of your flocks under me.*
30 *For you had few when I came; now they have increased enormously, and Yahweh has blessed you wherever I turned.*
But now I must finally take care of my own household.
31 *Then he said: What shall I give you?*
Jacob answered: You shall give me nothing.
If you will do for me what I tell you,
I will again feed and guard all your flocks.
32 *I will go through all your flocks today, and will pick out all the speckled and spotted animals*
[and all the black animals among the sheep
and the speckled and spotted animals among the goats],
and these shall be my wages.
33 *And my honesty will answer for me later*
when you come to check my wages.
Then everything that is not speckled
[among the goats and the black among the sheep]
shall be counted as stolen by me.
34 *The Laban replied: Good, let it be as you have said.*
35 *Now on the same day he picked out the speckled and spotted animals*
[and the speckled and spotted goats—all that had white on them—and all the black among the sheep]
and gave them to his sons to look after.

36 *And he put a journey of three days between himself and Jacob,*
while Jacob tended the flocks of Laban that remained.

37 *Then Jacob took fresh rods of poplar*
[and of almond and plane tree]
and peeled white stripes on them
[so that he laid bare the white on the rods].

38 *Then he placed the rods that he had peeled in the troughs*
[at the watering places where the flocks came to drink]
facing the animals
[and they came into heat when they came to drink].

39 *Thus the animals bred in front of the rods and gave birth to young that were*
[striped and] speckled and spotted.

40 *[And Jacob picked out the sheep, and he turned the faces of the animals*
toward the striped and all the black in Laban's flock. Thus he bred flocks for
himself that he did not add to Laban's animals.]

41 *And whenever the stronger animals were in heat,*
Jacob placed the rods in the troughs before the eyes of the animals, so that they
bred in front of the rods.

42 *But when it came to the weaker animals, he did not place them there. Thus*
the weaker animals fell to Laban's lot, the stronger to Jacob's.

43 *Thus the man spread abroad mightily,*
and had much cattle, male and female servants, camels and asses.

This passage recounts an agreement between Laban and Jacob (vv. 25b-34) and what came of it (vv. 35-42). The agreement, introduced by a conversation, formally resembles Babylonian dialogue contracts (cf. Gen. 23). The text as a whole is difficult to understand because a relatively simple process has been complicated by the technical notes of an expert (bracketed in the translation). If these interpolations are removed, the narrative goes back to J, who incorporated an originally independent herdsman narrative into the Jacob-Laban cycle.

25-30   The agreed term of fourteen years of service having ended, Jacob asks Laban to release him. He points out the quality of his work, which Laban confirms (vv. 26b, 27). Laban, however, hopes to benefit still from Jacob's ability. His implicit request is clear enough: he even leaves it up to Jacob to name his price for continuing to work. Jacob merely repeats more insistently his request to be released (vv. 29-30). It is a particularly nice touch that Jacob's reason—"I must finally take care of my own household"—plays on Laban's "watching out for his own" at the beginning. He reminds Laban that he has multiplied Laban's wealth through his honest labor, of which he is proud and which he knows has been blessed by Yahweh. Now Laban can no longer deny him the right to his own household.

31-34   In the second exchange Laban ignores Jacob's request and repeats his offer. Now Jacob realizes that his request has been rejected. He must find another solution; now, on his own initiative, he offers to stay on as Laban's herdsman. When Laban offers to let him name his own price, he replies initially with the amazing words: "You shall give me nothing" (v. 31a). But this is like Ephron's statement in a similar bargaining session: "I will give you the property" (Gen. 23). One knows how to take such statements. Jacob makes only one condition, but it indicates what he has in mind (30:32-33): he will segregate the abnormally colored animals from the herd. Then, after a certain length of time, he will keep from the herd—which now comprises only normally colored animals—only those that are abnormally colored as his payment. It is hard to recognize this clear and unambiguous condition in verses 32-33, because several additions have been made with the intention of defining the condition more precisely, with particular attention to the difference between sheep and goats. Laban agrees, because he smells a profit for himself (v. 34).

35-43 The carrying out of the agreement is divided into two parts: the actions of Laban (vv. 35-36) and the actions of Jacob (37-42). Laban takes certain precautions: he himself segregates the abnormally colored animals and gives them to his sons to look after (v. 35); staying a three days' journey distant should prevent any incursions on Jacob's part. Now that Jacob realizes that Laban does not plan to let him go, he see no other possibility than a stratagem. But this is meant in a positive sense: it reflects the ability of someone in a weak position to outwit someone strong and powerful. Jacob remains within the terms of the agreement; his stratagem is not a deception (vv. 37-42). He places peeled (and therefore multicolored) rods in the drinking troughs, with the result that the animals give birth to multicolored offspring (vv. 38-39). This describes the clever device of an astute herdsman, who uses the visible environment at the moment of conception to breed for a certain result. There are magical notions in the background, but the critical element in the case of Jacob is his intention to breed for a specific purpose by using his knowledge of animal behavior. The description of his stratagem ends with verse 39. Verse 40 is a different experiment, added by the interpolator, which achieves the same result. In verses 41-42, however, the method employed in verses 38-39 is continued and refined by being restricted to the stronger animals, so that the stronger of the young will belong to Jacob.

The conclusion in verse 43 is inconsistent with the preceding narrative, which speaks only of sheep and goats. Probably a redactor added this ending after the model of Genesis 26:13-14.

31:1-54 JACOB'S SEPARATION FROM LABAN

2 *And Jacob saw from Laban's expression*
that he no longer thought of him as before;
1 *and he heard the words of Laban's sons: Jacob has taken everything that*
belonged to our father;
all his wealth has come
from what belonged to our father.
3 *[And Yahweh said to Jacob: Return to the land of your fathers and to your*
family; I will be with you.]
4 *Then Jacob sent for Rachel and Leah*
and called them to the field where his flock was.
5 *And he said to them: I see by your father's expression*
that he no longer thinks of me as before;
[but the God of my father has been with me].
6 *And you yourselves know that I have served your father with all my*
strength.
7 *But your father has cheated me and has changed my wages ten times; but*
God has not allowed me to suffer harm.
8 *If he said: The spotted ones shall be your wages,*
the whole flock bore spotted;
if he said: The striped ones shall be your wages,
the whole flock bore striped.
9 *[So God has taken the flock from your father*
and given it to me.]
10 *[In the animals' mating season, I lifted up my eyes and saw in a dream how*
the he-goats mounting the flock were striped and speckled and dappled.]
11 *And the angel of God said to me in a dream:*
Jacob! And I said: Here I am.
12 *And he said: [Lift up your eyes and see how all the he-goats mounting the*
flock are striped and spotted and dappled; for] I have seen all that Laban has
done to you.
13 *I am the God who appeared to you at Bethel,*
where you anointed the pillar and where you made a vow to me. Now rise, go
from this land and return to the land of your family.
14 *Then Rachel and Leah answered him and said:*
Do we still have any part or inheritance in our father's house?
15 *Are we not regarded by him as foreigners? For he has sold us and long since*
consumed the money.
16 *For all the wealth that God has taken from our father—*
it belongs to us and our children.
And now, all that God has told you to do, do!
17 *Then Jacob made ready, put his children*
and his wives on camels,
18 *and drove off all his cattle and all his property*
that he had acquired, his cattle and his possessions

that he had acquired in Paddan-aram,
to go to his father Isaac in the land of Canaan.

19 But when Laban had gone to shear his sheep,
Rachel stole her father's teraphim;

20 [but Jacob stole the heart of Laban the Aramean
by concealing from him that he intended to flee].

21 And he fled with all that he had;
he set out and crossed the River
and made in the direction of the mountains of Gilead.

22 On the third day, Laban was told that Jacob had fled.

23 Then he took his brothers with him, pursued him for seven days, and caught
up with him in the mountains of Gilead.

24 [But God came in a dream by night to Laban the Aramean and said to him:
Take care to say not a word to Jacob.]

25 When Laban had overtaken Jacob—Jacob had pitched his tent on Mount . . . ,
but Laban had pitched his tent in the mountains of Gilead—

26 then Laban said to Jacob: What have I done to you,
that you have [stolen my heart and] taken away my daughters like prisoners
of war?

27 Why did you flee secretly and deceive me and say nothing to me, that I might
send you on your way with songs and rejoicing, with tambourine and zither,

28 and did not even allow me to kiss my grandchildren and daughters? You
have acted foolishly!

29 [Indeed I would have had the power to do you harm;
but the God of your father spoke to me last night and said:
Take care to say not a word to Jacob.]

30 But now—you have gone away because you longed so much for your father's
house.
But why have you stolen my god?

31 Then Jacob answered and said to Laban:
[Because I was afraid], because I thought that you would take your daughters
away from me by force.

32 Whoever you find in possession of your god shall not live. In the presence of
my brothers point out what they have that is yours and take it.
But Jacob did not know that Rachel had stolen it.

33 Then Laban went into Jacob's tent and Leah's tent
and into the tent of the two maids.
Then he went out of Leah's tent into Rachel's tent.

34 But Rachel had taken the teraphim, put it in the camel's saddle, and sat down
upon it.
And Laban searched the whole tent and did not find it.

35 And she said to her father: Do not be angry with me, sir,
that I cannot rise in your presence;
the lot of women is upon me.
And he did not find the teraphim.

36 And Jacob became angry and quarreled with Laban; Jacob retorted and said to
Laban: What wrong have I done? What is my offense that you have come
after me?

37   *For you have searched all my possessions; what have you found belonging to*
     your household?
     Lay it here before my brothers and before your brothers,
     that they may decide between us.

38   *It is now twenty years that I have been with you.*
     Your sheep and goats have not miscarried,
     and the rams of your flock I have not eaten.

39   *What was torn by wild beasts I was not allowed to bring you;*
     I had to replace it myself, from me you demanded what was taken by day or
     by night.

40   *By day the heat consumed me and the cold by night,*
     and sleep fled before my eyes.

41   *Twenty full years now I have served you in your house;*
     fourteen years for your two daughters
     and six years for your flock,
     and you have altered my wages ten times.

42   *If the God of my father*
     [the God of Abraham and the Refuge of Isaac]
     had not been with me, even now you would have sent me away empty-
     handed!
     God saw my affliction and the labor of my hands
     and spoke justice to you last night.

43   *Laban answered and said to Jacob:*
     The daughters are my daughters
     and the children are my children, the animals are my animals,
     all that you see here belongs to me!
     But what can I do for these my daughters now,
     or for the children that they have borne?

44   *Come now, let us make an agreement with each other,*
     I and you; let us make a cairn
     to stand as a witness between me and you.

45   *[And Jacob (Laban) took a stone and set it up as a monument.]*

46   *And Jacob said to his brothers: Gather stones.*
     And they took stones and erected a cairn
     [and had a meal there beside the cairn].

47   *[And Laban called it Jegar-sahadutha;*
     Jacob called it Galeed.]

48   *And Laban said: The cairn is a witness today between me and you;*
     [therefore it is called Galeed and Mizpah, because it is said:]

49   *May Yahweh watch between me and you*
     when we are out of each other's sight;

50   *If you ever ill-treat my daughters*
     or take other wives besides my daughters,
     even if none of us learns of it,
     God is a witness between me and you.

51   *[And Laban said to Jacob: Behold, this cairn and this monument that I have*
     erected between me and you,

52   *this cairn is a witness and a witness is this monument*
     that I will not pass beyond this cairn to your side

> *and that you will not pass beyond this cairn*
> *and this monument on my side to do harm.*
> 53a *Let the God of Abraham and the God of Nahor be judge between us (the God*
> *of their fathers).]*
> 53b *And Jacob swore by the Refuge of his father Isaac.*
> 54 *And Jacob slaughtered a sacrifice on the mountain,*
> *and he summoned his brothers to share the meal.*
> *And they ate the meal and passed the night on the mountain.*

In the larger context of chapters 27–33, Jacob's flight (27:41-45) is now followed by his return. In the Jacob-Laban episode, arrival (ch. 29) is now followed by departure, for Jacob once again a flight. The conclusion of this chapter (31:43-54, the agreement) also concludes the Jacob-Laban episode. The chapter is organized as follows: Jacob's flight, Laban's pursuit, Laban's charge and Jacob's countercharge, agreement and Laban's return (vv. 43-54 plus 31:55). The nucleus of the episode is the quarrel (Hebrew *rîb*) between Laban and Jacob and its resolution through a formal agreement. The entire chapter is pervaded with legal language and procedures.

1-16 Jacob's flight is introduced by the reason for it (vv. 1-3) and Jacob's ensuing conversation with his wives. Verse 2 should precede verse 1. Again the first impression is visual: Jacob sees hostility in Laban's expression (v. 2); he also hears the hostile words of Laban's sons (v. 1). He feels threatened; now he must do something. He decides to flee, but first he needs his wives' agreement; this is the subject of verses 4-16. The divine directive to return (v. 3) seems abrupt; the verse is probably a late addition.

4-13 Jacob's conversation with his wives is given in great detail; it has also undergone some expansion. It consists of Jacob's statement (vv. 4-13) and his wives' response (vv. 14-16). He summons them and describes the situation: Laban is hostile to him, but he defends himself by saying he is not to blame (vv. 6-7). He explains the background in detail in verses 8-12, summarizing the events of 30:25-43. In this discourse, his emphasis on God's governance in what took place does not contradict 30:25-43; it arises from the situation and the purpose of the discourse. This explanation could have ended with 31:9. In verses 10-13, which are very corrupt, two different revelations to Jacob have been combined; both are late additions. The first seeks to ascribe the increase of Jacob's flock to a divine revelation.

The second revelation is a directive to return coupled with a promise; in other words, it is a doublet of verse 3. It, too, could be reconstructed. It is clear that Jacob's statement to his wives ends with his saying that God has commanded him to return. This confronts his wives with the question of whether they will go with Jacob.

14-16   The answer of the wives is straightforward and decisive. Its first part consists in renouncing their father's house in a formal act of renunciation, like that in 2 Samuel 20:1 and 1 Kings 12:16 (also renunciation of a "house"). In stating their reason, they charge their father with having transgressed family law by taking the "compensation" (Hebrew *mōhar*) he received for them in the form of labor and spending it all on himself, thereby treating them as strangers rather than members of the family. Their accusation is justified: "He has sold us" (v. 15). The daughters' renunciation of their father's house creates a new "house" (another instance of the importance of women in this form of society); on behalf of themselves and their children, the women lay claim to the property Jacob has acquired in the house of their father against Laban's claim (v. 43). This means separation, and so they consent to Jacob's planned flight (v. 16).

17-21   As soon as his wives have agreed, Jacob sets out. His departure is described in the form of an itinerary in verses 17, 18, 21; the style of 18b shows that it comes from P. A parenthetical statement in verse 19 lays the groundwork for verses 25-30; the theft of the teraphim is possible because Laban is away shearing his sheep, which always includes a celebration. Teraphim are household gods such as are found in many religions; in the Iliad, for example, Aeneas takes the Penates with him when leaving Troy. The household gods give protection and blessing; their possession also has legal significance, so that Rachel's motive for the theft arises from the charges made by the women in verses 14-16. They are addressing a wrong that has been done them. The statement that Jacob "stole the heart of Laban" (that is, deceived him) is an interpolation based on the word "steal"; it is as out of place here as in verse 26.

22-30   These verses record Laban's pursuit and accusation. He receives the news that Jacob has fled, collects his people, and catches up with Jacob in the mountains of Gilead (vv. 22-23). The description demonstrates Laban's superior resources: he has his people along, with whom he quickly overtakes the fugitive; Jacob is in his hands. The superiority of the powerful Laban has triggered the interpolation of verses 24 and 29, countering this superiority with God's protection. Laban has caught up with Jacob; they are encamped on two opposing heights like hostile armies before battle (v. 25). But Laban attacks Jacob only with words, bringing two charges against him. The first is Jacob's secret flight, the second the theft of the household god (teraphim). It is an especially nice point that verse 30b mentions only the teraphim as having been stolen, whereas it is clear from the preceding narrative that Laban really is thinking of the whole flock that Jacob has taken with him. But he has no grounds for any charges having to do with this flock! Here, too, Laban appeals to the proprieties. It is disgraceful that Jacob has taken his daughters away "like prisoners of war" (v. 26). For this very reason it was of the utmost importance to Jacob that they were fully agreed to go. This charge is developed in verses 27-28; we learn in passing that such a departure was accompanied by singing and the playing of musical instruments. With his concluding rebuke—"You have acted foolishly!"—Laban tries to demean Jacob in the presence of his wives; the charge of foolishness is a serious matter. It loses its gravity, however, because Laban conceals the fact that he could easily compel Jacob to stay. Again the narrator's skill is revealed: it is left to the listener to discern how hollow the charges are. For the interpolator, however, this is a golden opportunity to recall God's warning to Laban to do nothing to Jacob (cf. v. 24). The interpolation, however, is out of place here, because Laban is doing precisely what he had been warned in a dream not to do: "Take care to say not a word to Jacob." The secondary nature of verse 29 is also clear from the fact that verse 30 makes more sense directly following verse 28. Verse 30a sounds like an attempt to exonerate Jacob with respect to the first charge; now, however, Laban shifts all the weight to his second point: You have robbed me! (cf. v. 27a).

31-35 Jacob responds to both charges. His answer to the first (v. 31) reveals the real situation. In verse 43 Laban himself unwittingly confirms Jacob's interpretation: "The daughters are my daughters. . . ." The second charge Jacob, who knows nothing of the theft, denies totally, sure of his innocence; he allows Laban to conduct the search and himself decrees the death penalty for the thief (v. 32). Laban's thorough search proceeds in vain, because Rachel has used a trick to prevent the image from being found. The episode is recounted in a bantering tone, but in the background stands the deliberate rebellion of a daughter against her father: she knows she is in the right. A theological aspect of the episode is barely hinted at: the impotence of wooden idols (cf. Isa. 46:1-2).

36-42 In Jacob's countercharge the Jacob-Laban episode reaches its climax. It begins in verses 36-37 with an ironic denial of the charge of theft; Jacob demands that Laban present his evidence—only thus could formal charges be brought. Then Jacob gives an accounting of his service to Laban (vv. 38-41a). This section is framed (vv. 38a, 41a) by an emphatic reference to the lengthy duration of this service: twenty years! This account gives us an insight into the work of a herdsman of the period: careful attention when the animals give birth and respect for the owner's property (v. 38) as well as the obligatory replacement of losses (v. 39). There was a herdsman's law with specific regulations governing such replacement; cf. Exodus 22:10-13 and Codex Hammurabi §§ 261-66. Also necessary was a willingness to endure bodily hardships (Gen. 31:40). We see that Jacob went far beyond the expected duties of a herdsman in caring for the property of his employer—an outstanding example of proud professionalism. Jacob's summary of his labors helps us understand what the New Testament metaphor of the good shepherd is meant to express. Jacob's passionate emotion finds expression in poetic language, as is so often the case at the climax of a narrative. The climax leads to a contrast: for twenty years, Jacob has undergone the hard life of a herdsman for his employer and for his employer's benefit. Had Laban had his way (vv. 41-42), Jacob would have gone away empty after these twenty years of hard labor! Thus Jacob's words conclude with a serious accusation. From the Covenant Code on, through the Deuteronomic Law and the prophets of judgment and into the New Testament, it was considered a serious transgression if an employer did not immediately pay his workers the wages they had earned. If we look back to the charges brought against Jacob by Laban (vv. 26-30), the contrast is extreme and speaks for itself.

At this climactic point, Jacob speaks of God and God's work: "If the God of my father had not been with me . . ." (v. 42a). This is the God who intervenes on behalf of the weak and takes the side of the poor (v. 42b). Thus Jacob's countercharge concludes by praising God: "God saw my affliction and the labor of my hands." This statement and the following words, "He spoke justice last night," suggest the language of the Psalms (Ps. 124:1; 34:6; 26:1); in them, this individual experience becomes the language of prayer for many. Jacob's final statement in Genesis 31:42 shows also that the promise of God's presence (v. 42a), which is characteristic of the Jacob story, belongs together with words of praise spoken by one who has experienced this presence (v. 42b). The rhythm of this clause is interrupted by the words "the God of Abraham and the Refuge of Isaac," which are probably a secondary addition. The phrase *paḥaḏ yiṣḥāq* appears only here and in verse 53b, where it is also secondary. It was interpreted formerly as "Dread of Isaac," an early divine appellative from the patriarchal period.[1] But this meaning is inappropriate for a patriarchal deity, both in general and in this passage. The meaning "Kinsman of Isaac" was therefore proposed,[2] but has been rejected. Recently, on the basis of Arabic, the meaning "refuge" has been suggested; it appears more probable.

43-54   Laban's agreement with Jacob. The text is very difficult

1. Albrecht Alt, "The God of the Fathers," pp. 1–100 in *Essays on Old Testament History and Religion* (Garden City: Doubleday, 1968).
2. William Foxwell Albright, *From the Stone Age to Christianity*, 2nd ed. (Garden City: Doubleday, 1957), p. 248.

because in it two different agreements have been conflated: one in verses 43-50, 53b-54 terminating the encounter between Laban and Jacob and another in verses 51-53a. The former is structured as follows: Laban proposes an agreement to Jacob, with a cairn as witness (vv. 43-44); Jacob accepts and has his people erect a cairn (v. 46); Laban formulates the agreement (vv. 48-50); Jacob confirms the agreement and ratifies it with a meal (vv. 53b-54); Laban takes his leave and returns home.

Initially Laban answers Jacob by insisting on his claim to ownership, justifying Jacob's fears. He finally yields, however, admitting that he cannot support his claim (v. 43). Clearly he cannot deny Jacob's words in verse 42. But he disguises his admission as concern for his daughters and grandchildren: he will do for them all that is left for him to do, implying that he will no longer stand in the way of their leaving. He therefore proposes an agreement to Jacob, with a cairn as witness. The Hebrew word translated "agreement" is $b^e r\hat{\imath}t$; in this context it does not mean "covenant," because it refers to a unique settlement limited to a single point in time. Jacob's answer comes in verse 46. The statement in verse 45 that "Jacob took a stone and set it up as a monument" is an interpolation. Verse 46 follows verse 44: Jacob assents to Laban's proposal and tells his people to build a cairn. The statement in verse 46b that they held a meal there comes too early; it belongs at the end of the ritual, where it is in fact repeated (v. 54). Now follows the actual agreement (vv. 48-50), formulated by Laban. The cairn will bear witness to the oath (v. 53b) Laban demands of Jacob, that he will treat his daughters well and will not take any additional wives. This event gave the cairn its name: "Therefore it is called Galeed ['heap'—'witness']." This was later expanded upon. One such expansion is all or part of verse 49, where the place is given the name "Mizpah," "because it is said: May Yahweh watch [Hebrew *ṣāpāh*] between. . . ." The other expansion, probably a learned gloss, appears in verse 47: Jacob called the place "Galeed," whereas Laban called it (in Aramaic) "Jegar-sahadutha."

Verse 50 should be followed by Jacob's oath, which does not appear until verse 53b. The oath sworn by Jacob alone in verse 53b follows verse 50 and belongs to the first agreement (vv. 48-50). It is followed in turn by a fellowship meal (v. 54), which Jacob provides because in it he ratifies the resolution of the quarrel. When he summons "his brothers" to share the meal, he includes Laban and Laban's people. Now Laban can be content; he says farewell to his daughters and returns home (v. 55).

The intervening verses (vv. 51-53a) are clearly an interpolation. Its structure is: cairn (and monument) as witness (vv. 51-52a); agreement (v. 52b); God is judge between us (v. 53a). It is a mutual agreement; each party undertakes not to enter the other's territory with hostile intent. While the first pact (vv. 48-50) deals with family matters, these verses deal with tribal matters. In this addition, "cairn" and "monument" have been combined. Once again, the text is very difficult; probably two formulations of the pact have been conflated. It must of course be agreed to by both parties; this is the clearest difference between it and the first agreement. Since both parties are tribes or nations, each (that is, its representative) must swear by its own god (v. 53a): "The God of Abraham and the God of Nahor be judge between us." The designations have been adapted to the context; a gloss adds: "the God of their fathers."

The health of a community clearly includes the quarrel as a way of resolving conflicts, so long as it remains within the limits defined by law. Such "peace under law" is endangered, however, when the strength and power of one party make it possible to discriminate against a weaker party under the guise of legality. In such a situation the narrator speaks of God's intervention on behalf of the weaker party. This intervention (v. 42) is the climax of the narrative. It appears again in the laments of the poor in the Psalms, in the social indictments of the prophets, and in the message of Jesus.

31:55–32:21 PREPARATIONS FOR THE MEETING WITH ESAU

31:55 *Early the next morning, Laban kissed his grandchildren and his daughters and blessed them;*
then Laban departed and returned to his place.

32:1 *Jacob, too, went his way.*
Then angels of God met him.

2 *And Jacob said, when he saw them:*
Here is an army of God!
And he called that place Mahanaim.

3 *And Jacob sent messengers on ahead to his brother Esau*
to the region of Seir, to the territory of Edom.

4 *And he ordered them: Thus you are to say to my lord Esau:*
Thus says your servant Jacob: I have been sojourning with Laban and have dwelt there until now.

5 *I have acquired cattle, asses, and sheep, male and female servants,*
and now I send message to my lord,
to tell my lord, that I may find favor in your sight.

6 *When the messengers returned to Jacob, they said:*
We came to your brother Esau,
he is already coming to meet you, and four hundred men are with him.

7   Then Jacob was very much afraid and distressed,
    [and he divided the people that were with him,
    the sheep and the cattle (and the camels) into two companies.

8   He thought: If Esau comes upon one company and destroys it,
    the other camp can escape.]

9   And Jacob said:
    [God of my father Abraham and God of my father Isaac], Yahweh,
    [who said to me: Return to your country and to your kinsmen and I will do
    well by you—

10 I am not the least worthy of all the mercy and all the fidelity that you have
    shown to your servant. For only with my staff did I cross the Jordan here,
    and now I have grown into two companies.]

11 Save me, I pray, from the hand of my brother,
    from the hand of Esau. For I am afraid of him,
    lest he come and strike me, the mothers with the children.

12 [You yourself have said: I will do well by you and make your descendants
    numerous as the sand by the sea,
    which cannot be counted for numbers.]

13 And he passed the night there.

    Then he took from what he had acquired
    a present for his brother Esau:

14 two hundred she-goats and twenty he-goats,
    two hundred ewes and twenty rams,

15 thirty milch camels with their young, forty cows
    and ten bulls, twenty she-asses and ten he-asses.

16 And he put them into the care of his servants, each herd separately,
    and he said to his servants: Go before me and put a space between the separate
    herds.

17 And he gave orders to the first: When Esau my brother approaches you and
    asks you: To whom do you belong, where are you going, and to whom do
    these belong?

18 then answer: To your servant Jacob; it is a present
    that he is sending to his lord,
    and he himself is coming behind us.

19 He gave the same orders to the second and to the third
    and to all who went behind the herds:
    Thus you are to speak to Esau
    when you meet him.

20 You are to say: Your servant Jacob himself is coming
    behind us. For he thought:
    I will appease him with the gift that goes ahead of me;
    only then will I see him in person.
    Perhaps he will receive me favorably.

21 So the present went on ahead of him,
    but he spent the night in the camp.

Verse 55 of chapter 31 is 32:1 in the Hebrew Bible; 32:1 is verse 2. In this
and the following section, English verse numbers are given.

31:55–32:2   In these verses a divine encounter is linked with the
conclusion of the Jacob-Laban episode. At the conclusion of many
narratives or episodes, we are told that the two parties go their separate ways after a meeting (Gen. 18:33; 33:16-17; 1 Sam. 24:22, etc.).
Thus Genesis 31:55–32:2 is a bridge concluding chapter 31 and introducing chapter 32. Laban says farewell to his daughters and grandsons; like the evening meal in 31:54, the farewell blessing confirms
that the agreement has ended the quarrel. Laban and Jacob go their
ways in peace. "Jacob, too, went his way"—now his way is no longer
flight. His encounter on the way (vv. 1-2) is reduced to a brief note
attached to the itinerary, like the notes about wells in chapter 26;
it is therefore not a fragment (cf. 33:16-17). Jacob's return after
his separation from Laban is introduced by a divine encounter: he
meets angels of God (32:1b); his response is an exclamation that
results in his naming the spot. Verse 1b clearly recalls 28:10-22,
which can help elucidate this abbreviated episode; the Hebrew
phrase *mal'ak̲ê 'elōhîm* appears only here and in 28:12. There is also a
parallel in Joshua 5:13-15: Joshua encounters a commander of the
"army of Yahweh"; in both passages, this divine encounter precedes
a perilous venture. This parallel is also suggested by Jacob's exclamation: "Here is an army of God!" Both recall the divine appellative
Yahweh Sabaoth ("Yahweh of hosts," "Yahweh of armies"). Jacob is
anticipating a threatening meeting with his brother. In this situation,
he is met by angels of God, which suggest to him an "army of God":
God's might will protect him from danger. He preserved this memory and passed it on to future generations in the name of the site:
Mahanaim (literally, "military camp," a dual form with singular
meaning). A city in Gilead with this name is mentioned in 2 Samuel
2:8 and elsewhere.

3-13a   Jacob prepares for his meeting with his brother by sending advance messengers to him; between this group of messengers
and the second group in verses 13-21b comes a prayer (vv. 9-12).

3-8   These verses constitute a classic example of sending a messenger, the most important medium of communication over a distance in a preliterate age. It is an ancient institution with its own
language, developed through long tradition—an especially important example of the *Sitz im Leben* of fixed forms of speech. The language of messengers continued to live on for a long time in the
language of letters. The message is addressed to the recipient as
though its sender were standing in his presence. The words of a
messenger are the words of the sender, just as the words of a herald
are the words of the king. Thus messenger formula "Thus says . . ."
has the function of bringing the words of the sender to life in the
presence of the recipient. "Thus says . . ." therefore has both perfec-

tive and present meaning. This is the reason why the prophets later made use of messenger language.

Jacob sends his messengers to the land of Edom (or Seir; cf. Gen. 25:30). As is usually the case, the message has two parts: a narrative section (32:4a, 5a) and an imperative or statement of purpose (v. 5b). The purpose of the message is grounded in what the narrative section reports. For Jacob, the purpose is "to find favor in your sight." Thus he indicates that he is willing to subordinate himself to his brother and forgo the privileges deriving from the blessing he obtained by trickery. Instead of an answer from Esau, however, the messenger brings the news that Esau is on his way to meet Jacob with four hundred men (v. 6). The size of the retinue shows (cf. Gen. 14:14; Judg. 7:6) that Esau is now a military commander (cf. Gen 27:40: "By your sword you shall live"). Jacob's reaction to this news (32:7a) is fear. He is still not certain whether Esau is coming to meet him with hostile intent; but he knows that in the fact of such overwhelming force he is lost, and that the relative immobility of his caravan, which includes women, children, and animals, prevents him from fleeing. His fear is the natural reaction of someone threatened by superior strength. In the face of this threat, he prays to God to save him. In an earlier form of the text, this prayer probably followed verse 7a immediately. The interpolated material in verses 7b-8 is intended to explain the name "Mahanaim" (vv. 1-2) on the basis of Jacob's separation of his people into two camps. It is a late addition.

9-12   In its present form, Jacob's prayer is out of harmony with both the style and the substance of the old narrative. In its original form, it is an elemental cry to God for help in the face of mortal danger:

> Yahweh, save me, I pray, from the hand of my brother,
> from the hand of Esau. For I am afraid of him,
> lest he come and strike me,
> the mothers with the children.

In the present text, the prayer has been expanded by the addition of divine predicates in verse 9a, retrospective references to God's directive and promise in verse 9b and to God's favor shown to Jacob in verse 10, and the promise in verse 12. A later tradent, recognizing perceptively that the old narrative reaches its climax in Jacob's cry for help, underscored it further by interpreting it at length as the heart of the story of Jacob's return. He did this by using the theme "recollection of God's saving acts" found in the Psalms, which is often coupled with an appeal for help, especially in the communal laments of the Psalter (Ps. 80). The tradent who thus expanded Jacob's simple cry for help in danger succeeded thereby in creating a work of art, a prayer in the religious language of a later age that concentrates the story of Jacob into a few sentences in this central passage. The extended invocation places the history of Jacob in the broader context of the Patriarchal History: "God of my father Abraham, God of my father Isaac." Like his fathers, Jacob has received directives and promises (Gen. 31:3) from this God. Here, however, the promises are reduced to general terms: "I will do well by you." This statement (which appears only in vv. 9 and 12 of ch. 32) is meant to summarize a variety of promises. Jacob's retrospective confession of faith summarizes his story impressively (v. 10). The introduction—literally, "I am too small . . . "—suggests the beginning of chapter 27; in its two sections, the statement in 32:10b summarizes Jacob's flight and return. His way has demonstrated the mercy and fidelity of the God to whom he cries for help in his hour of need. In Jeremiah 32 a short prayer has been expanded similarly. This expansion is clearly distinct from the cry for help that issues directly from fear in the face of danger. Such cries for help appear elsewhere in Old Testament narratives, e.g., Judges 10:15 and 1 Samuel 12:10. Genesis 32:11b illustrates what Jacob is afraid of: "Lest he come and strike me." This is a vision of impending battle, in which not only is the opponent "struck" that is, killed), but also the helpless and innocent victims are slain without mercy: "Lest he strike the mothers with the children."

13-21   A second group of messengers serves to bring an advance present to Esau with the same purpose: that Jacob may find favor in his sight. To understand this detailed passage, clearly of great importance to the narrator, it is necessary to know that Hebrew *berākāh* can mean both "blessing" and "present." In a column comprising three sections, the *berākāh* from Jacob moves toward his brother. Thus Jacob gives him back the blessing that he had tricked him out of. The narrator does not state this explicitly, but lets the action speak for itself; neither does the implicit confession of guilt need to be made explicit.

Carefully and precisely Jacob gives his instructions to his servants (vv. 16-19); the division of the column into three parts serves to intensify the request implicit in the gifts. Now Jacob's purpose is expressed openly by his reflection in verse 20b: "I will appease him with the gift." (Only here and in Prov. 16:14 is the verb *kipper*, "appease," used for reconciliation between two human beings.) Only then will Jacob come into his brother's presence, in the hope that he will treat him mercifully. There is an implicit connection between Jacob's cry of distress to God and his present readiness to restore to his brother that which he has deprived him of. The relationship to God intended by the narrator is so obvious that it does not need to be reduced to theological language.

32:22-32 JACOB AT THE JABBOK

22 *That same night he arose, took his two wives*
and his two maids and his eleven children
and crossed the ford of the Jabbok.

23 *He took them and sent them across the wadi,*
and all his possessions he sent across.

24 *But Jacob stayed back alone.*
Then a man wrestled with him until daybreak.

25 *When he saw that he was unable to overcome him,*
he touched his thigh [joint so that Jacob's thigh joint was dislocated as he
wrestled with him].

26 *Then he said: Let me go, dawn is breaking!*
But he answered: I will not let you go
unless you bless me.

27 *[Then he asked him: What is your name? He answered: Jacob.*

28 *He said: You are no longer to be called Jacob,*
but Israel, because you have wrestled with God and with a mortal man and
have prevailed.]

29 *And Jacob asked him and said: Now tell me your name.*
But he said: Why do you ask my name?
And he blessed him there.

30 *And Jacob named the place [Peniel, because (he said)*
I have seen God face to face and have survived].

31 *And the sun rose on him as he passed by Penuel;*
he was limping because of his thigh.

32 *[Therefore the sons of Israel even to this day do not eat*
the sinew of the nerve along the thigh joint,
because he had touched the sinew of the nerve along Jacob's thigh joint.]

See the note in the previous section on the verse numbers of chapter 32.

The text of 32:22-32 is a single literary unit, but the brackets mark several secondary additions. All exegetes agree that the basic narrative is very ancient; it displays animistic traits and is inseparable from its setting, the river and the ford. It is a typical local tale, in which the danger of a ford is personified in a spirit or demon that will not permit the traveler to cross. Such narratives are associated with many places. It must have been recounted in the vicinity of the Jabbok ford, as the wordplay in verse 24 shows. This ancient local tale was associated with Jacob by means of the itinerary in verses 22, 23, 31a, which traces Jacob's route after his break with Laban and before his meeting with Esau. The additions all date from a later period. An outline of the narrative without the additions runs as follows: introductory and concluding itinerary (vv. 22-23, 31a); attack (v. 24); outcome of the struggle (vv. 25-29); naming of the place (v. 30).

22-23   These introductory verses turn the following events into something that happens to Jacob as he travels. He arrives at the ford of the Jabbok, which he crosses with his people and property. The words "that same night" belong to what was originally an independent itinerary note, where they referred to a previous event, probably arrival at the ford. Verse 23a arranges for Jacob to be alone when he is attacked. The Jabbok ("the blue river") is a tributary of the Jordan from the east, a raging torrent that flows through a deep ravine; the topography plays a part in the narrative.

24   Verse 24a makes a transition to the beginning of the action, for which it is essential that Jacob be alone. The following statement, "A man [that is, 'someone'] wrestled with him," is meant to suggest a surprise attack resembling a robbery or murder. We are not dealing with a wrestling match agreed to by both parties. Like a robber who must avoid being caught, the attacker must avoid the light of dawn; like a robber, too, he must keep his identity secret. These three features are appropriate to hostile demons such as appear in many narratives throughout the world. Here it is a night or river demon, who embodies the peril of the ford. This widespread notion has animistic roots. Exodus 4:24-26 is similar; the nature of the attack is the same, it takes place when the protagonist is traveling, it ends with the attacker's letting go and a naming, and the attack precedes a dangerous meeting. The statement of time at the end of Genesis 32:24, "until daybreak," means that the struggle remained undecided until then.

25-29   The first clause of verse 25 makes this point: the attacker realizes that he cannot overpower Jacob. Thereupon he touches his opponent's thigh joint; this touch is meant as a magic gesture to break off combat. The Hebrew text shows that verse 25b is a secondary addition; it has no syntactic connection with its context. This addition goes with verse 32; its purpose is to establish the latter as part of the text.

The attacker's request to be released (v. 26a) thus follows verse 25a. The reason for the request is that the demon possesses power only during the night and loses it at daybreak; this, too, is a widespread motif (Plautus' *Amphitryon*; the first act of Hamlet). Jacob imposes a condition (v. 26b): the attacker must bless him. In this context, such a blessing can mean only that the attacker must give him some of his superhuman power. The attacker agrees to this condition in verse 29, but first there is an interpolation in verses 27-28. In this secondary addition, Jacob is given a new name and the reason for this name is stated. It is a secondary addition, because the renaming of Jacob as Israel presupposes the existence of Israel as a nation. It is a later interpretation of the narrative, which sees in Jacob a representative of the nation Israel. This is the point of verse 28b, which exalts Jacob: he has fought "with gods and mortals" (a pair of opposites designating a whole) and been declared victorious; in the narrative, on the contrary, the struggle remains undecided. Here we see the late tendency to exaggerate the virtues of the patriarchs; this is the motive behind the addition. The rare Hebrew word *śārāh*, "wrestle," is chosen because of the name "Israel." The theme of renaming is otherwise unique to P (ch. 17 and 35:10ff., which 32:27-28 echo).

The request in verse 26 is followed by a request for the attacker's name. This question, too, presupposes animistic notions: if the demon's name is known, it can be invoked; this, too, is a common theme. But for this very reason the attacker refuses to tell his name (cf. Judg. 13:18). The other request, however, the attacker is able to grant in order to be set loose; he imparts some of his power to Jacob. The statement "And he blessed him there" already leads into the naming of the place: because the struggle ended with Jacob's being endowed with power, the place is important to him.

30-32   The ancient narrative closes with the naming of the place. But the explanation given in verse 30 does not fit the narrative: it presupposes instead a theophany and reflects a common idiom of a later period (Judg. 6:22; 13:22; Exod. 33:20; Deut. 34:10). The name "Peniel" (given as "Penuel" in Gen. 32:31) actually has a different etymology: "God's face" is a toponym (Hermann Gunkel: "originally the outline of a ridge"); Strabo cites it as the name of a Phoenician foothill. But the narrative provides clear evidence for the name to which it originally led: the name of the river at whose ford the struggle took place. This evidence is the Hebrew verb *ʾābaq*, "struggle," found only here in verses 24-25 (the addition in v. 28 uses a different verb!), undoubtedly chosen on account of the name "Jabbok." But if the naming and its explanation in verse 30 have been changed, this late alteration cannot be used to interpret the narrative as Jacob's encounter with God. In the narrative, it is not God but a hostile demon who attacks the traveler. All the profound theological conclusions drawn from the fact that Jacob's attacker was God depend for their support solely on this secondary addition, not on the narrative itself.

With verse 31 the narrative merges once more into an itinerary. Having given the place a name, Jacob continues on. The statement "The sun rose on him as he passed by Penuel" echoes verse 26; the name "Penuel" here belongs to the itinerary, not the narrative. Until the first rays of dawn, Jacob has persevered in a life and death struggle—now day breaks. The attacker has lost his power. Jacob is delivered from the terror of the night and can continue on his way. He has escaped from his encounter with an attacker having superhuman powers; now he can meet his brother without fear. The touch on his thigh has left its mark; his limping reminds him of the mortal danger he has escaped. In a very late addition (v. 32), the attacker's touching of his thigh is used to explain a food taboo for the "sons of Israel"; as in verses 27-28, this presupposes the existence of the nation Israel. Israelites are forbidden to eat the sinew of the nerve along the thigh joint (the sciatic nerve). The prohibition is not mentioned elsewhere in the Old Testament. In the rabbinic period, it became the practice to base commandments not found in the laws of the Pentateuch on other biblical passages. That is what this late postexilic addition does. The interpolation in verse 25b is an attempt to integrate it more firmly into the text.

33:1-20 THE MEETING OF THE BROTHERS

1 *When Jacob lifted up his eyes, he saw Esau coming*
   and four hundred men with him.
   Then he divided the children amongst Leah and Rachel
   and the two maids.
2 *Then he put the maids with their children in front,*
   followed by Leah with her children, and Rachel with Joseph last.
3 *He himself went on before them and bowed to the ground seven times, until*
   he came near his brother.
4 *But Esau ran to meet him and embraced him,*
   and fell on his neck and kissed him, and they wept.
5 *And when he raised his eyes and saw the women and the children, he asked:*
   Who are these with you? He said:
   They are the children with whom God has graciously favored your servant.
6 *And the maids drew near with their children*
   and bowed down.
7 *Then Leah and her children also drew near*
   and they bowed down. Then Joseph and Rachel drew near
   and bowed down.
8 *And he said: What do you intend with all this host*
   that I have met? He answered:
   To find favor in the eyes of my lord.
9 *But Esau said: I have enough, my brother;*
   keep what you have.
10 *Jacob replied: By no means! If I have found favor in your eyes, accept the*
   present from me.
   For I have seen your face,
   seeing as it were the face of God,
   and you have received me favorably.
11 *Accept then my gift that I have brought you,*

231

for God has favored me and I have enough.
So he pressed him and he accepted it.

12 *Then he said: Let us depart and go on our way;*
I will go ahead of you.

13 *But he said to him: My lord knows that the children are frail and that I must*
care for the sheep and cattle giving suck; if we overdrive them for one day, all
the animals will die.

14 *Let my lord go on ahead of his servant; I will push on by easy stages,*
according to the pace of the flocks before me
and according to the pace of the children,
until I come to my lord in Seir.

15 *And Esau said: Then of the people*
I have with me, let me leave some with you.
And he said: Why so? Let me only find favor
in the eyes of my lord.

16 *So Esau turned around on this day and went his way back to Seir.*

17 *But Jacob set out for Succoth*
and built himself a house, but for his cattle
he made sheds; therefore the place is called Succoth.

18 *And Jacob came to Salem, the city of Shechem in the land of Canaan,*
when he came from Paddan-aram, and he camped before the city.

19 *And he bought the piece of land where he had pitched his tent*
from the sons of Hamor,
the father of Shechem, for a hundred qesitas.

20 *And he set up an altar there*
and called it: El, God of Israel.

Chapter 33 is a narrative episode concluding the story of Jacob and
Esau; it recounts the return of Jacob and the reconciliation of the
brothers. The narrator has elaborated the conclusion, which actually
records only a greeting (vv. 1b-11) followed by a separation (vv.
12-17), by detailing the contrast between the two greetings, in which
the tension is effortlessly resolved.

1-7   Jacob lifts his eyes; this gesture frequently introduces a narrative episode (Gen. 18:2; 24:63; 31:10). What began with Jacob's flight
after tricking Esau out of his blessing now comes to its resolution.
What is described here is a ceremony of submission; the episode
could well be a transaction between a sovereign and his guilty vassals. The narrator clearly has in mind some such courtly ritual, like
that described in the Amarna Letters: "At the feet of my lord I fall
down, seven times and seven times." Court ceremonial is also reflected in the arrangement of the three groups according to their
status; Jacob comes to meet his brother before them all. His gesture of
submission is repeated by the three groups of women and children.

Esau's greeting in 33:4-5 is that of a brother seeing his brother
after a long separation, totally heartfelt and natural. He runs to meet

him (cf. 18:7; 24:17) and falls on his neck. The contrast speaks for itself; it does not have to be stated. The fearful tension with which Jacob has been looking forward to this moment is resolved, because forgiveness is implicit in this heartfelt welcome. The absence of any explicit statement of forgiveness on Esau's part follows from the situation; it would ruin the story if we heard him say: "I forgive you, dear brother." This illustrates the narrator's profound knowledge of human nature; under some circumstances, forgiveness can be more honest and genuine if it is not spoken but concealed in an action or gesture. Now Esau asks about the people in Jacob's entourage (33:5a). Jacob's reply (v. 5b) is of enormous importance: these are the first words he says to his brother. What he wishes to tell his brother is expressed in the verb of the clause ". . . with whom God has graciously favored your servant." We would expect Hebrew *bārak*, "bless"; but Jacob is saying that it was God's forgiving favor that gave him these children in the course of a long and difficult history. This is not expressed by the verb *bārak*, but it is expressed by *ḥanan*, "favor," as we see, for example, in Psalm 103. In this statement, too, Jacob only intimates what he wants to say; his meaning is clear from the course of the history that has brought him to this moment. The narrator uses silence to express the implications of the statement just made, a silence in which only the gestures speak (Gen. 33:6-7).

8-11 Now Esau asks more questions about "this whole army," the flocks, the advance presents. Jacob's answer (v. 8b) silently echoes his first words: "To find favor in your eyes." Following Esau's brief statement declining the gift ("I have enough"), it is this echo that Jacob picks up and underscores: ". . . your face, as it were the face of God" (v. 10b). For Jacob, acceptance by his brother depends on his brother's acceptance of the gift: in it he is giving back the blessing he has stolen. He has come before the face of his brother "to find favor," but this includes repossession of the blessing. In repeating his request, therefore, he once more calls his gift a "blessing" (Hebrew *berākāh*), indicating that he wishes to give the blessing back to his brother. Because Esau accepts this explanation, he can now accept the gift (v. 11). He has already said clearly enough (v. 9) that the loss of the blessing bestowed upon the firstborn has made little difference to him. Even without it he has become great and powerful.

12-17 The concluding verses recount how the brothers separate once more, a common conclusion to a meeting; cf. the discussion of 31:55–32:1. Since we are dealing here with the conclusion of the whole chain of events that started with chapter 27, we should expect Jacob and Esau to return to the same place. Esau makes the same assumption when he suggests to Jacob that they go on together (33:12). Jacob, however, does not wish to go with Esau. Even now, in spite of Esau's impulsive brotherly welcome, he addresses Esau as "my lord" (v. 13), a form of address indicating a continued distance. Jacob asks Esau to be understanding, noting the difference between the two companies: Esau is leading a group of four hundred men, whereas Jacob is leading a group that includes flocks, women, and children; it is better for them to remain apart (vv. 13-14). The conclusion of his statement, ". . . until I come to my lord in Seir," is merely a polite formula; he does not wish to contradict his brother, as Esau naturally understands. A reconciliation between brothers, the narrator is saying, does not necessarily always lead to their living side by side; it is sometimes better for them both to part in peace, each to live his own way of life. Jacob refuses Esau's generous offer of an escort (v. 15); it would be a foreign body in his group of herdsmen. In his answer, however, he is able to tell his brother a third time that all that matters to him is his brother's acceptance (v. 15).

And so they separate (vv. 16-17). Each goes his own way, but they part in peace. Esau goes on to Seir; his story is concluded by the genealogy of chapter 36. Jacob sets out for Succoth; here the narrative becomes an itinerary. Genesis 33:17, however, contains a surprising conclusion: Jacob builds a house for himself and sheds for his cattle. This statement, too, is part of the itinerary, but constitutes its conclusion; it is a formula of settlement, which records the most primitive form of fixed habitation: house and stall. The former nomad establishes a settlement with housing for his people and the animals. Here the naming is particularly important: he calls the place Succoth, "sheds." The name points to the settlement of the nomadic patriarchs in the land of Canaan at the end of the patriarchal period.

18-20   These verses are a later addition in the form of an itinerary. By mentioning Shechem, they lead into chapter 34. The first clause presents no difficulties and does not require emendation: "And Jacob came to Salem, the city of Shechem," a site in the plain east of Shechem. This clause is continued in verse 18b: "and he camped before the city." The whole statement has been expanded by the interpolation of the relative clause "[which is located] in the land of Canaan, when he came from Paddan-aram." A redactor added this statement from P to make it clear that Jacob has come from Paddan-aram in Mesopotamia and is now entering the land of Canaan. Here he purchases a piece of land on which he had pitched his tent. Since this passage pictures Jacob as a nomad, verses 18-20 cannot be the original continuation of verse 17, which has him building a house. The land purchase recalls chapter 23 (P). It is therefore probably the burial place of Joseph referred to in Joshua 24:32. He buys it from the "sons of Hamor," who is called the father of Shechem, as in chapter

34; Joshua 24:32; and Judges 9:28. The price is given in terms of an unknown but undoubtedly ancient unit: one hundred qesitas.

To conclude Jacob's journey to Canaan, verse 20 is added to the interpolated relative clause in verse 18; it is based on an ancient itinerary note about the setting up of a monument. At the end of his journey, Jacob sets up an altar, which he names "El, God of Israel." Thus El, the supreme god of the Canaanite pantheon, becomes El, God of the people Israel: the worship of the God of Israel replaces the El cult of Canaan (cf. Josh. 8:30). The statement is a confession of faith in the God of Israel, linking the end of the Patriarchal History with the history of the people and nation.

34:1-31   DINAH AND THE SHECHEMITES

1   *Dinah, the daughter of Leah, whom she had borne to Jacob,*
    once went out to visit the women of the land.
2   *Then she saw Shechem, the son of Hamor the Hivite,*
    the chief of the land. He seized her, lay with her,
    and thus did violence to her.
3   *But his heart remained true to Dinah, Jacob's daughter;*
    he loved the girl,
    and he spoke feelingly to the girl.
4   *And Shechem said to his father Hamor:*
    Get me this girl for a wife.
5   *But Jacob heard that he had disgraced his daughter Dinah.*
    But since his sons were with the cattle in the field,
    Jacob kept silent until they came back.
6   *Then Hamor, the father of Shechem, went out to Jacob*
    to speak with him.
7   *Now when the sons of Jacob came in from the field and heard it,*
    the men were indignant and became very angry
    that he had committed an outrage in Israel
    by sleeping with Jacob's daughter;
    such a thing ought not to be done!
8   *But Hamor spoke with them and said: My son Shechem is completely in love*
    with your daughter;
    give her to him as a wife, I beg you.
9   *Make a marriage alliance with us; give us your daughters*
    and take our daughters.
10 *Settle amongst us; the land lies open before you.*
    Stay, move about freely in it, and settle.
11 *And Shechem said to her father and to her brothers:*
    Let me find favor in your eyes.
    What you ask of me I will give.

12   *Even if you ask of me a very high brideprice and gifts, I will give what you ask of me;*
    only give me the girl as wife.

13   *Then Jacob's sons answered Shechem*
    and his father Hamor with deceitful speech,
    because he had disgraced their sister Dinah.

14   *They said to them: We cannot do such a thing*
    as to give our sister to one who is uncircumcised,
    for that would be a disgrace to us.

15   *Only under this condition will we come to terms with you,*
    that you become like us by having all the males among you circumcised.

16   *Then we can give you our daughters*
    and take your daughters; we will dwell among you
    and become one people.

17   *But if you do not agree*
    to be circumcised,
    then we will take our daughters and leave.

18   *Their words pleased Hamor and Shechem, the son of Hamor.*

19   *The young man did not hesitate to do what they said,*
    for he was taken with Jacob's daughter,
    and he was held in the highest respect in his father's house.

20   *So Hamor and his son Shechem went into their city gate*
    and addressed this word to the men of their city:

21   *These men have peaceful intentions. Let them dwell amongst us in the land*
    and move about in it. The land is broad enough for them. We can take their
    daughters as wives and give them our daughters.

22   *But only on this condition will the men agree*
    to dwell amongst us and become one people:
    that we circumcise all the males among us,
    as they are circumcised.

23   *Their flocks, their possessions, and their cattle*
    will then belong to us. Let us agree
    so that they will settle amongst us.

24   *Then all who went in and out at the gate*
    agreed with Hamor and his son Shechem,
    and they were all circumcised, every male,
    on the flesh of their foreskin.

25   *But on the third day, when they were still in pain,*
    Jacob's two sons Simon and Levi, Dinah's brothers,
    each took his sword, boldly entered the city, and killed every male.

26   *And Hamor and his son Shechem they also killed*
    with the blade of their sword; then they took Dinah
    from Shechem's house and went away.

27   *Then Jacob's sons fell upon the slain*
    and plundered the city,
    because they had disgraced their sister.

28   *Their sheep, cattle, and asses, all that was in the city*
    and in the field, they took away.

29 *All their possessions, all their children and wives they took away*
    and plundered everything that was in the houses.
30 *Then Jacob said to Simeon and Levi:*
    You have brought me misfortune by making me hated among the inhabitants
    of the land, the Canaanite and Perizzites, where I have only a few people.
    If they join forces against me, they will strike me down, and I shall be
    destroyed, I and my house.
31 *But they answered:*
    Should he treat our sister like a harlot?

The structure of the chapter is as follows: Shechem's crime (vv. 1-5); negotiations (vv. 6-24); revenge (vv. 25-29, plus 35:5); Jacob's reaction (34:30-31). The second section is disproportionately long and contains several doublets and discrepancies. We can trace each step in the effort to combine two narratives into one; for example, Hamor and Shechem are both treated as protagonists, even when that is inappropriate to the context. We conclude, therefore, that Genesis 34 is a secondary conflation of two different narratives. The earlier is a family narrative, into which a tribal narrative has been incorporated.

1-7   The introduction shows that Genesis 34 is an independent narrative taking place much later than the events of chapters 27–33. The characters are reintroduced in verse 1. Jacob's family is encamped before the city of Shechem; a long stay must have been involved. Dinah, Jacob's daughter, wants to visit other girls who live there. Shechem, the son of the local chief Hamor, takes her by violence (v. 2) but then falls in love with the girl (v. 3) and asks his father to request Dinah's family for permission to marry her (v. 4). Acting on this request, Hamor goes out to Jacob—that is, outside the city gate—in order to speak with him (v. 6). The negotiations follow in verses 8-10. Verses 5 and 7 interrupt the chain of events: Jacob hears what has happened to his daughter but waits until his sons return from the field. In this situation, it is up to the brothers to take action (as in 2 Sam. 13). Genesis 34:7 continues verse 5; in verses 4-8 the change of locale with each verse shows the composite nature of the text. When Dinah's brothers return, they hear what has happened and are enraged because their honor has been impugned. No other reason is needed to account for their anger, but the late author has added two on the basis of his own perspective. First, "He has committed an outrage in Israel" (Deut. 22:21; Judg. 20:6, 10; Josh. 7:15). This presupposes an age in which Israel was in existence; it is also inappropriate here because the person committing the outrage is not an Israelite. The other reason, "Such a thing ought not to be done," appears along with the first in a similar situation in 2 Samuel 13:12, where both are more apposite. Probably the late author borrowed them from 2 Samuel 13.

8-10   These verses follow verse 6. Hamor proposes the marriage of Dinah to his son without mentioning the rape. As head of his city, however, he is not content with this proposal; more important to him is his offer of intermarriage and permission for Jacob's group to settle in his territory, for which the proposal of marriage furnishes an occasion. In this speech by Hamor in verses 8-10, we can clearly see the step from interfamily negotiations to political negotiations: Hamor is interested in increasing the size and importance of his city by bringing into it a nomadic group and its flocks, a process that took place frequently during the occupation of Canaan by the tribes. This is in fact how small groups of Israelite tribes actually did settle in Canaan. Hamor offers the newcomers mutual intermarriage (prohibited in Deut. 7:3) together with the right to settle and move about freely in his territory (Gen. 34:10).

11-12   These verses record Shechem's request to marry Dinah without mentioning Hamor's proposal. Unlike the latter, it is based entirely on Shechem's earlier act, on account of which he is prepared to pay any price the brothers may name to make restitution (Hebrew *mōhar* is the brideprice, *mattān* probably a gift to the bride).

13-17   This detailed response was composed by the late author to answer both Hamor's proposal in verses 8-10 and Shechem's request in verses 11-12; it is therefore addressed to Shechem and Hamor, although according to verse 6 Shechem is not present. Verses 13-17 are therefore a secondary conflation of two different answers. In verse 14 we can still see the answer to Shechem in response to verses 11-12: the only demand is that a single man be circumcised. Shechem accepts this condition (v. 19a). Verses 15-16 contain a different answer: circumcision of all males is required as a condition for accepting Hamor's proposal in verses 8-10. Here we are dealing with a political matter. The style of these verses also bears a striking similarity to that of P (Gen. 17:10; Exod. 12:48; Lev. 12:3). The late conflator is close to the language of P. The concluding clause of the answer in Genesis 34:17 serves as a bracket linking the political offer with the proposal of marriage.

18-19   These verses recount the acceptance of the condition twice. The agreement of Hamor, the chief of the city, in verse 18 is continued in verse 20; it must be ratified by the city council. This continuity is interrupted by verse 19, which deals with the question of interfamily relationships; it contains Shechem's agreement, which refers solely to verse 14. When the young man unhesitatingly accepts the condition (v. 19a), it can only mean circumcision of himself and his household. For this he does not need approval from the city council; his position within his own household suffices (v. 19b). It is in verses 18 and 19 that we see most clearly how two different negotiations, one dealing with family matters and the other with political matters, have been linked by a later hand.

20-24   Hamor's address to the city council. The elders are assembled in the city gate; Hamor ("and Shechem" is secondary) speaks his mind to them. Nothing more is said of Shechem's personal interest; the question at issue concerns the community as a whole. There is evidence that in this period, when tribal groups of the Israelites were settling in Canaan, such discussions of including a nomadic group within the city precincts did in fact take place. When Hamor, recommending inclusion, begins by saying: "These men have peaceful intentions," this is important, unimpeachable evidence that some tribal groups of Israelites entered Palestine peacefully (the theory of Albrecht Alt). In this period, at the beginning of the occupation, there was still plenty of room for settlement: "The land is broad enough for them" (v. 21). In verse 23 Hamor seeks to make the offer even more attractive: the wealth of cattle belonging to the newcomers will have a favorable effect on the city's economics. But the condition imposed by the Jacob group is dubious in this context. It is highly unlikely that, at the beginning of the occupation, a Canaanite city would have accepted circumcision of the entire male populace as the price for incorporation of the new group into the community. Here we see the concern of the later author, speaking from the perspective of his own period and saying what should have taken place. In verse 24 the spontaneous agreement of all the men of the city to Hamor's proposal makes sense only if verse 22 is removed from the demand.

25-26   These verses continue the interfamily drama. Having agreed unhesitatingly to the condition (v. 19), Shechem has all the males of his household circumcised. It is to them alone that verse 25 refers as being still in pain on the third day, that is, not ready for battle. The treacherous plan of Dinah's brothers in verse 13 had foreseen this result; it gave them the chance to avenge their sister's disgrace. They take sword in hand, boldly enter the city, kill Shechem and his men, rescue their sister, and escape. It is so at least according to the original narrative; the later editor added "They killed every male" in verse 25 and "Hamor" at the beginning of verse 26, thus turning two different events into two acts of the same drama.

27-29   What now follows is a totally different event. Now the actors are the sons of Jacob, a nomadic tribal group, who fall upon a defenseless city; in this version it is all the men of the city who were circumcised (vv. 15b, 24b); all are killed and the city is looted. The true motive for this bellicose act on the part of a tribe is clear from verses 28-29: these verses recount a raid in which the looters capture a wealth of booty. The detailed list suggests the rejoicing in the wake of a successful surprise attack. This is not the family drama of verses 25-26. Such a list of booty is possible only in a military operation, as we see from the similar list in Numbers 31:9-10, which the author probably used as his source.

35:5   Most exegetes believe that the conclusion of the narrative to which verses 27-29 belong is found in 35:5, having been incorporated into the next section (35:1-7). The first clause of 35:5, "Then they set out," would then follow 34:29 directly: having looted the city, they departed. The following sentences explain why they were not followed: a "terror from God" that fell upon the surrounding cities prevented pursuit; cf. Exodus 23:27 and Joshua 2:9.

34:30-31   The conclusion of the (family) narrative in verses 30-31 is quite different; it follows verses 25-26 and ends with Jacob's rebuke to his sons Simeon and Levi: "You have brought me misfortune by making me hated [literally, 'making me stink'] among the inhabitants of the land." Jacob knows he is at their mercy if they seek to avenge the death of Shechem; his group is much too small to stand up to the populace of the city (as in Ps. 105:12). This reproof from Jacob describes precisely the situation of the nomadic patriarchs, who had to avoid military confrontation. Jacob would have accepted Shechem's offer in Genesis 34:11-12 and found it sufficient compensation. The response of his sons Simeon and Levi illustrates the difference not between two generations but between two eras. They share a sense of group solidarity that is irreversible. It is dominated by considerations of honor and disgrace; killing to avenge one's honor has become a necessity. The disgrace inflicted on a member of their family must be avenged with blood.

Deuteronomy 7:2-3 commands the Israelites entering the land of Canaan not to marry the inhabitants of the land or make treaties with them:

> . . . then you must utterly destroy them.
> You shall make no treaty with them
> and show no mercy to them.
> You shall not make marriages with them,
> giving your daughters to their sons
> or taking their daughters for your sons.

The later author who combined the history of the patriarchs with the history of the tribes had these words before him. He used them to construct a model of obedience to this Deuteronomic commandment. Here the execution of the ban is explicitly contrasted to the possibility of joining the inhabitants of the land by treaty and intermarrying with them: ". . . you must utterly destroy them." We might call this story a midrash, dating from a time when intermarriage in particular had once more become a danger or a temptation for Israelites.

In the tribal narrative, before it was altered by the later narrator, we have a valuable witness from the early history of the occupation. Hamor's offer (Gen. 34:8-10), ratified by the city council (vv. 20-23, omitting 22), reflects an historical event in the period of the occupation.

The family or patriarchal narrative with which the tribal narrative was combined belongs to neither J nor P; it is preserved only here. This shows that patriarchal narratives were preserved outside these two works. It is a narrative from the transitional period between the patriarchal age and the beginnings of settlement. In the family narrative, the transition may be seen most clearly in the statement "Simeon and Levi, Dinah's brothers, each took his sword" (v. 25) and Jacob's reaction (v. 30). With this act of vengeance begins the era of war and violence. A variant of this narrative appears in Genesis 49:5-7, the oracle concerning Simeon and Levi, only here they represent tribes. The sharp contrast between Jacob's lament and the final form of the text, which commands total destruction of the enemy, looks ahead to the prophets of judgment, who finally repudiate war (Isa. 9:2-7). The king to come will reign over a kingdom of peace.

35:1-29   JACOB AT BETHEL AND HEBRON; JACOB'S SONS; ISAAC'S DEATH

1   *Now God said to Jacob:*
    Arise, go up to Bethel, stay there
    and build there an altar to the God who appeared to you
    when you were fleeing from your brother Esau.
2   *Then Jacob said to his household and to all*
    who were with him: Put away the foreign gods
    that you have with you, purify yourselves and change your clothes.
3   *We will arise and go up to Bethel.*
    There I will make an altar to the God
    who heard me in the time of my distress
    and has been with me along the way I have gone.

4   *Then they handed over to Jacob all the foreign gods that they had with them*
    and the rings they wore on their ears,
    and Jacob buried them under the terebinth
    that stands near Shechem.
5   *[Then they set out, but a terror from God came upon the cities round about,*
    so that they did not pursue the sons of Jacob.]

6   *Then Jacob came to Luz in the land of Canaan [that is, Bethel],*
     he and all the people with him.

7   *And he built an altar there and called the place El-bethel,*
     for there God had revealed himself to him
     when he was fleeing from his brother.

8   *Then Deborah, Rebekah's nurse, died,*
     and she was buried under the oak below Bethel,
     and he named it the oak of tears.

9   *And God appeared again to Jacob*
     when he came from Paddan-aram.

10   *And he blessed him, and God said to him:*
     Your name is Jacob, but no longer shall your name be Jacob;
     Israel shall be your name.
     And he called him Israel.

11   *And God said to him: I am God Almighty;*
     be fruitful and increase.
     A nation, indeed a host of nations shall spring from you,
     and kings shall come forth from your loins.

12   *And the land that I gave to Abraham and Isaac*
     I give to you, and to your seed after you I give the land.

13   *Then God went up from him at the place*
     where he had spoken to him.

14   *And Jacob set up a monument at the place*
     where he had spoken to him, a pillar of stone,
     and he poured a drink offering over it and poured oil on it.

15   *And Jacob called the place where he had spoken to him Bethel.*

16   *And they set out from Bethel,*
     and when they were still some distance from Ephrath,
     Rachel gave birth, and the birth was difficult for her.

17   *And when she was having so difficult a birth, the midwife said to her: Be of*
     good cheer, you will have yet another son.

18   *But when her breath was departing from her—for she was dying—*
     she called him Ben-oni ['son of my pain'],
     but his father called him Benjamin ['son of fortune'].

19   *And Rachel died and was buried on the way to Ephrath, [that is, Bethlehem].*

20   *And Jacob set a monument over her grave.*
     That is the monument of Rachel's grave until this day.

21   *Then Israel journeyed on and pitched his tent*
     further away beyond Migdal-Eder.

22a *At the time when Israel was living in this region,*
     Reuben went and slept with Bilhah, his father's concubine. When Israel
     heard of it. . . .

22b *Jacob had twelve sons.*

23   *The sons of Leah were: Reuben, Jacob's firstborn,*
     Simeon, Levi, Judah, Issachar, and Zebulun.

24   *The sons of Rachel: Joseph and Benjamin.*

25   *The sons of Bilhah, Rachel's maid: Dan and Naphtali.*

26	*The sons of Zilpah, Leah's maid: Gad and Asher.*
	These are the sons of Jacob who were born to him in Paddan-aram.
27	*And Jacob came to his father Isaac at Mamre,*
	Kiriath-arba—[that is, Hebron]—
	where Abraham and Isaac had dwelt as sojourners.
28	*But Isaac was 180 years old.*
29	*Then Isaac departed; he died and was gathered to his people, old and*
	fulfilled in life.
	And his sons Esau and Jacob buried him.

The story of Jacob and Esau ended with chapter 33; chapter 34 is an interpolation. Chapter 35 is a concluding chapter that brings together texts of various nature and origin; it does not contain any narratives. The redactor begins in verses 1-7 with his own account of how Jacob built an altar at Bethel; cf. 11:27-32. What follows is a mixture of itinerary and genealogy such as we find elsewhere at the beginning and ending of sections of the Patriarchal History. The text records departures and arrivals, births and deaths. It concludes with a list of Jacob's sons (35:22b-26) together with the life span and death of Isaac (vv. 28-29). The P material (vv. 6, 9-13, 22-29) constitutes a clearly conceived unit; the non-P texts, like verses 1-7, have been adapted to an itinerary.

1-7　Jacob receives a command from God in verse 1 and carries it out in verse 7; the almost identical language of the two verses shows that verses 1-7 constitute a single unit. Jacob gives the same directive to his household in verse 3 (introduced by the first clause of v. 2); verse 5 records their departure, verse 6 their arrival, and verse 7 the carrying out of the order. Jacob's directive to his household to put away foreign gods and purify themselves is interpolated in verse 2; the first part is carried out in verse 4.

The language of the command God addresses to Jacob in verse 1 is unusual: he speaks of himself in the third person, modified by a relative clause: "the God who . . ."; the natural wording would be: "And build me there an altar." It is also noteworthy that nowhere else is a command from God necessary for the building of an altar. Clearly we have here an allusion, put in God's mouth, to the promise at Bethel in 28:10-22. Genesis 35:3b and 7b are similar allusions. The narrator's purpose is to conclude the story of Jacob with the fulfillment of the prediction recorded in chapter 28.

In 35:2a, 3 Jacob transmits this directive to his household. The people respond in the first clause of verse 3: "We will arise and go up to Bethel." This statement echoes the beginning of a pilgrimage psalm: "We will go up to the house of Yahweh" (Ps. 122:1), a call to set out on a pilgrimage. This is followed by an agreement to build an altar (as in Gen. 35:1), which again echoes the language of the pilgrimage psalms: "To the God who heard me in the day of my distress" (cf. Ps. 120:1). The model is a pilgrimage to fulfill a vow (Gen. 28:20-22). The author's purpose is to recount the fulfillment of this vow. Genesis 35:2b, however, immediately introduces another directive from Jacob, such as might be spoken by a priest, ordering his household to make themselves ready for a cultic ceremony. The command to bathe and change clothes appears in Exodus 19:10-11, and that to put away foreign gods in Joshua 24:14. There are parallels to both in many religions. The execution of the first is recounted in Genesis 35:4; that of the second is not described, because it must take place immediately before the ceremony and here the journey or pilgrimage intervenes. Both commands (as well as the pilgrimage) really presuppose a regular cult at a sacred shrine; by adding verses 2b and 4, which are at odds with the religion of the patriarchs, the author wishes to state that all foreign idols or images must be put aside and all cultic impurity removed when the people enter the land. He probably has in mind the teraphim of Rachel (ch. 31) and thinks of the earrings as amulets. Burying them under a tree probably has a ritual basis.

The redactor's purpose in interpolating 35:5, which originally followed 34:29 and concluded chapter 34, is to integrate his conclusion more closely with the preceding narrative; the statement "Then they set out . . ." fits neatly between the command in verse 3 and the arrival in verse 6. The language of the itinerary note in verse 6 suggests that it belongs to P. The redactor, however, incorporates it firmly into its new context, thus joining the latter to the P material that follows (vv. 6, 9-13, [23-29]). The place names, however, reveal the composite nature of the text: verse 6 already refers to the place as Bethel, although at the beginning of the verse it is called Luz and is not renamed as Bethel until verse 7. Finally (v. 7), Jacob carries out the command of verse 1 by building an altar; in addition, he names not only the altar but also the sacred site brought into being by the altar. The name "El-bethel" is unusual: the usual form, even for the redactor, is "Beth-el," as verse 1 shows. The name may indicate identification of the place with the deity worshipped there (cf. Assyrian *Ilu-bayti-ili*). The etymology cited for the name is another allusion to Genesis 28:10-22: the establishment of the sanctuary is based on the divine revelation Jacob received there.

8   There follows in verse 8 an itinerary note, apparently independent of both verses 1-7 and 9-12, (15). It would be quite appropriate, however, before verse 16; in both form and content, verses 8 and 16-20 belong together.

9-13   This section comes from P; it goes with verses 6 and 23-29. It begins and ends with almost the same words as the address to

Abraham (17:1, 22); both passages include a promise and a new name. P's point is that the election of Abraham continues on in Jacob. Abraham represents the patriarchal period; Jacob, with his new name (35:9-10) and his twelve sons (vv. 22b-26) represents the people of Israel.

When he says "again," the redactor means that, in addition to the divine revelation in chapter 28 "when Jacob was fleeing from his brother" (vv. 1-7), there is now a new revelation at the same place, where he fulfills his vow. God's words are introduced by: "And he blessed him and said to him"; the word "bless" has become a term for the promise, as in Genesis 48:3. There are some inconsistencies in the divine address; the self-revelation ("I am . . ."), for example, does not come at the beginning, as in Gen 17:2, but in verse 11. The reason is that, in P, 35:9-13 was a parallel to 28:10-20; R moved it here and altered it accordingly. The language of the renaming is also convoluted; the LXX omits both "your name is Jacob" and "he called him Israel." The redactor (R) may be responsible for the change of Jacob's name to Israel, because P continues to call him Jacob. The promise of increase and the promise of the land are both renewed to Jacob (35:11-12); the promise of God's presence and the covenant ceremony are unique to Abraham. That the promises continue those made previously is explicitly stated by the clause "that I gave to Abraham and Isaac" (17:8; 26:3). The concluding verse, 35:13, repeats 17:22.

14-15 These verses are problematical, because the naming has already been recounted in verse 7 (as well as 28:19). R may have wanted to include the setting up of the monument pillar and its ritual anointing on the basis of 28:18; there this act was followed by the naming (28:19), which he therefore repeated here. Some unknown ritual explanation must exist for the drink offering.

8, 16-21 Verses 1-7 are an interpolation by R, intended to record the fulfillment of Jacob's vow in chapter 28. In 35:6, 9-13, he links them with P's parallel to chapter 28, from which he constructs a second divine revelation. Genesis 35:14-15 constitute an addendum to 1-7. The whole is set in the context of a journey: departure (vv. 1, 3), arrival at Bethel (v. 6), departure from Bethel (v. 16). Verse 8 then must belong to this itinerary: Deborah, Rebekah's nurse, died at or near Bethel. Verse 8 is thus set in the context of this itinerary, which continues in verses 16-21. Genesis 24:59 also speaks of Rebekah's nurse, but not by name. It is typical of the Patriarchal History that the tree beneath which Deborah was buried (cf. the "palm of Deborah" in Judg. 4:5) should be given a name. The "tree of tears" so named will be recalled by future generations; the nurse of the ancestress is part of the family, to be remembered long after her death.

16-21 These verses constitute a self-contained unit based on an itinerary. Verse 16a records the departure from Bethel, verse 21 a halt at Migdal-Eder; the intervening verses describe the death of Rachel during the birth of a son. The entire section (vv. 8, 16-21) is clearly distinct from verses 1-7, 14-15 and 9-13 (P); it comes from the earlier narrator J. The journey is interrupted (v. 16a) by Rachel's severe labor pains. This illustrates the truly harsh conditions under which the patriarchs lived: Rachel must travel with the flocks even though she is many months pregnant. In the middle of the journey, labor begins and the birth is inevitable. Rachel dies by the wayside and is buried. Then the caravan sets out again, leaving the mother's grave behind; the newborn infant, bereft of its mother, is taken along. The record notes that the birth was very difficult and took place "some distance from Ephrath" (v. 16). Ephrath is not far from Ramah (1 Sam. 10:2; Jer. 31:15). The nurse says to the mother in her agony: "Be of good cheer" (Gen. 35:17). She can take comfort from having borne a son (cf. 1 Sam. 4:20). "Yet another"—the nurse recalls Rachel's desire to have a second son, a desire enshrined in the name of her first (Gen. 30:24). With her dying breath, the mother gives her child a name meaning "son of my pain." His father, however, changes his name, calling him "son of the right (hand)," which can also mean "son of fortune," in order to preserve in the child's name what its mother meant to him (v. 18). This brief episode illustrates eloquently that naming is an essential element in the history of a community: names preserve the memory of events.

The account of Rachel's death in verses 19-20 belongs to both genealogy and itinerary: the life of the patriarchs was a nomadic life, from birth (vv. 16-18) to death (vv. 19-20). The words of Jeremiah, "A voice is heard in Ramah, lamentation . . . ," show that Rachel's grave was a living memory for centuries, as late as Matthew 2:17-18: "Rachel weeping for her children." Jacob sets up a monument (Hebrew *maṣṣē-bāh*) on Rachel's grave. The narrator adds the etiological formula "until this day." In Genesis 35:19 a later gloss adds "that is, Bethlehem," because a "Rachel's grave" was also pointed out in the vicinity of Bethlehem.

Jacob travels on from the place of birth and the place of death. He is called "Israel" here and in verse 22a, probably because of a revision based on the renaming in verse 10. He pitches his tent (as in 26:25) at a stopping place called Migdal-Eder ("herdsman's tower"). The site has not been identified; it could be a common name.

22a   This verse is a fragment. A narrative emerges from the itinerary, because something important took place during a stay in a particular place. But only the beginning of the narrative has been preserved. It recounts a crime committed by Reuben, "Jacob's eldest son": he slept with his father's concubine. "His father heard of it. . . ."

The same words appear in the same context in 34:5; they show that the narrative dealt with the crime and its punishment, but here the text breaks off. In 49:3-4 Reuben is stripped of the right of primogeniture on account of this act.

22b-26   P's conclusion, which follows, consists of a list of Jacob's sons (vv. 22b-26) together with an account of Jacob's return (v. 27) and Isaac's death (vv. 28-29). This genealogical conclusion is characteristic of P's work. Jacob's sons are listed according to their mothers, as in Genesis 29–30: the sons of Leah (35:23), Rachel (v. 24), Bilhah (v. 25), and Zilpah (v. 26a). The number twelve is important for P: Dinah is not mentioned, and Benjamin is included among the sons born in Paddan-aram. The list may be compared especially to that in Exodus 1:1-5.[1]

27-29   Jacob returns to his father at Mamre (v. 27; cf. 28:1-5; 31:18). P was familiar with the earlier narrative of J; for him, however, all that matters is that Jacob took a wife there; he says nothing of the rivalry between the brothers. This is typical of the difference between the later P document and the earlier Yahwistic history: the social dynamics central to J's narrative are totally peripheral for P, for whom religion is limited to worship and doctrine. For this reason, too, the difference between the nomadic way of life and settlement has lost its importance for P. When Jacob returns "where Abraham and Isaac had dwelt as sojourners," this can mean only that he, too, settles where Abraham and Isaac lived. Now Isaac's life span and death are noted (35:28-29), in almost the same words as in the case of Abraham. Isaac, too, is gathered to his people; he, too, dies "old and fulfilled in life." Like Abraham's sons, Esau and Jacob, now reconciled, peacefully bury their father. Isaac is also buried in the cave at Machpelah (cf. ch. 23), as we are told in 49:31. The statement in 35:28 that Isaac lived long after Jacob's return contradicts chapter 27, which speaks of Isaac as a dying man.

36:1-43   ESAU'S DESCENDANTS

1   *These are the descendants of Esau [that is, Edom]:*
2   *Esau took his wives from the daughters of Canaan,*
    Adah, the daughter of Elon the Hittite, and Oholibamah the daughter of Anah, the son of Zibeon the Horite,
3   *and Basemath, the daughter of Ishmael, the sister of Nebaioth.*

---

1. On the various lists of the sons of Jacob, see Helga Weippert, "Das geographische System der Stämme Israels," *Vetus Testamentum* 23 (1973): 76-89.

4   *Adah bore to Esau, Eliphaz; Basemath bore Reuel;*
5   *and Oholibamah bore Jeush, Jalam, and Korah.*
     These are the sons of Esau that were borne to him in the land of Canaan.
6   *And Esau took his wives, his sons, his daughters, and all the members of his*
     household, as well as his possessions, and all his cattle, and all his property
     that he had acquired in the land of Canaan, and went into the land of Seir,
     away from his brother Jacob.
7   *For their possessions were too great for them to dwell together, and the land*
     of their sojournings
     could not support them because of their herds.
8   *So Esau settled in the hill country of Seir;*
     [Esau; that is, Edom].
9   *These are the descendants of Esau, the father of Edom,*
     in the hill country of Seir.
10   *These are the names of Esau's sons:*
     Eliphaz, the son of Adah, the wife of Esau,
     Reuel, the son of Basemath, the wife of Esau.
11   *The sons of Eliphaz were:*
     Teman, Omar, Zepho, Gatam, and Kenaz.
12   *And Timna was the concubine of Eliphaz, Esau's son;*
     she bore Amalek to Eliphaz.
     These are the sons of Adah, the wife of Esau.
13   *And these are the sons of Reuel: Nahath, Zerah, Shammah, and Mizzah.*
     These are the sons of Basemath, the wife of Esau.
14   *And these are the sons of Oholibamah, the wife of Esau, the daughter of*
     Anah, the son of Zibeon. She bore to Esau Jeush, Jalam, and Korah.

15   *These are the chiefs of the sons of Esau:*
     the sons of Eliphaz, the firstborn of Esau:
     the chief of Teman, the chief of Omar,
     the chief of Zepho, the chief of Kenaz,
16   *the chief of Korah, the chief of Gatam, the chief of Amalek.*
     These are the chiefs of Eliphaz in the land of Edom,
     these are the sons of Adah.

17   *These are the sons of Reuel, the son of Esau:*
     the chief of Nahath, the chief of Zerah,
     the chief of Shammah, the chief of Mizzah.
     These are the chiefs of Reuel in the land of Edom,
     these are the sons of Basemath, the wife of Esau.

18   *These are the sons of Oholibamah, the wife of Esau:*
     the chief of Jehush, the chief of Jalam, the chief of Korah.
     These are the chiefs born of Oholibamah, the daughter of Anah, the wife of
     Esau.
19   *These are the sons of Esau, and these are their chiefs—*
     [that is, Edom].

20   *These are the sons of Seir, the Horite,*
     who were settled in the land: Lotan, Shobal, Zibeon, Anah,
21   *Dishon, Ezer, and Dishan. These are the chiefs of the Horites, the sons of*
     Seir in the land of Edom.

22   *The sons of Lotan were: Hori and Hemam.*
     And Lotan's sister was Timna.

23   *These are the sons of Shobal: Alvan, Manahath, Ebal, Shepho, and Onam.*

24   *These are the sons of Zibeon: Aiah and Anah.*
     This is the Anah who found the springs in the wilderness
     when he was pasturing the asses of his father Zibeon.

25   *These are the sons of Anah: Dishon and Oholibamah, the daughter of Anah.*

27   *These are the sons of Ezer: Bilhan, Zaavan, and Akan.*

28   *These are the sons of Dishan: Uz and Aran.*

29   *These are the chiefs of the Horites: the chief of Lotan, the chief of Shobal, the*
     chief of Zibeon, the chief of Anah,

30   *the chief of Dishon, the chief of Ezer, the chief of Dishan.*
     These are the chiefs of the Horites,
     according to their chiefdoms in the land of Seir.

31   *These are the kings who reigned in the land of Edom,*
     before any king ruled in Israel:

32   *Bela the son of Beor became king over Edom,*
     his city was called Dinhabah.

33   *When Bela died, Jobab the son of Zerah of Bozrah became king in his stead.*

34   *When Jobab died, Husham from the land of the Temanites became king in his*
     stead.

35   *When Husham died, Hadad the son of Bedad became king in his stead; he*
     defeated the Midianites in the fields of Moab. His city was called Avith.

36   *When Hadad died, Samlah of Masrekah became king in his stead.*

37   *When Samlah died, Shaul of Rehoboth on the River became king in his stead.*

38   *When Shaul died, Baal-hanan the son of Achbor became king in his stead.*

39   *When Baal-hanan the son of Achbor died, Hadad became king in his stead;*
     his city was called Pau, and his wife was called Mehetabel, the daughter of
     Matred, daughter of Mezahab.

40   *These are the names of the chiefs of Esau according to their families, accord-*
     ing to their places, according to their names:
     the chief of Timna, the chief of Alvah, the chief of Jetheth,

41   *the chief of Oholibamah, the chief of Elah, the chief of Pinon,*

42   *the chief of Kenaz, the chief of Teman, the chief of Mibzar,*

43   *the chief of Magdiel, the chief of Iram.*
     These are the chiefs of Edom according to their dwelling places in the land of
     which they had taken possession.
     [That is, Esau, the father of Edom.]

This is one of the chapters of the Old Testament that the modern reader finds not only uninteresting but also unedifying—uninteresting because we cannot cope with the multiplicity of names; unedifying because the chapter deals "only" with the descendants of Esau, leading to the Edomites and the kings of Edom, the later enemies of the people of God. Nevertheless, this chapter has major significance in the Old Testament. This significance lies on the one hand in the simple fact that it traces the descendants of Esau from Isaac's son to the kings of Edom. The God of the patriarchs is not concerned solely with a single lineage that runs through Jacob and his twelve sons to the people of Israel. He is concerned also with Esau's other son and his descendants; they, too, are sons of Isaac, sons of Abraham. The sons of Esau are also created by God; they, too, share in the dignity and rights of the human race.

Chapter 36 is organized according to a conscious plan. It leads up to the section listing the kings of Edom in verses 31-39; verses 40-43 are an appendix. Two lines converge on this section: the first comprises the sons of Esau (vv. 1-14) and the chiefs of Esau (vv. 15-19); the second comprises the sons of Seir the Horite (vv. 20-28) and the chiefs of the Horites (vv. 29-30). In both cases, the names of the chiefs are identical with those of the sons; the names of the sons are recorded in a genealogy (the earlier form), those of the chiefs in a list (the later form). Seen from the tribal perspective, the sons become chiefs. This development finally leads to the third form of tradition: the historical form of the royal chronicle. Here we can trace clearly the historical development from families or clans through tribes to the state.

1-8   P concludes the story of Jacob and Esau with the genealogy of their descendants: the twelve sons of Jacob in 35:22-27 and the descendants of Esau in chapter 36 (cf. the genealogy of Ishmael in 25:12-18). The genealogy names the wives of Esau and the sons borne to them. It attempts to harmonize the various traditions concerning the names of Esau's wives in 26:34; 28:9; 36:9-14. The conclusion formula in verse 5b leads into the following section.

Verses 6-8 constitute an itinerary recounting Esau's journey with his family and possessions from Canaan into the land of Edom (the hill country of Seir), the uplands south of the Dead Sea. The same reason is given for their departure as for the separation of Abraham and Lot in 13:15-16; both passages are intended to suggest a peaceful separation. The final three words, "from his brother Jacob," are meant to emphasize that Esau leaves the promised land to his brother.

9-14   While verses 1-5 limit themselves to Esau's immediate family, the genealogy in verses 9-14 includes the next two generations: the sons and grandsons of Adah in verses 10b-12, those of Basemath in verse 13, and those of Oholibamah in verse 14. Thus the Edomite people arose from the family of Esau.

15-19   There follows a list of the tribal chiefs of Esau, framed by introductory (v. 15a) and concluding (v. 19) formulas. Without exception, the list comprises the same names as verses 9-14; the only new element is the term "chiefs." The Hebrew word *'allûpîm* probably derives from the number *'elep*, "thousand," but later referred to a smaller number. The title is used only among the Edomites and

Horites (Exod. 15:15) and is probably an Edomite term. The list reflects the transition from familial to tribal organization.

20-28 Following the list of the sons of Esau, verses 20-28 list "the sons of Seir, the Horite." They are called "inhabitants of the land," that is, the inhabitants already settled there when the "sons of Esau" arrived. They trace their descent to their father Seir (elsewhere a toponym). Deuteronomy 2:12-22 also speaks of the Edomites' subjugation of the Horites. The name "Horites" might suggest cave dwellers (< Hebrew *ḥōr*, "cave"). Genesis 36:20b-21 list seven sons of Seir the Horite; the mention of "chiefs" probably means that verse 21 is secondary. Their sons, eighteen in all, are listed in turn in verses 22-27; verse 22 also mentions a daughter Timna, the concubine of Eliphaz. A daughter is also mentioned in verse 25: Oholibamah, who became one of Esau's wives. In each case, the name of a daughter refers to a marriage between an Edomite man and Horite woman.

Verse 24 speaks of Anah as one of the sons of Zibeon and recalls a story about him: "This is the Anah who found the springs in the wilderness when he. . . ." When we recall 26:32b—"We have found water!"—this material preserved in a genealogy or an itinerary shows how important an event the discovery of a source of water was in this period. It was discussed long afterwards. This brief note proves that 36:20-28 preserves a very ancient genealogy, at first transmitted orally.

29-30 The genealogy of the sons of Seir the Horite is followed in verses 29-30 by a list of the chiefs of the Horites. They have the same names as the sons in verses 20b-21a; family history is followed by tribal history.

31-39 The chronicle of the kings of Edom is a valuable document, an historical document in the strict sense. The chronicle comprises a series of names and events. The reigns of eight kings are recorded according to a fixed schema: . . . became king over Edom—(the name of his city)—he died— . . . became king in his stead (exactly as in 1 Kgs. 16:22; 2 Kgs. 1:17; 8:15; 12:22; 13:24). In contrast to the preceding passages, this schema describes the new form of political power: a man comes to rule over the entire nation as an adult and remains its ruler until his death. He is not born king; there is as yet no dynastic kingship, and the royal residence changes with different kings, each residing in his own city (like Saul in Israel). The only chronological information appears in Genesis 36:31b: "before any king ruled in Israel," an early form of synchronism. This statement must have been added by a tradent at the court of David or Solomon. An important event from the reign of one king is included: "He defeated the Midianites in the fields of Moab" (v. 35b). This addition shows how royal annals developed into historical accounts. During the reign of the last king named, Hadad II, David conquered Edom (2 Sam. 8:13b-14), putting an end to the history of the Edomite kingdom.

40-43   This passage is an appendix listing eleven names, four of which are new.

The historical importance of chapter 36 lies in its bearing witness to the same three stages in the development of society found in the structure of the historical books of the Old Testament: from family through tribe to the state (in the form of a monarchy). This significance extends also to the history of the chapter's growth and transmission, the three stages of which are accounted for by its *Sitz im Leben*, the need to govern a conquered land. Thus the Edomite king list came to the chancery of the king at Jerusalem. But it also includes lists of the regions of Edom, in the form of lists of chiefs; Isaiah 34:12 mentions the chiefs of Edom alongside its king. The genealogies of the families represent an even more detailed subdivision. The doublets and contradictions in these lists were not harmonized; their authenticity was thus preserved.

In chapter 36 Edom appears as the nation most closely related to Israel. The same is true in Deuteronomy 23:7: "You shall not abhor an Edomite, for he is your brother." The familial bond proved stronger over generations than political enmity. By the time Genesis 36 came into being, Edom had often been Israel's enemy; but that did not change the fact that Esau was Jacob's brother, that Esau had married Oholibamah and his son Eliphaz had married Timna. This is the reason why Israel continued to have an interest in the history of Edom. The documents in chapter 36 had long lost their usefulness; but they retained their significance, because Jacob and Esau were part of Israel's history. We learn from them that the Horites inhabited the land before the Edomites entered it, that they were conquered by the Edomites but nevertheless intermarried with them. We learn that the Edomites had a monarchy 150 to 200 years before Israel and much about the nature of this monarchy.

The theophorous personal names have much in common with those of Israel; they include praise names, just as in Israel, and the name of the Edomite king Shaul (or Saul), like that of his Israelite counterpart, expresses the experience of having a prayer for a child answered.

CONCLUDING REMARKS ON GENESIS 12–36

THE ORIGINS OF THE PATRIARCHAL HISTORY

Behind the texts as we have them stands a complex oral tradition, comprising lists (genealogies and itineraries) and narratives. The

Patriarchal History in its written form is substantially more unified than was assumed in the period of the classical documentary hypothesis. Only two works are represented in Genesis 12–36: that of the Yahwist and that of the Priestly Document. Many more texts in these chapters are homogenous than was previously supposed.

The Yahwist brings together traditional narratives and reports from the patriarchal period, placing them in two groups: one concerning Abraham, the other concerning Jacob and Esau. In both he adds a wealth of additional material. The composer of this work is simultaneously tradent, author, and theologian. Out of the elements at his disposal he forms a unified whole, within which the individual narrative is dominant in chapters 12–25, the overall structure (flight—return) in chapters 25–36. The narrator is also a theologian, because he cannot speak of the patriarchs without speaking at the same time of God's words and acts.

The former theory of a written Elohistic document cannot be maintained for Genesis 12–36: there is no perceptible independent conception of the story of Abraham or that of Jacob and Esau besides that of the Yahwist. The texts in Genesis 12–25 formerly ascribed to the Elohist (E) consist almost entirely of secondary additions placed after the conclusion in Genesis 21:1-7; they differ among themselves. In Genesis 25–36 some texts exhibit more than a single stratum; but secondary expansion accounts for all of these.

The Priestly Document in Genesis 12–36 largely reduced the Patriarchal History to genealogies and itineraries outlining the lives of Abraham, (Isaac), and the two brothers Jacob and Esau. At the heart of both stands a revelation discourse with a promise and a change of name (Gen. 17; 35:6, 9-13). P uses three narrative expansions to establish precultic rituals, all concerned with family continuity: circumcision (ch. 17), intrafamily marriage (27:36–28:9), and burial on one's own soil (ch. 23). P reshaped the Patriarchal History markedly from the viewpoint of his own theology.

The redactor (R) shaped the two documents J and P into a single connected presentation of the Patriarchal History, as in Genesis 1–11. His hand appears particularly in introductions and conclusions. Elsewhere he generally left the texts of J and P intact, thus preserving the theological uniqueness of each, as well as that of the expansions.

CONCLUDING REMARKS ON THE PATRIARCHAL HISTORY

In the patriarchs we see people living a prepolitical and precultic way of life. Abraham and his family face elemental dangers that threaten their survival over generations: infertility, hunger and thirst, natural catastrophes, tests imposed by powerful lords or by God. They live the life of nomadic herdsmen without economic or political security.

Jacob and Esau are pictured living in fraternal coexistence, which is threatened by conflicts. These conflicts move from the family circles into the economic and social realm until they reach the point of settlement by force, but with a built-in tendency toward peaceful resolution. In his period, under the cloud of war, J sees in this tendency toward peace a heritage of the patriarchal period; for him, blessing and peace go hand in hand. The same tendency appears in the relationship between the patriarchs and other peoples; in the prepolitical form of society, the patriarchs have no hostility toward the peoples through whose territories they travel. Their relationship to the Canaanites is entirely peaceful. Genesis 34 is different: here we have the beginnings of battle and bloody vengeance. Above all, this attitude may be seen in 12:3, the promise of blessing for the nations.

The term "the God of the fathers" (or "the God of my father") is characteristic of the people whose story is told in the Patriarchal History. The religion of the patriarchs differs markedly from the later religion of the people of Israel. It is characterized by a personal relationship with God that is congruent with the way of life of the patriarchs and their form of society. In their common life, traveling with their flocks, the patriarchs are dependent on God's blessing, which enables them to live. God crowns their labor with success; he causes children and flocks to grow and thrive. God is with them on their way, he sustains them by enabling them to find and control sources of water, by causing the work of the herdsmen to succeed. He helps them find their way by giving directives about where to go, when to set forth, when to stop. Since they have no security, they trust in God's promises. In contrast to a later age (Deuteronomy), neither blessing nor promise is conditional. Curse is not yet the counterpart of blessing; proclamation of judgment is not yet the counterpart of promise.

In all the narratives of the period, the patriarchs are concerned with just *one* God. It would be out of place to speak of a conscious monotheism, but there is no trace of polytheistic influence from the surrounding world. What was later to become the first commandment of Israel's religion and the heart of its confession of faith (Deut. 6:4) does not yet require a commandment. It is *one* God to whom they cry and in whom they trust. Only so is it possible to move from the patriarchs through Moses to the people of Israel.

Prayer emerges as a simple, brief cry to God, expressing praise, complaint, petition, or trust, and growing out of life. Its meaning and necessity derive from the particular situation; it is therefore a natural element of the relationship with God. This is illustrated by the lament of Abraham (Gen. 15:2-3) or Rebekah (25:22), by Jacob's plea for deliverance (32:11), by the servant's plea for success (ch. 24). Praise of

God is commemorated in the name of a place (ch. 22); the name given a child may reflect praise or petition. The absence of any institutional cult is characteristic of worship in the patriarchal stories. Transactions between God and mortals are direct; there are no priests (*pace* ch. 14). With respect to holy places, we can clearly trace the process leading from places holy by nature to those made holy by human action. We can see the transition from the religious practices of nomads at a stopping place (building an altar and calling upon God) to the sanctuaries of settled groups. The later expansions of the narratives seek to trace cultic institutions of the later, settled period to the patriarchal age (14:18-20; 28:20-22).

Theological reflection appears first in later retellings of the old stories, an outgrowth of such reflection (for example, 18:16-33). Only here do theological concepts such as faith, righteousness, and testing come into their own. Another late feature is the tendency to exalt the figures of the patriarchal stories and emphasize their rewards. Later this exaggeration of Abraham's greatness in particular becomes even more expansive. In the history of the promises, the emphasis on what they meant to the patriarchs themselves is shifted to their meaning for the people of Israel. Thus the promises to the patriarchs become a bridge, first to the rest of the Old Testament, then finally to the New Testament.

THE JOSEPH STORY   37–50

The narrative begins with a quarrel between Joseph and his brothers; it ends in chapters 45–46 with their reconciliation and reunion. The subsequent material in chapters 46–50 is too long to be part of the conclusion. These chapters in fact conclude the story of Jacob, as is particularly clear in 46:1-7, a text with affinities to the Patriarchal History but not to the Joseph story. This analysis is confirmed by the observation that texts from P appear in chapter 37 but do not appear again until chapters 46–50. All these P passages concern Jacob, even when they mention Joseph. Within chapters 37–50, therefore, we must distinguish the conclusion to the story of Jacob from the Joseph story in the narrow sense. The latter (chs. 37; 39–45; parts of 46–50) is a single seamless and complete unit by a single author; it differs in both style and content from the Patriarchal History. This conclusion solves a problem in the exegesis of chapter 37, in which source analysis found its strongest evidence: different names for the same person, doublets, and repetitions. These are explained by the fact that in this chapter the beginning of the Joseph story in the narrow sense is interwoven with elements of the Jacob story. Two narrative strands run in parallel because the Joseph story is linked here with the Jacob story. This also explains why the Joseph story per se lacks any exposition. Its author used the existing story of Jacob as exposition; his purpose is to continue the story of the patriarchs.

The Joseph story does not use the itinerary, genealogy, or directive and promise form; these forms do appear, however, in chapters 46–50. The conclusion of the Jacob story tells how Jacob arrives in Egypt with his family. This accounts for the repetition of 45:5-8—Joseph's interpretation of what has taken place for his brothers—in 50:17-21. Chapter 45 was the original locus of this passage; it is repeated in 50:17-21 to link the conclusion of the Jacob story more tightly with the Joseph story. At the same time, repetition lends weight to the interpretation. Finally, chapters 38 and 49 may be understood as additions to the Jacob story; they have nothing to do with the Joseph story.

THE COMPOSITION AND ORIGIN OF THE JOSEPH STORY IN THE NARROW SENSE

In the Joseph story the author has combined a family narrative with a political narrative.[1] The family narrative moves from the threatened breach within Jacob's family (ch. 37) to the healing of this breach. The political narrative shows how Joseph's rise to high position in the Egyptian court makes possible the restoration of peace. The narrative includes two expansions: the rise of Joseph (chs. 39–41), based on the tale motif of the rise of the youngest to power and wealth at the royal court; and the two journeys of the brothers (chs. 42–45), which link the family narrative with the political narrative. The delay caused by the two journeys heightens the tension, which is resolved in chapters 45–46. The author combined a family narrative with a political narrative in order to connect the familial way of life with the political life of the Monarchy. They reflect two stages in the historical path of the Israelite people: the patriarchal period and the beginning of the Monarchy. The latter period vigorously debated whether one brother might or should reign over his other brothers (37:8); this question constitutes the background for the two parts of the Joseph story.

THE LITERARY FORM OF THE JOSEPH STORY

The Joseph story has been called a tale, a short story, and a didactic wisdom narrative. The term "short story" (German *Novelle*) used by such scholars as Hermann Gunkel and Gerhard von Rad was meant to indicate that it is a unified independent literary work. So much is true; but, since modern criticism considers the short story to be essentially fictional and individualistic, the Joseph story should not be called a "short story," for it is neither. It is not fictional, because it claims to tell of Israel's ancestors; it is not individualistic, because it concerns a family and deliberately develops the contrast between two forms of society: family and monarchy. It is indeed a work of literature, the product not of oral tradition but of an author's conception. It should be called simply a narrative or story. Moreover, it is far from being a didactic wisdom narrative, as exegesis will show. When the theme of wisdom appears (especially in chs. 40–41), it is because the setting demands it: wisdom is associated with the royal court because wise counselors are there.

---

1. Hugo Gressmann, *Ursprung und Entwicklung der Josephsage.* Forschungen zur Religion und Literatur des Alten und Neuen Testaments 36 (Göttingen: Vandenhoeck & Ruprecht, 1923): 1-55.

The Joseph narrative as a single, self-contained document came into being during the Early Monarchy as the work of a literary author who was also a theologian. We do not know who this author was. It cannot have been the Yahwist, whose approach and style differ fundamentally from those of the author.

THE EGYPTIAN BACKGROUND

Since the Joseph story in chapters 39–50 is set in Egypt, its Egyptian background is not surprising; what is surprising is the totally positive and favorable picture of Egypt and the fact that one of the patriarchs of Israel was a great man at the court of Pharaoh. This consists best with the time of Solomon, when the Israelite monarchy was on good terms with the Egyptian court and borrowed much from Egyptian civilization. No other narrative of the Old Testament reflects such an astonishing interest in a foreign land—above all the court and its institutions, its officials and their titles, its ceremonies, rituals, and practices. It is noteworthy that the only aspect of Pharaoh's rule dealt with is the political economy of Egypt; there is no mention of foreign policy, nor is there any interest in the architecture of the ancient Egyptians. The depiction of the Egyptian background seems to reflect a first encounter. This points once again to the time of Solomon. It is only natural that the author's knowledge should be somewhat limited, with many minor inaccuracies and many generalities. What he considered important was above all the contrast between the life of a simple family of nomadic herdsmen and life at the Egyptian court to which they come from far away, dazed to discover that their brother has become a great man at the court of Pharaoh.

The Egyptian section (chs. 39–41) is also characterized by Egyptian themes. Chapter 39 has a familiar Egyptian parallel. In chapter 40 we find the common theme of the rise and fall of court officials, and in chapter 41 the theme of the wise counselor as deliverer, who in time of trouble gives the king advice that averts disaster.

GENESIS 37–50: THE JOSEPH STORY

37:1-36 JOSEPH AND HIS BROTHERS

1   *But Jacob dwelt in the land where his father had sojourned, the land of Canaan.*

2   *This is the story of Jacob:*
When Joseph was seventeen years old,
he was a herdsman with his brothers guarding the sheep,
he was an assistant to the sons of Bilhah and Zilpah, his father's wives.
And Joseph informed their father
of the bad things said about them.

3   *But Israel loved Joseph more than all his other sons,*
because he had been borne to him in his old age,
and he made him a sleeved tunic.

4   *Now when his brothers saw that their father loved him more than his other*
sons, they became hostile to him
and could not so much as greet him.

5   *Once Joseph had a dream and told it to his brothers;*
[then they hated him more].

6   *And he said to them: Listen to this dream that I have had.*

7   *Behold, we were binding sheaves outside in the field,*
and my sheaf rose up and stood upright,
but your sheaves gathered round
and bowed down before my sheaf.

8   *Then his brothers said to him: Are you going to be king over us, or are you*
going to lord it over us?
Then they hated him still more because of his dreams and his words.

9   *And he had yet another dream, and he told it to his brothers, saying: Behold,*
I have had another dream: the sun and the moon and eleven stars were
bowing down before me.

10   *When he told it to his father and brothers,*
his father rebuked him and said to him:
What kind of dream is this that you have had?
Am I and your mother and your brothers to come and fall down before you?

11   *And his brothers were incensed at him,*
but his father pondered the matter.

12   *When his brothers had gone to pasture their father's sheep at Shechem,*

13   *Israel said to Joseph: You know, your brothers are pasturing at Shechem.*
Come, I will send you to them.
He said: Here I am.

14   *Go and see if all is well with your brothers and if all is well with the sheep,*
and bring me back word.
So he sent him out of the valley of Hebron, and he came to Shechem.

15   *Then a man met him as he was wandering in the fields.*
And the man asked him: What are you looking for?

16   *He answered: I am looking for my brothers; tell me, please, where they are*
pasturing.

17   *Then the man said: They have moved on from here;*
I heard them saying: Let us go on to Dothan.
Then Joseph went after his brothers and found them at Dothan.

18   *When they saw him in the distance, and before he drew near to them, they*
plotted against him to kill him.

19   *They said to each other: Here comes this dreamer!*

20   *Now is our chance to kill him and throw him into one of these cisterns and say that a wild animal has eaten him. Then we will see what use his dreams are.*

21   *When Reuben heard this, he tried to save him from their hands and said: We must not take his life.*

22   *[And Reuben said to them:] Do not shed blood!*
    Throw him into this cistern in the wilderness,
    but do not lay a hand on him. He planned to save him from their hands to bring him back to his father.

23   *Now when Joseph came up to them they took off his tunic [the sleeved tunic that he was wearing].*

24   *Then they took hold of him and threw him into the cistern.*
    But the cistern was empty; there was no water in it.

25a   *Then they sat down to eat.*

25b   *[When they looked up, they saw a caravan of Ishmaelites coming from Gilead, and their camels were carrying gum, balm, and resin, and they were on their way down to Egypt.*

26   *Then Judah said to his brothers: What have we gained if we kill our brother and cover up his blood?*

27   *Come, let us sell him to the Ishmaelites and not lay our hands on him; after all, he is our brother, our flesh! And his brothers agreed (with him).]*

28a   *But some Midianite merchants passed by,*
    who drew Joseph out of the cistern.

28b   *[And they sold Joseph to the Ishmaelites for twenty silver pieces,*
    and they brought Joseph down to Egypt.]

29   *Now when Reuben came back to the cistern,*
    behold, Joseph was no longer in the cistern.

30   *And he tore his garments, went back to his brothers, and said: The boy is not there!*
    Now what shall I do?

31   *Then they took Joseph's tunic, slaughtered a goat, and dipped his tunic in the blood.*

32   *Then they [sent the sleeved tunic] brought it to their father and said: We have found this. See whether it is your son's tunic or not.*

33   *When he had examined it, he said:*
    It is my son's tunic. A wild animal has eaten him. Joseph has been torn to pieces!

34   *And Jacob tore his garments and put sackcloth about his loins. And he mourned his son for many days.*

35   *Then all his sons and daughters arose to console him.*
    But he refused to be consoled, and said:
    No, I will go down to the realm of the dead mourning for my son. Thus his father wept for him.

36   *But the Midianites sold Joseph in Egypt to Potiphar, one of Pharaoh's chamberlains, the head of the bodyguard.*

Chapter 37 is based on an earlier narrative, belonging to the story of Jacob, which dealt with a quarrel within Jacob's family. In its present form this chapter has become the introduction to the Joseph story; it comprises three episodes, each with a different setting. In the second episode (vv. 18-30), the author has deliberately interwoven two narrative strands in such a way that any listener can tell them apart by the different names they use: Reuben/Judah, Ishmaelites/Midianites. The author shows his audience that he is using two variants of the existing narrative. The first episode accordingly combines two motives for the brothers' hatred. The third episode is homogeneous.

1-2   These verses are P's introduction (cf. 25:19-20); they comprise a transition (37:1), the heading for the conclusion of the Jacob story (v. 2aα), and the beginning of a story about Joseph (v. 2aβ-2b), which then breaks off.

1   The location of Esau's dwelling place (36:8) is followed by that of Jacob. This statement concludes the story of Jacob and Esau in P and at the same time leads into the conclusion of the Jacob story (cf. 47:27a).

2   The *tôlᵉḏōṯ* (here "story") of Jacob, which ends in 49:29-33 with his death and burial, begins here with a story about his sons. The exposition includes Joseph's age and the two following statements: at the age of seventeen, Joseph was a shepherd boy or assistant (the meaning of Hebrew *naʿar* here) to his brothers, the sons of Bilhah and Zilpah. What he told his father about these brothers has to do solely with the sons of Jacob's two concubines: the rivalry between Jacob's wives (chs. 29–30) continues in their sons. Nothing is said about whether the slanderous reports were true or not; since P generally tends to mitigate quarrels between brothers, it is possible that Joseph was trying to mediate between the brothers. Only the association with 37:3-11 makes Joseph look like a malicious informer. Here the narrative breaks off.

3-4   An event is related that leads to enmity between the brothers. In both form and content, verses 3-4 resemble the narratives of the Patriarchal History in chapters 12–36. This passage might derive from J, having been borrowed without alteration by the author of the Joseph story.

3   We are told of the father's preference for his youngest son (cf. 25:28), a "child of his old age." For the author, it is natural that a father should have a special relationship with the child borne to him at a time when his life is already beginning to decline. Neither is it the father's preference for Joseph that arouses his brothers' ire, but rather the privileged position Joseph has with respect to the others, declared openly in his father's gift. It is a special garment: a sleeved tunic (not a "coat of many colors"), according to 2 Samuel 13:18 the

costume of a princess, an ankle-length tunic (Koehler-Baumgartner *Lexicon*) that designates high rank. This gift to Joseph is the first occurrences of the clothing motif, which will turn up repeatedly throughout the narrative. The author presupposes the great social significance of clothing, for millennia one of the most striking evidences of social stratification. It is this tunic, not Joseph's dreams, that first poses the question: May a brother be thus exalted above his other brothers?

4 The events that follow are governed by this question; the father's preference expressed in the form of privilege evokes the hatred of Joseph's brothers. The Hebrew verb translated "they became hostile to him" or "they cast hatred upon him" refers neither to an attitude nor to a status, but to an act. This "casting of hate" introduces a tension that must lead to action. The statement that the brothers became hostile to Joseph rather than to their father, who is actually responsible for Joseph's elevation, reveals a deep understanding of human nature: the hatred of the disadvantaged is often directed not against those who bestow privilege unjustly but against those who receive it (cf. ch. 4). The brothers' enmity is expressed by their refusal to favor Joseph with a friendly greeting. Greetings were very important in this period. Even today, refusal to greet someone can mean social ostracism. The importance of greetings as a social phenomenon is a primary theme throughout the Joseph story. With verse 4, the peace of Jacob's household has been shattered. Here begins the narrative arc that ends with the healing of the breach by the reconciliation of the brothers in chapters 45 and 50.

5-11 Joseph's dreams. In Joseph's dreams, the author of the Joseph story follows his principle of doubling by adding a second cause of dissension within Jacob's family to that already stated in verses 3-4. The dream motif runs through the entire Joseph story; chapters 40 and 41 also record two dreams each. They share an element of tension between prediction and fulfillment, but in each case the effect on the course of the story is different. The author's overall conception appears in the increasing importance of each pair of dreams; any other sequence would be out of the question.

5-8 Verses 5-6 introduce the story of the dream. The youth's dreams are based on a widespread motif, especially common in tales: the youngest brother outstrips his older brothers. The charged language, almost poetic, in which Jacob recalls his dream shows how excited he is by it, how he longs to recount it. The dream consists of an exposition (v. 7a) followed by an act of standing upright and an act of bowing. The actions speak for themselves and need no interpretation; the brothers understand at once. Their anger is expressed in the two synonymous verbs in parallelism that constitute the climax of this section: the youngest brother wants to reign over his older brothers! This runs counter to the familial structure of society, in which all authority derives from seniority. The brothers represent this old order, which they see threatened by Joseph's arrogant dreams.

9-11   The second dream is only an augmentation of the first and is therefore much shorter; it is an augmentation, because it includes the parents. The dream is described as a single momentary image. "Stars" does not mean constellations but eleven individual stars, corresponding to the eleven brothers. The father's reaction to Joseph's dream is anger and indignation; he rejects such a perversion of the existing order as vigorously as Jacob's brothers. But "he ponders the matter" (cf. Luke 2:19); he does not rule out any future possibilities.

12-17   These verses constitute a bridge that serves to separate the *dramatis personae* of the first three episodes. What takes place now involves only Joseph and his brothers. Verses 12-14 lay the groundwork for an encounter between Joseph and his brothers without their father's presence. Jacob sends his son away without sensing the danger he is facing. His instructions twice use the Hebrew word *šālôm* ("peace, well-being"; cf. 29:6); what is intended to maintain peace is about to shatter it. The place names in this passage present problems; they probably come from a prototype in which they made more sense. The interlude in 37:15-17 shows how helpless Joseph is apart from his father and his father's protection; the stranger's information takes him even further away. Only at Dothan (2 Kgs. 6:13), some eight miles from Shechem, does Joseph meet up with his brothers.

18-30   Two narrative strands have been interwoven in this section. In verses 18-25a, 28a-30 (omitting v. 28b), Reuben is the eldest son and the foreigners are Midianite merchants; in verses 25b-27, 28b, Judah is the eldest and the foreigners are Ishmaelites. Here we clearly have two narrative strands recounting the same sequence of events: the proposal of the eldest brother—its motivation—his advice to the others—Joseph's arrival in Egypt.

18-22   Joseph's brothers see him coming, and their anger is aroused once more (cf. v. 4); now, while he is in their power, they decide to kill him. A plan is quickly worked out, which includes concealing the deed; but consensus is necessary. Then Reuben opposes the plan. He, too, wishes to do something about Joseph, but he wants to avoid murder. Verse 22 states another reason: "to bring him back to his father." Here Reuben assumes the duties of the eldest brother, which are his in the absence of their father. During this brief period of time, he is responsible. Here we see the origin of the concept of "responsibility": someone must respond to the father's questions when he returns.

23-25a   All the brothers participate in what follows. They strip Joseph of the detested tunic and throw him into an empty cistern. There is no murder; his fate is left open. We are told in 42:21 that Joseph pleaded with his brothers. The absence of such entreaty here is deliberate: the author wishes to make it clear that insensitivity to the pain and pleas of the victim is part of the offense. After the deed, the brothers therefore calmly sit down to eat.

25b-27, 28b   The interpolated variant involving Judah and the Ishmaelites is included in such a way as not to interrupt the narrative flow. While the brothers are enjoying their meal (an element from the other narrative strand), a caravan of Ishmaelite merchants passes by. Their place of origin, the goods they are carrying, and their destination are described in detail (v. 25b). The merchandise (cf. also 43:11) comprises medicaments and cosmetics. The importation of such goods to Egypt from Transjordan by the trade route through Dothan is well attested. Judah wants to avoid murdering his brother; the caravan inspires him to sell Joseph to the Ishmaelites as a slave (37:26-27). Urgently he warns his brothers not to commit the terrible crime of fratricide. His brothers agree and so sell Joseph to the Ishmaelites for 20 shekels (v. 28b), the going price. The Ishmaelite merchants take Joseph with them to Egypt. Then follows the beginning of chapter 39.

28a, 29-30   Now the other narrative strand (Reuben and the Midianites) is developed, following verse 25a. These verses clearly have a different story to tell than verses 25b-27, 28b, with which they have been skillfully linked by verse 28b. While the brothers are eating, Midianite merchants pass by; they probably hear Joseph's screams, draw him out of the cistern unbeknownst to his brothers, and make off with him. When Reuben comes back to rescue Joseph from the cistern, it is empty. Overcome with fear and regret, he tears his clothes and admits openly to his brothers that he had planned to rescue Joseph. He cannot conceal his lament for his youngest brother from the others: "The boy is not there!" His desperate question, "Now what shall I do?" suggests that he is answerable to his father.

During the period when the stories of the patriarchs were being transmitted orally, it was normal for such stories to have variants (cf. chs. 16 and 21). One can often say which is earlier and which is later, but one can never say which is "right" and which is "wrong." In the case of 37:18-30, also, the audience would not ask: What really did happen? Was the eldest brother Reuben or Judah? Did the passing caravan consist of Ishmaelites or Midianites? These questions were not asked because stories were strictly distinguished from historical accounts; the question "What really did happen?" the question of names and dates, can be asked of an historical account but not of a story. Stories have a certain freedom; they are not fixed in every detail, not even with respect to names. The overall course of the story of how Joseph came to Egypt is not disrupted but enriched. The author of the Joseph story here uses these variants as a form of doubling to underline a theme. In *both* brothers who seek to prevent the murder, the author emphasizes the special nature of the eldest brother's authority, which under certain circumstances he must exercise. It differs from the sovereign authority of the monarchy: it is limited to a definite period of time and is based on responsibility. In essence, it represents the difference between democracy and autocracy.

31-35   The third episode is set once more in the father's house; it recounts the concealment of the crime and the father's lamentation. The brothers, acting once more in concert, fake an accident. What cannot be undone is set forth starkly in an account that deceives the father and plunges him into mourning. The tunic provides the means to conceal the crime. Without any words of explanation or reflection, the leitmotif of the tunic speaks through the contrast alone. The gift given as an expression of paternal love, which aroused the hatred of the brothers, they now hold dripping with blood before their father's eyes in order to conceal their crime. But they have gained nothing. The father recognizes his son's tunic; the trick has worked: "A wild animal has eaten him." His anguish speaks in his agonized cry: "Joseph has been torn to pieces!" (v. 33). The old man's life is now marked by grief for his youngest son, expressed in the rites of mourning (v. 34). He will not allow his children to comfort him. He will remain in mourning until he dies; then he will be reunited with his son. The brothers can get rid of Joseph, but things will never be the same. The peace of the family remains breached.

36   This verse, which forms a bridge to chapter 39, shows that chapter 39 is the continuation of chapter 37.

38:1-30   JUDAH AND TAMAR

1   *At that time, Judah left his brothers*
     and joined with a man from Adullam named Hirah.
2   *There Judah saw the daughter of a Canaanite named Shua.*
     He married here and went to her.
3   *She conceived and bore a son,*
     and she called him Er.
4   *Then she conceived again and bore a son,*
     and called him Onan.
5   *Yet again she bore a son, and called him Shelah.*
     But she was in Chezib when she bore him.

6   *For his firstborn Er, Judah took a wife named Tamar.*

7   *But he, the firstborn of Judah, was wicked in Yahweh's eyes,*
      and Yahweh caused him to die.

8   *Then Judah said to Onan: Go to your brother's wife and do the duty of a brother-in-law,*
      that you may raise up issue for your brother.

9   *But Onan knew that the children would not be his;*
      and so whenever he went to his brother's wife
      he destroyed his seed (by spilling it) on the ground,
      so as not to raise issue for his brother.

10   *But what he did was wicked in the eyes of Yahweh,*
      so he caused him to die.

11   *The Judah said to his daughter-in-law Tamar:*
      Go back to your father's house as a widow
      until my son Shelah has grown up. For he feared
      that he, too, would die like his brothers.
      So Tamar went and lived in her father's house.

12   *After a long time had passed, Shua's daughter, Judah's wife, died. When the period of mourning was over, Judah went with his friend Hirah from Adullam to the sheep-shearing at Timnah.*

13   *But when Tamar was told: Your father-in-law is going up to the sheep-shearing at Timnah,*

14   *she put off her widow's clothes, covered herself with a veil, and sat at the gate of Enaim, on the way to Timnah.*
      For she knew that Shelah had grown up
      and she had not been given to him in marriage.

15   *When Judah saw her, he thought she was a prostitute,*
      for she had veiled her face.

16   *He turned off to her from the road and said: Come, let me lie with you.*
      For he did not know that she was his daughter-in-law.
      She answered: What will you give me to lie with me?

17   *He said: I will send you a kid from the flock.*
      She replied: If you will give me a pledge until you send it.

18   *He said: What sort of pledge shall I give you?*
      She answered: Your signet ring, your cord, and the staff in your hand. He gave them to her and went to her,
      and she became pregnant by him.

19   *Then she rose and went away. She took off her veil and put on her widow's clothes again.*

20   *When Judah sent the kid by his friend from Adullam to recover the pledge from the woman, he could not find her.*

21   *Then he asked the people of the place: Where is the prostitute who sits by the roadside at Enaim? They said: There was no prostitute here.*

22   *Then he returned to Judah and said:*
      I did not find her, and the people of the place said:
      No prostitute has been here.

23   *Then Judah said: So she can keep it for herself!*
      If only we are not mocked! I did send the kid, and you did not find her.

24 *About three months later, Judah was told:*
    Your daughter-in-law Tamar has played the prostitute
    and is pregnant because of her immorality.
    Then Judah said: Bring her out to be burnt.
25 *As she was to be brought out,*
    she sent to her father-in-law and said:
    I am pregnant by the man to whom these belong.
    And she also said: See if you recognize
    to whom this signet ring, this cord, and this staff belong.
26 *When Judah saw the items, he said: She is within her rights rather than I.*
    Why did I not give her to my son Shelah!
    From that time on he had no further relations with her.
27 *When the time came for her to give birth,*
    there were twins in her womb.
28 *But during the birth, one of them put out a hand.*
    The midwife then took a scarlet thread and tied it to his hand, saying: This
    one came out first.
29 *But when he drew back his hand and his brother came out, she said: What a*
    breach you have torn!
    And she named him Perez.
30 *Then his brother came out, who had the scarlet thread on his hand; she called*
    him Zerah.

Chapter 38 was appended to the conclusion of the story of Jacob (not the Joseph story) because it deals with one of Jacob's sons and could therefore be included at this point. Previously it had been transmitted independently, as is suggested by the extensive genealogical framework in verses 1-11 and 27-30, similar to that in the book of Ruth. It is a story about Judah's family, which later became the tribe of Judah. It recounts how a childless widow daringly guarantees her right to have a child. It is set on Canaanite soil during the transition to settlement. It originated as an oral narrative among the descendants of Judah and Tamar in the territory of the tribe of Judah, near the towns of Adullam and Timnah.

1-11   The introductory genealogy comprises two generations, the first in verses 1-5, the second in verses 6-11. After a redactional bridge in verse 1, the first begins by saying that Judah, having separated from his brothers, took a Canaanite wife (v. 2). Such an event could be stated straightforwardly at an early period without appearing offensive. Her father Shua lived in Adullam, a town ten miles northwest of Hebron. Three sons are borne to him. The statement that their mother named them is also a sign of an early date.

6-11   These verses introduce the second major character in the story: Judah gives his son a wife named Tamar (cf. 2 Sam. 13:1; 14:27). Judah's firstborn dies prematurely, which is interpreted as a punish-

ment from God (38:7). Tamar is left as a young, childless widow
(v. 8). Now, as local custom requires, Judah is responsible for seeing
that the family of the departed is continued. This practice (levirate
marriage) appears elsewhere in the Old Testament in Deuteronomy
25:5-10 and in Ruth; it is also found among other peoples. It requires a
surviving brother to beget a child (or children) with his sister-in-law;
such a child is considered the child of the departed. Originally, the
widow could demand only a child, not marriage with her brother-in-
law. Therefore Judah tells Onan, his second son, to raise up seed for
his brother. Tamar does not become Onan's wife; her sole concern
throughout the story is to get a son. But Onan only feigns obedience
to his father's demand; in reality, he refuses to perform his duty. He,
too, dies prematurely; his death, too, is explained as God's punishment (vv. 9-10). Now Judah has only one son left, and he is concerned for his life. He puts off the decision and has Tamar return to
her father's house.

12-14   Now begins the action proper. Tamar, who is living as a
widow in her father's house, realizes that she is being deprived of her
rights. She therefore undertakes to obtain her due on her own initiative. She contrives a daring but risky plan. Judah, whose wife has
died, gives her her chance when he and his friend Hirah from
Adullam go into the mountains near Timnah for the sheep-shearing.
Tamar sits down by the side of the road he must travel and disguises
herself as a prostitute (cf. Jer. 3:2; Ezek. 16:25).

15-19   What now takes place is recounted solely as a story about
a woman who is determined to obtain her rights, without any moral
judgment. She conceives a child through Judah and takes a pledge
that enables her to prove that he is the father. The pledge consists of
an aristocrat's insignia, attested in both Babylonia and Canaan: a
signet ring with a cord (a cylinder seal) used to sign contracts and a
staff carved with his own mark.

20-23   The brief but vivid interlude in verses 20-23 is inserted to
explain why the insignia remain in Tamar's possession until the
critical moment: Tamar has prudently seen to this. In addition, the
scene is meant to depict Judah as a man of honor: he does all he can to
discharge his debt.

24-26   In these verses the story reaches it climax. Tamar becomes pregnant. In the presence of Judah, the head of the family, she
is charged with adultery. He at once pronounces the sentence
decreed by ancient family law: she is to be burnt. The death penalty is
to be carried out in front of the gate, outside the town (cf. Deut.
22:21-24). All the citizens are involved in the execution (Deut. 22:24).

Tamar has waited until this moment. She has said nothing in her own defense and has not asked for mercy. At the very last moment, condemned to be burnt to death and about to be led out of the city to be executed, she sends Judah the insignia that prove he is the father of the child. He himself must now bear witness to her innocence. Here is celebrated the courage of a woman who ventured everything to fight for her own rights (Gen. 38:25). Even in this situation, Judah demonstrates that he is a man of honor, declaring publicly: "She is within her rights rather than I." Her conduct is justified by his own injustice. In Judah's justification of Tamar the story reaches its goal.

27-30 In this final section the story returns to its genealogical framework. It recounts the birth and naming of twins. Tamar once more has an honored position in the family. The twins she expects are legitimate; begotten by a member of the family, they are accounted the children of her departed husband (v. 27). The birth and naming of the twins (vv. 28-30) has been expanded by an allusion to a quarrel over the precedence of the firstborn; the names of the children preserve a recollection of this dispute (cf. 25:21-26). The midwife marks with a scarlet thread the arm of the first one to emerge (38:28); he is accordingly named Zerah. The verb means "shine forth"; the name has scarcely any recognizable connection with the scarlet thread. The other twin is nevertheless born first; he thrusts himself forward and is given the name Perez (from the verb "break through"), on the basis of the midwife's exclamation, "What a breach you have torn." An earlier form of the text probably told only of this single son Perez, born to Tamar, who continues her line, in which David will one day be born. This original conclusion was later expanded to reflect the tradition of the two Judahite families of Perez and Zerah, mentioned in the lists of Genesis 46 and Numbers 26. Only with this addition does the genealogical conclusion of Genesis 38 acquire a tribal perspective.

Genesis 38 belongs to the group of narratives concerning childless women. Here it is a childless widow, who obtains her rights through a daring and clever act. The questionable means she uses are justified by the reestablishment of justice. Tamar thus belongs among the women in the patriarchal stories who rebel against the common ethos when it causes injustice. In each case, the narrative justifies such self-defense. Judah, too, sees the preservation of the community in the justice of Tamar's cause. But Genesis 38 is also a biblical story, because it speaks in these secular terms of God's providence, which preserves the life of the community. Only in a later context (Ruth 4:18-22) does it become significant that Tamar's son is one of David's ancestors.

39:1-23   JOSEPH AND HIS MASTER'S WIFE

1   *When Joseph had been brought down to Egypt, [Potiphar, one of Pharaoh's chamberlains, chief of the guard] an Egyptian bought him from the Ishmaelites*
    who had brought him there.
2   *But Yahweh was with Joseph, and all went well with him,*
    so that he remained in the house of his master, the Egyptian.
3   *Now when his master saw that Yahweh was with him*
    and that Yahweh through his hand gave success to all that he undertook,
4   *then Joseph found favor in his eyes; he became his personal attendant.*
    Then he set him over his house,
    and he entrusted all his property to him.
5   *But from the time that he had entrusted all his property to him, Yahweh blessed the house of the Egyptian because of Joseph, and Yahweh's blessing rested on all that he had, both in house and field.*
6   *So he left all his property in Joseph's care and concerned himself personally with nothing but the food he ate.*
    But Joseph was of fine figure and of fine appearance.

7   *After these events, his master's wife began to cast her eye upon Joseph and said to him: Sleep with me.*
8   *But he refused and said to his master's wife:*
    Behold, with me around my master does not concern himself with his household, and he has entrusted all his property to me.
9   *He himself is not greater in this house than I,*
    and nothing has he withheld from me except you,
    because you are his wife. How could I do anything as wicked as this and sin against God?
10 *And although she kept asking Joseph day after day, he would not listen to her to lie with her [to have intercourse with her].*
11 *On one occasion when he came as usual to the hous*
    to do his work,
    and none of the members of the household was inside,
12 *she seized hold of his cloak and said: Sleep with me.*
    But he left his cloak in her hand and fled and ran out.
13 *Now when she saw that he had left his cloak in her hand when he ran out,*
14 *she summoned the members of the household and said to them:*
    Look! He has brought a Hebrew to us to sport with us!
    He came to me to sleep with me,
    but I screamed loudly.
15 *When he heard my screaming, he left his cloak beside me and fled and ran out.*
16 *And she kept his cloak by her until his master came home.*
17 *And then she spoke to him in the same fashion and said:*
    The Hebrew slave whom you brought to us came to me to sport with me.
18 *But when I raised my voice and screamed,*
    he left his cloak beside me and fled outside.

19 *Now when his master heard the words of his wife that she spoke to him: This*
is what your servant did to me,
he was very angry.

20 *And he took Joseph and had him thrown into prison, where the prisoners of*
the king were held.
And he remained there in prison,

21 *but Yahweh was with Joseph and showed him favor.*
He won him the favor of the governor of the prison.

22 *So the governor of the prison entrusted to Joseph all the prisoners who were*
in the prison; everything that they did there was done through him.

23 *The governor of the prison did not concern himself any further with what*
was entrusted to him, because Yahweh was with him and Yahweh gave
success in all that he undertook.

The second part of the story, Joseph in Egypt (chs. 39–41), begins
with chapter 39: Jacob's son, sold in Egypt as a slave, becomes a high
official of Pharaoh. Verse 1 is a transitional verse; the rest of the
chapter recounts Joseph's rise (vv. 2-6), fall (vv. 7-20), and new rise in
prison (vv. 21-23).

1 This transitional verse links with 37:28; it is prepared for by
37:36. The identification of the purchaser in 39:1b seems wordy: "Potiphar, one of Pharaoh's chamberlains, chief of the guard" is an addition, identical to 37:36b. His name is mentioned only in these two
passages, not in the narrative itself. "Potiphar" appears once again
in a somewhat different form as the name of Joseph's father-in-law
in 41:45-50; 46:20. It means "one given by Re." The Hebrew word
sārîs means "eunuch"; later it became a general term for a court
official.

2-6 Together with verses 21-23, these verses constitute the
theological introit to the Joseph story, introducing the leitmotif of
Yahweh's being with Joseph (vv. 2, 3, 21, 23). It has a counterpart in
the interpretative passages 45:5-8; 50:17-21. The name "Yahweh" appears only here, and in the mouth of the narrator; his intent is to
make a connection with the formula of Yahweh's presence with the
patriarchs in chapters 25–36. The God of the patriarchs is now with
Joseph in far-off Egypt, just as he was with Joseph's fathers. As in the
case of Jacob, God's support also affects those around him; his master therefore shows him special favor (39:3-4), and God blesses the
house of the Egyptian (vv. 5-6). The master of the house has complete confidence in him and puts everything in his charge. Verse 6b
leads into the next episode. One of the blessings God bestows upon
Joseph is physical attractiveness (cf. 1 Sam. 16:18); that is why the wife
of his Egyptian master desires him.

7-26 The following episode involving Joseph and the wife

of his Egyptian master resembles the Egyptian Story of the Two Brothers.[1]

> Two brothers lived together; the elder, Anubis, had a house and a wife; the younger, Bata, worked for him in the fields. One day Bata entered the house to get seed for the sowing; his brother's wife wanted him to sleep with her. Very angry, he rejected her suggestion out of loyalty to his brother, who had been like a father to him, and expressed his abhorrence at the "great sin" that she wanted him to commit. He promised to say nothing and returned to his brother. Anubis came home in the evening and discovered his wife covered with self-inflicted wounds; she brought a false charge against her brother. . . .

The author of the Joseph story made the Egyptian narrative (which has a different conclusion) into an episode in his story, with appropriate changes.

7-9 Joseph cites his relationship with his master as his reason for refusing. He must not commit a breach of trust. To do so would be a serious crime (the same term as in the Egyptian story; cf. 2 Sam. 13:16) as well as a sin against God, for the confidence his master has in him is due to the fact that God has been with him.

10-12 The woman's first attempt is followed by others; she never stops trying, and finally grabs Joseph by the cloak. Joseph is taken by surprise, the story emphasizes, stressing his innocence. Since his position prevents him from raising his hand against his master's wife, all he can do is run away.

13-15 The story limits itself strictly to outward actions. The effect is so powerful that it does not need to say a word about what is going on in the participants' minds: events speak for themselves. They began when the woman "saw" Joseph (v. 7); now in verse 13 she "sees" again: she notices that Joseph has left his cloak in her hand (that is, in her power). This perception precipitates the crisis; nothing more need be said. Once again, Joseph's clothing is the corpus delicti, albeit in a totally different way; once again, it is an instrument of deception. The woman uses Joseph's cloak as evidence to back up her accusation before the household (vv. 14-15). Skillfully she puts them on her side: "He has brought a Hebrew to us. . . ." With this fabrication she forces her husband to intervene on her behalf; otherwise he would have to admit publicly that she has lied.

16-20 In verse 16 the author introduces an effective pause: the woman lies down with Joseph's cloak beside her. When her husband

---

1. For an abridged translation, see James B. Pritchard, ed., *Ancient Near Eastern Texts*, 3rd ed. (Princeton: Princeton University, 1969), pp. 23-25.

returns, she angrily tells him the same story (vv. 17-18). Its effect on him is merely suggested by the words "he was very angry"; at whom his anger is directed is left open. In any case he is angry to be put in this position. He is acting under duress. His responsibility for administration of justice within his house requires him to give Joseph a hearing, but this he cannot do. The punishment he decrees, however, makes it clear that he is not convinced of Joseph's guilt. If he were to impose the appropriate sentence, he would have Joseph put to death or sold into base slavery.

Now Joseph's fortunes are once again at a nadir. His reaction is not described. He knows that he has no recourse against his master's decree. But the very fact that he is assigned to the prison for "prisoners of the king" implies the possibility of a change of fortune.

21-23 These verses, which with verses 2-6 constitute the framework of the episode, reintroduce the leitmotif of God's help. The reason why another rise follows Joseph's fall is that God once again "shows Joseph favor." The same idiom appears in Psalm 40, a hymn of praise and thanksgiving for deliverance: "He inclined to me and heard my cry." God's help and presence can continue even for someone who has fallen. And once again Joseph experiences God's loving care in the friendship a stranger shows him. The governor of the prison entrusts its entire administration to Joseph (Gen. 39:22-23a). This was possible because Yahweh gave him success in all that he undertook. God's presence makes itself felt in this success, but also in Joseph's unswerving loyalty.

40:1-23 JOSEPH INTERPRETS THE DREAMS OF THE CUPBEARER AND BAKER

1 *Some time after this, the king's cupbearer and baker offended their master,*
   the king of Egypt.
2 *Then Pharaoh became angry with his two courtiers,*
   the chief cupbearer and the chief baker,
3 *and had them put in custody in the house of the chief of the guard, into*
   prison,
   the place were Joseph also was held.
4 *And the chief of the guard entrusted their oversight to Joseph.*
   They remained some time in custody.
5 *Then on the same night they both had a dream,*
   each a dream with its own meaning,
   the cupbearer and the baker of the king of Egypt,
   who were held in prison.
6 *When Joseph came to them in the morning, he saw*
   that they were dismayed.

7   Then he asked the courtiers of Pharaoh who were in custody with him:
     Why are your faces downcast today?
8   Then they answered him: We have had a dream;
     but there is nobody to interpret it.
     Joseph answered them: Interpretation of dreams belongs to God,
     but tell me.

9   Then the chief cupbearer told Joseph his dream, and said to him:
     In my dream I saw a vine in front of me,
10   and there were three branches on the vine. And when it began to bud, it
     blossomed
     and its clusters ripened into grapes.
11   I had Pharaoh's cup in my hand and took the grapes;
     I squeezed them into Pharaoh's cup and handed Pharaoh the cup.
12   Then Joseph said to him: This is its interpretation:
     the three branches mean three days.
13   Within three days Pharaoh will raise your head and restore you to your post.
     You will hand Pharaoh his cup as you used to do when you were his
     cupbearer.
14   But remember me when things go well with you again.
     Do me this favor—mention me to Pharaoh and get me out of this house.
15   For I was abducted out of the land of the Hebrews,
     and I have done nothing here
     that they should put me in a dungeon.

16   When the chief baker saw that he had interpreted favorably,
     he said to Joseph: In my dream I was carrying three wicker baskets on my
     head.
17   In the first basket were all sorts of baked goods for Pharaoh; but the birds were
     eating them from the basket on my head.
18   Joseph answered and said: This is its interpretation:
     the three baskets are three days.
19   Within three days, Pharaoh will raise your head (from you).
     He will hang you on a gallows
     and the birds will eat your flesh from you.

20   And it happened on the third day, on Pharaoh's birthday,
     he gave a feast for all his courtiers.
     Then he raised the head of his chief cupbearer
     and the head of his chief baker in the presence of his servants.
21   The chief cupbearer he restored to his post,
     and he was allowed once more to place the cup in Pharaoh's hand.
22   But the chief baker he ordered to be hanged,
     as Joseph had it interpreted to them.
23   But the chief cupbearer gave no further thought to Joseph,
     but forgot him.

The second episode in Egypt exhibits a carefully conceived structure, beginning with the encounter in verses 1-4 and ending with the cupbearer's forgetting in verse 23; Joseph's request is placed in the middle (vv. 14-15).

1-4   The introduction (vv. 1-4) brings Joseph into contact with two courtiers. There were undoubtedly stories of the fall and rise of courtiers in Egypt; the theme is common. The words "he had them put in custody" do not refer to a prison sentence but to detention pending trial; Pharaoh will decide the punishment later. The encounter is made possible by the guard chief's assignment of Joseph to take care of their needs.

5-8   What takes place next begins with a friendly question. To ask how someone is feeling is common to all languages and all peoples; here it takes on special weight. It is not an empty formula but a living expression of concern. Joseph's observation of sadness in the faces of his fellow prisoners stands at the beginning of the way that brings him before Pharaoh. In response to his question, both say they have had dreams which there is no one to interpret. In this context Joseph's reply, "Is dream interpretation not God's affair?" means that a trained expert is not absolutely necessary; God can endow anyone with the gift of dream interpretation.

9-11   The author exhibits all his artistry in these dreams, which provide an insight into life at Pharaoh's court: one is an image of success, the other an image of failure. This contrast itself implies the interpretation. The first dream comprises an image (vv. 9b-10a) and an event (v. 10b). In verse 11 the cupbearer himself enters the picture. Pharaoh's presence in each of the three actions the cupbearer performs illustrates the bond between this servant and his master, which continues to exist despite his imprisonment.

12-15   The interpretation comprises an explanation of the dream and a prediction growing out of it. The statement "The three branches are three days" is typical of allegorical interpretation, which probably originated in professional oneiromancy. But that is not the important point here. In his prediction, Joseph understands the dream more as being symbolic: the content of the cupbearer's dream reflects the reality that lies behind it. Because Joseph shares the fate of the prisoners, he thinks about their transgressions and their fate; therefore he can interpret their dreams. Joseph does not arrive at the interpretation "within a short time" (three days) on the basis of mantic knowledge but through the maturing process that takes place instantaneously within the dream itself. In the imminent audience, Pharaoh will raise the cupbearer's head in a ceremonial gesture (2 Kgs. 25:27).

Joseph does not claim the usual reward for his interpretation; instead, he requests the cupbearer, when he is restored to the honor of his office, to mention before Pharaoh that Joseph is languishing innocent in prison (Gen. 40:14-15). Here for the first time Joseph declares his innocence.

16-19   As in chapter 37, the second dream is shorter and simpler. It is an image of failure; the dream says clearly that it conveys a message of calamity. To the baker, too, Pharaoh will give personal attention at the audience; his head, too, will be "raised." But here the expression refers to the penalty of death by hanging. The additional profanation of the corpse makes it clear that the baker must have committed a serious offense.

20-23   Everything turned out as Joseph had predicted in his interpretation. But the hopes expressed in his request to the cupbearer are disappointed.

In the first episode, Joseph's rise was followed by his fall; in the second, his justified expectation that he would be set free is bitterly disappointed. Can God still be with him?

41:1-57   PHARAOH'S DREAMS AND JOSEPH'S ELEVATION

1   *It happened after the passage of two years*
    that Pharaoh had a dream.
    And behold, he was standing by the Nile,
2   *when seven cows came up out of the Nile, sleek and fat, and grazed among*
    the reeds.
3   *Then seven other cows came up out of the river after them, gaunt and lean;*
    they stood by them on the bank of the Nile.
4   *Then the gaunt and lean cows devoured the sleek and fat cows.*
    Then Pharaoh woke up.

5   *And he fell asleep again and had a second dream.*
    And behold, seven ears of grain were growing on a stalk, full and good.
6   *Then seven more ears grew up after them,*
    thin and shriveled by the east wind.
7   *And the thin ears swallowed up the seven full and good ears. Then Pharaoh*
    woke up,
    and behold, it was a dream.

8   *The next morning, when he was troubled in mind,*
    he sent and summoned all the soothsayers of Egypt and all his sages, and
    Pharaoh told them his dream. But there was no one who could interpret it for
    Pharaoh.
9   *Then the chief cupbearer said to Pharaoh:*
    Today I must recall my fault.
10 *Pharaoh was angry with his servants, and he put them in custody in the*
    house of the chief of the guard,

11   *me and the chief baker. And we had a dream in the same night, he and I,*
     each had a dream with its own meaning.

12   *There was with us a young Hebrew man, a slave of the chief of the guard; we*
     told him our dreams, and he interpreted them for us, a special interpretation
     for each.

13   *And it turned out just as he interpreted to us.*
     I was reinstated in office, but he was hanged.

14   *Then Pharaoh sent and had Joseph summoned.*
     Hurriedly they brought him out of the dungeon. He shaved and changed his
     clothes, then appeared before Pharaoh.

15   *And Pharaoh said to Joseph: I have had a dream, and no one can interpret it*
     for me. But I have heard it said of you
     that you need only hear a dream,
     and then you can interpret it.

16   *Joseph answered Pharaoh: I can do nothing.*
     But God will announce good fortune for Pharaoh.

17   *Then Pharaoh said to Joseph:*
     In my dream I was standing on the bank of the Nile.

18   *And behold, seven cows came up out of the river,*
     sleek and fat,
     and grazed among the reeds.

19   *Then seven more cows came out,*
     gaunt, ugly, and lean.
     I have never seen such ugly cows in the whole land of Egypt!

20   *And the thin and ugly cows devoured the first seven, the fat ones.*

21   *And though they ate away at them, one could not see that they had swal-*
     lowed them up; they looked as ugly as before. Then I woke up.

22   *Then I saw in my dream: Seven ears of corn were growing on a stalk, full and*
     good.

23   *Then there grew up after them seven more ears,*
     withered, thin, and shriveled by the east wind.

24   *And the withered ears swallowed up the seven good ears.*
     I told this to the soothsayers,
     but none could explain it to me.

25   *Then Joseph said to Pharaoh:*
     Pharaoh's dreams are one and the same;
     God has told Pharaoh what he is going to do.

26   *The seven good cows mean seven years,*
     and the seven good ears are also seven years.
     It is a single dream.

27   *The seven gaunt and lean cows that came up after them are seven years.*
     And the seven withered ears, shriveled by the east wind, mean seven years of
     famine.

28   *This is what I meant when I said to Pharaoh:*
     God has let Pharaoh see what he is going to do.

29   *Behold, seven years are coming*
     during which there will be great plenty throughout the whole land of Egypt.

30   *And after them will come seven years of famine,*
     when all the plenty in the land of Egypt will be forgotten,
31   *and the famine will destroy the land. There will be no sign of plenty in the*
     land because of the famine that follows, for it will be very severe.
32   *But the fact that Pharaoh has dreamed twice*
     means that God has decided the matter
     and that he will soon bring it about.

33   *Now let Pharaoh look around for a wise and intelligent man and put him in*
     charge of the land of Egypt.
34   *And let Pharaoh appoint supervisors over the land,*
     [and take one-fifth of the produce of the land of Egypt
     during the years of plenty].
35   *They should collect all the produce of these good years that are coming and*
     store the grain under Pharaoh's control, bringing it into the cities and
     guarding it.
36   *Thus the grain will serve as a reserve in the seven years of famine that will*
     come in the land of Egypt. Thus the land will not be wiped out by the famine.

37   *These words pleased Pharaoh and all his servants.*
38   *And Pharaoh said to his servants:*
     Can we find a man like this,
     in whom there is the spirit of God?

39   *And Pharaoh said to Joseph:*
     Since God has made all this known to you,
     there is no one as wise and intelligent as you.
40   *You shall be placed in charge of my house,*
     and all my people shall obey your word;
     only with respect to the throne will I be higher than you.
41   *Then Pharaoh said to Joseph:*
     Behold, I hereby appoint you over the land of Egypt.
42   *Thereupon Pharaoh took his signet ring from his hand and put it on the hand*
     of Joseph;
     he dressed him in garments of fine linen
     and placed the chain of gold around his neck.
43   *He had him ride on his second chariot,*
     and the cry went before him: Abrek!
     Thus he set him over the whole land of Egypt.
44   *And Pharaoh said to Joseph: I am Pharaoh.*
     Without your consent, no one shall move hand or foot throughout the whole
     land of Egypt.
45   *And Pharaoh gave Joseph the name Zephenath-paneah,*
     and he gave him as wife Asenath, the daughter of Potiphera, the priest of On.
     [Then Joseph went out over the land of Egypt.]
46   *Joseph was thirty years old when he stood before Pharaoh, king of Egypt.*
     And Joseph left Pharaoh's presence
     and went throughout the land of Egypt.

47   *The land produced an abundance of grain in the seven years of plenty.*
48   *He gathered up all the food of the seven years of plenty in the land of Egypt*

and brought the grain into the cities. Into each city he had the harvest
brought from the surrounding fields.

49 *So Joseph stored up large quantities of grain, like the sand of the sea, until he*
ceased measuring it, because it could not be measured.

50 *Before the famine came, two sons were born to Joseph. Asenath, the daughter*
of Potiphera, priest of On, had borne them.

51 *Joseph named the firstborn Manasseh, for:*
God has made me forget all my hardship
and my father's house.

52 *The second he named Ephraim, for:*
God has made me fruitful in the land of my hardship.

53 *When the seven years of plenty in the land of Egypt came to an end,*

54 *there began seven years of famine, as Joseph had said;*
[and there was a famine in all countries,
only throughout the land of Egypt was there bread].

55 *But when the whole land of Egypt began to hunger,*
the people cried out to Pharaoh for bread.
Then Pharaoh said to all the Egyptians:
Go to Joseph and do what he tells you.

56b *Then Joseph had all the reserves of grain opened and sold grain to the*
Egyptians, when the famine became severe in the land of Egypt.

56a *And famine spread over the land,*

57 *and the whole world came to Joseph in Egypt to buy grain,*
for the famine was severe everywhere.

In chapter 41 the author has combined three narrative strands. The
first tells of a dream, its interpretation, and the realization of what
was predicted in the interpretation. The second tells of a man of
humble rank who, in the presence of a dignitary, answers a question
no one else had been able to answer and is rewarded for his answer.
The third is the larger context of the Joseph story, in which chapter 41
represents the turning point.

1-7   Pharaoh's dreams. Verse 1 is a bridge connecting this section with 40:23 and saying to the listener: Joseph had to wait two
whole years more! But when told that a dream of Pharaoh is about to
be recounted, the listener suspects that the turning point is at hand.

There are many stories about dreams of kings in the ancient
world, e.g., Ashurbanipal (seventh century B.C.), Nabonidus (sixth
century), Hattusilis III (thirteenth century), and Thutmose IV (fif-
teenth century). They are of great importance for the king's whole
realm, because the king stands in a special relationship to the deity
(so-called sacral kingship). In addition, he is responsible for the prosperity of his land; he is the mediator of blessing. In dreams he can
receive divine directives or announcements of things to come.

In his dream Pharaoh is standing on the bank of the Nile, which
makes the land of Egypt fertile; this is what his dream is about. It is a

symbolic dream, like that of the cupbearer in chapter 40. In such a dream, the dreamer sees a chain of events reflecting a chain of events in the real world. Because it is the same chain of events, Joseph says that the two constitute a single dream. They have to do with cattle-breeding and agriculture, both of which depend on the Nile. The dreams themselves with their bizarre contrastive imagery suggest danger—so much Pharaoh can see. The second, shorter dream about the ears of grain complements and underlines the first dream about the cows. Pairs of dreams were also the subject of chapters 37 and 40; such pairs are common. Only when he wakes up does Pharaoh realize that it was a dream. He is deeply shaken and realizes that he must do something.

8-13   Pharaoh suspects that the dream may mean some threat to his kingdom, so he summons "all the soothsayers of Egypt and all his sages." He tells them his dream, but no one can interpret it. This does not mean that they all had nothing to say; their suggestions could not convince Pharaoh. Then the cupbearer, long since reinstated in office, recalls how the dreams he and the baker dreamt in prison were interpreted. He tells Pharaoh what took place then (vv. 10-13), and Pharaoh immediately has Joseph brought from prison.

14-16   This artful connection takes up the thread once more; the story of Joseph continues. He had to wait two years; now he must suddenly hurry. But the text says nothing about what goes through his mind. The author leaves this to the listener's active imagination by introducing a brief pause with a statement describing preparations for the audience: "He shaved and changed his clothes" (cf. 2 Kgs. 25:29). Thus he can summarize the change in Joseph's fortunes after these long years with a single sentence: "He appeared before Pharaoh."

The meeting between Joseph and Pharaoh is summarized in a few words. Pharaoh says what he wants of Joseph; he credits him with great expertise in dream interpretation. Joseph is prepared to interpret Pharaoh's dream, but refuses the accolade. What he is about to say is not a proof of his skill. Interpretations, like dreams themselves, come from God. It is especially important to emphasize this point in the present case, because, as Pharaoh already suspects, the dream bodes ill. But now Joseph adds one further statement, on which all the stress lies: even if he conveys a message of disaster, ultimately it will bring good fortune for Pharaoh and his land.

17-24   Pharaoh tells Joseph his dream. The repetition of verses 1-7 in these verses shows clearly that the author has a purpose in mind; such repetitions always have a special function in the total narrative. Here this function is brought out by Pharaoh's emphasis on "gaunt, ugly, and lean" (v. 19) and his additional comment that no change could be seen in the thin and ugly cows after they had eaten the fat ones (v. 21). This subjectively biased recollection of the dream brings out the threat Pharaoh perceives in the ugly cows. Thus the repetition of the dream is already a step in the direction of its interpretation. The author makes it easy to see why Pharaoh accepts Joseph's interpretation. This is the point of the concluding statement in verse 24b: none of the soothsayers saw this.

25-32   Joseph's interpretation is not a detailed allegory but more like a parable, in which what happens in the dream parallels events in the real world. Both dreams address the same message to Pharaoh (v. 25). The interpretation of the four groups of seven in verses 26-28 appears allegorical, but it actually evolves from the dream as a whole. Common sense and alertness enable Joseph to recognize the meaning; he does not need the erudition of the Egyptian sages. Therefore his interpretation, which mentions only the bare essentials, can be very brief.

The interpretation (vv. 26-28), framed by the statement "God has let Pharaoh see what he is going to do," is followed in verses 29-31 by an explicit prediction. All the emphasis is on the prediction of disaster: the dream foretells a famine. There are clear echoes of the language used by the prophets in prophesying disaster. The severity of the famine is described in terms that reflect Pharaoh's premonitions (v. 21). The conclusion in verse 32 underlines the urgency of the situation expressed by the double dream.

33-36   Immediately following his interpretation, Joseph gives Pharaoh advice that makes it possible to avert the disaster facing the land during the years of famine. Thus—but only thus!—can Pharaoh's dream ultimately yield good fortune (v. 16). Joseph urges on Pharaoh one particular preventive measure (v. 33), to be carried out in three ways (vv. 34-35). He advises Pharaoh to appoint "a wise and intelligent man" over Egypt (that is, a vizier) to be responsible for carrying out the necessary measures. The word "wise" (Hebrew *ḥākām*) appears in Genesis only here and in 41:8, where it refers to the professional sages of Egypt. Here "wise and intelligent" refers to aptitude for a specific job (cf. Solomon in 1 Kgs. 3:12; also Isa. 10:13; Prov. 8:14-15; Job 12:2-3),[1] the ability to plan and execute an economic program of great importance. What is needed is not academic erudition or intellectual brilliance. Joseph was never trained in a wisdom school; what enables him to carry out the job is his God-given intelligence, matured in the school of hard knocks.

Detailed instructions follow in Genesis 41:34-35. Supervisors are

---

1. See also Magne Sæbø, "*ḥkm* weise sein," cols. 557-576 in *Theologisches Handwörterbuch zum Alten Testament*, ed. Ernst Jenni and Claus Westermann, I (Munich: Christian Kaiser, 1971).

to be appointed throughout the whole land. When Joseph says, "Let Pharaoh . . . ," he means that Pharaoh's authority must stand behind the vizier's program. The supervisors are to collect all the surplus grain and store it in granaries. This, too, is to be done under Pharaoh's authority. These granaries are a characteristic institution of ancient Egypt; they were well known and greatly admired throughout the ancient Near East. The clause ". . . and take one fifth . . ." (v. 34b) is a secondary interpolation intended to lay the groundwork for the later addition of 47:13-26, which also deals with the contributed fifth. Genesis 41:35 originally followed verse 34a directly.

Joseph concludes his advice by assuring Pharaoh that this program can preserve the land from famine (v. 36).

37-46 Joseph's elevation. Pharaoh and his court agree with Joseph's words; they accept both his interpretation and his advice (v. 37). Pharaoh concludes that Joseph himself is the man for the job (v. 38). He had dared to convey the message of disaster while also showing a way to meet the threat. Now Pharaoh turns to address Joseph (vv. 39-40): he declares his intention to place him in charge of his house and his people, a position inferior only to that of Pharaoh himself. Joseph's ability ("wise and intelligent," as in v. 33) is ascribed explicitly to God ("the spirit of God" [v. 38]). Verse 40 uses an idiom from the language of the court to describe Joseph's position.

41-46 Joseph's ceremonial installation follows immediately: his appointment (vv. 41 and 44) is combined with his investiture (vv. 42-43), in which a ring is placed on his finger, he is clothed in a festal robe, and a golden chain is placed about his neck. Similar ceremonies are found throughout the world when someone is appointed to high office. The description resembles Ashurbanipal's seventh-century account of his appointment of Necho as vassal-king of Egypt.[2] Esther 3:12 and 8:8 also speak of a signet ring as part of an investiture. It is associated with the office of vizier, who is also the custodian of the royal seal. The robe of fine linen (Greek *býssos*) is depicted in many ancient Egyptian paintings, as is the gift of a golden chain, which recalls the conferring of an order. Many illustrations give us an idea of what the chariot looked like that Pharaoh placed at Joseph's disposal; a similar one was found in the tomb of Tutankhamon. The cry of the heralds as the chariot goes it way is a demand for homage. Genesis 41:44 reconfirms Joseph's position. He is given unlimited executive power, but his authority has a limit: the sovereignty of Pharaoh.

At the same time as he is installed officially in office, Joseph is ennobled (v. 45). He is given an Egyptian name, "Zephenath-pan-

---

2. James B. Pritchard, ed., *Ancient Near Eastern Texts,* 3rd ed. (Princeton: Princeton University, 1969), p. 295.

eah," which means "God speaks and it lives"; the name never appears again. The daughter of a noble house is given him as wife: Asenath, the daughter of Potiphera, the high priest of On (Heliopolis, northwest of Cairo).

Joseph assumes his office as vizier by traveling through the territory in his charge (v. 46b; cf. 13:17). The statement of his age in 41:46a has probably been incorporated from P.

47-49 What Joseph had predicted now comes to pass. In the first seven years the land yields a surplus of grain. This also marks the beginning of Joseph's program of collecting and storing grain to guard against famine.

50-52 Here has been interpolated a note from the conclusion of the story of Jacob, very much in the style of the patriarchal stories. It follows the statement about Joseph's marriage and paves the way for chapter 48. Two sons are born to Joseph; their naming is also described, as in chapters 29–30. The names of the sons enshrine the memory of their father's life far from home. The name "Manasseh" is explained as meaning "God has made me forget all my hardship" far from his father's house. The second son's name, "Ephraim," means "God has made me fruitful in the land of my hardship," an echo of the promise in Genesis 17:6, 20; 28:3. These names give thanks to the God who preserves and blesses; they both confirm the promise of God's help and presence in chapter 39.

53-57 These verses continue verses 47-49: the seven lean years begin. The famine extends to the surrounding lands, but now only Egypt has bread (v. 54). At Pharaoh's command, those without food turn to Joseph (v. 55), who opens the granaries and provides food for the land (v. 56). Many come from far away to buy grain in Egypt (v. 57). The text of verses 53-57 is corrupt; it makes more sense if verse 54b is taken as a late addition and verse 56a is read at the end of verse 56 before verse 57.

In chapter 41, which stands in the center of the Joseph story, the two strands that determine the story as a whole converge. Joseph's elevation to a position of authority, the reversal of fortunes in the life of an obscure slave from a foreign land, preserves the life of his family and heals the breach within it. The other strand is the blessing bestowed by God, which preserves the great Egyptian nation through Joseph's counsel.

42:1-38 THE FIRST JOURNEY OF THE BROTHERS TO EGYPT

1 *And Jacob learned that there was grain in Egypt,*
[and Jacob said to his sons: Why do you stand looking at each other?]

2 *And he said: Behold, I have heard that there is grain in Egypt; go there and*
 buy grain for us there that we may live and not have to die.

3 *So Joseph's brothers, ten of them, went down*
 to buy grain in Egypt.

4 *Benjamin, Joseph's brother, Jacob did not allow to go with his brothers, for he*
 thought that some harm might happen to him.

5 *[So among those who went there also went the sons of Israel to buy grain,*
 for there was famine in the land of Canaan.]

6 *But Joseph [was governor in the land; he] it was*
 who sold grain to all the people of the land.
 Now when Joseph's brothers came,
 they bowed to the ground before him.

7 *When Joseph saw his brothers, he recognized them;*
 but he pretended not to know them and spoke harshly to them.
 He asked them: Where do you come from? They answered:
 From the land of Canaan to buy food.

8 *Whereas Joseph recognized his brothers, they did not recognize him.*

9 *And Joseph remembered the dreams he had dreamt of them, and said to them:*
 You are spies!
 You have come to spy out the weakness of the land!

10 *But they said to him: No, my lord. Your servants have come to buy food.*

11 *All of us, we are sons of one man; we are honest people, your servants are not*
 spies.

12 *But he answered them: No, you have come to spy out the weakness of the*
 land.

13 *They responded: We, your servants, were twelve brothers, sons of one man*
 in the land of Canaan. The youngest is still with our father, and one is no
 more.

14 *But Joseph said to them: It is as I have said to you; you are spies.*

15 *By this you shall be tested, by the life of Pharaoh:*
 You shall not leave this place
 until your youngest brother comes here.

16 *Send one of you to bring your brother; the rest of you shall remain in*
 custody. So shall your words be tested to see whether you have spoken the
 truth or not.
 By the life of Pharaoh, you truly are spies!

17 *Thereupon he had them put in custody for three days.*

18 *But on the third day, Joseph said to them:*
 If you wish to remain alive, this is what you must do
 (I am a man who fears God):

19 *If you are honest people, then one of your brothers is to remain in custody*
 where you are. But the rest of you can go and take grain for your hungry
 households.

20 *But you must bring your youngest brother to me,*
 that your words may be confirmed
 and you shall not die. [And they agreed.]

21 *Then they said to each other: Truly,*
 we are guilty with regard to our brother.
 We saw his anguish of heart when he pleaded with us,

but we did not listen.
That is why this disaster has befallen us.

22 *Then Reuben spoke and answered them:*
   Did I not say to you: Do not do the boy any wrong?
   But you did not listen.
   Now his blood is required!

23 *But they did not know that Joseph understood them,*
   because an interpreter communicated between them.

24 *And he turned away from them and wept.*
   Then he turned back to them and spoke to them.
   And he took Simeon away from them
   and had him bound before their eyes.

25 *Joseph then gave orders that their sacks be filled with grain, that each one's money be put back in his sack, and that they be given provisions for their journey. And it was done.*

26 *But they loaded their grain onto their donkeys and went off.*

27 *When one of them opened his sack at the stopping place*
   to give his donkey some provender,
   he saw his money lying at the top of his sack.

28 *And he said to his brothers: My money is back!*
   Behold, it is lying in my sack!
   Then their hearts sank. They looked at each other appalled and said: What has God done to us!

29 *Now when they came to their father Jacob in the land of Canaan, they told him all that had happened to them. They said:*

30 *The man who is lord of the country spoke harshly to us;*
   he had us put in custody, alleging that we were spying out the land.

31 *We said to him: We are honest people,*
   we are not spies.

32 *We are twelve brothers, sons of the same father.*
   One of us is no more, and the youngest is still with our father in the land of Canaan.

33 *Then the man who is lord of the country said to us:*
   By this I shall know that you are honest people:
   One of you brothers shall stay behind with me;
   the rest of you take the grain that your hungry households need and go.

34 *But bring your youngest brother down here to me, that I may know that you are no spies but honest people.*
   Then I will give your brother back to you
   and you shall be free to move about the country.

35 *[Now when they emptied their sacks, each found a bag with his money in his sack. But when they—they and their father—saw the bags of money, they were afraid.]*

36 *And Jacob their father said to them:*
   You are making me childless! Joseph is no more, and Simeon is no more, and now you want to take Benjamin as well! Everything has come upon me!

37 *Then Reuben said to his father:*

You may kill my two sons if I do not bring him back to you. Entrust him to
me and I will return him to you.
38 But he said: My son shall not go down with you;
for your brother is dead, and he alone is left.
Some harm could happen to him on the way he travels.
Then you would bring my gray hairs down to Sheol in sorrow.

Chapter 42 follows chapter 37; it is the theme of famine that connects
this chapter with the interlude in chapters 39–41. It is the same famine that threatens both Jacob's family in Canaan and the people of
Egypt. In Egypt, it is viewed from the perspective of a king's responsibility for his people; in Canaan, it is viewed from the perspective of
those who are starving. The chapter has the structure of a travel
account in three parts (vv. 1-5, 6-24, 25-28). There must have been
many such accounts; the coming of groups from foreign lands to buy
grain in Egypt is well attested. It is possible that the author of the
Joseph story was using such a document. Here it has been turned
into an episode in the total story of Joseph.

1-5   We would expect the chapter to begin with an account of
the famine, as in 12:10. Such an account is anticipated by 41:57, which
links chapter 42 with 41. Verse 1a is continued by verse 2; verse 1b is
an intrusive fragment. It belongs to another version in which the
brothers initially refuse to follow their father's orders, possibly because they are afraid to go to Egypt. The father justifies his command
(v. 2) by saying that the survival of the family is at stake, and so the
ten brothers set out (v. 3). The number is explained by the father's
refusal to let Benjamin go along (v. 4), on the grounds that some
harm might befall him. This lays the groundwork for what follows.
As at the beginning of chapter 37, we again have three players: the
father, the brothers, and the youngest brother. Genesis 42:5 is out of
place here; it takes the place of a statement that the brothers arrived
in Egypt. This verse, however, would go well with 41:57; "among
those who went" would then refer to the statement that "the whole
world went to Egypt" (41:57). This would also introduce the destination, which does not appear in 42:5. The striking expression "sons of
Israel" in verse 5 appears also in 46:5, 8 in the context of a journey to
Egypt.

6-20   The first sojourn of the brothers in Egypt begins with their
meeting with Joseph in 42:6-17; the second ends with a parallel meeting in 45:1-16. The contrast between the two is deliberate on the part
of the author. His point is that the second meeting would not have
been possible without the first; the road to reconciliation must pass
through this abyss. The author alludes to the parallel by introducing
a reflection at the beginning of the audience: the brothers bow down

(42:6) and Joseph recognizes them (v. 7), "and Joseph remembered the dreams he had dreamt of them." This reflection links the beginning (chapter 37) with the end (chapter 45); the narrative context justifies Joseph's harsh words to his brothers. In these harsh words and in his false accusation, he is preparing the resolution in chapter 45.

The brothers bow down before the foreign lord; the gesture speaks for itself. The brothers know they must humble themselves before this powerful figure in order to obtain bread (42:6). But worse is to come. The man who controls the sale of grain takes them by surprise, accusing them of being spies. The brothers are totally defenseless against this charge. The interrogation takes place in two phases (vv. 7b-11, 12-13). The brothers assert their innocence, to no avail. The man repeats his accusation (vv. 9, 12, 14, 16). The brothers insist that they are honest people, the sons of one man (v. 11). They are helpless to do more than explain at somewhat greater length that they all belong to a single family. This is in fact the only way they can defend their honorable intentions, by insisting that they belong to a family unit; families do not wage war and therefore have no interest in espionage. In the course of their argument they mention their youngest brother, who has stayed behind, not suspecting that this gives Joseph the chance to take his next step. The interrogator immediately seizes upon this concrete fact, which can be tested. The brothers as yet have no suspicion that proof of their statement will absolve them of the charge of espionage. Thus the turning point is already at hand, although the interrogation ends with the imprisonment of all the brothers. A second directive from the foreign lord follows in verses 18-20. Although the brothers have no idea why, it represents a mitigation. It is also deliberately different in language from the first: it is more friendly. The brothers are surprised by the potentate's concern for their families at home, whose hunger he mentions. Now just one, not all, must remain in custody; the others may depart and bring grain to their families. Then, however, they must return with their youngest brother.

21-24 Now follows a brief interlude, a conversation amongst the brothers in custody, which constitutes a deliberate parallel to Joseph's reflection in verses 8-9. The brothers, too, have reflected. What has befallen them in Egypt has brought home to them a realization that may long have been forming. Their conversation is conducted in deep dismay. They recognize that they are guilty with regard to their brother. Like Joseph, they, too, recall the beginning and recognize a connection: the punishment they are now undergoing is appropriate to the guilt they have brought upon themselves. They tried to conceal what they had done, but did not succeed: "That is why this disaster has befallen us." Joseph is listening; what moves him to tears is this recognition of the connection, a recognition that now makes reconciliation possible. But Joseph must still remain in character. Verse 24b follows verse 20; the directive must be carried out, and Joseph is once again the harsh Egyptian lord.

25-38 The third part of the travel account (vv. 25-38) records the brothers' return to their father. An incident on the journey strikes them with consternation. While they are spending the night at a lodging place (cf. Exod. 4:24), one of the brothers discovers his money at the top of his feed bag. The vivid scene makes use of a common technique, describing the experience of a group in terms of an individual. The dramatic effect is heightened: a single person finds the money in his sack and exclaims in astonishment; his consternation spreads to the others. The audience understands that all the brothers discovered their money. The scene is so interpreted in Genesis 43:21. The author can expect a high degree of involvement on the part of his audience.

29-38 Arrival. The brothers return to their father (v. 29) and give their report (vv. 30-34). They say only what their father absolutely has to know, and they do as much as possible to protect him. Therefore they do not yet say anything about the discovery of their money. Verse 34 should be followed by the father's reaction, which does not come until verse 36. Verse 35 appears awkward and intrusive. It is a secondary addition on the part of someone who understood verses 27-28 as meaning that only one of the brothers had discovered his money. The father's response (v. 36) expresses grief and consternation, but it also has an accusatory tone. There are clear echoes of the effect the brothers' report had on their father at their previous return (37:31-35). Reuben's offer of surety for Benjamin (42:37) cannot alter his father's grief; it only results in Jacob's explicit refusal to allow Benjamin to go along. Again we hear his love for Rachel's son; his lament echoes the words of 37:35. The chapter closes in dark despair.

In the middle of chapter 42, in the conversation of the brothers (vv. 21-24), the author finally records Joseph's reaction to what his brothers did to him. Nothing was said of this reaction in 37:24; now the brothers recall how they remained unmoved by his suffering, as he begged them and they refused to listen. Now they have come to see the connection between crime and punishment; now they, too, know that there is a connection, grounded in God's providence: "What has God done to us!" (42:28). The hand of God is seen in the realization that in the incomprehensible ups and downs in human life there is a connection between crime and punishment, and therefore also meaning.

43:1-34 THE SECOND JOURNEY OF THE BROTHERS TO EGYPT

1   *But the famine still weighed heavily upon the land.*

2   *Now when they had used up all the grain they had brought from Egypt, their*
father said to them:
Go back and buy us a little more grain.

3   *Then Judah said to him: The man expressly warned us:*
You shall not come into my presence
unless your youngest brother is with you.

4   *If you will allow our brother to go with us, we will go down and buy grain for*
you.

5   *But if you do not allow him, we will not go down; for the man said to us:*
You shall not come into my presence
unless your brother is with you.

6   *Then Israel said: Why have you hurt me so badly*
as to tell the man that you had another brother?

7   *They answered: The man interrogated us in detail about ourselves and our*
family, and asked:
Is your father still alive? Have you another brother?
We answered these questions of his.
How were we to know that he would say:
Bring you brother down here?

8   *The Judah said to Israel his father:*
Entrust the boy to me; then we will be up and on our way so that we may live
and not die, we and you and our small children.

9   *I myself will be surety for him. From my hand you shall require him. If I do*
not bring him back and restore him to you, I shall bear the guilt before you
through all my life.

10   *Had we not delayed, we had already been there and back twice!*

11   *Then Israel their father said to them:*
If it must be so, then do this:
take some of the best products of the land in your sacks and bring them to the
man as a present:
a little balsam, a little honey,
tragacanth gum and myrrh, pistachios and almonds.

12   *Take double the amount of money with you;*
also the money that was on top of your sacks you must take with you.
Perhaps it was a mistake.

13   *Take your brother along, too; up and go back to the man.*

14   *And may God Almighty be merciful to you before the man,*
that he may send back your other brother with you,
and Benjamin too. But I am bereaved, bereaved!

15   *Then the men took the gift and double the amount of money with them, and*
Benjamin also, and set out;
they went down to Egypt and presented themselves before Joseph.

16 *When Joseph saw Benjamin with them, he commanded his steward: Bring these men into my house,*
kill a beast and make ready,
for the men are to eat with me at noon.

17 *The man did as Joseph had commanded him,*
and the man brought the men into Joseph's house.

18 *And the men were afraid because they were brought into Joseph's house; they thought: Because of the money that found its way back into our sacks the last time we have been brought in, that we may be overpowered and seized and taken into slavery with our donkeys.*

19 *Therefore they approached the man who was in charge of Joseph's house, spoke to him at the entrance to the house, and said:*

20 *Please, my lord! We came down once before to buy grain.*

21 *When we arrived at the lodging place and opened our sacks, each found his money on top of his sack, our money in full measure. This we have brought back with us.*

22 *We have brought more money with us to buy food. We do not know who put our money in our sacks.*

23 *He replied: Rest assured and do not be afraid.*
Your God, the God of your father, must have put a treasure in your sacks. Your money came to me.
Then he brought Simeon out to them.

24 *And he brought the men into Joseph's house,*
handed them water to wash their feet,
and gave their donkeys fodder.

25 *But they kept their present ready until Joseph's arrival at noon, for they had heard that they were to dine there.*

26 *When Joseph entered the house, they presented him with the gift they had brought with them,*
and bowed to the ground before him.

27 *But he greeted them and asked: How is your old father, about whom you spoke to me? Is he still alive?*

28 *They answered: Your servant, our father, is well and is still alive. And they bowed and prostrated themselves.*

29 *And when he raised his eyes and saw his brother Benjamin, the son of his mother, he said:*
Is this indeed your youngest brother, about whom you spoke to me? And he said: May God be gracious to you, my son.

30 *Then Joseph hurried, for his heart was deeply moved at the sight of his brother, and he was on the verge of tears, and he went into his private room and wept there.*

31 *Then he washed his face, went out, controlled himself, and commanded: Serve the meal.*

32 *Then he was served separately and they were served separately and the Egyptians who dined with him were served separately.*
For the Egyptians may not eat with the Hebrews, because that is an abomination to the Egyptians.

33   *But they were seated opposite him,*
     from the eldest to the youngest, strictly according to age.
     And they looked at each other in astonishment.
34   *Then he had them served from the dishes that were before him; the portion*
     placed before Benjamin was five times as large as that of all the others.
     And they drank with him and were merry.

The second journey encompasses chapters 43–45; not until the end of chapter 45 do the brothers return to their father. Chapters 42 and 43–45 are similar in structure, but 43–45 is interrupted by 44:4–45:24. This interruption marks the turning point.

1-2   Like chapter 42, chapter 43 begins with famine and the father's command. The second journey is necessary because the grain brought back the first time has been used up.

3-14   The command is not carried out until verse 15; verses 3-14 deal with whether Benjamin will be allowed to go along. In verses 3-5, Judah makes the journey to Egypt conditional on his father's permitting Benjamin to go, citing the demand made by the man who controls the purchase of grain. This crucial insistence on the part of Judah is the counterpart to Reuben's offer, which his father had rejected (42:37-38). Reuben's offer could not go beyond personal surety; now another brother must bring up the crucial demand of the man in Egypt. Judah's words make his father relent; from this point until the end, therefore, Judah speaks for the brothers. Their father realizes he must give in, but tries once more to argue with the brothers (43:6-7); they insist, however, that it was impossible to avoid mentioning Benjamin to the man. Now Judah again asks his father to entrust Benjamin to him, since the survival of the family is at stake. He will himself be surety for Benjamin; he will take full responsibility for him (vv. 8-10). These words anticipate Judah's speech in 44:18-34.

11-15   Now that Jacob has bowed to the inevitable, he wants to contribute his part to the success of the venture. He counsels his sons to take local products along as gifts: balsam, tragacanth gum and myrrh (cf. 37:25), almonds and pistachios. He also has his sons take twice the amount of money along. He allows Benjamin to go and now he himself tells them to be on their way. All that he has left to say he puts in the prayer that God will be merciful to them before "the man." At his sons' departure, he himself feels his loss—the loss that is part of his past and the loss he fears is yet to come: "But I am bereaved, bereaved!" The brothers set out and arrive in Egypt.

16-25   The brothers' sojourn in Egypt (vv. 16-34) is divided into two scenes: one with the steward (vv. 16-25) and one with the master of the house (vv. 26-34). In contrast to the previous occasion, their reception by the steward is remarkably friendly. Joseph has given orders to have the men brought into the house, and the steward obeys (vv. 17 and 24, the beginning and the conclusion of the episode). The scene itself (vv. 18-23) is played in the courtyard. The brothers are terrified that they will be overpowered in the house; while still in the courtyard, they beg the steward for a hearing. When their request is granted, they tell him what really happened with the money. Tense and fearful, they await his answer; then they hear it: "Peace be with you, do not fear." These words, which take the brothers totally by surprise, introduce the turning point, even if they only constitute the prelude. The steward gives the reason for his reassuring reply: "Your God must have put a treasure in your sacks." To help the brothers understand, he is more explicit: he received the money. To confirm his words, he brings Simeon out to them in the courtyard; the suspicion of espionage is banished.

The action that begins in verse 17 is concluded in verse 24. The brothers are welcomed into the man's house with the gifts of hospitality: water to wash their feet and fodder for their donkeys. Verse 25 makes it clear that they are fully reassured: in the house, they set out the gifts they have brought with them.

The steward's reply to the brothers structurally resembles a salvation oracle: "Fear not, God has . . ." This resemblance is not immediately apparent; the story does more to conceal it than to stress it. The brothers have asked in fear about the money; in the answer, "God in his kindness did it," with its echo of a salvation oracle, the author suggests the meaning of the story as a whole, as Joseph finally restates it in his own interpretation in chapters 45 and 50.

The scene in 43:16-25 is a particularly refined and eloquent example of the narrative artistry found in the story of Joseph. It is not readily apparent to us, because we have different criteria. It is also almost impossible to explain; it must be absorbed through an alert ear and willing participation. The scene is intended to be climactic, but the climax is more indirect and concealed than apparent. Characteristic of this indirection is the next to last sentence, which ends with the donkeys' being fed. Anyone who understands why this statement is placed here has understood the significance of the scene.

26-34 Verses 26-31 describe a welcome that can be understood properly only in its place between the first meeting in chapter 42 and the third meeting in chapter 44. But even so it can be understood only if every word and every gesture is allowed to declare its significance in the larger context. The first meeting, in chapter 42, was beclouded by the political suspicion of espionage; this cloud is removed in the second. Joseph's inquiries give it a familiar and friendly atmosphere; there is still some reserve, however, in comparison to the third meeting. In the sequence of these three meetings, the author draws attention to the juxtaposition of these three possibilities. He has much to say, but not explicitly: he shows, for example, that mere prostration is submission, but accompanied by gifts it represents homage (cf. Matt. 2:11). If the leitmotif of this meeting is "peace," the author makes it clear that the meaning of this word encompasses a wealth of possibilities that cannot be defined in detail and are authentic only in the situation from which they emerge. To describe peace as a "state" is therefore impossible. What is meant here by "peace" clearly does not require equal treatment for all; the author consciously distinguishes Joseph's welcome of Benjamin from that of the other brothers by use of the special formula "May God be gracious to you, my son" (cf. Gen. 33:5, 11). Once again, the author does not elaborate on the meaning of these words at this moment; we are only told that Joseph is deeply moved.

The conclusion (43:32-34) describes a meal in which the joy of a feast is singularly interwoven with an element of strangeness that points to a resolution yet to come. Moments before, the brothers had trembled before this potentate in Egypt; now they are his guests. But they are still separated by a wall that prohibits Egyptians from dining at the same table as Canaanites (a custom also noted by the Greek historians Herodotus, Diodorus, and Strabo). Joseph is still an Egyptian, a foreigner on the other side of the wall. There is also the man's uncanny knowledge: he assigns the brothers their places according to age and makes the youngest the guest of honor. There is still estrangement, a mysterious uneasiness. The festive meal is just a preliminary.

44:1-34   THE GOBLET

1   *Then Joseph gave orders to his steward: Fill the men's sacks with grain, as much as they can carry, [and place each one's money in the top of his sack].*
2   *But my goblet, the silver goblet, put in the top of the sack of the youngest [together with his money for the grain].*
    And he did as Joseph had commanded him.

3   *In the morning, at first light, he sent the men away with their donkeys.*
4   *They had hardly left the city when Joseph said to his steward: Up and after them! And when you have caught up with them, say to them:*
    Why have you returned evil for good?
5   *Why have you stolen my silver goblet?*
    Is it not the one from which my lord drinks and in which he practices divination? You have done wrong in doing this.
6   *When he caught up with them, he said this to them.*
7   *But they said to him: How can my lord say such a thing!*
    Far be it from your servants to do such a thing!

8   *Behold, the silver we found in the top of our sacks we brought back to you from the land of Canaan; how could we have stolen silver or gold from your master's house?*

9   *With whichever of your servants it is found, he shall die, and we shall be your master's slaves.*

10   *He replied: Well then, be it as you say.*
      Whichever of you has it shall be my slave, but the rest of you will be free.

11   *Each quickly lifted his sack to the ground and each opened his sack.*

12   *But he searched them. He began with the eldest and finished with the youngest.*
      And the goblet was found in Benjamin's sack.

13   *Then they tore their garments. And each loaded his donkey, and they returned to the city.*

14   *When Judah and his brothers arrived at Joseph's house*
      (he was still there),
      they prostrated themselves before him.

15   *And Joseph said to them: What is this that you have done?*
      Did you not know that a man such as I practices divination?

16   *Then Judah said: What can we say to my lord?*
      What reply can we make to justify ourselves? God has discovered the wickedness of your servants.
      Behold, we are my lord's servants, both we and the one who was found to have the goblet.

17   *He answered: Far be it from me to do this.*
      The one who was found with the goblet,
      he shall be my slave. But you can return to your father in peace.

18   *Then Judah approached him and said: Please, my lord,*
      may your servant have a word in your ear,
      and let not your anger flare against your servant,
      for you are as Pharaoh.

19   *My lord had asked your servants:*
      Have you a father or a brother?

20   *We answered my lord: We have a father who is old and a younger brother who was born to him in his old age. His brother is dead;*
      and so he is his mother's only surviving child,
      and his father loves him.

21   *You commanded your servants: Bring him to me,*
      I would like to see him with my own eyes.

22   *Then we answered my lord:*
      The boy cannot leave his father.
      Were he to leave his father, his father would die.

23   *Then you said to your servants:*
      If your youngest brother does not come here with you,
      you shall not come into my presence.

24   *When we returned to your servant, my father,*
      we recounted to him the words of my lord.

25   *When our father said: Go back again*
      and buy us some food,

26 *we said: We cannot go back.*
   Only if our youngest brother is with us can we go back.
   For we cannot enter the man's presence
   unless our youngest brother comes with us.

27 *Then your servant, our father, said to us: You know*
   that my wife bore me two sons.

28 *The one has departed from me.*
   I cried out: He has been torn to pieces!
   I have never seen him since.

29 *And now you will take this one from me as well.*
   If any misfortune should happen to him, you will bring my gray hair in
   sorrow to Sheol.

30 *Now were I to come to your servant, my father,*
   and the boy with whom his life is bound up were not with us,

31 *he would die when he saw that the boy was not with us, and your servants*
   would have brought the gray hair of your servant, our father, in sorrow to
   Sheol.

32 *Now because your servant has made surety for the boy before his father,*
   saying:
   If I do not bring him back, then I will bear the guilt before my father all my
   life,

33 *therefore let your servant remain in place of the boy as the slave of my lord;*
   but let the boy return with his brothers.

34 *For how could I go back to my father*
   if the boy is not with me! I could not bear to look on the distress that would
   come upon my father.

Within the account of the brothers' second journey (42:1–45:28), chapter 44 describes an interruption on the trip back, caused by a false accusation. All the emphasis is on Judah's speech in verses 18-34. The whole narrative trajectory that begins in chapter 37 leads up to this speech, in which it reaches its climax. In Judah's explanation, this climax also represents the entire story (beginning with ch. 37) in a nutshell.

1-17   The action in these verses, like that in chapter 43, is structured as two scenes: one with the steward (45:1-13), the other with Joseph (vv. 14-17). As in 42:25, before the brothers' first return, Joseph gives his steward instructions: the first time, money was involved; now it is something even more important, one of Joseph's personal possessions. The inclusion of the money in 45:1b and 2b is secondary, as we can see from verses 11-12, which do not mention it. Joseph's instructions are intended to set up a situation like that in chapter 37. The second set of instructions (45:3-4) uses the language of the messenger form: Joseph places in the steward's mouth the words he is to speak to the brothers. The question "Why have you stolen my silver goblet?" in verse 5 is supplied from the Septuagint;

the charge is so serious as to seem almost fantastic. The whole scene borders on unreality; the turning point is close at hand. Divination by means of drinking vessels is often attested in the ancient world. Isaiah 19:3 speaks of it in a prophecy of judgment against Egypt, and it is forbidden in Israel (Lev. 19:26; Deut. 18:10). The brothers, shocked and alarmed, respond to the accusation by rejecting it totally. Have they not just proved that they are honest people? They even demand the harshest possible punishment for the thief (Gen. 45:7-9). With the brothers' consent, their sacks are searched; their shock when the goblet is discovered in Benjamin's possession is expressed by their tearing their garments. The blow strikes them all (vv. 10-13).

The next scene (vv. 14-17) takes place in the house of the Egyptian potentate. Judah is the spokesman. Once again the brothers prostrate themselves before Joseph. One question spoken by this potentate shows how totally they are at his mercy: "Did you not know that a man such as I practices divination?" The brothers must be thinking to themselves: if so, he would know that we are innocent! The tension has reached its limit. Now Judah turns to the man with words that openly express the impossibility of being found innocent, while honorably refusing to admit that his brother has stolen anything. The blow that has struck them all he accepts meekly as God's punishment for a crime whose seriousness they have only recently affirmed (42:21): "God has discovered the wickedness of your servants." By admitting the old crime, he places the false condemnation in its larger context, where not the Egyptian potentate but God holds sway. With these words, spoken by Judah on behalf of all the brothers, they have passed the test. But the man refuses Judah's request that all the brothers be punished, together with the one who has been unjustly accused; only the youngest brother is to suffer punishment. Now we are back to the initial situation: father—brothers—youngest brother. Now Judah makes his offer.

18-34   Judah's speech. Once more Judah requests a hearing, in a manner that shows that something vital is at stake, of which he must speak (v. 18). He wishes to address a request to the mighty lord (vv. 33-34), which he justifies proleptically by describing the chain of events that has brought about the present situation. He begins with the first conversation between the lord and the brothers (42:7-20). He repeats as much as serves to support his request, omitting everything that might antagonize the lord, whose human sensibilities he appeals to by adding that the youngest son is especially dear to his father. Summarizing the conversation between his father and his brothers before their second departure, Judah also includes only what supports his request (45:24-29). He wants to make it clear to the lord that in this conversation they adhered strictly to his injunction.

In the words that follow, Judah seeks to explain what the loss of Benjamin would mean to his father. This is why he mentions Benjamin's brother and the son who was lost previously (vv. 27-29).

In verses 30-32 Judah moves on to his request. With the "Now . . ." at the beginning of verse 30, he describes to the lord what will happen if the brothers return without Benjamin. He says ". . . were I . . . ," because he now accepts responsibility for whatever happens. He cannot enter his father's presence without the boy; his father would die of grief. He says also that he has himself made surety for his brother. In this justification of his request, Judah has extended the story into the past (from the first meeting with the lord down to this second meeting; vv. 27-29) and the future, all to lend force and credence to his request. Thus at this climactic moment just before the imminent turning point, he summarizes the entire Joseph story. The foreign lord he is addressing hears it also through the ears of a brother. He hears that there has been a momentous change.

33-34   Now Judah can put forward his request to stay on as the lord's slave instead of Benjamin. It is a fervent appeal addressed to the lord: "I could not bear to look on the distress that would come upon my father." In this sentence Judah drops the polite form "your servant." It is Jacob's son and Benjamin's brother who speaks. In the brothers' experience, they have discovered a profound connection between crime and punishment. They sought to conceal their transgression; now God has revealed it. He has pursued them (Gen. 3:9). They have learned that God still cares for them, but the hour was long in coming. Repentance is authenticated by the course of one's whole life; sometimes the road is long.

Here, at the end of the Joseph story and the Patriarchal History, the Bible speaks for the first time of vicarious suffering. Judah would rather take the punishment upon himself than cause his father further grief. This differs from the "servant of God" at the end of the history of the prophets of judgment and from Christ in the New Testament. But there is a trajectory that leads to these from the Joseph story. It is possible that a breach within a community can be healed only if someone is ready to suffer for others.

45:1-28   JOSEPH REVEALS HIMSELF TO HIS BROTHERS

1   *Then Joseph could no longer control himself in the presence of all who stood about him, and he cried out:*
    Let everyone leave my presence!
    So there was no one with Joseph when he made himself known to his brothers.

2   *And he wept loudly, so that all the Egyptians heard it and it was noted in the house of Pharaoh.*

3   *Then Joseph said to his brothers: I am Joseph!*
      Is my father still alive? But his brothers were not able to answer him, so stunned were they before him.

4   *And Joseph said to his brothers:*
      Come closer to me. When they had come closer, he said: I am Joseph, your brother, whom you sold into Egypt.

5   *Now then, do not be distressed or reproach yourselves that you sold me here; for God sent me ahead of you to save lives.*

6   *For there has been a famine in the land for two years,*
      and for five more years there will be neither plowing nor harvest.

7a   *But God sent me ahead of you*
7b   *[to preserve you a remnant in the land*
           and to keep you alive,
           a great host of survivors].

8b   *He made me a father to Pharaoh*
      and master over his whole house
      and ruler over the whole of Egypt.

8a   *Now then, it was not you who sent me down here, but God.*

9   *Hurry, go back to my father, and say to him:*
      Thus says Joseph, your son: God has made me ruler over the whole land of Egypt.
      Come down to me, do not delay!

10   *In the land of Goshen you shall dwell and be near me,*
      you, your sons and grandsons, your sheep and your cattle and all that you have.

11   *I will take care of you there (for there are still five years of famine to come), lest you be reduced to poverty,*
      you and your family and all that is yours.

12   *You see now with your own eyes, and your brother Benjamin sees, that it is my mouth that speaks to you.*

13   *And tell my father of my position of honor in Egypt and of all else that you have seen.*
      But then hurry to bring my father here!

14   *Then he fell upon Benjamin's neck and wept,*
      and Benjamin wept on his neck.

15   *Then he kissed his brothers as well and wept and embraced them.*
      Only then did his brothers speak to him.

16   *The news spread also to Pharaoh's palace:*
      Joseph's brothers have arrived.
      And Pharaoh and his servants were pleased.

17   *And Pharaoh directed Joseph to say to his brothers:*
      Do this: load your donkeys
      and go to the land of Canaan.

18   *And bring your father and your families and come to me.*
      I will give you the best of the land of Egypt,
      and you shall eat of the fat of the land.

19   *But you are to instruct them: This is what you are to do:*

*take wagons from the land of Egypt for your children and your wives, and let
your father rise up and come here.*

20 *And have no regrets over your household possessions,
for the best of all the land of Egypt will be yours.*

21 *The sons of Israel did so.
And Joseph gave them wagons to take along at Pharaoh's command,
and he gave them provisions for the journey.*

22 *To each of them he gave a festal robe,
but to Benjamin he gave three hundred pieces of silver and five festal robes.*

23 *But to his father he likewise sent ten donkeys,
loaded with the best of Egypt, and ten she-asses,
loaded with grain, bread, and provisions
for his father for the journey.*

24 *Then he bade his brothers farewell, and they set out, after he had urged them:
Do not quarrel on the way.*

25 *They departed from Egypt and came to the land of Canaan,
to their father Jacob.*

26 *And they told him: Joseph is still alive!
He is ruler over the land of Egypt!
But his heart remained cold, for he did not believe them.*

27 *But when they had told him everything that Joseph had said to them, and
when he saw the wagons that Joseph had sent to fetch him,
then the spirit of their father Jacob revived.*

28 *And Israel said:
Enough, Joseph my son is alive.
I will go down and see him before I die.*

Instead of a response to Judah's request, we have a change of fortunes for the entire family, precipitated by the Egyptian potentate's revelation that he is their brother (vv. 1-8). There follow his instructions concerning his father (vv. 9-13), confirmed by Pharaoh (vv. 16-21), Joseph's welcome to his brothers and their departure (vv. 14-15, 22-24), and their return to their father (vv. 25-28).

1-8   The introduction (vv. 1-2) manages the transition from political history back to family history; the scene changes with the departure of the servants and officials. Joseph is deeply moved; now he can give free rein to his tears. His excitement appears in his first words: "I am Joseph! Is my father still alive?" This is not the same question he asked previously as a high official engaging in polite dialogue. The brothers cannot understand what is happening; they are speechless. Words and actions paint a vivid picture of how they all draw closer. Now Joseph once more discloses his identity as their brother, but this time—as was inevitable in their reunion—he recalls their common history: "Your brother, whom you sold into Egypt." This statement conjures up the old offense once more, and the first words Joseph addresses to his brothers are designed to allay their fear. The context gives these words a heightened importance.

5-8   A secondary addition (v. 7b) makes it more difficult to understand what Joseph says to his brothers; this addition led in turn to
the reversal of verses 8a and 8b.

With regard to verse 7b: The reference to Jacob's family as a
"remnant" makes no sense here; what are they supposed to be a
remnant of? This is the only occurrence of the word in the entire
Pentateuch. When it appears elsewhere, especially in the prophets,
it refers to the remnant of the nation.[1] The words "remnant" and
"survivors" appear in parallel in late prophecies of deliverance (cf.
Isa. 37:32 and 2 Kgs. 19:31: "Out of Jerusalem shall go forth a remnant,
and out of Mount Zion a band of survivors"). In this late period, the
statement in Genesis 45:7b was added by someone who saw here an
allusion to this promise; one may compare the late additions to the
promises to the patriarchs. The interpolation caused the following
statements to be reversed. Joseph's words to his brothers should
therefore be read in the order of the translation: verses 5-7a, (7b), 8b,
8a. The use of the same phrase ("Now then . . .") to begin both the
first and the last sentence is an example of the rhetorical device called
inclusio.

Joseph is concerned to relieve his brothers' fears. His words of
reassurance (v. 5) have the structure of a promise of salvation (cf.
50:21; 43:23): "Fear not, for God has. . . ." In contrast to Deutero-
Isaiah, this promise is here pre-cultic in form. The author does not
put a universal, eternal truth in Joseph's mouth, as is often claimed;
his purpose is to direct his brothers' attention to an act of God: only
thus can he allay their fears. In Genesis 45:6-8 he explains to them
how God has acted. Behind what they have experienced stands
God's purpose: "to save lives." God sent him ahead—an oblique
turn of phrase that spares the brothers' feelings—so that the famine
in Egypt might be averted through his efforts. In Egypt, God had him
appointed to an office that made it possible to undertake a program
preventing starvation. In verse 8a, which concludes his explanation,
he reiterates that his brothers should see all that has happened from
the broad perspective of God's providence. It is also the author's
purpose to link the two elements of the Joseph story through God's
providence: it is the same God who saves lives in Pharaoh's kingdom
and heals the breach in Jacob's family.

9-13   Joseph includes in his welcome to his brothers a message
for their father, whom he yearns to see once more (cf. v. 3). Here the
author uses the messenger form (cf. 32:4-6) because it enables him to

---

1. See E. Ruprecht, "*plṭ* pi. retten," cols. 420-27 in *Theologisches Handwörterbuch zum Alten Testament*, ed. Ernst Jenni and Claus Westermann, II
(Munich: Christian Kaiser, 1976).

use direct address for the words of the sender. As the form requires, an indicative section (45:9b) is followed by an imperative (vv. 10-12), his invitation to his father to come to Egypt. The land of Goshen is a region of the Nile delta near the desert, Wadi Tumilat. His father's "nearness" is meant relative to his present vast distance.

14-15 Only now does Joseph welcome his brothers with all his heart—first Benjamin, then the others. This welcome seals his forgiveness, which no longer needs to be stated explicitly. Now the breach is healed, and the brothers can address Joseph once more as their brother.

16-21 Joseph's invitation of Jacob's family needs to be ratified by Pharaoh. The scene in verses 16-21 follows verses 1-2. News of the event had come to Pharaoh's ears; he and his court generously second the invitation, rejoicing that Joseph has been reunited with his family. Pharaoh sanctions the invitation as his own directive; now when the brothers bring their father, it will be at Pharaoh's behest (v. 21a). Pharaoh restates the invitation in more general terms; he offers them "the best of the land of Egypt"—the choice is theirs. Pharaoh's instructions are carried out; when Joseph places wagons and provisions at their disposal for the journey, it means that they are to set out immediately.

22-24 Having showered his brothers with gifts, Joseph bids them farewell. The gifts, which are a *berākāh,* a blessing, confirm the reconciliation. He sends along gifts for his father, which bear witness to his love and concern and also to his high position.

25-28 The brothers return and report to their father. Just as they could not comprehend at first that "the man" was their brother (v. 3), so their father cannot believe their report: "His heart remained cold." Here the narrator echoes the beginning in 37:31-36. But Joseph's words and gifts finally convince him, and his spirit revives (cf. Ps. 22:26; 69:32). Joseph's urgent desire to see his father again now is matched by his father's desire to see his son. Then he can die in peace.

46:1-30 JACOB'S JOURNEY TO EGYPT AND REUNION WITH JOSEPH

1   *And Israel set out with all that he had.*
    And when he came to Beer-sheba,
    he offered sacrifice to the God of his father Isaac.
2   *Then God spoke to Israel in a vision by night.*
    He said: Jacob, Jacob!
    And he said: Here I am.

3 *And he said: I am God, the God of your father.*
Do not be afraid to go down to Egypt,
for I will make you a great nation there.
4 *I will go down to Egypt with you.*
And I will bring you up again,
and Joseph shall close your eyes.
5a *Then Jacob set out from Beer-sheba.*

5b *And the sons of Israel lifted Jacob, their father, and their little ones, and their*
wives onto the wagons that Pharaoh had sent to fetch them.
6 *And they took their cattle and their possessions,*
which they had acquired in the land of Canaan,
and they came to Egypt,
Jacob and all his descendants with him;
7 *and his sons and his grandsons, his daughters and his granddaughters,*
and his entire family
he brought with him to Egypt.

8 *These are the names of the sons of Israel,*
who came to Egypt, Jacob and his sons:
Reuben was Jacob's firstborn.
9 *The sons of Reuben: Hanoch, Pallu, Hezron, and Carmi.*
10 *The sons of Simeon: Jemuel, Jamin, Ohad, Jachin, Zohar, and Shaul,*
the son of the Canaanite woman.
11 *The sons of Levi: Gershon, Kohath, and Merari.*
12 *The sons of Judah: Er, Onan, Shelah, Perez, and Zerah.*
Er and Onan died in the land of Canaan.
The sons of Perez were Hezron and Hamul.
13 *The sons of Issachar: Tolah, Puvah, Iob, and Shimron.*
14 *The sons of Zebulun: Sered, Elon, and Jahleel.*
15 *These are the sons of Leah, whom she bore to Jacob in Paddan-aram, and*
his daughter Dinah;
altogether thirty-three sons and daughters.
16 *The sons of Gad: Ziphion, Haggi, Shuni· Ezbon, Eri, Arodi, and Areli.*
17 *The sons of Asher: Imnah, Ishvah, Ishvi, Beriah, and Serah their sister.*
And the sons of Beriah were Heber and Malchiel.
18 *These are the sons of Zilpah, whom Laban gave to Leah his daughter.*
These she bore to Jacob, sixteen souls.
19 *The sons of Rachel, Jacob's wife: Joseph and Benjamin.*
20 *To Joseph were born in the land of Egypt Manasseh and Ephraim, borne*
to him by Asenath, the daughter of Potiphera the priest of On.
21 *The sons of Benjamin: Bela, Becher, Ashbel, Gera, Naaman, Ehi,*
Rosh, Muppim, Huppim, and Ard.
22 *These are the sons of Rachel, whom she bore to Jacob, altogether four-*
teen souls.
23 *The sons of Dan: Hushim. . . .*
24 *And the sons of Naphtali: Jahzeel, Guni, Jezer, and Shillem.*
25 *These are the sons of Bilhah, whom Laban gave to Rachel his daughter.*
These she bore to Jacob, altogether seven souls.
26 *All the souls belonging to Jacob who came to Egypt, all his bodily*

> *descendants, not including the wives of Jacob's sons, altogether came to*
> *sixty-six souls.*

27   *The sons of Joseph, born to him in Egypt, were two. All the souls of*
> *Jacob's family who came to Egypt were seventy.*

28   *And he sent Judah ahead of him to Joseph,*
> *asking whether he would come to meet him.*
> *And they came into the land of Goshen.*

29   *Then Joseph had his chariot made ready*
> *and went up to Goshen to meet his father Israel.*
> *And when he saw him, he fell about his neck*
> *and cried for a long time on his neck.*

30   *Then Israel said to Joseph: Now I am ready to die,*
> *now that I have seen your face and know that you are still alive.*

While the Joseph story in chapters 37–45 (omitting ch. 38) is a single unit, its conclusion in chapters 46–50 is intertwined with the conclusion of the story of Jacob, which also constitutes the conclusion to the Patriarchal History (Gen. 12–36). J and P contained a concluding section, following chapters 25–36, which recounted how Jacob came to Egypt after his son Joseph (ch. 37). This constituted the transition from the Patriarchal History to the book of Exodus. In Genesis 46–50 in their present form the conclusion of the Joseph story has been combined with this conclusion to the Jacob story (from J and P). To the Joseph story belong the arrival of Jacob in Egypt and his reunion with Joseph, the account of how they were provided for in Egypt during the famine, and Jacob's death and burial. The other sections of chapters 46–50 belong to the conclusion of the story of Jacob. In chapter 46 these include an itinerary in verses 1–5a, into which a promise has been inserted, an itinerary in the language of P in verses 6–7, and a list of names in verses 8–27. In both form and content, all these passages belong to the Patriarchal History.

1–5a   This introductory text in particular shows that we are in a different world from that of the Joseph story. The association of an itinerary (vv. 1, 5a) with a promise (vv. 2–4), coupled with an act of worship during the journey (cf. 12:1–7), is typical of the Patriarchal History. It never occurs in the Joseph story.

The itinerary in verses 1a and 5a has the structure departure—arrival and location—halt—departure. The place from which Jacob sets out is not specified; it was obvious from its context in the Jacob story. According to 37:14, Jacob had been at Hebron. As in 12:8 and 28:18, the halt includes an act of worship, here a sacrificial meal. The statement that Jacob offers the sacrifice to "the God of his father Isaac" is meant to indicate that even in a foreign land he remains linked with the God of his fathers. The divine oracle addressed to Jacob in 46:2–4 consists of an introduction (v. 2) and a directive joined to a promise (vv. 3-4), reminiscent of 12:1-5. The introduction is highly formulaic. The expression "vision by night" is actually inappropriate here, because Jacob does not see anything; the Hebrew word (a plural form) is a later term for "revelation" (cf. Job 4:13; Ezek. 1:1; 8:3; 40:2; 43:3). Genesis 46:2b is a call followed by a response, as in 22:11 and 31:11.

In the directive and its associated promise, God reveals himself as "the God of your father." The statement of reassurance "Do not be afraid" here refers to the dangers inherent in the journey to Egypt; they are countered by the promise (46:3b) that there God will make Jacob a great nation—in other words, a promise of increase (cf. 18:18). In Egypt, then, Israel is to become a great nation. The fulfillment of this promise is cited explicitly in Exodus 1:7; both passages presuppose that the history of the patriarchs and the history of the nation (Exodus) have been joined. To the promise of increase, Genesis 46:4 adds the promise of God's presence (cf. 31:3; 35:3), which here already associates Jacob's journey to Egypt with Israel's exodus from Egypt. It is through the action of the same God that the journeys of the patriarchs are connected with the exodus of the nation from Egypt. There follows, strangely, the highly personal promise to Jacob that Joseph will close his eyes when he dies (46:4b); it is meant to link the far-reaching promise to the patriarchs with the Joseph story (cf. 45:28; 46:30; also 15:13-16).

The formulation of the promise in 46:2-4 exhibits several features suggesting a late date. It has probably been substituted for an earlier, simple promise of God's presence coupled with a directive, such as are typical of the Jacob story.

5b   There follows in verse 5b a statement from the Joseph story; it, too, tells how Jacob's family sets out for Egypt from Canaan, but in totally different terms. In contrast to the itineraries, which reflect a nomadic way of life, this verse speaks of wagons used for transport. The account of verse 5b follows the return of the brothers to their father in 45:25-28. In the Joseph story, it is continued by 46:28-30.

6-7   In verses 5-6, P's version of Jacob's migration to Egypt with his entire family is added. All exegetes agree that these verses exhibit the style of P; cf. 12:5; 31:18; 36:6; 17:7-10; 35:12. Furthermore, taking "all their possessions" (46:6) does not chime with 45:20. The listing of all the members of Jacob's family in 46:7 (the only mention of Jacob's daughters) is meant to indicate that Jacob's journey to Egypt marks a new epoch, the transition from family to nations: all Jacob's descendants are included.

8-27   For this reason, a list is interpolated in verses 8-27, which expands on the summary statement in verse 7 by giving numbers and individual names. It is a list of Jacob's descendants over three generations; to fit the present context, it has been reworked as a list of Jacob's sons who came from Canaan to Egypt. This revision is responsible for minor discrepancies and inconsistencies. The list is organized according to the mothers of Jacob's sons, as in chapters 29 and 30: the sons of Leah, totalling thirty-three (46:8b-15); the sons of Zilpah, totalling sixteen (vv. 16-18); the sons of Rachel, totalling fourteen (vv. 19-22); the sons of Bilhah, totalling seven (vv. 23-25). Each of these sections begins and ends with a caption, indicating that they originated as separate traditions. The concluding summary cites a total of sixty-six in verse 26 and seventy in verse 27; the figures are arrived at by counting in different ways. The number seventy was part of the tradition used by the author of the list (Exod. 1:5; Deut. 10:22; Exod. 24:1-9); it is a round number, as in Judges 8:30; 12:14 (the seventy sons of Gideon). The individual numbers are clearly artificial: the sons of Leah constitute half the total, and each maidservant has half as many sons as her mistress.

The parallels to this list in Exodus 1:1-7; 6:14-16; and Numbers 26, together with the names in 1 Chronicles 2–8, show that we are dealing with an independent tradition unconnected with the Joseph story; it probably dates from the period before settlement. The conclusion of the list (Gen. 46:26-27) shows that two forms of it have been interwoven. The original conclusion appears in verse 27b: "All the souls of Jacob's family who came to Egypt were seventy." All the other statements offer corrections or additions to account for the combination of two lists. Since Joseph and his sons (v. 27a) were not involved in the journey, the total could only be sixty-seven. And since the list comprises only the *sons* of Jacob, we arrive at a total of sixty-six for the journey to Egypt. All the other statements are attempts at harmonization.

As for the names, with few exceptions they are personal names; the list is not a list of tribes. We find names of animals, names reflecting physical or psychological characteristics, names that express the joy or hopes of a child's parents, and theophorous names.

28-30   The account of Jacob's arrival in Goshen (vv. 28-30) follows the departure from Canaan (v. 5b; a sentence has been omitted), which is preceded by Jacob's desire to see his son again (45:28). Jacob sends Judah ahead to Joseph to announce his arrival. Genesis 46:28b is an itinerary fragment, which follows verses 1a and 5a. Joseph comes to meet his father in Goshen (v. 29a). The reunion of father and son follows in verse 29b, described in a simple gesture. (The correct reading is "When he saw him.") Finally Jacob says what this reunion means to him. The father's lament for his beloved son has been silenced; now Jacob can die in peace.

The inclusion of the Joseph story at the end of the story of Jacob in chapters 46–50 declares it to be part of the Patriarchal History, which began in 12:1-5 with God's command to Abraham to set out for Canaan. It concludes here with God's reassurance of Jacob as he returns to Egypt (46:1-5). Both passages include promises. Here, however, the promise looks forward to the history of the nation (the list of seventy descendants) in a prediction of the later exodus from Egypt. The God who guided and preserved the patriarchs will one day lead the children of Israel out of Egypt into the land through which their fathers traveled, where they received the promises.

46:31–47:28 JOSEPH PROVIDES FOR HIS FAMILY

46:31 *Then Joseph said to his brothers*
[and to his father's family]:
I will go up and inform Pharaoh and say to him: My brothers and my family,
who were in the land of Canaan, have come to me.

32 *The people are shepherds, [for they breed cattle].*
They have brought their sheep, their cattle,
and all their possessions.

33 *Now if Pharaoh summons you and asks:*
What is your occupation?

34 *then say: Your servants have been cattle breeders from youth up to now, we*
and our fathers. Thus you will be able to remain in the land of Goshen.
For all shepherds are an abomination to the Egyptians.

47:1 *And Joseph went and told Pharaoh. He said:*
My father and my brothers have come from the land of Canaan with their
sheep and cattle and all their possessions; they are now in the land of Goshen.

2 *From the number of his brothers he had taken five along,*
whom he presented before Pharaoh.

3 *And Pharaoh asked the brothers: What is your occupation?*
Then they answered Pharaoh: Your servants are shepherds, we and our
fathers.

4 *And they said further to Pharaoh: we have come to sojourn in the land. For*
your servants can find no more feed for their sheep, since the famine is severe
in the land of Canaan. So please allow your servants to settle in the land of
Goshen.

5 *Then Pharaoh said to Joseph:*
So your father and your brothers have come to you.

6 *The land of Egypt lies open to you. Settle your father and your brothers in the*
best part of the land; they may remain in the land of Goshen. And if you
know that there are competent people among them, put them as overseers
over my own herds.

7 *Then Joseph brought in his father Jacob*
and presented him to Pharaoh.
And Jacob blessed Pharaoh.

307

8	And Pharaoh asked Jacob:
	How many are the years of your life?
9	And Jacob answered Pharaoh: The years of my sojourning are 130 years.
	Short and hard has been the time of the years of my life,
	and it has not reached the years of the life of my fathers in the time of their sojourning.
10	And Jacob blessed Pharaoh.
	And he left Pharaoh's presence.
11	And Joseph settled his father and his brothers in the best part of the land . . . , as Pharaoh had commanded,
	and he gave them property in the land of Egypt . . . ,
	in the land of Rameses.
12	And Joseph provided his father and his brothers and the whole of his father's family with bread according to the number of their children.
27a	So Israel dwelt in the land of Egypt, in the land of Goshen,
27b	and they established themselves in it, and were fruitful, and became very numerous.
28	And Jacob lived another seventeen years in the land of Egypt, so that his life span covered 147 years.
13	[Now there was no bread anywhere in the land,
	for the famine was very severe, so that the land of Egypt and the land of Canaan languished on account of the famine.
14	Then Joseph collected all the money
	that was in the land of Egypt and in the land of Canaan
	in return for the grain that was bought.
	And Joseph deposited the money in Pharaoh's palace.
15	Now when the money in the land of Egypt and in the land of Canaan had run out, then all the Egyptians came to Joseph and said: Give us bread! Why should we die before your eyes? The money has all run out.
16	Then Joseph said: Hand over your cattle, and I will give you bread in exchange for your cattle, if your money has run out.
17	Thereupon they brought their cattle to Joseph, and Joseph gave them bread in exchange for their horses, their herds of sheep and cattle, and their donkeys. Thus in that year he provided them with bread in exchange for their cattle.
18	But when the year was ended, they came again in the second year and said to him: My lord, we cannot hide it from you: the money has run out.
	Our herds, too, belong to our lord.
	We have nothing left to offer our lord
	except our bodies and our land.
19	Why should we now die before your eyes, we and our fields? Buy us and our fields for bread, and we and our fields will be in bondage to Pharaoh.
	But give us seed so that we may live and not die and our fields not become a desert.
20	So Joseph bought up all the farmland of the Egyptians for Pharaoh. For the Egyptians sold all their fields, because the famine lay heavy upon them. Thus the land came into the possession of Pharaoh.
21	But the people he put in servitude to him,
	from one end of Egypt to the other.

22 Only the land of the priests he did not buy. For the priests had a fixed income
    from Pharaoh, and they lived on the income Pharaoh gave them.
    Therefore they did not need to sell their fields.
23 And Joseph said to the people: Today I have bought you and your land for
    Pharaoh; here is seed for you, that you may sow the land.
24 But of the produce you must hand over a fifth to Pharaoh.
    Four parts are yours to sow your fields and to provide food for you and for
    those in your houses and for your children.
25 Then they said: You have saved our lives!
    May we find favor in the eyes of our lord;
    we will gladly be slaves to Pharaoh.
26 Thus Joseph made it a statute for the land of Egypt until this day, that they
    must hand over a fifth to Pharaoh. Only the farmland of the priests did not
    become Pharaoh's property.

In 46:31–47:28 we may distinguish three components of different
origin. The Joseph story includes the audience with Pharaoh (46:31–
47:6), Joseph's provisions for his brothers, and Israel's settling in
Egypt (47:11*, 12, 27a). The conclusion of the Jacob story (P) comprises Jacob's blessing of Pharaoh, his settling in Egypt, and his life
span (verses 7-10, 11*, 27b, 28). Finally, an appendix deals with the
fifth owed Pharaoh (verses 13-26).

46:31-34 Now Joseph must report the arrival of his family to
Pharaoh, whose prior approval of their coming is presupposed
(45:16-20). Joseph emphasizes that his brothers are shepherds; the
words "for they breed cattle" (46:32) are an accidental duplication of
verse 34. He counsels his brothers to say the same thing (vv. 33-34).
Pharaoh is to understand that the brothers have no ambitions to rise
to high office under their brother's protection. This, too, is an example of Joseph's wisdom: he maintains the distinction between the
court and providing for his family. The explanatory statement that
"all shepherds are an abomination to the Egyptians" probably refers
solely to non-Egyptian nomads.

47:1-6 The audience with Pharaoh proceeds as expected. After
Joseph presents his brothers to Pharaoh (vv. 1-2), Pharaoh has a
conversation with them (vv. 3-4) distinct from his conversation with
Joseph. Pharaoh answers the brothers' request indirectly by granting
approval through his minister (vv. 5-6). Pharaoh is glad to see Joseph
reunited with his family; he generously grants them free choice of
where to settle and, at the brothers' request, affirms their choice of
Goshen. In addition, however, he offers the most competent among
them the chance to rise in the world.

7-10 Here the redactor inserts a second audience, which comes
from P. Joseph presents his father to Pharaoh; the highest court
official wishes to introduce his father, who has come to Egypt at
Pharaoh's invitation. The author of P attaches special importance to

this meeting, which he solemnly frames with the statement: "And Jacob blessed Pharaoh" (vv. 7b, 10a; cf. 2 Sam. 14:17). The words refer to a formal greeting, but the sense of "blessing" dominates the passage: the priestly author is thinking of a liturgical blessing. The solemnity of this blessing is evident: Jacob, an alien shepherd from the steppes, who must ask Pharaoh for bread, appears before the powerful king of a mighty empire—and blesses him. It is this contrast that lends the blessing its substance here. Jacob is on the point of death when he imparts his blessing to Pharaoh; we see this clearly in the conversation in Genesis 47:8-9. Pharaoh inquires how old Jacob is. Jacob responds to this sympathetic question by sharing his life experience. His life span is long in years, but it has been "short and hard." Its shortness is not measured in days; his long periods of suffering have shortened his life (37:35; 45:27). He uses the unique expression "years of sojourning" to describe his life span; elsewhere we find only the phrase "land of sojourning" (17:8; 28:4; 36:7; 37:1; Exod. 6:4). This idiom associates his life with that of his fathers.

Jacob knows that death is approaching. Before he dies, he wishes to bless his children (Gen. 48–49). But the blessing of the dying man is extended to include the king of Egypt, in whose kingdom his family found refuge from famine. Here we find a distant echo of J's introduction to the Patriarchal History, which states that the blessing promised Abraham will extend to all the "families of the earth." We are told at the end of the Patriarchal History that the blessing that extends through the chain of the patriarchs is not limited to the fathers of Israel or to the nation of Israel to which they give birth. It is a blessing intended for the entire human race.

11-12, 27-28   Pharaoh's approval, stated in verses 5-6, is put into effect by Joseph; verse 11 contains an interpolation from P: "And he gave them property in the land of Egypt . . . , in the land of Rameses." Because the famine is still raging, Jacob's family must be furnished with food (v. 23; cf. 45:11). They are given enough to provide for their needs (literally, "according to the number of the mouths of their children"). The conclusion in 47:27-28, displaced by the appendix in verses 13-26, is a composite comprising the last sentence of this section of the Joseph story (v. 27a) and the conclusion from P (vv. 27b-28). According to P, the members of Jacob's family in Egypt acquire property, upon which they increase in number (v. 27b; cf. 35:11), a statement that looks forward to Exodus 1:7. Finally, P characteristically records Jacob's age (Gen. 47:28).

13-26   The fifth in Egypt. This text originated as an independent unit; it interrupts the continuity between verses 11-12 and 27-28 of the Joseph story, where it has been inserted secondarily. It serves no function in the narrative trajectory of the Joseph story. It is an etiological narrative (cf. "until this day" [v. 26]) intended to explain a remarkable feature of the Egyptian economy, which the author ascribes to the work of Jacob, which he knows from the Joseph story. The author is only vaguely familiar with property ownership in Egypt, a subject also discussed by Herodotus and Diodorus. He makes no distinction between crown lands and the sovereign authority exercised by Pharaoh over the entire land of Egypt. Furthermore, the Egyptian peasantry was never made up entirely of serfs; there were free landowners in all periods.

The organization of the text is obscure and its style very awkward, as all exegetes state. An introduction (vv. 13-14) is followed by a first (vv. 15-17) and then a second, more severe (vv. 18-26) year of famine. The second section is longer than the first; the outcome is related twice (vv. 20-22 and 26). As a result, the structure is confused. Verses 13-15a deal with Joseph's program in Egypt and Canaan; afterwards only Egypt is mentioned. Verses 13-22 have to do with food, verses 23-24 with grain for sowing.

13-14 In these introductory verses, the author links his narrative with the Joseph story, especially 41:53-57. His reference to both Canaan and Egypt (only in 47:13-15a) is intended as a bridge from the Joseph story (41:57). The first element of Joseph's program, which the author found described in the Joseph story, he mentions only in passing, drawing the conclusion that Joseph collected all the money from Egypt and Canaan and turned it over to Pharaoh.

15-17 When their money is used up, the Egyptians once more beg for bread; Joseph demands their cattle in return (v. 16). His demand is met in verse 17: the Egyptians bring Joseph all their cattle, horses, and sheep, and Joseph in return provides food for them. The author does not deal with the problem of how all the livestock of Egypt could actually be brought together.

18-26 The third act begins again with a petition, combined with the Egyptians' offer to transfer all their lands to Joseph and become his serfs, lest they perish (vv. 18-19). At this point we would expect Joseph's reply to their request; instead verses 20-21 already describe the outcome. Joseph's reply appears as an awkward afterthought in verses 23-24. Verses 20-21 clearly constitute a conclusion. Verse 22 adds that the priests were an exception because they had special income from Pharaoh. These priestly privileges roughly reflect the historical situation. Joseph's reply to the Egyptians in verses 23-24, which should really follow verses 18-19, has been adapted to harmonize with the outcome in verse 26. Joseph grants the Egyptians' request and accepts their offer (vv. 23-24); now, however, it is not bread but seed that he gives them. Of their harvest, the Egyptians must give Pharaoh a fifth; four fifths are for their personal use. They gratefully agree; this agreement in verse 25 can refer only to verses 23-24. The conclusion in verses 20-22, on the other hand, refers only to the three increasingly severe stages of the famine, and say nothing about the tax of a fifth, which would make no sense here, because the Egyptian peasants have lost everything. In the context of the tax of a fifth, their loss is much smaller. Verse 26b is a late addition linking the two versions.

47:29–48:22 JACOB'S TESTAMENT

47:29 *Now when the time drew near that Israel was to die,*
he summoned his son Joseph and said to him:
If I have found favor in your eyes, put your hand under my thigh and be loyal and true to me,
and do not bury me in Egypt.

30 *When I lie with my fathers, bring me out of Egypt and bury me in their grave.*
He answered: I will do as you have said.

31 *And he said: Swear to me. And he swore to him.*
Then Israel inclined toward the head of the bed.

48:1 *Now after these events Joseph was told:*
Behold, your father is ill. Then he took his two sons Manasseh and Ephraim with him and went to Jacob.

2 *And Jacob was informed: Behold, your son Joseph is coming to you.*
Then he summoned up his strength and sat up in bed.

3 *And Jacob said to Joseph:*
God Almighty appeared to me in Luz in the land of Canaan. He blessed me

4 *and said to me: Behold, I will make you fruitful and multiply you, and I will make you a host of nations.*
I will give this land to your seed after you
as an everlasting possession.

5 *But now your two sons, who were born to you in the land of Egypt before I came to you in Egypt, are to belong to me. Ephraim and Manasseh, they are to belong to me like Reuben and Simeon.*

6 *But the children born to you after them, they are to belong to you. They shall be called after the name of their brothers in the matter of their inheritance.*

7 *When I was coming from Paddan, I lost Rachel;*
she died on the way in the land of Canaan, when there was still some distance to go to Ephrath. And I buried her there on the way to Ephrath (that is, Bethlehem).

8 *When Israel saw Joseph's sons, he said: Whose are these?*

9 *And Joseph answered his father: These are the sons whom God has given me here. And he said:*
Bring them here to me; I will to bless them.

10   *But Israel's eyes had grown dim with age,*
     and he could not longer see well.
     But when he brought them to him,
     he kissed and embraced them.

11   *And Israel said to Joseph: I had not expected to see you again; and now God has even allowed me to see your children.*

12   *Then Joseph lifted them from his knees and bowed with his face toward the ground.*

13   *Then Joseph took the two of them: Ephraim on his right, Israel's left, and Manasseh on his left, Israel's right, and brought them to him.*

14   *And Israel stretched forth his right hand*
     and laid it on the head of Ephraim—he was the younger—
     and his left hand on the head of Manasseh,
     crossing his arms—for Manasseh was the firstborn.

15   *And he blessed Joseph and said:*
     The God before whose face my fathers Abraham and Isaac walked, the God who has been my shepherd
     my whole life long to this day,

16   *the angel who ransomed me from all distress,*
     may he bless these boys so that my name may live in them and the name of my fathers Abraham and Isaac,
     that they may grow and become many in the land.

17   *When Joseph saw that his father had laid his right hand on Ephraim's head, he was displeased,*
     and he grasped his father's hand so as to lift it from Ephraim's head to Manasseh's head.

18   *Joseph said to his father:*
     No, my father, this is the firstborn,
     lay your right hand on his head.

19   *But his father refused and said:*
     I know, my son, I know well. He, too, shall become a nation; he, too, shall become great.
     But his younger brother will be greater than he,
     and his seed will become a host of nations.

20   *And he blessed them that day, saying:*
     In you will Israel bless itself with these words:
     May God make you like Ephraim and Manasseh.
     Thus he gave Ephraim precedence over Manasseh.

21   *And Israel said to Joseph: Behold, I am about to die. But God will be with you, and will bring you back into the land of your fathers.*

22   *But I give you one shoulder in preference to your brothers, which I took from the Amorites with sword and bow.*

Genesis 47:29 marks the beginning of the events that center on the death of Jacob; these include preparations for his death as well as his burial. The Joseph story concludes with the death of Jacob, already spoken of in several passages (37:35; 42:38; 43:27-28; 44:22, 29, 31; 45:9, 13, 28; 46:30), all of which focus on whether Jacob will "be brought in sorrow to Sheol" or will be able to die in peace (45:28). But the death of the patriarch Jacob also belongs to the conclusion of the Jacob story, which is part of the Patriarchal History. Here it is an expanded genealogical entry recounting the last will, death, and burial of Jacob. Jacob's final arrangements before his death are an element of the larger complex 47:29–50:14, which comprises texts of various origin. This is clear in the case of chapter 49, the "Blessing of Jacob." The entire section is bracketed by the promise in 47:29-31 and its fulfillment in 50:1-14. Joseph's visit to his sick father (48:1-12) constitutes an independent unit, which is interrupted by verses 3-7, Jacob's adoption of Ephraim and Manasseh. The continuation in verses 13-20, which deals with Ephraim's precedence over Manasseh, was originally also an independent unit; it has been reshaped as the continuation of verses 1-12. Verses 13-20 have also been expanded secondarily by the addition of verses 15-16. Two independent traditions have been appended in verses 21 and 22.

47:29-31 The account of a person's death often includes his last will, which is always considered very important (cf. Gen. 27). Before he dies, therefore, Jacob makes a request of his son Joseph: he does not want to be buried in Egypt. The words in which he states his desire are almost deferential. The old man feels himself a stranger in Egypt, and so his last will concentrates on his desire to be buried where he is at home (cf. 2 Sam. 19:37; Ruth 1:17). He knows that Joseph alone has the power and ability to carry out this wish. Because it is so important to him, he makes Joseph swear to comply (cf. Gen. 24:2, 9). Joseph's assent, sealed by oath, removes this anxiety from him. The author has Jacob express his sense of release by the gesture of bowing; cf. 1 Kings 1:47, where bowing in the same situation is coupled with praise of God. It is possible that, with this urgent desire on the part of Jacob to be buried in Canaan, the author wishes to suggest the dying man's presentiment that the history of his descendants will continue there.

48:1-12 A new episode in the story begins with Genesis 48:1. Joseph is informed that his father is ill, and sets out with his two sons to visit him. His father hears that he is coming and prepares to receive him (v. 2). In this visit, it is the ailing Jacob who will be the giver.

3-7 Verse 8 continues verse 2; verses 3-7, an interpolated text from P, interrupt the continuity. Verses 3-4 recall the revelation and promise at Bethel (35:9-12), which are cited to support the declaration in 48:5-6. For P, Joseph's two sons still need legitimation as tribal ancestors, since they were born in Egypt of an Egyptian mother. Only Jacob can do this; he does so by declaring Joseph's two sons to be his own, thus setting them on a par with Reuben and Simeon, the two eldest sons of Jacob. This is not an act of adoption in the strict sense, since the sons remain with their parents. It is intended as a belated legitimation of their future as tribal ancestors. Only Jacob can perform this act of legitimation, because it is he who received the revelation and the promise. Verse 6 serves only to define more precisely what is said in verse 5: the legitimation is limited to these two, and does not apply to any sons why may be born subsequently.

7   A later tradent familiar with chapter 35, for whom the revelation at Bethel was associated with the death of Rachel, copied 35:16, 19 almost word for word at this point.

8-12   These verses go with verses 1-2, which they should follow directly. Jacob's question about Joseph's two sons presupposes that he has not yet seen them. The Joseph story assumes that Jacob died shortly after arriving in Egypt; P has a different idea (47:28). Here Joseph's sons are still young boys. This agrees with the overall character of the Joseph narrative, in which the action takes place from beginning to end in a single series of events. An interval of seventeen years (47:28 [P]), indicated only by a date, is typical of P's chronology.

Now comes the blessing, which follows a fixed ritual, similar to that in chapter 27. The statement that Jacob could no longer see well really belongs with 48:13-20; it has been inserted here because verses 13-20 have been revised to follow verses 8-12. After Joseph brings his two sons to Jacob, the latter kisses and embraces them; bodily contact is part of the blessing ceremony. Just as Joseph sees God's hand at work in the gift of sons in a foreign land (v. 9), so Jacob sees the same in being allowed to see Joseph's sons (cf. 45:26-28). It is God's help and presence that have bridged the vast distance. The account concludes with 48:12; Joseph goes out again with his sons. His gesture of bowing expresses his thanks to his father and his reverence for God. But this episode lacks the formula of blessing, which should follow verse 11; a blessing must include words as well as actions. It has been omitted here because of the blessing formula in the following section (vv. 15-16).

13-20   These verses are concerned with Ephraim's precedence over Manasseh. The episode lacks an introduction; it has been added secondarily to verses 1-12, more specifically to the command in verse 9b. Verse 10a already belongs to 13-20; it is continued directly by verse 13. The repetition of "he brought them to him" in verses 10b and 13b shows that we are actually dealing with separate episodes.

In this episode, too, the ritual of blessing is suggested by the elements of approach, identification, imposition of hands, and blessing formula. In both episodes it is Jacob who blesses and the sons of Joseph who are blessed. Joseph brings his sons before Jacob in such

315

a way as to make the ceremony easier for him, because he can no longer see well (v. 13). Quite unexpectedly, however, Jacob crosses his hands, with the intention (explained in v. 19) of touching Ephraim, the younger son (v. 14), with his right hand. Here for the first time we have a blessing that involves imposition of hands, later to become standard in the cult.[1]

15-16   The formula of blessing has been introduced secondarily at this point; this is clear from verses 17-19, which originally followed 13-14, because the correction Joseph requests in verses 17-19 would be meaningless once the formula has been pronounced. The introductory words "And he blessed Joseph and said" probably indicate that an earlier text contained a blessing of Joseph at this point, followed by a blessing of his sons. The triple predication of God (vv. 15a, 15b, 16a) echoes the language of the Psalms. The triple invocation of God resembles the Aaronic blessing in Numbers 6:24-26 (cf. also Ps. 80:1; 50:1-2), which is also reflected clearly in the structure of the blessing formula. This echo of the Aaronic blessing, which is certainly intentional, is meant to connect the patriarchal blessing, associated with the blessing before the death of the last of the three patriarchs, with the liturgical blessing of the period when it was pronounced in the context of Israel's worship. Thus this interpolated blessing formula serves to link the tradition of the patriarchs with Israel's worship.

This blessing summarizes God's actions in the lives of the patriarchs Abraham, Isaac, and Jacob, which are pictured as a journey before the face of God. As in a confession of faith, Jacob summarizes what God's blessing and deliverance have meant for him. To picture this double aspect of God's work he uses the image of the shepherd, which appears here for the first time; initially, it referred to Israel as a nation (Ps. 80:1), later the individual (Ps. 23:1). God's deliverance is described by the clause: "The angel who ransomed me from all distress." This is likewise the first occurrence in the Bible of the Hebrew word *gāʾal*, "ransom, redeem." God is referred to as an "angel" (*malʾāk*) because of the passages in the Patriarchal History where God's messenger brings deliverance from distress. The use of "ransom" with an individual as object also reflects late usage (Ps. 19:14; Job 19:25; Jer. 31:10-11). Jacob adds to the blessing a wish that his name and the name of his fathers may live on in his grandsons (cf. Gen. 21:12). This does not so much mean continual glorification of the patriarchs on the part of later generations as the continuation in the grandsons of the patriarchs' history and their experience of God. So

---

1. See Joseph Coppens, "Handauflegung," cols. 632-36 in *Biblisch-Historisches Handwörterbuch*, ed. Leonhard Rost and Bo Reicke, II (Göttingen: Vandenhoeck & Ruprecht, 1964).

understood, the blessing in 48:15-16 is a valuable witness from a later period that constitutes a theological summary linking the patriarchal period with the history of Israel. Since, however, the secondary material belonging to this period is clearly identifiable as such, it is still possible to reconstruct the original form of the blessing, a simple promise of increase in the form of a poetic benediction: "The God of my fathers [or: 'father'], may he bless the boys, that they may grow and become many in the land."

17-20   These verses continue verses 13-14; verse 17 follows verse 14 directly and shows that verse 10a also belongs to this episode. Because his father can no longer see well, Joseph assumes that he has confused the two boys and seeks to correct his mistake. This presupposes that the right hand conveys the more powerful blessing. The gesture suffices to express precedence. But Jacob replies with quiet superiority that he knows what he is doing. The dying man is looking into the distant future. Verse 19b alludes to a formula of blessing, the traditional bipartite promise of increase. No distinction is made between blessing and promise: the younger will be greater than the elder. The episode concludes in verse 20b: "Thus he gave Ephraim precedence over Manasseh." The episode was constructed as an appendix to legitimate this precedence from the mouth of one of the patriarchs. It is an etiological appendix like many found in the stories of the patriarchs. In it, Manasseh and Ephraim are conceived of as representatives of tribes. The historical process through which Ephraim achieved this precedence is presupposed. Another blessing formula has been interpolated in verse 20a, which interrupts the continuity of verses 19 and 20b. The introductory words, "And he blessed them that day, saying," are inappropriate after verse 13. An editor has added a familiar blessing formula that he felt was appropriate here: "May God make you like Ephraim and Manasseh" (cf. 12:3; 18:18; 22:18).

21-22   The Jacob story concludes with an accumulation of appendices and additions; it was the logical place to record individual, independently preserved sayings of Jacob. Jacob's promise to Joseph, in which he predicts the exodus of the Israelites from Egypt back to the land of their fathers, plays an important role in the Pentateuch as a link connecting the exodus from Egypt as recounted in Exodus and Numbers with the tradition of the patriarchs. The Exodus was already promised by the patriarch Jacob! This statement is repeated in 50:24, of which 48:21 is an abbreviated version. Here the promise of the Exodus to Joseph is lent even greater weight by being ascribed to one of the three patriarchs. The second appendix in verse 22 is an isolated tradition recorded here because it, too, has the form of a bequest to Joseph by Jacob. Jacob bequeaths to his especially beloved son Joseph the territory of Shechem (Hebrew *šᵉ̱kem*), above and beyond the portion of the brothers. This refers not to the city of Shechem but to a small region known as "The Shoulder." When Jacob adds that he took this region from the Amorites "with sword and bow," Jacob is thought of as the leader of an armed band (cf. chs. 14 and 34), a conception appropriate to the period of the judges. The tradition must have originated in Canaan.

Jacob's death brings the patriarchal period to a close. This situation is common to all the various texts brought together here. The blessing of the patriarch extends from one generation to the next, establishing continuity between them. It takes on even greater importance at the transition from one era to another. The various texts of chapter 48, with their various origins, show how this continuity was maintained from the patriarchal period through the later period. How the link between the history of the patriarchs and the history of the nation is established by God's action is summarized in the form of a benediction by verses 15-16.

49:1A, 28B–50:14: JACOB'S DEATH AND BURIAL

49:1a *And Jacob summoned his sons.*
28b *And he blessed them, each with a special blessing.*
29 *Then he commanded them and said to them:*
    Now when I am gathered to my kindred,
    bury me with my fathers in the cave
    on the plot of land of Ephron the Hittite,
30 *in the cave on the plot of land at Machpelah*
    opposite Mamre in the land of Canaan, which Abraham bought as a burial place from Ephron the Hittite.
31 *There they buried Abraham and his wife Sarah;*
    there they buried Isaac and his wife Rebekah,
    and there I buried Leah,
32 *on the plot of land with the cave on it,*
    bought from the Hittites.
33 *When Jacob had given his sons all these directives,*
    he drew his feet up onto the bed.
    Then he departed and was gathered to his kindred.
50:1 *Then Joseph bent over his father's face;*
    he wept over him and kissed him.
2 *Then Joseph ordered the physicians who were in his service to embalm his father.*
    And the physicians embalmed Israel.
3 *It took forty days;*
    that is how long the embalming took.
    And the Egyptians mourned for him for seventy days.

4   *Now when the period of mourning was over,*
      Joseph spoke to Pharaoh's court:
      If I have found favor in your eyes,
      speak on my behalf to Pharaoh and say to him:
5   *My father made me take an oath, and said:*
      When I die, in my grave that I hewed out for myself in the land of Canaan,
      there you shall bury me.
      And now I would like to go up and bury my father.
      Then I will return.
6   *Pharaoh answered: Go up*
      and bury your father as he made you swear to do.
7   *So Joseph went up to bury his father,*
      and with him went up all Pharaoh's servants, the elders of his house, and all
      the elders of the land of Egypt,
8   *together with all the house of Joseph, his brothers and the house of his father.*
      Only their children, sheep, and cattle did they leave behind in the land of
      Goshen.
9   *With them went chariots and horsemen,*
      so that it was a very large train.
10   *And they came to Goren-atad on the far side of the Jordan,*
      where they raised a loud and solemn lament.
      He observed mourning rites for his father for seven days.
11   *And when the people of the land, the Canaanites, saw the lamentation at*
      Goren-atad, they said:
      There is a great mourning ceremony of the Egyptians!
      Therefore the place was called Abel-mizraim;
      it is on the far side of the Jordan.
12   *And his sons did to him*
            as he had commanded them.
13   *His sons brought him to the land of Canaan*
            and buried him in the cave on the plot of land at Machpelah, opposite
            Mamre, that Abraham had bought as a burial place from Ephron the
            Hittite.
14   *Then Joseph returned to Egypt,*
      he and his brothers and all who had gone up with him to bury his father, after
      they had buried his father.

The death and burial of Jacob bring both the story of Joseph and the
story of Jacob to an end. The redactor has recounted them with
intentional doublets: Jacob gives the command to bury him in Canaan to Joseph in 47:29-31 and to all the brothers in 49:29-32 (P).
Jacob's death and burial, however, are recounted only once (49:33,
together with 50:12-13 [P]), like the death of Abraham (25:8-9) and
Isaac (35:29). The so-called "Blessing of Jacob" (49:1b-28a) has been
interpolated into P's conclusion to the Jacob story (49:1a, 28b-33;
50:12-13). The framework (49:1a and 28b) introduces chapter 49 as
well as 49:28b-33 and 50:1-14.

    49:28b-33   The dying Jacob gives each of his sons a special blessing (replaced by the tribal oracles in ch. 49) and then commands them to bury him in the cave at Machpelah. He announces his death with the words "I am being gathered to my kinsmen," as in 25:8. The place of burial is then described in the very circumstantial language typical of P; it agrees with chapter 23. The last words spoken by Jacob (49:31) summarize the history of the patriarchs in the triad of names Abraham—Isaac—Jacob; its course comes to an end in their common burial place. The grave is their property in the land promised to their descendants—an impressive conclusion to the Patriarchal History in its three generations. Now verse 33 recounts the death of Jacob in a few dispassionate words.

50:1-14 The account of Jacob's burial brings the Joseph story to an end: Jacob has died in peace; now, as he wished, he is buried where he had journeyed while alive. The account of the burial echoes his charge.

1-3 The language of the Joseph story reappears in Joseph's reaction to the death of his father, in the spontaneous gesture of love that expresses his grief. Then Joseph makes arrangements for the funeral rites; he orders the physicians in his service (not previously mentioned) to embalm Jacob. Embalming is mentioned in the Old Testament only here and again in 50:26, with reference to Joseph himself. In Egypt as elsewhere, physicians were originally priests. A special subgroup became expert in the art of embalming, which was highly developed in Egypt. The mourning period in Israel lasts seven days (1 Sam. 31:13). The period of seventy days may be connected with Diodorus' statement that kings were mourned for seventy-two days.

4-14 Joseph delegates representatives of the court (probably on account of the funeral ceremonies) to ask Pharaoh's permission to bury his father in Canaan; this permission Pharaoh grants. In making this request, Joseph informs Pharaoh that his father has made him swear an oath, by which he is bound. His father wished to be buried with his own people. The formulation of this request ("in the grave that I hewed out for myself in Canaan") echoes the Egyptian practice of seeing to the construction of a tomb before one's death.

7-9 With Pharaoh's approval, Jacob's burial is observed as a state funeral. Here once more the family narrative and the political narrative converge. The procession is accompanied not only by Jacob's family but also by Egyptian dignitaries; the repeated "all" is deliberate exaggeration. A military escort accompanies the train. Here in the procession to Jacob's burial there appears once more the splendor of the royal court. It is strange that, once Joseph is appointed to his office in chapter 41, the honor and glory of this office are not emphasized or even mentioned until this passage; and even here it is not Joseph himself but his father who receives these honors. Such funeral processions, especially to the sanctuary at Abydos, are frequently depicted in Egyptian tombs.

10-11 The departure in verse 9 is followed by an arrival. In the Joseph story, this referred to arrival at the place of burial, but because the burial in verses 12-13 follows P's account, verses 10-11 now appear as a stopover, during which mourning rites are observed. The arrival at Goren-atad ("Threshing floor of thorns") is noted; here a "loud and solemn lament" is held. These words must actually refer to the lament at the *end* of the procession in verses 7-9, that is, the rites associated with burial. Verses 10b-11 are an etiological appendix. Verse 10b marks a new beginning; the subject is Joseph alone, and the funeral rites are described in different terms. The mourning period of seven days follows Israelite custom (1 Sam. 31:13). This etiological appendix echoes the style of the patriarchal stories. This brief narrative reflects the impression made on the local inhabitants by the ceremonies of an Egyptian funeral procession. This event gave Abel-mizraim ("Lament of the Egyptians") in Transjordan its name. Both toponyms are found only here and are otherwise unidentified. Probably two traditions concerning the place of burial are presupposed, one located east of the Jordan and one in Canaan, west of the Jordan. The name "Abel-mizraim" belongs to a group of compound names in which "Abel" means either "pasture" or "stream."

12-13 These two verses derive from P and follow 49:29-33. The suffix in 50:12 ("*his* sons") refers to "Jacob" in 49:33; the words "as he had commanded them" refer to 49:29-32, in part quoting the latter passage exactly. P knows of no Egyptian participation in the burial or of any stopover (50:10-11). Here the sons as a group bury their father after bringing him from Egypt to Mamre.

14 This verse concludes the Joseph story's account of Jacob's burial. As he had promised Pharaoh, Joseph returns to Egypt with his brothers and their retinue. The words "after they had buried their father" are deliberately placed at the end: this final section of the Joseph story had begun with the announcement of Jacob's imminent death in 47:29; now he has died in peace and Joseph has carried out his final wishes.

50:15-21 CONFIRMATION OF THE RECONCILIATION

50:15 *When the brothers saw that their father had died, they thought: Suppose Joseph should be hostile to us and pay us back for all the evil that we did to him?*

16 *So they sent to Joseph, saying:*
Your father commanded before his death:

17 *Thus shall you say to Joseph: I pray you, now forgive your brothers their*
crime and sin, for they have done you wrong. But now forgive the sin of the
servants of the God of your father.
But Joseph wept when he heard them speak these words to him.

18 *Then his brothers themselves went in, prostrated themselves before him, and*
said: Behold, we are your servants.

19 *Then Joseph answered them:*
Do not be afraid! Am I in the place of God?

20 *You conceived evil against me, but God planned it for good,*
so as to bring about what is today,
to preserve the lives of many people.

21 *So do not be afraid;*
I will provide for you and your children.
So he comforted them and reassured them.

After the conclusion in 50:1-14, this continuation, which describes a
second reconciliation between Joseph and his brothers, is unex-
pected. It would have an important function in the story as a whole
only had it been previously said that the brothers feared Joseph's
vengeance. But there is no hint of such an eventuality. The only
explanation for the addition of this scene is that the connection with
the conclusion of the Jacob story has removed the climactic reconciliation between Joseph and his brothers in 45:5-8 so far from the
story's conclusion in the death and burial of Jacob that the redactor
who combined the conclusion of the two stories thought it necessary
to repeat this passage to interpret the Joseph story as a whole.

15-17   From the very beginning, the Joseph story involved three
parties: father, brothers, and a single brother. Now that their father is
dead, the brothers are afraid Joseph will have a free hand to take
vengeance. But this possibility is only raised by the redactor: there
are no grounds for this fear in the preceding narrative. The reconciliation in chapter 45 was undoubtedly intended as absolute. Once
again, the importance of the father in this situation is illustrated: the
brothers, who send a message to Joseph reflecting their fear, cite
their father's command to ask Joseph to forgive his brothers' transgression. It is characteristic that this secondary repetition should
speak twice of the forgiveness of sin—a concept deliberately avoided
in chapter 45, and in the formulaic language of prayer. But the brothers' appeal to their father implies also that they are bound together by
the God of their father. Joseph weeps to see this new evidence of
suspicion on the part of his brothers; his very tears show that he had
entertained no thought of vengeance.

18-21   Now the brothers themselves appear before Joseph.
Their concern speaks from their gesture and their expression of sub-

servience. Joseph's response, which is the reason this scene was added, is framed by the formula of reassurance: "Do not be afraid" (vv. 19, 21; cf. 45:5; 43:23). Joseph's first reason, "Am I in the place of God?" (50:19b), allays his brothers' fear by pointing away from his own person to the providence of God, which he interprets once more for them (v. 20; cf. 45:5-8). He speaks openly of his brothers' crime: "Indeed, you conceived evil against me!" But he counters this admission with the statement that God planned it to come to good. The meaning of the Hebrew verb he uses (ḥāšab, "think, plan, devise") includes the execution of whatever is planned. God's plan has put the evil planned by the brothers to good use, so that it can finally be forgiven. But the long road that leads to this forgiveness includes God's forgiveness, which makes reconciliation possible, together with God's providence in saving the lives of many. This explanation, reduced to a single sentence, includes God's providential work in both realms of the Joseph story, his universalistic life-saving work in the great kingdom of Egypt and his forgiving work within a small human circle, the family of Jacob. This explanatory scene so clearly expresses the theological meaning of the Joseph story as a whole that the addition of 50:15-21 can be justified. Jacob then repeats his reassurance, "Do not be afraid" (v. 21), and tells his brothers that he will continue to provide for them as he promised his father. The famine is not yet over, but his brothers do not need to worry about their children. This concern for children pervades the entire Joseph story. The two verbs in the final sentence, "comfort" and "speak to the heart," appear again in Isaiah 40:1-2, at the beginning of Deutero-Isaiah's message of comfort. In both cases, this comfort involves more than words. The brothers know that Joseph has forgiven them and that he will provide for them.

50:22-26 EPILOGUE: JOSEPH'S OLD AGE AND DEATH

50:22*But Joseph remained in Egypt, he and the family of his father.*
And Joseph lived 110 years.
23 *And Joseph saw Ephraim's sons to the third generation. And the sons of Machir, Manasseh's sons, were recognized as Joseph's children.*
24 *And Joseph said to his brothers:*
I am dying. But God will certainly come to your aid,
and he will bring you up from this land to the land that he swore to Abraham, to Isaac, and to Jacob.
25 *And Joseph made the sons of Israel take an oath, saying:*
When God comes to your aid, then take my bones with you from here.

26 *Then Joseph died, 110 years old.*
    He was embalmed and put in a coffin in Egypt.

In 50:22-26 two different appendices have been combined to form an epilogue. The first records the twilight of Joseph's life (vv. 22-23); the second tells of Joseph's final words, followed by his age and his death. The repetition of his age in verses 22 and 26 shows that we are dealing with two appendices.

22-23   Verses 22-23 might follow verse 14: following Joseph's return (v. 14), he stays in Egypt (v. 22). Joseph's life span is clearly different from the much longer lives of the three patriarchs; he attains an age reached by many. In ancient Egypt, 110 years was considered the ideal life span. It is also a ripe old age that enables Joseph to see the third generation of his descendants grow up (cf. Job 42:16). In Genesis 50:23b an etiological note has been added: the sons of Machir, Joseph's grandson, are adopted by him. As in 48:13-20, this refers to an event of tribal history. Judges 5:14 incudes Machir among the tribes of Israel.

24-26   The report of Joseph's death could follow verse 23, but it has been expanded in verses 24-25 after the model of Jacob's death. Almost all the clauses of this section echo other passages. As in the case of Jacob, death is preceded by a request to be buried in Canaan, altered to fit the circumstances (v. 25). This command is associated with the promise of a future exodus from Egypt (v. 24; cf. 48:21). The poetic language shows that it is the original nucleus of the text. Reflecting the language of the Psalms, the first clause expresses God's favor, the second his intervention. The words "God will come to your aid" (literally, "visit") appear again in the same context in Exodus 3:16; 4:31; 13:19. This observation alone shows that the promise is intended to forge a link between the history of the patriarchs and the history of the Exodus. Here, therefore, for the first time the promise is addressed to all three of the patriarchs Abraham, Isaac, and Jacob.

The promise is "sworn" to the fathers, as in the oath ceremony in Genesis 15:7-21, as well as 22:16; 26:3; 24:7—all late passages in which the oath refers to the promise of the land (cf. Exod. 13:5, 11; 32:13; 33:1). To the promise is joined a command (Gen. 50:25), modeled after the same command given by Jacob before his death. The promise in verse 24 is presupposed. In Exodus 13:19 Moses takes the bones of Joseph with him, citing Genesis 50:25. The burial of Joseph's bones is recorded in Joshua 24:32; cf. Genesis 33:19.

The epilogue concludes with the death of Joseph (50:26). Here, too, death is followed by embalming, which is only noted in passing. The comment that the body was put in a coffin in Egypt also points ahead to the exodus from Egypt.

49:1-28A: THE BLESSING OF JACOB

1 *And Jacob summoned his sons and said:*
   Gather round! I will make known to you
   what will take place at the end of days.

2 *Come together and listen, you sons of Jacob,*
   listen to your father Israel.

3 Reuben, *you are my firstborn,*
   my strength, the firstling of my manly vigor.
   Preeminent in pride, preeminent in power!

4 *You foamed over like water,*
   you shall be preeminent no more,
   because you climbed into your father's bed,
   then you defiled my couch.

5 Simeon *and* Levi *are brothers,*
   instruments of violence are their swords.

6 *[I will not dally in their council,*
   I will not share in their assembly.]
   For in their anger they murdered men,
   and in their recklessness they hamstrung oxen.

7 *Cursed be their anger, for it was fierce,*
   their wrath, for it was cruel!
   I will scatter them in Jacob,
   I will disperse them in Israel.

8 Judah *are you; your brothers praise you.*
   Your hand seizes your enemies by the neck.
   The sons of your father bow before you.

9 *A young lion is Judah, from the kill in the valley he comes up.*
   He lay down, crouched like a lion,
   like a lioness, who dares rouse him?

10 *The scepter shall not pass from Judah, nor the staff from between his feet,*
   until his ruler comes,
   and the nations are obedient to him.

11 *He tethers his ass to the vine,*
   his ass's colt to the grapevine.
   He washes his cloak in wine,
   his garment in the blood of grapes.

12 *His eyes are darker than wine,*
   his teeth whiter than milk.

13 Zebulun *dwells by the shore of the sea,*
   he shall become a haven for ships.
   His flank is upon Sidon.

14 Issachar *is a bony ass,*
   who crouches between the cattle pens.

15 *When he saw that the resting place was so good,*
   the land so pleasant, then he bent his back to the burden and submitted to
   forced labor.

325

16 Dan *executes justice for his people as one of the tribes of Israel.*

17 *Dan (shall be like) a serpent on the way,*
    a viper on the road, who bites the horse's fetlock, so that its rider falls
    backward.

18 *[I hope for thy salvation, Yahweh!]*

19 Gad—*raiders raid him,*
    but he raids on their heels.

20 Asher—*his food is rich,*
    and he provides royal delicacies.

21 Naphtali—*a hind in flight,*
    who bears comely fawns.

22 *A young fruit tree is* Joseph,
    a young fruit tree by the spring;
    its branches climb up the wall.

23 *They harassed and shot at him,*
    archers pressed him hard.

24a *But his bow remained firm,*
    flexible his arms and hands.

24b *By the hands of the Strong One of Jacob,*
    by the name of the Shepherd, the Stone of Israel,

25 *by the God of your father—may he help you,*
    by God Almighty—may he bless you
    with the blessings of heaven above,
    with the blessings of the deep that crouches below,
    with the blessings of breast and womb.

26 *The blessings of your father are richer*
    than the blessings of the ancient mountains,
    the splendor of the eternal hills.
    May they come upon the head of Joseph,
    upon the crown of the blessed among his brothers.

27 Benjamin *is a ravening wolf;*
    in the morning he devours his prey, in the evening he divides the spoil.

28a *All these are the twelve tribes of Israel.*
    And this is what their father said to them.

Genesis 49 is a collection of tribal sayings like the "Blessing of Moses" in Deuteronomy 33. It originated as an independent collection, belonging to neither the Patriarchal History nor the story of Joseph. The text deals with the tribes of Israel in the land of Canaan during the period of the judges; it was included here because the tribes are named after the sons of Jacob. The number twelve is a separate tradition with its own history;[1] the individual sayings originated

1. See Martin Noth, *Das System der zwölf Stämme Israels.* Beiträge zur Wissenschaft vom Alten und Neuen Testament 4/1 [52] (1930; repr. Stuttgart: Kohlhammer, 1966).

apart from the tradition of the twelve. The sayings characterize each of the tribes, usually using an animal metaphor (Gen. 49:9, 14, 15, 17, 21, 22, 27; Deut. 33:17, 20, 22). Comparison of Genesis 49 with Deuteronomy 33 shows that in the former the original form of the sayings predominates, whereas in the latter expansions and variations predominate.

A preliminary stage in the development of these tribal sayings appears in Judges 5:14-18, a passage in the "Song of Deborah" in which the tribes of Ephraim, Benjamin, Machir, Zebulun, Issachar, and Naphtali (vv. 14-15, 18) are extolled as heroes for following Deborah and Barak, whereas Reuben, Gilead, Dan, and Asher (vv. 16-17) are castigated for refusing to take part in the battle. The setting of these sayings is a strategic critique after the battle led by Deborah. In Genesis 49 and Deuteronomy 33, on the other hand, the sayings are not associated with a specific situation; their praise and censure are meant as general truths. The locus where these sayings originated and were preserved was a convocation of tribal representatives held on various occasions (cf. Josh. 24; Judg. 20:1). The sayings came into being independently or in small groups; the collection is a secondary phenomenon.

1-2   The collection has been interpolated into P's account: "And Jacob summoned his sons . . ." (v. 1a), ". . . and he blessed each of them with a special blessing" (v. 28b). This device legitimizes them as the words spoken by Jacob before his death. Thus they became the "Blessing of Jacob." Verse 2 constitutes the introduction to the collection proper; it has the same poetic form as the sayings themselves. A third introduction, in prose, has been added in verse 1b, according to which Jacob wishes to make known to his sons "what will take place at the end of days" (cf. Deut. 32:1; 31:28). It is a late addition to the introduction; the phrase "at the end of days" points to the distant future, as in Isaiah 2:2; Micah 4:1; Jeremiah 48:47; 49:39; Numbers 24:14. This addition chimes with Genesis 49:10-12, which, like Numbers 24:14, predicts a future ruler; the redactor interpreted Genesis 49:10-12 as a messianic prophecy.

3-7   The sayings regarding Reuben and Simeon-Levi differ from the rest: they are addressed directly to Jacob's sons, and are structured in terms of crime and punishment. They announce a punishment for a transgression, recalling the judgment oracles of the prophets.

3-4   The father addresses his son as his firstborn, extolling him as the offspring of his father's youthful vigor; the two nouns in verse 3b are also meant to be laudatory. On account of his transgression (35:22), however, he is denied the preeminence of primogeniture. In this saying, the predicates used to extol Reuben are striking in their

327

force (49:3). Perhaps we are hearing echoes of an earlier saying in which Reuben was praised. In a period when the tribe of Reuben no longer existed, it was revised on the basis of 35:22.

5-7   This saying, too, is a secondary composition. Simeon and Levi had to be included because they were part of the list of twelve. They are probably called "brothers" only because they cooperated in the escapade of verse 6b. They are accused of an act of violence; the form of the accusation recalls the accusations of the prophets. The motivation for the charge is stated in verse 6b. Here, as in verse 4, the author is borrowing from tradition; it is generally accepted that the reference is to the surprise attack on Shechem in chapter 34. But a variant of that account must be involved, because 34:30 and 35:5 look upon the brothers' action in avenging their sister as an honorable deed; furthermore, chapter 34 says nothing of hamstringing oxen. The punishment combines a curse (49:7a) and a prediction of judgment (v. 7b)—not against two individuals but against two tribes. It is not Simeon and Levi who are cursed, however, but the violence of their anger. According to verse 7b, the same punishment is to strike both tribes; this does not agree with historical facts: Simeon was absorbed into the tribe of Judah, and Levi became a priestly tribe, extolled in Deuteronomy 33:11. The saying is a literary fiction: the author had before him a tradition concerning a tribe of Levi that once engaged in battles together with Simeon.

Genesis 49:6a is a parenthetical interpolation, a marginal comment by a reader of a later period, couched in the language of the Psalms and religious wisdom. In it the reader distances himself from the cursed tribes, like the devout man in Psalm 1:1, who turns aside from the "counsel of the wicked" and the "seat of scoffers."

8-12   The series of tribal sayings proper begins with Judah; it comes first on the basis of the ancient muster order in Numbers 2:3; 10:14 (cf. Josh. 15:1). In Genesis 49:8-12 three independent sayings concerning Judah have been brought together; verses 8 and 9 are tribal sayings, whereas verses 10-12 are a promise of a blessing.

8   The saying concerning Judah in verse 8 reflects the name of the tribe: "Judah are you," that is, you are what your name implies; an explanation is added: "Your brothers praise you." His brothers praise him for some heroic deed, which is only alluded to: he seized his enemies while they were fleeing. Also in response to this deed, his brothers bow before him, recognizing him as leader in battle on account of this heroic exploit. The saying resembles those in Judges 5 in that a tribe is extolled for its courage in battle against a common enemy (Judg. 5:18). This saying, then, probably dates from the period of the judges.

9   This verse, too, is an independent tribal saying. It also praises

the tribe of Judah for its performance in battle, this time using an animal metaphor. Verse 9a likens the tribe to a young lion; the metaphor is developed in the following clauses. The change to the second person in the Hebrew text of verse 9a ("from preying . . . you have come up"), together with the vocative "my son," is a secondary assimilation to verse 8. He has torn his prey and gone up with it to his cave; there he crouches, and no one dares to disturb him (cf. Num. 24:9). The lion was considered the strongest and bravest beast of prey (cf. Deut. 33:20, 22; Num. 23:24; 24:9; Jer. 4:7; Prov. 30:30); no interpretation is needed.

10-12 These verses are a promise to the tribe of Judah; they resemble the oracles of Balaam. Verse 10 is a bipartite prediction: sovereignty will remain with Judah—in the period of the judges there were many changes of leadership—until there comes one who will gain the obedience of the nations, that is, exercise far-ranging authority. Two periods in the future history of Judah are distinguished. The first section declares that the temporary hegemony of Judah over the tribes will remain in effect; the second predicts the Judahite monarchy, for only under a monarchy is the subjugation of other nations possible, and the figure described in verses 11-12 can only be a king. As in Judges 5:14, scepter and staff (synonymous parallelism) refer to the "commander's staff" of the tribal leader. The Hebrew text of Genesis 49:10b reads: "Until Shiloh comes." The word "Shiloh" has been the subject of much debate; the literature is enormous. The context shows that the toponym "Shiloh" makes no sense here; the word can only refer to the future ruler. The simplest explanation assumes that the text is corrupt and that we should read *mšlh*, "his ruler," instead of *šlh*.

11-12 The advent of the ruler is followed by victory, a victory that ushers in a time of blessing and plenty. This blessing is prefigured in the person of the ruler. The noble vine with its grapes is a symbol of fertility (v. 11). "There is so much wine that. . . ": this is undoubtedly meant as an exaggeration (cf. Num. 24:5-7) and should not be taken literally. The ass is the royal mount (Zech. 9:9). Genesis 49:12 extols the king's physical beauty, the beauty of his face. His eyes and teeth are likened to milk and wine—again symbols of blessing. In Psalm 45, too, the blessing bestowed by God on the king is exemplified by his beauty[2] (cf. also 1 Sam. 16:18).

It is usually assumed that Genesis 49:10-12 originated in the time

2. See Claus Westermann, "Das Schöne im Alten Testament," pp. 479-497 in *Beiträge zur Alttestamentlichen Theologie*. Festschrift Walther Zimmerli, ed. Herbert Donner, Robert Hanhart, and Rudolf Smend (Göttingen: Vandenhoeck & Ruprecht, 1977).

of David as a *vaticinium ex eventu*. They could, however, have originated in the period of the judges, reflecting hopes for the institution of the monarchy.

13 Zebulun. The three sections of this saying refer to the geographical location of Zebulun. The first sentence reflects its location with respect to the Mediterranean (cf. Josh. 19:10-16). The second merely elaborates this statement: the ships go with the sea. The third section is also vague: "Sidon" refers to the territory of Phoenicia. The meaning is not entirely clear, but probably suggests censure (cf. Judg. 5:17b, clearly intended as a rebuke). The search for an outlet to the sea with its possibilities for trade and dependence on Sidon are probably meant to have negative connotations. The praise of Zebulun in Judges 5:18 does not rule out censure in a different period.

14-15 Issachar. This saying is based on an animal metaphor: "Issachar is a bony ass," that is, a strong ass. He is strong but lazy: he "crouches between the cattle pens" (the expression appears again in Judg. 5:16 in the same context and with the same meaning). Genesis 49:15 continues the metaphor in a brief narrative that tells how this lazy settling in came to pass. Like a donkey, the tribe looked for a quiet, pleasant place to settle. The price paid, however, was forced labor (cf. Josh. 16:10). The same word for forced labor appears in a letter from the archives of Amenophis IV, which also speaks of a place called Sunem, which is located in the territory of Issachar. This might be evidence from outside Israel for what Genesis 49:15 says about the tribe. The saying constitutes a harsh censure of Issachar for agreeing to provide labor for the Canaanites, even though forced to do so by its position in the midst of the chain of Canaanite fortifications. Judges 5:15, on the contrary, praises the tribe for its part in the battle led by Deborah.

16-17 Here are two originally independent sayings concerning Dan. The saying in verse 16 puns on the Hebrew verb *dîn*, "judge, execute justice." Dan executes justice for itself; the tribe holds its own against its enemies, and accomplishes this with the aid of its own people. It is as successful as any other tribe, even though it is small. Verse 17 is a vivid animal metaphor: Dan is compared to a serpent lurking by the wayside, which bites the leg of a passing horse so that its rider is thrown. While the powerful tribe of Judah can be compared to a lion (v. 9), the comparison of Dan to a serpent points to the tribe's small size. It cannot attack its opponents in open battle, but can only now and again chance an attack from ambush. Both sayings praise Dan, but the praise reflects the tribe's special situation. They undoubtedly originated during the period of the judges.

18 This exclamation—"I hope for thy salvation, Yahweh!"— can be recognized at first glance as a quotation from the Psalms, a

declaration of trust; it is identical with Psalm 119:166 and similar to Psalms 38:15; 39:7. The name "Yahweh" appears only here in Genesis 49. The verse is a marginal comment by a reader of the exilic or postexilic period, a comment on the tribal sayings as a whole (being placed in the middle), in which the reader counters what he considers the terrible spirit of the tribal sayings with the spirituality of his own day. He will put his trust solely in God's help. This marginal comment is an impressive example of critical exegesis!

19   This saying about Gad plays on the tribe's name: four of the six Hebrew words in the sentence contain the root *gdd*, "harry." Raiders harry Gad, but Gad harries hard on their heels, warding them off aggressively. The brief saying describes the situation of the tribe succinctly: Gad was in perpetual danger from its neighbors to the south and east. According to Deuteronomy 33:20-21, it was obviously able to improve its position. Both passages praise the tribe.

20   The saying about Asher comprises only two parts and also involves a play on words (Hebrew *'ešer*, "good fortune"; cf. 30:13). The statement "Asher, his food is rich" refers to the fertility of the tribe's land, on the coastal plain between Carmel and Phoenicia. The fertility of this region is also extolled in Deuteronomy 33:24. The second half of the verse ("He provides royal delicacies") is usually also interpreted in a positive sense: he has a surplus, from which he can provide food for kings (cf. Ezek. 27:17). Probably, however, this statement suggests censure: "*But* he provides royal delicacies." Asher is censured for catering to the Canaanite courts. This interpretation is supported by Judges 1:32, where the statement "Asher dwells among the Canaanites" suggests political dependence. Cf. also the censure of Asher in Judges 5:17.

21   The saying about Naphtali also comprises just two clauses; it is an animal metaphor. Naphtali is "a hind in flight" (or, according to another interpretation, a terebinth), "who bears comely fawns." Another reading of the second clause, "who gives beautiful words," is hardly possible. The saying praises Naphtali for its mobility and love of freedom. It will flourish in the freedom of the mountains.

22-26   Three sayings about Joseph have been combined: a metaphor (v. 22), a panegyric (vv. 23-24a), and a blessing (vv. 24b-26). Verse 22 is an independent metaphor, comparing Joseph to a young fruit tree by a spring. The second part of the metaphor is textually uncertain; the most likely reading describes the branches of this tree climbing a wall. The spring suggests fertility, the wall security. Since there is particular emphasis on the Hebrew word *pārāh*, "be fruitful," a pun on "Ephraim" is probably intended. If so, the saying applied originally to the tribe of Ephraim; cf. the naming of Ephraim in 41:52: "God has made me fruitful."

23-24a   The second saying describes Joseph's courageous defense again enemy attack. It has been appended to verse 22 without mention of the tribe's name (which may have been dropped when the sayings were combined). The three verbs in v. 23 vividly describe the attack on the tribe, but without naming the enemy; all that is clear is that they are the aggressors. The saying thus describes battles in which Joseph defended itself courageously (v. 24a). The text of verse 24a is very difficult; the Septuagint differs from the Masoretic Text. Both clauses describe the defense: the weapon, the bow, remained firm; arms and hands (literally, "arms of his hands") remained flexible. The saying involves neither a pun nor an animal metaphor (although one may have been omitted from its beginning), but resembles other tribal sayings in praising the tribe for its valor.

24b-26   Verses 25-26 are a blessing on the tribe; cf. verses 10-12. Verses 24b-25a constitute a transition. Most exegetes treat verse 24b as a continuation of verse 24a, so that the "firmness" of verse 24a is ascribed to God's help (v. 24b). Considerations of style and content almost rule out this interpretation; the tribal sayings speak a secular language and do not mention God's help. The plethora of divine names is stylistically at odds with the tribal sayings, which know nothing of the gods of the fathers. In fact, verses 24b-25a are a bridge to the blessing formula in verses 25b-26. This bridge resembles 48:15-16 in both form and content, above all in its use of several divine appellatives. The redactor is here using late liturgical language. The collocation of divine appellatives in 49:24b-25a derives from a late period. The blessing upon Joseph in verses 25-26 is very similar to the Joseph saying in Deuteronomy 33:13-16; they are two variants of the same blessing. The blessing is developed in three clauses. Joseph is to be blessed with agricultural fertility, nourished by rain from the heights of heaven and by the springs and streams that rise from the depths of the earth, together with the procreative fertility of human beings and livestock, symbolized by breast and womb, and finally with the blessing that comes from the mountains and hills. Here Deuteronomy 33:15 preserves the earlier form: "the finest produce of the ancient mountains, the abundance of the everlasting hills." Genesis 49:26a, however, clearly resists any possible divinization of the forces of nature. Such blessing formulas were probably borrowed from Israel's Canaanite environment. Similar blessings are found in Deuteronomy, as well as Genesis 27:28. The final clause of 49:26b resembles Deuteronomy 33:16b. The language reflects the ceremony of imposition of hands: "May they come upon the head of Joseph." Joseph is called "the blessed among his brothers," which means that he is singled out for a special deed.

27   The Benjamin saying is an animal metaphor, developed in a

noun clause (v. 27a) and two verbal clauses (v. 27b). The comparison of Benjamin to a ravening wolf in a laudatory saying is especially striking, because no other passage in the Old Testament speaks of wolves in a positive manner. Elsewhere the ravening wolf is always a dangerous enemy, especially in prophetic oracles of judgment (Jer. 5:6; Ezek. 22:27, etc.). The metaphor praises Benjamin's military prowess and/or love of pillage (cf. Judg. 5:14). How little that befits the Benjamin of the Joseph story! The succinct expansion in the two verbal clauses artfully builds on the sequence capture—divide—devour; the combination "in the morning, in the evening" means that Benjamin is indefatigable. By contrast, the Benjamin of Deuteronomy 33:12 probably reflects a later stage in the process of settlement: "He dwells secure amongst his mountains."

28a   The first clause of the concluding verse (v. 28a) refers to the tribal sayings, while the second (v. 28b) makes the transition to the frame, Jacob's blessing of his sons.

The tribal sayings are a genre with fixed form and content and a recognizable setting. The animal metaphors are related to the larger body of metaphorical sayings found in Proverbs; they embody knowledge and experience in the comparison of human beings to animals. The precision and accuracy of the metaphors suggest that the sayings originated in the period of the occupation or the judges. The puns show that the names of the tribes were already thought to reflect their character. The "name" is interpreted with reference to the interests of the community, its meaning for or against others. The name may have positive or negative implications. In this interpretation of the name, we can trace the process by which smaller units came to form a larger whole. A good name signifies recognition on the part of others: "Judah, your brothers praise you. . . ." A bad name threatens relationships with the larger whole. This way of interpreting names also points to an early date.

The inclusion of the blessings (vv. 10-12, 25-26) with the tribal sayings indicates that the two forms went hand in hand even in the preliterary period. It is possible that when the tribes or their representatives convened, the ritual included a solemn dismissal in which such blessings on a tribe may have had their locus. The meaning given the tribal sayings by their present setting is far different from their original meaning. In verses 1 and 28b a redactor has interpolated the sayings into the narrative of P, thus turning them into formulas of blessing pronounced by Jacob over his sons and reassigning them to the time of Jacob's death. The redactor's purpose, however, was to lend the sayings the status of words spoken by one of the patriarchs. Thus the tribal sayings, which would certainly have perished in isolation, were preserved. The redactor also had a broader purpose: to link the patriarchal period solidly with the period of the tribes and their traditions. This linkage, strictly speaking, is "unhistorical"; indirectly, however, it achieved great historical significance.

The second framework in verses 2 and 28a came into being as the setting for the tribal sayings when they were brought together. Here, too, they are presented as the words of Jacob. In this case, however, another element was added: the emphasis on the twelve tribes of Israel, from which the nation of Israel developed. The purpose is to trace the unity of Israel back to its beginnings: the fathers of the tribes are the sons of a single father.

Only in a later addition (v. 1b) are the sayings interpreted as prophecy for the end of days, and this interpretation refers solely to verses 10-12. On the other hand, the first two sayings (vv. 3-4 and 5-7) reflect the language of prophetic oracles of judgment. Finally, two marginal glosses echo the spirituality of the Psalms, influenced by the wisdom tradition. In verse 6a we hear the voice of a devout reader who refuses to associate with the wicked; in verse 18 another devout reader opposes the militant spirit of the tribal sayings by avowing his trust in the help that comes from God alone.

CONCLUDING REMARKS ON THE STORY OF JOSEPH

THE NARRATIVE ART OF THE JOSEPH STORY

While the Patriarchal History in chapters 12–36 evolved from individual narratives, linked by means of genealogies and itineraries, the Joseph story is a single, self-contained story. It is aimed primarily at listeners, not readers; for a long time it existed only in a few manuscripts, and it was known for the most part through recitation and listening. This demanded a high degree of involvement on the part of the listeners; it was therefore necessary that the structure of the story be clear and obvious, so that it was easy to know at any moment where one was in the story. The introduction and conclusion show that the Joseph story was interpolated into the Patriarchal History. The course of the narrative is clearly delineated by journeys from Canaan to Egypt and back again. It is a natural consequence that the two major elements should be a story set within Jacob's family and a story set at the court of Pharaoh. The sequence of major sections follows: chapters 37, 39–41, 42–45. Each individual episode is organized so tightly and clearly as to fit naturally into the whole.

The author also uses leitmotifs as a compositional technique: for example, the dream motif in the three pairs of dreams of Joseph, the courtiers, and Pharaoh. The sequence of these three pairs, which could not possibly be different, exhibits a deliberate climactic structure. Another leitmotif is that of clothing; it crops up repeatedly, without needing any particular explanation. We might also mention such motifs as the welcomes expressed in words and gestures. The motif of famine links the Joseph story with the Patriarchal History.

An important stylistic device used by the author is doubling, on both a large and small scale. Two journeys by the brothers connect the settings of the story; Joseph, the courtiers, and Pharaoh have two dreams; Pharaoh's dream is recounted twice. Twice the wife of Joseph's master tries to seduce him. The same event is often recounted twice, as in 42:30-34 and 43:3-7. The repetition is never mechanical; deliberate differences are introduced. This doubling technique might be considered a kind of parallelism in prose, comparable to the parallelism employed by poetry. The purpose of such repetitions can vary. The two journeys of the brothers serve to increase the tension, which leads up to a resolution at the end of the second journey. An event may be silently emphasized by repetition or illuminated by being recounted from a different perspective. The repetition of God's presence with Joseph at the beginning and end of chapter 39 underlines the theological leitmotif. Above all, however, such repetitions make it possible for the author to avoid introducing his own comments on what is happening and let events speak for themselves. This is a very demanding and elegant style of narrative, which respects the listener's involved participation.

THE JOSEPH STORY AND WISDOM

Our exegesis has shown that the Joseph story is not a didactic wisdom narrative. Its only clear connection with the wisdom tradition is in chapters 39–41, which is dictated by the subject matter: the wisdom of the statesman at the court of the king. Pharaoh calls Joseph a wise statesman, which he turns out to be. But Joseph's wisdom is not an acquired academic wisdom, it is wisdom bestowed by God (41:38) and nurtured by adversity. Joseph makes this point when confronting the unsuccessful representatives of academic Egyptian wisdom before Pharaoh (41:16). God has opened his eyes to reality, and this wisdom that comes from experience continues to prove successful. The interpretative passages in chapters 45 and 50, which Gerhard von Rad and others single out to support the wisdom background of the Joseph story, cannot be expressions of wisdom because they exhibit the structure of a salvation oracle. They do not speak timeless generalities about God and human beings, but address a unique situation in the context of a story.

FAMILY AND MONARCHY IN THE JOSEPH STORY

The two settings of the Joseph story contrast two forms of society: the family and the royal court. At the beginning, the brothers brusquely reject monarchy; at the end, monarchy makes the deliverance of Jacob's family possible. This reveals the author's attitude toward a conflict of his own day, the rejection or affirmation of monarchy at the time of its beginnings in Israel. He brings to light the positive contributions of monarchy, while making it clear that the values of the traditional family organization can be preserved under a monarchy. The Joseph story also exhibits a lively and varied interest in the forms of human society and interpersonal relationships. It is informed by the contrast between the simple life of the fathers and the elaborate way of life at the royal court of Egypt, with the imminent changes in Israel's way of life always in the background. The author exercises his artistry in describing the figures and events that surround Joseph's rise at court, letting this different world unfold before his audience. It is noteworthy that he plays down the role of the king in international politics in favor of his social and economic function, his responsibility for the well-being of his people. It is this responsibility of the king that the author seeks to bring home to his own people. A special role is played by the phenomenon of rising at court. In contrast to the brusque rejection by the brothers at the beginning, the author maintains that it is right and proper for someone who is able and intelligent to achieve high rank in this other world for the good of the whole. But he brings out the risks of such a rise and indicates the danger that lies in abuse of power.

WHAT DOES THE JOSEPH STORY SAY ABOUT GOD?

The theological introit to the Joseph story declares that God was with Joseph (39:1-6, 21-23). At the end, Joseph affirms that "God has brought me here" (45:8). This holds true for both his fortunes and his achievements. His way passes through the depths, but God's presence accompanies him even there. God's presence makes itself known in his ability to interpret dreams: "Interpretation of dreams is from God." But since the dreams are Pharaoh's dreams, God's providence goes beyond Joseph's personal fate and leads to the preservation of an entire nation from famine. Another demonstration of God's providence is the way traveled by the brothers, who are burdened by the guilt of a crime. God goes after them on this way until they realize that "God has discovered out the wickedness of your servants" (44:16). The hour came when they could confess their guilt; thus forgiveness and reconciliation were made possible. God's work includes both blessing and deliverance. The interpretative passages (45:5-8; 50:19-21) speak of both; Joseph can allay his brothers' fears because God has acted. His words of comfort here are meant to summarize the narrative from beginning to end. God's providence includes what happens both within the family and at the court of Pharaoh. The author is also thinking of the transition from the form of society based on the family to that reflected in the monarchic state. There is also a change in the realm of religion. The religion of the patriarchs, in which God spoke directly to the fathers, in which there were as yet no mediators, cultic or otherwise, between God and human beings, has come to an end. Joseph no longer belongs to the world of the patriarchs; he receives no revelation. He is a transitional figure. With what the author says of God's providence, he wishes to show that what was fundamental to the patriarchs' relationship with God can be preserved in the new era of a spirituality based primarily on a local cult.

THE INFLUENCE OF THE JOSEPH STORY

The story of Joseph had little influence on the literature of the Old and New Testaments. The Old Testament mentions Joseph elsewhere only in Psalm 105, in a retrospective summary of God's saving acts in history. Similar references appear in the Apocrypha in Sirach 49:15; 1 Maccabees 2:53; Wisdom 10:13-14, and in the New Testament in Acts 7:9-16 and Hebrews 11:21-22. In all these passages, Joseph has a place in a traditional series of figures from Israel's history. He appears in this series in a variety of contexts, but always as an individual; the story of Joseph is never mentioned. The same holds true when Joseph appears outside the Bible. It is not the story but the figure of Joseph that lives on, interpreted as suits the thought of the period in question. In Jewish, Christian, and Muslim tradition, Joseph is an outstanding figure, often viewed as a model, whether as provider, counselor, or paragon of chastity. In later Christian typology, from the Church Fathers through the nineteenth century, he came to represent Christ, prefiguring his life and passion. The Joseph story as such did not survive in these traditions.

Two novels with Joseph as their central figure deserve mention. *Joseph and Asenath* dates from the time of Philo; it recounts the conversion of Joseph's Egyptian wife Asenath (Gen. 41:45). It is an expression of the great missionary efforts of the Jewish diaspora in that period. Thomas Mann's novel *Joseph and His Brothers* (1933-1944) attempts to make the ancient biblical story of Joseph accessible to people of the twentieth century. But while the author of the biblical Joseph story is concerned to let events speak for themselves, Mann constantly introduces intellectual reflections, strongly influenced by later Jewish literature.

The Joseph story speaks of God and his providence in different terms than Jewish religious polemic or the enlightened syncretism of the modern novel. When we speak of the later influence of the Joseph story, the day when it will be listened to for what it is and says still lies before us.